Baseball's Great
Hispanic Pitchers

DISCARDED

ALSO BY LOU HERNÁNDEZ

Memories of Winter Ball:
Interviews with Players in the Latin American
Winter Leagues of the 1950s (McFarland, 2013)

The Rise of the Latin American Baseball Leagues,
1947–1961: Cuba, the Dominican Republic, Mexico, Nicaragua,
Panama, Puerto Rico and Venezuela (McFarland, 2011)

Baseball's Great Hispanic Pitchers

Seventeen Aces from the Major,
Negro and Latin American Leagues

LOU HERNÁNDEZ

McFarland & Company, Inc., Publishers
Jefferson, North Carolina

ISBN 978-0-7864-7975-7 (softcover : acid free paper) ∞
ISBN 978-1-4766-1545-5 (ebook)

LIBRARY OF CONGRESS CATALOGUING DATA ARE AVAILABLE

BRITISH LIBRARY CATALOGUING DATA ARE AVAILABLE

© 2015 Lou Hernández. All rights reserved

*No part of this book may be reproduced or transmitted in any form
or by any means, electronic or mechanical, including photocopying
or recording, or by any information storage and retrieval system,
without permission in writing from the publisher.*

On the cover: Juan Marichal (National Baseball Hall of
Fame Library, Cooperstown, New York)

Printed in the United States of America

*McFarland & Company, Inc., Publishers
Box 611, Jefferson, North Carolina 28640
www.mcfarlandpub.com*

To the memory of
Margarita Bichara (1926–2013),
the matriarch of our family.

Table of Contents

Acknowledgments

The thorough study on Ramón Bragaña done by Dr. Layton Revel and Luis Muñoz for the Center for Negro League Baseball Research provided an invaluable source of information to me as I prepared his profile in Chapter 1.

The center's compilation of Adolfo Luque's managerial record in Mexico likewise helped me add a finishing brushstroke to that multitalented individual's career.

A variety of magazines and newspapers were consulted as I fleshed out all of the player profiles. But for much of the 20th century, the *Sporting News* was surely the greatest single source for baseball information and I made continuous use of it throughout the research and writing of this book.

Retrosheet.org was of immeasurable help with its treasure trove of box scores. And baseball-reference.com provided all of the WAR, WHIP and ERA+ statistics cited, as well as other useful data.

The Elias Sports Bureau and Stats, LLC provided the statistics used within the player profiles of Mariano Rivera, Johan Santana and Félix Hernández.

Personal thanks to Dr. Layton Revel and the late Charles Monfort for photograph contributions.

Preface

Warren Spahn noted that pitching was all about upsetting a hitter's timing. I believe no one should be upset with the choices of the greatest Hispanic pitchers identified in this book. My ranking of these pitchers may draw out dissenting discussion. That can only shine more positive light on the men involved.

Most of the names of the men spotlighted in this book are familiar ones to baseball fans. But perhaps their individual accomplishments may not be so well known. That is where, with this work, I hope to enlighten a broader audience—as I was enlightened—to the achievements each pitcher's dedicated labor to his craft produced.

My goal in writing this book is to provide a comprehensive look at baseball's all-time best Hispanic pitchers. Bringing expanded attention to these particular athletes of the diamond by recognizing their grand exploits was another desired objective of this project.

All of the pitchers headlined in these pages were born in Latin America. I use the term "Hispanic," rather than the interchangeably used "Latino," because I feel Hispanic is the more appropriate term when referring to a Spanish-speaking person of Latin American descent residing in the United States. All of these players lived, at one time or another, in the United States. (It should be noted, for reference sake at least, that not all countries in Latin America have Spanish as their primary language. And that the root word of Hispanic suggests the Spanish culture and language much more definitively than the outmoded language root of Latin.)

For 80 of the roughly 100 years covered in this book, pitchers in all professional leagues throughout the Western Hemisphere did not concern themselves with a pitch count. Whether that was a good or bad philosophy will be left open for debate. The men of these complete-game-centric pitching eras unquestionably drew greater personal satisfaction—and deeper admiration from peers and fans—with their extended performances than the six-inning starters of today.

How did I choose the pitchers? What was the selection process? I used a minimum of 250 career wins for selection of all the 20th century profiled stars—all leagues inclusive. (Orlando "El Duque" Hernández and Fernando Valenzuela each came up a little short.)

I also included Mariano Rivera, one of the most gifted and respected major league players of the past 20 years. As a relief pitcher, he warrants a different perspective from that of a starter. Yet, as a testament to how staggeringly good his body of work was, it seemed apparent to me that his placement alongside the conventional pitchers could not be denied, though there was no viable method of ranking him with the others.

I feel compelled to elaborate here on my classification of Adolfo Luque's 1923 season as the greatest season ever produced by a Hispanic major league pitcher. More contemporary fans and Sabermetrics followers may point to Pedro Martínez and his 2000 campaign ranking as the best by *any* pitcher all time. But I contend statistical dominance over hitters should not be the bellwether. Martinez's 2000 campaign consisted of only 29 starts, 18 wins, seven complete games, four shutouts, and 217 innings, all vastly diminished numbers in comparison to many of the greatest pitching seasons on record.

Luque, in 1923, threw 322 innings and had nearly as many complete games (28) on the season as Martínez had starts in 2000. Luque won 27 games and tossed six shutouts—in a 154-game schedule. (Luque was denied seven other shutouts simply due to unearned runs!) Martinez bettered Luque in ERA, 1.74 to 1.93, and strikeouts, 284 to 151. The strikeout difference is not as large as it appears, as the players of past eras were far more disciplined at the plate compared to the hacking free-swingers of modern times.

Had Martínez pitched more often, made more starts, thrown more innings, would he have been as dominant—*or effective*? Not likely.

Martinez supporters, of course, may argue that the competition of an integrated, designated-hitter, performance-enhanced, drug-permeated league was tougher than what Luque had to face. That may be, but one-third of the argument then leaves Martínez under the cloud of suspicion hanging over the game during his dominant time. Another third of the contention, I view, as a boomerang effect that would then, for debate's sake, allow one to question the overall caliber of play in the Negro and Winter Leagues. For example, did Cool Papa Bell and Buck Leonard have to bat against Satchel Paige and Hilton Smith every game? No. Josh Gibson and Willard Brown set home run records in Mexico and Puerto Rico. Does anyone want to examine the won-lost records of the pitchers faced by these record-setting men in those leagues? The one concession, therefore, that can be given is the fact that Martinez had to face a "legitimate" hitter four times a game, whereas Luque did not.

Comparing players from different baseball eras has always been a spirited but difficult endeavor. In the end it came down to Luque's quantity and quality over Martínez's singular quality.

This side note aside, I believe the book's main goal has been accomplished. I will leave it up to the reader to decide how thoroughly.

Introduction

The internationalization of baseball in the United States can be traced to the early part of the 20th century with the appearances of the first Hispanic ballplayers in both the Negro and major leagues. Latin American athletes of the time established the first toe-holds of advancement for future generations of foreign-born players to follow.

Hispanic pitchers excelled ahead of Hispanic position players at the outset of the prior century. The 21st-century bumper crop of multi-national players who now represent various countries from two hemispheres at the big league level owe a debt to early Hispanic pitchers who first tilled the unaccommodating soil of the North American baseball landscape.

A handful of these early pitchers, José Méndez, Martín Dihigo, and Ramon Bragaña, were denied access into organized baseball in the United States because of their skin tones. That did not prevent these talent-laden hurlers from making superlative contributions to other vibrant leagues that existed apart from the major leagues. Those contributions validated the Latin American sportsman and kept the door open for similar men of color.

In the Negro Leagues, black Hispanics constituted a small subset of players who were challenged by both a language barrier and institutional racism not encountered in their native countries. Since salaries of the era were minimal, it is a testament to the strength of character of these men that they not only overcame these daily obstacles abroad but thrived in spite of them.

No one thrived more as a Latin American pitcher in the initial decades of the 20th century than Adolfo Luque, at least when it came to the mainstream press. The Cuban right-hander blazed the earliest trails from the mound of any big league Hispanic moundsman. Blessed with exceptional ability and acceptable skin pigmentation, Luque was one of only a handful of Hispanic pitchers to play in the pre-integrated major leagues. (Contrast that to the number of Hispanic pitchers on today's major league rosters.) Hispanic Caucasians, like Luque, made up the first minority class within organized baseball. In 1930, Luque, after starring with the Cincinnati Reds during the 1920s, became the first Hispanic player for what would evolve into the progressive Brooklyn Robins/Dodgers franchise.

Starting in the early 1940s, the Washington Senators ball club was to Hispanic Caucasians what Brooklyn became for African Americans beginning in 1947. But opportunity sometimes came with a price. In 1939, Venezuelan pitcher Alejandro Carrasquel's name was changed to Alex Alexandra by Washington's hierarchy to make it more fan friendly for the North American ear and tongue. Carrasquel persevered and his pitching eventually earned him the "right to get all the credit that's coming to him under his own name," a quote that was attributed to Senators owner Clark Griffith.

Less than two decades following the erosion of the color barrier, black Hispanic pitchers

Luis Tiant and Mike Cúellar embarked on stellar big league careers that reaped multiple 20-game-winning seasons. Earlier than that, light-skinned Dominican pitcher Juan Marichal established his place among elite major league hurlers.

The spring training obstacles of the Jim Crow South did not deter these Hispanic pioneers from establishing their own worthy place from the pitching mounds at baseball's highest level. They, along with their African American counterparts, changed for the better the face of major league baseball, improving its quality while better reflecting the game's overall fan base.

In the past 20 years, Hispanics have far surpassed African Americans as the majority minority of baseball at the major and minor league level. As society in general made significant strides toward racial equality in the closing decades of the last century, ironically, baseball lost (and continues to lose) many black athletes to rival sports. During that time, Asian ballplayers have supplemented the minority ranks of big league baseball with a diversifying excellence that Hispanic pitchers and players originally delivered.

On the field, the impact of Hispanic pitchers in the post-segregated major leagues has been far-reaching. Pitchers from Latin America have won Cy Young and Most Valuable Player Awards, have hoisted World Series MVP trophies. Baseballs from no-hitters and perfect games reside on their mantels. In short, every pinnacle achievement on an individual and team basis has been conquered.

I have selected to trumpet the exploits of 17 of these ethnic conquerors in the following chapters, with the intention of giving much needed—and well deserved—historic perspective to the enduring and enriching legacy they have left behind and continue to perpetuate.

PART I

Outside the Major Leagues

1

The Negro Leagues: Ramón Bragaña, Martín Dihigo

Ramón Bragaña

During a wide-ranging, 30-year career in which he pitched and played in Cuba, the Dominican Republic, Venezuela and the U.S. Negro Leagues, Ramón Bragaña made his most indelible mark from the baseball mounds of Mexico.

Bragaña was most notably a right-handed mound authority, though he began his career in his native Cuba as an 18-year-old infielder for team Cuba during the 1927–28 winter league season. Bragaña played in only three games with team Cuba. But he had evidently shown enough promise as to earn an invitation that summer to come to the United States to play for the Cuban Stars East of the Eastern Colored League. The ballclub was owned by impresario Alejandro "Alex" Pompez. After his internship abroad, Bragaña returned to Cuba over the winter of 1928 and debuted as a pitcher, appearing in four games. He chalked up a loss in his only decision.

Before his Negro League career had hardly commenced, Bragaña, along with a group of other players, were suspended by Pompez for not honoring their contracts and reporting to the team in 1929. Having a change of mind, or weighing other considerations, Bragaña decided to cast his lot in the Dominican summer league and joined the Licey Tigres.

Back in Cuba that winter, the 20-year-old registered his first victories from the hill as a member of the Santa Clara Leopardos. The young pitcher, with a 5–3 record, trailed only teammates Basilio "Brujo" Rosell (6–7) and Leroy "Satchel" Paige (6–5), and Almendares hurler Johnny Allen (7–4) for most victories in the league. It was Paige's only winter season pitching in Cuba.

In the summer of 1930, Bragaña returned to the Cuban Stars. Following that campaign, the itinerant pitcher, who stood just under six feet and weighed 195 pounds, did not return to the U.S. until 1935. He formed part of Pompez's redesigned entry into Negro League baseball called the New York Cubans, which maintained the high profile of outstanding Hispanic talent as had the Cuban Stars East. Among Bragaña's teammates that 1935 season were Martín Dihigo and Luis Tiant, Sr.

In 1936, the Havana product made ingresses into both the Venezuelan and Dominican Leagues. In an early summer session in Caracas, with a team called Senadores, Bragaña notched a 4–2 record in six games, helping to hoist the 12–4 squad to the Venezuelan National Series League title. For Estrellas Orientales of San Pedro de Macoris in the Dominican Republic, Bragaña posted a 9–1 mark, lifting the Eastern Stars team to the island championship. He was also named Most Valuable Player of the circuit. Over the winter of 1936, the busy moundsman won another nine games and lost five in 16 appearances for the Cuban League Almendares squad; he tossed 11 complete games.

That 9–6 performance came after a five-year absence from Cuban baseball. (In one of those years, 1933, the Cuban League had no season due to the economic repercussions of the Depression.). Bragaña had apparently become content with the playing commitments he had established in Mexico starting in 1930, pitching for several teams loosely tied to the Mexican League.

In the spring of 1937, the New York Giants traveled to Havana to condition themselves for the upcoming U.S. campaign. The Giants played four exhibition games against three Cuban teams, Almendares, Habana and Fortuna, an amateur club. The visiting New York team managed one victory—against the amateurs. Bragaña was one of two Almendares pitchers to defeat Bill Terry's club, Rodolfo Fernández the other. At Tropical Park on March 1, Bragaña tossed a six-hitter over the defending National League champions and took home a 6–1 victory.

In a rematch later during the Giants' stay, Bragaña, starting for a squad of Cuban All-Stars, matched three Giants hurlers over 11 innings in a 1–1 tie. He allowed only five hits to the New Yorkers.

Bragaña seemed in tip-top form when he joined the Estrellas team for their title defense in 1937. The Eastern Stars were not as dominant as in the prior year, as Dominican baseball enjoyed its most celebrated season of the first half of the 20th century. The stellar competition provided by the other two teams in the league resulted in Estrellas' third-place finish at 11–14 and Bragaña's 4–7 record. Packed with Negro League talent and sometimes featuring a battery of Satchel Paige and Josh Gibson, the famed Cuidad Trujillo team triumphed as league champions with an 18–13 record over Estrellas and Águilas Cibaeñas (13–15).

In 1938, the 29-year-old Bragaña joined the Agrario team of Mexico's premier league, beginning an 18-season, star-studded career in the land of Montezuma. He won eight games in each of his first two seasons in the league, and then won 12 games or more in eight of the next nine campaigns.

In 1940, Bragaña joined Veracruz and excelled. He registered a 16–8 win-loss ledger, and his 2.58 ERA in 233⅔ innings topped the league. The Veracruz team, purchased by Mexico's irrepressible business tycoon, Jorge Pasquel, was moved to the capital city and altered the team nickname to Azules. Pasquel also installed himself as manager. The Blues won the pennant with a 61–30 record, six games better than the Mexico City Reds. Bragaña established a 12-year pitching residency with Veracruz and developed a close friendship with Pasquel.

Veracruz repeated as league champions the following season, this time under the helm of player-manager Lázaro Salazar, one of many Cuban stars in the league. Bragaña contributed 13 wins as Veracruz (67–35) ran away with the pennant by 13½ games over the second-place Mexico City Reds. Also propelling the Blues' cause was the record-setting 33 home runs catcher Josh Gibson hit in 94 games.

Salazar assumed the reins of Monterrey in 1942, and Veracruz coincidentally fell on hard times, finishing last in the league and winning only 39 games. Amazingly, Bragaña won *22* of the games while losing ten. Bragaña tied Martín Dihigo of pennant-winning Torreón for most wins in the league.

Ramon Bragaña with the Dominican Republic's Estrellas Orientales team in 1936 (photograph from Dr. Leyton Revel).

Bragaña's season may not have appeared amazing for those who had seen him pitch the prior winter in Cuba. The right-hander led the Cuban Winter League in games (21), wins (9), complete games (11, tied with Dihigo) and shutouts (5), in furnishing a major assist to the Almendares Scorpions' championship campaign. Four of Bragaña's shutouts were pitched consecutively, and he established a league record for scoreless innings at 39⅔. The goose-egg streak ended January 3, on an error by shortstop Antonio Rodríguez.

The circuit's top pitcher was involved in two extra-inning games that both ended in 1–1 ties. The first was on October 22, 1941. Facing Habana, Bragaña tossed 13 innings, matching the combined efforts of Habana hurlers Santiago "Sandy" Ulrich and Gilberto Torres. Bragaña and Torres permitted the contest's only runs in the 12th inning. On November 8, also against Habana, Bragaña held Mike González's team to one eighth-inning run over 12 frames. Mound opponent Manuel "Cocaína" García equaled Bragaña's exceptional labor. Lamentably, no ERA records were officially kept or preserved for the league that season.

The following winter, the pitcher managed a 6–6 record for Almendares while leading the league in appearances once again with 22.

In 1943, pulling in another 17 victories for another poor Veracruz contingent, Bragaña helped his 39–51 team barely stay out of the circuit's cellar.

In 1944, Bragaña literally did it all for his Mexican club, which made a return to championship form. He was appointed manager, guided Veracruz to their third pennant in five years, and won a remarkable 30 games on the hill. The historic 30th win for the pitcher occurred on October 5, versus the Nuevo Laredo Owls, a 6–0 six-hitter, Bragaña's fourth shutout, that clinched the pennant for Veracruz. The right-hander amazingly accounted for 30 of his team's 52 victories.

Veracruz slipped in the standings the following season, and Bragaña experienced his first losing campaign with them (15–16). The Blues, with a 42–48 record, dropped to fifth place in the six-team league. After skipping the previous two hibernal campaigns, Bragaña was back competing in Cuba over the winter of 1945. Hurling for a 29–31, third-place Almendares squad, his 9–6 record topped all other Scorpions pitchers.

Nineteen-forty-six was the grand coming-out year of Jorge Pasquel. The Mexican mogul shook the contractual foundation of baseball's ivory towers with his free-market challenge of the reserve clause. Pasquel's high-priced signings of major league players unnerved the game's North American hierarchy and provided a tumultuous side-show during much of the Mexican and major league baseball seasons. The tumult did not escape Pasquel's own Veracruz club and its multiple managers. Four field bosses directed the team, starting with Bragaña and ending with the big boss himself. In an expanded eight-team circuit, Veracruz finished seventh, 16 games under .500. Bragaña must have been bothered by the external turmoil, judging by his 9–16 record despite a 3.66 ERA.

Pasquel's bold foray had repercussions in winter baseball. In Cuba, a new independent league, with players supporting Pasquel's way of thinking, was formed. The new league competed against the established Winter League, whose players preferred to remain loyal to Organized Baseball. Ramón Bragaña sided with Pasquel's high-salary brand of baseball. The veteran pitcher joined the short-lived Federation League and won the last six games of his Cuban Winter League career with the team that carried the Winter League knock-off name of Alacranes (Scorpions).

At age 38, Bragaña recorded a strong bounce-back season upon his return to Mexico in 1947. An 18–12 record placed him at the head of his team's squadron of pitchers. Once again, Bragaña was the only stabilizing pitching force for a last-place Veracruz team (52–67).

Veracruz improved to 43–43 in 1948, with the five-time Mexican League All-Star infusing a positive 12–9 record into the club's otherwise mediocre totals. A 3.06 ERA accompanied Bragaña's seventh straight season of 200 or more innings and his eighth in nine years.

The Mexican League began experimenting with split season formats in 1949. For the next two seasons, Veracruz watched from the sidelines as other playoff teams vied for the ultimate prize. Bragaña won eight and ten games in successive seasons for his also-ran teams.

A few days into the 1950 season, "Ramón Bragaña Day" was held, on March 26, prior to a game at Mexico City's main baseball venue, Delta Park. Celebrating his 25th year in professional baseball, Bragaña was honored and bestowed with gifts by teammates and fans. The pitcher did not disappoint the latter, taking the mound after the ceremonies and tossing an 11–3 victory over the rival Mexico City team.

On May 31, an automobile accident sidelined the well-respected hurler for more than a month of the season. The vehicle he was in rolled over twice and he was reportedly critically injured. He obviously made a fast recovery from his injuries and returned to action in mid–July.

In 1951, Veracruz returned to glory once more. The team won the second half-season of play and faced off against the first-half winner, San Luis Potosí. During the team's second-half run, Bragaña had taken to working some games behind the plate, due to a shortage of catchers on the squad. From his natural position on the mound, Bragaña excelled in the championship round between the two split season victors.

In a best-of-seven series, Veracruz won four games out of five, including a forfeited contest in Game 3. The gift win for the Blues came as the result of an outright riot by San Luis Potosí fans in their Twentieth of November home ballpark. Bragaña was involved in a physical altercation with fans outside the park after the game was declared a forfeit by the umpires. Jorge Pasquel had to be hospitalized with a head injury following a hazardous clash with rock-throwing belligerents. Pasquel had witnessed the hostile encounter involving Bragaña and was coming to the defense of his favorite pitcher when he was struck on the head by a granite missile.

Back in Mexico City, Bragaña picked up victories in the last two games. (The remainder of the series was ordered played at Delta Park by league officials.) Bragaña pitched a two-hit, 6–

As a long-time pitcher with the Veracruz Blues, Ramon Bragaña was the first Mexican League pitcher to record 200 wins (photograph from Dr. Leyton Revel).

0 shutout in the fourth game, and then won the clincher with 3⅔ innings of scoreless relief, preserving a 3–2 triumph.

Jorge Pasquel withdrew from Mexican baseball the following year, 1952, and the Veracruz club was resettled back in its original port city, reborn as the Veracruz Eagles. Ramón Bragaña's lengthy association with the team ended, however, and he moved over to play for and manage the Jalisco Charros. It was for Jalisco that Bragaña recorded his 200th Mexican League win. At the Charros' Guadalajara ballpark, the 43-year-old defeated the Monterrey Sultans, 8–2, in early June. He allowed eight hits and walked two. The sentimental favorite was carried off by fans and placed at the head of a line of automobiles which paraded him around town. It was Bragaña's fifth win on the campaign, with only two more to be had for what was an average 46–44 Jaliso team.

Legacy

Ramón Bragaña was nicknamed "El Profesor" for the astute attributes he displayed on the mound, earning him many successes. However, it could not be said that he used any amount of "scholarly judgment" in 1946 during a one-on-one pitching exhibition against baseball's greatest living legend. In the hope of attaining greater legitimacy for his league, Jorge Pasquel invited Babe Ruth to Mexico in May. Ruth accepted and was coaxed into trying to demonstrate his long-gone splendor at Delta Park, in front of 22,000 fans. Wearing civilian clothes with spikes and a baseball cap, Ruth picked up a bat to hit. Bragaña was on the mound, clearly in no mood to allow the Bambino any easy swings. What ensued was an embarrassing repetition of swings and misses, or foul tips, by the 51-year-old Ruth against Bragaña's difficult tosses. Bragaña resisted being relieved by another pitcher and engaged in an argument with Mexico City manager Ernesto Carmona IV, one of the founders of the Mexican League in 1925. Bragaña eventually left the mound, but the heated exchange with Carmona continued inside the clubhouse, ending in fisticuffs. Bragaña was suspended, and Pasquel was forced to make his first managerial change of the 1946 season.

Bragaña closed out his 18-season, 211-win Mexican career in 1955, at age 46. He won another won 48 games in ten winter campaigns in Cuba. Roberto González Echevarria, Yale professor and Cuban baseball author, painted Bragaña on the mound as "a pitcher with great velocity, a wicked curveball and excellent control."[1]

In their published research for the Center for Negro League Baseball Research, Dr. Layton Revel and Luis Muñoz itemized 310 lifetime wins for Bragaña, amassed over the years in various countries. With the added speculation of incorporating "missing records," the pair believe Bragaña's career win total could top 400.

Many years prior to winning his 200th career game in Mexico, Ramón Bragaña had become a naturalized Mexican citizen. He not only maintained a special love for Mexico but he found a special love there as well, whom he married. Bragaña, along with other Cuban greats such as Lázaro Salazar and Santos Amaro, married and started families in Mexico, where they enjoyed the celebrity status of star athletes.

When Ramón Bragaña died on his 76th birthday, May 11, 1985, in Puebla, Mexico, he had been elected to the Halls of Fame of Cuba and Mexico.

He was rightfully inducted into the Latino Baseball Hall of Fame, as part of its third class of honorees, in 2012.

Bragaña and good friend Jorge Pasquel take a break during a hunting expedition (photograph from Dr. Leyton Revel).

Martín Dihigo

One of the greatest players who ever lived, and the acknowledged most exceptionally versatile, was Martín Dihigo Llanos. He stood 6'1" and weighed a lithesome 190 pounds in his playing prime. He played every diamond position and, except possibly at catcher, excelled at each. Dihigo's playing career stretched from 1923–1947.

Born May 24, 1906, in the Limonar municipality of Matanzas, Cuba, Dihigo began his baseball career at Almendares Park II, playing for the Habana Leones during the 1922–1923 Cuban Winter League season. The future superstar made his professional debut on January 21, 1923, against eventual league champion Marianao. He pinch-hit unsuccessfully in the ninth inning of a game won by Marianao, 8–5. The 16-year-old played sparingly, and when he did he was overmatched by the competition. In Dihigo's rookie year, six of his Habana teammates were former or current major leaguers.

After that season, in which Habana finished second, one of Dihigo's teammates, Adolfo Luque, traveled to the United States to play. Luque played for the Cincinnati Reds and produced one of the greatest pitching seasons on record. An opposing player in the Cuban League, Pelayo Chacón, convinced the young Dihigo to come abroad with him and play in the U.S. Negro leagues. Cuban historian Alfredo L. Santana Alonso, in his 1996 biography of Martín Dihigo, *El Inmortal del Béisbol,* quoted Dihigo, as follows, on what that period in his early baseball life was like:

> I had to ask my family for permission, since I was still under age. I'm grateful to Mike González [for letting me go] and Pelayo Chacón and Bartolo Portuondo [Cuban and Negro League players] who guided me [in the U.S.].
> I played for the Cuban Stars. I was paid $100 a month. I learned to unravel, bit by bit, the secrets of playing baseball well. But I also experienced, first hand, the contempt of gringos, the trying vexations of daily life and the stark realities of having to subsist day to day.[2]

Dihigo's team was Alex Pompez's Cuban Stars East of the newly formed Eastern Colored League. The following season, Dihigo received a monthly salary increase to $125 and hit ten home runs. In all, Dihigo participated in 12 campaigns in the Negro Leagues.

Dihigo was not only the quintessential all-around player—run, field, hit, throw—but he could also pitch, and pitch brilliantly.

In 1932, Dihigo commenced the first of three seasons in Venezuela. With the Concordia team, on August 21, 1932, Dihigo pitched a no-hitter with 14 strikeouts. In 1933, the 27-year-old was undefeated in six decisions and struck out 101 batters in 60 innings. As a member of Equipo Universidad, he threw his second one-hitter of the season on September 24, downing Royal Criollos and 21-year-old pitcher Alejandro Carrasquel, 1–0, in ten innings.

From 1935 forward, pitching became a regular facet of Dihigo's game. It was on the mound that year that Dihigo was involved in the best and most famous all-star game in Negro Leagues history. Pitching for the East squad, the all-purpose All-Star surrendered a game-winning, three-run home run in the bottom of the tenth inning to George "Mule" Suttles of the home team "Westerners."

The East-West All-Star Game, as it was known, pitted premium players from their regionally-based teams. The competing players were voted in by the fans. The *Chicago Defender,* a prominent black newspaper of the era, examined the player selections as ballots were pouring in. Dihigo's was recorded in the following manner: "Martin Dihigo is head and shoulders above his competition for the right field berth. He's the greatest in that position in the country. He has the greatest throwing arm in baseball, and when he hits one on the nose it's headed for distant parts."[3] The "superb ballplayer," as James A. Riley described Dihigo in his biographical encyclopedia on Negro Leagues players, received the second-most votes of any participant, behind only shortstop Willie Wells.

The Cuban virtuoso also played in Puerto Rico, the Dominican Republic, and Mexico, where he became a legendary figure in that county's baseball history.

In 1938, his second year in Mexico, the 32-year-old Dihigo recorded one of the greatest seasons by a pitcher in league history, winning 18 and losing but two for Águila de Veracruz. In the rarefied air of high-altitude Mexico, he compiled an unfathomable 0.92 ERA in 167 innings with 184 strikeouts. His .387 average, including six long balls and 27 RBI, in 42 games, won the circuit's hitting crown. Dihigo's Veracruz team won the pennant with a 40–9 record. He became the first player in circuit annals to record six hits in a game, on September 18. Dihigo's hits, a homer, double and four singles, were struck against the capital city's Agrario team, against North American pitching titan Satchel Paige and well-regarded Mexican hurler Alberto Romo Chávez. Two weeks earlier, on September 5, Dihigo and Paige faced each other on the mound for the first time. Dihigo won, 3–1, in a complete game effort, with Ramón Bragaña pinned with the loss in relief of Paige. These were two of the three games Paige pitched in the Mexican League.

During the schedule-reduced 1937 season, pitching for the same Eagles team, Dihigo had tossed the first no-hitter in Mexican baseball history, on September 16. He humbled the Nogales Cerveceros, 4–0. The right-hander saw pitching action in four games for the 20–4 Veracruz club, winning all of them. He contributed immensely to Veracruz being crowned champion of the league. During the playoffs between Southern Division victors Veracruz and Northern Division champs Agrario (21–4), Dihigo registered all three victories in the best-of-five series.

During his third Mexican campaign, Dihigo set a single-game strikeout record with 18 over nine innings. Defeating the Tampico Alijadores, 7–3, on August 5, 1939, the Águila right-hander whiffed the equivalent of two full rotations through the batting order. Veracruz (37–21) finished in second place, a distant nine games behind Lázaro Salazar's pennant-capturing Córdoba Cafeteros. Dihigo's year-end pitching numbers were 15–8 with a 2.90 ERA in 202 innings. He also hit .337 with five home runs and 31 RBI in 51 games.

In 1940, Dihigo was part of another veracruzano championship team. Dihigo's 8–6 mark took a back seat to teammates Ramón Bragaña's 16–8 and Barney Brown's 16–7 records for Jorge Pasquel's pennant-winning aggregation which had relocated to Mexico City. But the 34-year-old star hit to the loud tune of .364 with nine homers and 73 runs driven home in 78 games.

After four years with Veracruz, Dihigo moved over to Unión Laguna de Torreón in 1941. He slipped to 9–10 on the hill with a 4.08 ERA. But the versatile player recorded solid offensive statistics at the plate. Playing in 92 games, he powered 12 home runs, hit .310 and knocked 59 runs across the dish.

In 1942, Dihigo took home Triple Crown honors on the mound again, playing for the Blue Sharks of Torreón. He also managed the team, after taking over the club following a managerial change prior to the close of the 1941 campaign. Tying Ramón Bragaña for most wins in the league with 22, Dihigo guided Torreón to a tight pennant win over nearest competitor Monterrey (winning by 1½ games). The pitcher lost only seven times on the season; his ERA was a trim 2.53 in 245⅓ innings, a career high. His 211 strikeouts paced the circuit. Dihigo hit .300 or better (.319) for the sixth straight season.

The hitting title went to Bragaña's Veracruz teammate, Monte Irvin, with a .397 mark. It was the only year Irvin spent in Mexico as a player, and the Hall of Famer wrote the following about Dihigo in his 1996 autobiography: "Dihigo was a big, tall, regal guy and had a lot of confidence. He was the greatest Latin American player I had ever seen and a pleasure to be around."[4]

The next season, 1943, Torreón, at 51–36, finished one-half game behind pennant-winning Monterrey, with a record of 53–37. The league apparently made no effort to have Torreón rectify their inadequacy of games played. Dihigo's 16–8 pitching ledger, with a 3.10

ERA, was second-best on the club to the 18–6, 2.70 ERA compilation of teammate Manuel Fortes.

When the Torreón club did not field a team in 1944, Dihigo was enticed by Nuevo Laredo to be their new playing manager in 1944. The franchise was a new entry into the

Second from right, Martin Dihigo sits atop a Mexican League dugout in the uniform of Unión Laguna. The barbed wire is to keep overzealous fans in their seats. The photograph is purported to have been taken April 11, 1946, Dihigo's final season as manager of the Blue Sharks.

league, having taken the spot of the temporarily disbanded Torreón team. Dihigo won a dozen games, tying Fortes, who also joined the team, for top honors on the club. But Nuevo Laredo fell short of the title, five games behind Ramón Bragaña's Veracruz Blues, in fourth place, in a close pennant battle with three other clubs.

After a year away from Mexico during 1945, Dihigo came back to Torreón, once more at the team's helm. George Hausmann, a major leaguer persuaded by magnate Jorge Pasquel to come to Mexico in 1946, joined the Dihigo-managed Torreón club. Forty-four years later, the league-jumping player spoke of his first meeting with a gracious Martín Dihigo in a *Baseball Research Journal* article.

> I joined Torreon in Mexico City early in April, a few games into the season. When I arrived at the park, a photographer wanted to take a picture of me with Dihigo. Martin was very considerate. I would have been greatly honored to have a picture taken [with him]. But he wanted me to get the star treatment, and he stepped aside and told the photographer to take the picture of me by myself.[5]

Dihigo was 41 at the time and his playing career was quickly winding down. Even though he was the field boss, Dihigo had no reason to welcome Hausmann so courteously. He could have very easily and resentfully looked upon Hausmann as a representative of the institution that had for so long shunned him and other black players. But he did not, and that kindly act spoke volumes about Martín Dihigo the man.

Following two sub-.300 batting average seasons in 1943 and 1944, Dihigo hit .316 in 66 games in 1946. He knocked three balls out of the park and accounted for 32 runs driven home. Torreón languished in the middle of the eight-team pack with a 50–47 record.

Dihigo played ten seasons in Mexico, 1937–1944 and 1946–47, and one game in another, 1950. As a pitcher, throwing more than 1,500 innings, he assembled a 119–57 won-loss mark with an ERA of 2.84, and had a lifetime batting average of .317 with a slugging percentage of .490. He was the first pitcher to win 100 games and the first to send 1,000 men back to the bench on strikeouts.

Of course, Dihigo did not forsake his homeland. He lavished his baseball skills on Cuban baseball diamonds for more than two decades, pitching in nearly all of them. A four-time Most Valuable Player with a .296 lifetime average, Dihigo's mound exploits in the league were greater than those with the bat. "El Maestro," as he was appropriately nicknamed, won and completed more games than any other pitcher in Cuban League history. His victory total was 107 with 121 complete games. Only Adolfo Luque pitched in more campaigns than Dihigo (22 to 19). Biographer Santana Alonso stated that Dihigo wore the number 11 during all of his uniform-numbered campaigns in Cuba. Dihigo also managed for five seasons in Cuba, all as a player-manager.

LEGACY

As a pitcher, following the final out of games, Martin Dihigo was known to throw the last utilized baseball into the sun-drenched grandstand. "It's there the poorest of fans sit," he reasoned over his humble display of generosity.[6]

Cuban author Roberto González Echevarria raised Dihigo to the echelon of a DiMaggio in his encompassing baseball history, *The Pride of Havana*:

Dihigo, a man of truly superlative talents, and not just in baseball terms, was and is a revered figure in Cuba. He had something else difficult to describe, an intangible trait associated with bullfighting, a sport in which there are no numerical records to evaluate an individual: He had grace. His blend of style, dignity, and elegance was apparently unique.

Dihigo also had leadership qualities, was personable, well-spoken, and had a sense of humor. With the years Dihigo developed into a sharp dresser who wore his suits well. He eventually became a successful manager and the first Cuban ballplayer to become a sportscaster after retiring. Dihigo was also endowed with a social and political conscience: He supported and aided the Cuban Revolution in its early years. He was buried a hero when he passed away.[7]

Dihigo's ball-playing days ended after the 1946–1947 winter season, the same calendar year the majors commenced integration. In 1923, the young Dihigo had debuted in the Cuban Winter League as an unsuccessful, ninth-inning pinch-hitter in a game versus the Marianao Tigres. On December 26, 1946, the 23-season veteran collected his final base hit on a Cuban baseball field—a pinch-hit, ninth-inning, game-winning single off Almendares pitcher Max Lanier. The hit lifted Dihigo's Cienfuegos Elephants team to a 1–0 victory.

The former great player appeared in his last game on a Cuban diamond on January 11, 1947, as a mop-up relief pitcher in a 14–3 Cienfuegos loss to Marianao.

"The Man Who Did Everything"

Martín Dihigo, the player, left such lasting impressions as a ballplayer throughout Cuba, Mexico and U.S. black baseball that he was elected to the national Halls of Fame of these three countries. In 2010, he was enshrined as part of an inaugural class of 25 players, broadcasters and executives in the newly established Latino Baseball Hall of Fame in La Roma, Dominican Republic.

The National Baseball Hall of Fame, in accordance with the special Veterans Committee established to recognize great players from the Negro Leagues era, posthumously enshrined the Matanzas-born player in 1977, six years after his death.

Baseball writer Bob Broeg recognized Dihigo and John Henry "Pop" Lloyd, voted into the Hall with Dihigo, in a *Sporting News* article from their election year, subtitled "Black Beauties." Broeg mentioned, in the opening of the article, a recent story written by historian John B. Holway, researched for him by a former player.

> Pittsburgh man Ted Page, a loyal Hall of Fame Day visitor to Cooperstown and an opponent of Dihigo in the old Eastern Colored League of the 1920s and 30s, went all out for Holway in a piece the historian from Manassas, Va. did about Dihigo entitled aptly, *"The Man Who Did Everything."*
>
> As an admirer of Roberto Clemente, Page said Dihigo threw even harder than Clemente and, playing shortstop at times, covered short like Marty Marion. Once in Cuba, Martin watched a powerful-armed jai-lai player whip the horsehide from home plate against the centerfield fence on one bounce. Dihigo wound up and threw the darn ball over the wall.[8]

A decade after his death, a poll taken among his living peers and historians placed Dihigo as the greatest second baseman in Negro Leagues history. Dihigo, well-remembered by the reverent sobriquet "El Inmortal," also received accompanying votes as best all-time outfielder and third baseman, permanent testimonial to his masterful dexterity. Negro Leagues Hall of Famer Cool Papa Bell called Dihigo the most complete player he had ever seen.

Martín Dihigo was the only child produced by the marriage of Benito Dihigo and Margarita Llanos. He had two half-brothers, one each by his respective parents. Martín was raised in the Matanzas suburb of Pueblo Nuevo, where the family established itself when Martín was a toddler. Martín grew up not far from the historic Palmar del Junco baseball park and played many games as a youngster on its glorified terrain. (The ballfield, still preserved in Cuba today, was the site of the earliest, widely recorded professional game in Cuba, dating back to 1874. The field carries the same allegorical—but more tangible—equivalent of the Elysian Fields from early U.S. baseball history.)

At age 13, Dihigo began his participation in a youth league with a team called Oriente. He played with several youth teams in subsequent years, competing against other squads located in other towns, along what was a hotbed of baseball competition that existed between the 55-mile corridor from Matanzas east to Havana.

In 1922, Dihigo's great raw talent was made known to Habana manager Mike González, who added Dihigo to his team. Dihigo sat idly on the Leones' bench for two months until his pinch-hitting debut.

* * *

Upon Martín Dihigo's death in 1971, Prensa Latina, the state-run news agency of Cuba, reported his passing as the result of cerebral thrombosis. The report noted that Dihigo had in 1967 worked as sports commentator and baseball instructor for the Cuban Sports Ministry, better known by its acronym INDER.

During the 1960s, Dihigo helped raise, with his wife, his two children, Martín, Jr. and Gilberto. Martín, Jr. remains in Cuba, but youngest son Gilberto left the island in the 1990s. Gilberto has distinguished himself as a journalist in several Latin American countries since his departure. He remembered his father in a 1999 interview as a "thinker, idealist, and fierce nationalist ... someone who spoke out against discrimination and stood up for black players like himself before it became fashionable."[9]

Gilberto's grandfather, Martín's father, was named Benito and was a sergeant in the Mambises army—the Cuban ragtag equivalent of the U.S. colonial forces led by George Washington. The native army fought against Spain during Cuba's turn-of-the-20th-century War of Independence. Benito originally did not approve of Martín's ball-playing, believing that all men should learn a trade. (In his younger years, Martín took up wood-working, to try and appease his father.)

It is obvious that Martín Dihigo's developed social consciousness rose from his freedom-fighting father. Although, according to Santana Alonso, the social activist did not have more than a fifth grade education (having to forego school at a young age in order to earn supplemental income for his family), Dihigo later in life became a well-read man. He was well informed about the turbulent history of Cuba as a young republic.

A Cuban newspaper profile from the 1946–1947 CWL season indicated that Dihigo had assumed, at that point of his life, the comfortable station of a self-educated man:

> Martín rose at 8:00 a.m. to begin his day and read the newspapers, while his wife Africa, prepared his breakfast. Martín devoured the press reports of the day from nearly all of the city's daily papers.
> First, he reviewed the boxscores from the sports section, studying the accomplishments and frustrations of the recognized players.... Then he reads the political news on the homefront and then the section of world news.[10]

Needless to say, as a young adult, Dihigo experienced racial discrimination throughout his years in U.S. black baseball. As a mature man with sensibilities rooted against social unjust, he was thoroughly displeased by the strong-arm tactics of Fulgencio Batista's ascent to power in 1950s Cuba, enough to abandon Cuba, in protest, for an extended period of years. Two decades earlier, during the mid–1930s, Dihigo also voluntarily left Cuba for a few years, voicing his political objections to the supposed underhanded re-election tactics of Cuban president Gerardo Machado that fostered for him a second term in office.

After his playing days, to his immense credit, the self-educated Dihigo established himself as newspaperman, from 1948 to 1952, meriting a column in the Havana newspaper *Hoy* (Today). He also was heard as a color analyst during this period for Cuban Winter League games for stations Unión Radio and Cadena Oriental de Radio.

Dihigo left the broadcast booth and took the job managing Pablo Morales' Caracas Leones team over the 1952–1953 Venezuelan Winter League season. The Lions won the pennant and traveled to Havana to play in the V Caribbean Series. The team did not make a good showing, winning only one game in six in the famous round-robin tournament.

In the 1950s, while in self-imposed exile in Mexico, Dihigo was introduced to Argentine revolutionary Ernesto "Che" Guevara. The meeting may have been related to a ball-playing endeavor by Dihigo in Mexico in 1958. The 52-year-old former great suited up one final time to play right field for Torreón in an exhibition game to raise funds to benefit the Cuban Revolutionary movement.

Gilberto Dihigo currently maintains his own blog.[11] He sometimes reminisces about his father, who died in Cienfuegos in 1971, when Gilberto was a pre-teen.

While Martín Dihigo worked for the Cuban Sports Ministry and was sympathetic to the Cuban Revolution in the early years, his son points out that toward the end of his life his father, he feels, was disillusioned by it all. Gilberto Dihigo cited an example from a 1969 interview, involving famed Dodgers catcher Roy Campanella, who publicly lamented the death of Martin Dihigo to his interviewer. (Campanella had caught Dihigo in the 1945 East-West All Star Game.) In fact, Dihigo had not died, he had simply been cast aside by the Cuban propaganda machine for not following what Gilberto termed "the letter of the revolutionary law." According to Gilberto, when the very Sports Ministry in which Dihigo had worked was queried by the foreign press as to his father's whereabouts, the organization could not provide an answer.

Gilberto stresses today that his father deserves to be remembered as a man for all ages, rather than a man of his time. His youngest son laments that in Cuba there is not a sizable stadium or meaningful baseball tournament named after his late father, one of two fitting measures he feels his father's memory merits. (There is a modern day bust of Dihigo inside Estadio Latinoamericano in Havana and a museum exhibit dedicated to him in the Cienfuegos Municipality of Cruces.)

There are also places outside of Cuba dedicated to recognizing and preserving the memory of "superb ballplayers" like Martín Dihigo. One of the most impressive, if not the most impressive stop inside the Negro League Museum in Kansas City is the Field of Legends, where 10 life-size bronze statues adorn a condensed ballfield design. One can see the sculpted representations of Cool Papa Bell, Oscar Charleston and Leon Day that are on stationary patrol in the outfield. From the same left to right diamond placements, Ray Dandridge, Judy

Johnson, Pop Lloyd and Buck Leonard, man with immobility the four infield spots. Behind the plate is the permanently crouched Josh Gibson, wonderfully captured at the catcher's precise "rocking movement," as his spikes nestled him into a comfortable squatting position prior to receiving the pitched ball. On the mound, in a hands-at-the-belt "set position," an inflexible Satchel Paige prepares an undeliverable pitch to the plate.

And stepping a rigid foot into the batter's box, with motionless hands squeezing the bat handle, is the statue of Martín Dihigo.

Frozen in time as interminably as his legend.

2

The Latin American Leagues:
Ramón Arano, Rubén Gómez,
Orlando Hernández, Juan Pizarro

Ramón Arano

Ramón Arano rewrote Mexican League record books during a 32-year pitching career in which he competed for various teams, most recognizably the Mexico City Diablos Rojos and the Córdoba Cafeteros.

Arano hailed from Tierra Blanca, a south-central municipality in the state of Veracruz. When he was nine, his family moved farther southeast in the same state, to Cosamaloapan, where he was raised.

He was brought into the Mexican League as a 19-year-old by the Poza Rica Petroleros in 1959. (His first professional ballplaying occurred with Aguascalientes of the Mexican Central League in 1957. He lost his only decision in the league.) The Oilers of Poza Rica showed no patience with the youngster and released him. He was picked up by the neighboring Águila team. In 26 appearances, mostly as a starter, between the two clubs, the novice hurler fought off the more experienced challengers of the league and sported a win-loss ledger of 8–9. In 129 innings, Arano's ERA was 4.47.

A right-hander, Arano did nothing to reinforce the Veracruz Eagles' faith in him the following season. The sophomore pitcher did not win a game, while losing five. His ERA soared to 6.53 in 33 outings, all but seven of them in relief.

But in 1961, Arano found within himself the physical and intellectual qualities that make a successful pitcher and applied them to his craft. He won 11 and lost only three, in the dual role of reliever and starter. Tied with two others for second-most wins on the team, he was a boost to Águila as the team captured the pennant by four games over second-place Puebla.

During this time, the best team in the Mexican League faced the champions of the Texas League in what was called the Pan American Series. In a best-of-seven cross-border series, Águila was defeated by the San Antonio Missions, four games to two. Arano earned both of the Eagles' wins, including the opener, 4–2, played in Veracruz. Arano downed the Missions, allowing two runs on five hits, with five strikeouts. The 22-year-old pitcher postponed the San Antonio celebration with a victory in Game 5, stopping them on nine hits, 4–3, in another complete game effort. They were the only games a team from Mexico won against the Texas League in the three annual championship competitions played so far.

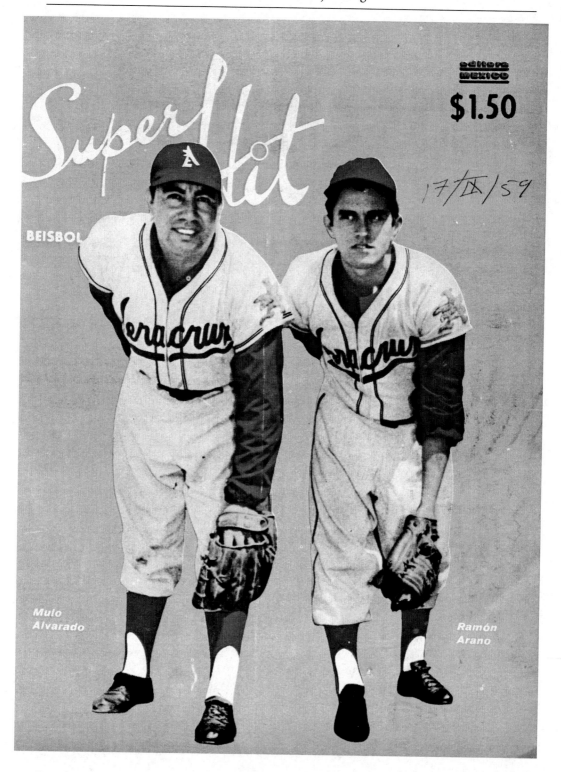

Ramón Arano, right, pictured as a 1959 rookie in tandem with teammate Rodolfo "Mulo" Alvarado of the Veracruz Eagles. Arano went on to become the winningest pitcher in Mexican baseball history.

Arano broke out with a 17-win campaign in 1962, the second-most wins in the league, behind two other pitchers. Six losses and a 2.60 ERA earned him the top spots in winning percentage and ERA in the circuit. Mike Cúellar's 134 strikeouts nudged Arano out of the strikeout title by ten.

The Oklahoma City 89ers of the American Association acquired Arano's rights from Veracruz prior to the close of the season. He debuted for Oklahoma City on August 26, and gained credit for a 10–5 win over the Denver Bears. Arano hurled six innings, surrendering two runs and five hits. His record was 1–1, with a high ERA, as a late addition to the team.

Oklahoma City took that late look at Arano in 1962, but early the next season the club had a change of heart and returned the pitcher to Veracruz in April. These were the only forays Arano would make into baseball in the great north. He was either not invited back to North American baseball or decided to concentrate solely on his career at home after that.

His recent successes led Arano into a contract dispute with the Eagles that same spring. Unable to come to terms with their burgeoning star, the club sold him to the Mexico City Red Devils for $10,000. Arano began a successful nine-and-one-half-year residency with the capital city team by winning 13 and losing only four. He led the league in winning percentage for the third year in a row and, over the past three seasons, had compiled a 41–13 record.

In 1964, the Mexican League celebrated its 40th season and added a team to the loop. For the first time since 1951, with the addition of the Jalisco Charros, eight clubs competed for the pennant. Led by 16-game-winners Aaron Flores (16–7) and Arano (16–9), the 82–58 Red Devils edged out the Puebla Parrots by three games in the final standings to lay claim as the top team in Mexico. It was the franchise's first pennant since 1956 and only their second in 25 years.

In a game on June 3, Arano faced younger brother Efraín, a pitcher for the Poza Rica Oilers, for the first time. Efraín, with relief help, bested his older sibling, 4–3. That season in the Mexican League, the biggest individual headlines belonged to Héctor Espino. The Monterrey Sultans slugger set a record for most home runs in a season with 46, playing for a second division team (66–74).

In 1965, Arano posted a 9–8 record in 22 starts, with a 4.80 ERA. Not surprisingly, the Red Devils slipped in the standings to fifth place, eight games below .500 and 16½ games off the pace of the league-topping Mexico City Tigers.

The following season, Arano started off slowly, winning only once in seven decisions. But he turned his season around from that point forward. On July 3, the pitcher evened his record at 11–11 with one of two shutouts he tossed on the campaign. He blanked the Mexico City Tigers, 7–0, on four hits. The right-hander won his final ten decisions and his season-ending pitching ledger was 16–11, third-best on the club. He appeared in 39 games, 29 as a starter. His ERA was a neat 2.96. In a split-season format, the Red Devils won the second half-season, but were defeated by their capital city brethren in the best-of-seven championship series in six games. Arano suffered one of the four losses.

In March of 1967, the Cleveland Indians continued a succession of visits the big league club made to Mexico City during spring training over the past several seasons. Social Security Stadium, Mexico City's main baseball venue, was packed for all three exhibition games Cleveland played against the stadium's inhabitants. One of Mexico's best-known sportswriter, Fernando M. Campos, summed up the festive atmosphere surrounding the first game in this report: "It's wonderful.... Look how the people cheer. Baseball certainly is a universal language, is it not? The only thing that can compare with the Indians coming here the last three years is a visit the late President Kennedy made to Mexico City."[1]

The Indians won two games against the Tigers and were defeated, 4–0, by the Red Devils. Arano hurled the shutout and was carried off the field by fans after the final out. Arano's younger brother Wilfredo smacked a three-run home run for the winning team. A few months into the regular campaign, Wilfredo came within one hit of tying the league record for consecutive hits. The youngest baseball-playing Arano brother accumulated nine hits in a row before his streak was stopped on May 16 by Veracruz. Arano, however, collected three more hits in his next three times up in the May 16 contest—a 4–1 Red Devils victory—leaving him 12-for-13.

A 15-game winner in 1967, Ramón Arano picked up his 100th career victory on June 20. He downed the rival Tigers, 10–5. His brother Wilfredo recorded a perfect 4-for-4 day at the dish. Arano pitched in 40 of the his team's 139 games, starting 31 games and completing 17. He was defeated 11 times and posted a 2.78 ERA for his third-place squad.

The New York Yankees took the international goodwill baton from the Cleveland Indians in the spring of 1968 and visited Mexico City. The Yankees played four games, winning three. Once again, Ramón Arano made Mexican fans' hearts beat hardest and their lungs bellow the loudest. Arano topped the New Yorkers in a jammed Social Security Stadium, 5–3, in the opener of the exhibition set on March 18. Arano gave up home runs to Andy Kosco and Frank Fernández among five hits surrendered. In a subsequent game, Mickey Mantle received a standing ovation when he clubbed one of the seven home runs the Yankees hit during their stay, which drew over 93,000 spectators.

Six days after defeating the Yankees, Arano notched his first win of the infant campaign. A home run by brother Wilfredo helped him ease past the Monterrey Sultans, 2–1. On April 23, Arano was the hard-luck loser, 1–0, in 11 innings to Jesús Robles and the Mexico City Tigers. Arano had set down 23 batters in a row entering the final inning when he was done in on a walk, sacrifice and base hit.

Winning 17 games in 1968 with a brilliant ERA of 2.02, Arano led his Mexico City team to the top of the circuit heap. In his 30th start of the season, Arano clinched the flag for the Red Devils with a 1–0 conquest of the Reynosa Broncos on the last day of the campaign. Pitching on two days' rest, the veteran hurler allowed only three hits and set down the final 13 batters in order. It was Arano's 15th complete game and third shutout. It came in the first game of a doubleheader, and a win in the second game by the Red Devils elevated the final victory margin to 2½ games over second-place Veracruz.

James Horsford accomplished the rare feat of winning 20 games for Reynosa in 1968. Horsford was then obtained from Reynosa by the Monterrey Sultans prior to the campaign in 1969. The Santurce, Puerto Rico, native matched up against the Mexico City Reds' star pitcher to open the new season. Ramón Arano came out on top, 2–0, to the cheers of a sellout crowd of 25,000 in Mexico's capital. Both runs scored against Horsford were unearned. It was one of the few highlights on the season for Arano, however. He was sidelined by injury for the first time in his career and his record slipped to 5–7 in only 82 innings of mound work.

Arano compiled a 15–14 record the following season, 1970. He started 35 games but completed only five. His ERA inflated to 3.95 in 198 innings. The Mexican League split its ten teams into two divisions. The Northern Division-winning Mexico City Red Devils played Southern Division victors Veracruz in the championship series. The Eagles were crowned champions with a six-game series triumph over the Red Devils. Arano lost two games in the circuit square-off, including the clincher.

In 1971, Arano developed some difficulties with Red Devils field general José Guerrero. Not helping his cause were Arano's own difficulties on the mound. After losing four games in a row, Arano became embroiled "in a row with manager Guerrero." The team then cut ties with Arano. On the surface, it was a rather shameful parting of the ways between the Red Devils and the pitcher who had won over 100 games for the team and had aided immensely in collecting two championship trophies for the franchise.

Arano latched on with the Saltillo Saraperos and posted a winning record with the team from the northeastern state of Coahuila. His winning record with Saltillo (but 12–15 overall) was a needed shot in the arm for the team, which won the Zona Norte by 3½ games over Monterrey.

The league had corrected a geographic oversight and relocated the Mexico City Red Devils into the Southern Division. It appeared the Red Devils would face Arano's Saltillo squad for post-season championship honors, but the Red Devils blew a ten-game lead and were overtaken late in the season by the Jalisco Charros, who won eight of their last ten games to close out the campaign. The Cinderella Charros then beat Arano's Saraperos in a seven-game series. Arano lost the sixth game, 3–2. He had a no-decision in Game 2.

The Mexican League expanded to 14 teams in 1972, with two new teams joining the Southern Division. The defending champions from Jalisco were moved into the Northern Division. One of the new franchises was the Córdoba Coffeegrowers, and the new team of Ramón Arano. The 33-year-old was an inconsistent pitcher for Córdoba, splitting his 26 decisions on the season. But Córdoba, which was an earlier member of the league before dropping out in 1940, made history as the first expansion team to win the Mexican League championship. Led by 21-game-winner Silvano Quezada, the 72–61 club won their Southern Division by 1½ games over the runner-up Mexico City Tigers, and elevated their game to take a six-game series over an 89-win Saltillo squad from the Northern Division.

Arano won two games in the championship round, both in relief. In the sixth game, Arano pitched five scoreless innings as Córboba held on for a 3–2 champagne-popping victory.

Baseball was experiencing enough of a boom in Mexico for the league to expand again in 1973. Two more teams, in the cities of Chihuahua and Juárez, were awarded franchises and joined a realigned four-division circuit.

Arano opened the season at home for Córdoba and defeated the Yucatán Leones, 8–4. A crowd of 13,500 cheered Arano on to his 168th lifetime win. Arano was then limited to only nine more starts all season. Recovery time from an emergency appendectomy in early May curtailed Arano's output. Absorbing a decision in each of his ten outings, he won six and had a splendid ERA of 1.66 over 76 innings. Córdoba finished at the bottom of the new Southeastern Division.

In a more common 26 starts during the 1974 season, Arano won 12 and lost 10. Most of them were quality starts, judged by the 2.55 ERA he posted in 197⅓ innings. One of the defeats was a 13-inning encounter on April 28, versus Saltillo. Two solo home runs were the difference in the 2–1 loss—one in the eighth inning by Saraperos outfielder Alfredo Mariscal, and the back-breaking blow by Marcelo Juárez in the 13th frame.

On July 11, Arano tied San Luis Potosí native Francisco "Panchillo" Ramírez for the second-most wins in Mexican League history. An 8–6 win over the Juárez Indians delivered Arano's 184th career victory.

Eight teams made the playoffs in the second year of the league's new 1974 expanded format. As the second-place team in the Southeastern Division, Córdoba's first round opponent was Jalisco, the champion of the Southwestern Division. (The Southeastern Division winners played the second-place team in the Southwestern Division. The Northeastern and Northwestern Division teams followed suit.) The Coffegrowers were ousted in four straight games by Jalisco, which displayed superior pitching. Arano absorbed a heart-breaking 1–0 loss, in 11 innings, in Game 2. The Charros, whose 84–50 record was the best of the eight qualifiers, twice defeated Cordoba's 13-game-winner Juan Pizarro, 2–0 and 2–1. When all was said and done, the Mexico City Red Devils emerged as the new champions of the league.

In February 1975, Arano was added to the roster of Mexican Pacific League champions, the Hermosillo Naranjeros, to compete in the Caribbean Series, held in San Juan, Puerto Rico. Arano lost his only Caribbean Series start, February 2, to the home country's representative club. Arano and his Orangegrowers team lost, 6–4, to the eventual Caribbean Series champions, the Bayamón Cowboys.

Arano began the 1975 Mexican League season within reach of 200 career wins. He started the season 9–1. His ninth victory was win number 194, a 5–3 decision over Saltillo. His 15th and final victory of the campaign was his 200th. Córdoba, with strong arms on their staff, including another 15-game-winner, Porfirio Salomon, 14-game-winner Juan Pizarro and 13-game-victor Vicente Romo, made it to the final series before bowing to the Tampico Dockworkers in five games. Arano won the only game for the Coffegrowers with a 7–0, two-hit shutout in the second game. It was Tampico's first championship since the turbulent 1946 season.

At the start of his 18th campaign in 1976, Arano had Ramón Bragaña's all-time wins record of 211 within his sights. On April 2, he tossed a one-hitter, defeating the Poza Rica Oilers, 2–0, for career win 202. Multiple starts later, Arano tied Bragaña's mark with a 2–1 win over the Nuevo Laredo Owls, and in his next start he gained the record all to himself with a victory over Coahuila.

Córdoba won the Southeastern Division for the second year in a row, and Arano's 14–9 record contributed to the accomplishment. The team was defeated in the second round of the playoffs by the division rival Mexico City Red Devils, four games to two. Arano handed the Red Devils one of their losses, 6–2.

In 1977, after becoming the all-time wins leader, Arano became the pitcher with the most lifetime strikeouts. He surpassed the 1,701 career mark of Ramón López in late May. He also had been named manager of Córdoba's two-time division-winning team. But Arano did not finish the season at the helm; he was replaced by experienced skipper Wilfredo Calviño. In a playoff repeat of the prior season, Córdoba exited in the second round to the Red Devils, this time in four straight games.

Following his 15-win campaign in 1977, Arano set a career high with 19 victories for a strong Córdoba team in 1978. The club posted a 95–50 record, best in the circuit, and ran away with their division by a 25½-game margin. Arano recorded the second-most wins on the staff, behind José Peña's 22. In 30 starts, the 20-year veteran completed 21 games and hurled five shutouts. But the Coffegrowers stumbled once more in round two of the championship engagement. The team from Aguascalientes took down Córdoba in a series that lasted six games.

Arano nearly duplicated his 19–10 showing of 1978 the following season with a 19–13 mark. In 1979, he also matched his complete game high of 21 and career-best five shutouts from the prior campaign. He improved his ERA from 2.51 in 1978 to 2.34 in 1979. To top it off, he set a personal single-season mark in innings with 269. Arano accomplished all these resplendent numbers at 40 years of age. Córdoba won their division for the fourth time in five years and for the fourth consecutive year did not make it past the second round of the playoffs. The Puebla Parrots continued the semifinal round jinx for the Coffegrowers, eliminating the team in five games.

Prior to the exit, Arano did shine in the opening series against Aguascalientes. He shut out the "Warm Springs' team, 1–0, in the opening game. Along with teammate Diego Seguí, Arano pitched his team back from a 3–1 deficit in the series. In three do-or-die games, Seguí won Games 5 and 7, 3–0 and 2–0 respectively. Arano was victorious in the sixth game, 3–0.

In 1980, after eight seasons with Córdoba, Arano was successfully courted by the Reynosa Broncos to ply his trade with their ball club. Reynosa was part of the Northeastern Division. Arano started 21 games for the border franchise; he won 12 and suffered nine setbacks, with an ERA of 2.96 and 15 complete games.

The Mexican League had accumulated 20 franchises at this stage, but evidently could not stand the prosperity. A strike by a majority of the players prevented the conclusion of the season. Only six teams were able to continue to the end, playing a schedule of less than 40 games each. Reynosa was one of the loyalist teams and finished in fifth place. Arano went 2–6 in those played games. All statistics from all the teams, including those participated in by the strikers, were counted in official records.

On the heels of a peace accord, a trimmed-down league of 16 teams began the 1981 championship campaign. Apparently with past differences forgotten as well, Ramón Arano returned to the Mexico City Red Devils. He was at the fore of the pitching corps with a staff-pacing 14 wins against only five losses. His 26 starts yielded 14 complete games and four shutouts. An ERA of 2.93 in 181 innings validated his exceptional pitching.

The Red Devils were the class of the Southeastern Division, and in the second round of the playoffs the team roared back from a three-games-to-one deficit against Campeche to go on to win the championship of the league. The memorable post-season turning point occurred on August 26. Mexico City was three outs away from elimination against Campeche when the squad rallied for three ninth-inning runs and an eventual extra-inning victory, 6–3. (The win, in 14 innings, was obtained the following day as play was stopped due to rain.) The Red Devils then beat Northeastern champion Reynosa in a series that went the full complement of seven games. For the fifth time in his long career, Ramón Arano had a hand in hoisting Mexico's ultimate championship trophy.

In 1982, Arano, being referred to in the local press as the Gaylord Perry of Mexico, closed in on the remarkable and unprecedented achievement of 300 wins. His 299th win came May 18, an 11–8 decision over Juárez. The big day arrived June 3, against Monclova. Arano edged the Northwestern Division team, 6–5. Arano finished the season with a 9–9 record in 29 games, 24 as a starter. The defending champion Red Devils did not make the playoffs.

In his 25th Mexican League campaign, Ramón Arano suited up for his seventh club.

Returning closer to home in 1983, Arano wore the uniform of the Coatzacoalcos Azules from his homestate of Verzcruz. He suffered through a losing record of 8–14, one of only a handful he experienced in his monumental career. The Blues were an also-ran in the league. One of the highlights of his season came May 14, when the long-in-the-tooth hurler recorded his 53rd career shutout with a 5–0 blanking of Tabasco.

At age 45 in 1984, Arano returned to his roots, pitching for his hometown Águila team. He topped all pitchers on the Eagles with 11 wins, but could not prevent his team from finishing below .500. Arano closed the campaign with 323 lifetime wins, more than 100 more than the previous record.

LEGACY

Arano hung on for two more seasons, winning another nine games. In 1995, in his mid-fifties, he came back and pitched with Águila, winning two more games. He also appeared in one game in 1998 for Córdoba. In 2001, at age 62, he completed a lone three-inning outing with Veracruz. Baseball-reference.com cites Arano and Hub Kittle as the only pitchers to pitch in six decades in organized baseball history.

Arano wanted to come back in 2010 to pitch in his seventh decade with Veracruz, but the league would not permit it. In a decision similar to Fay Vincent prohibiting Minnie Miñoso's major league intended appearance as a sexagenarian, the Mexican League would not entertain Arano's overtures to pitch as a 71-year-old.

In a television interview during this period, Arano addressed his dedication to the game in this manner: "My life in baseball is well written, but my life outside of baseball is not. Why? Because I went from the ballpark straight home after every game, and from home to the ballpark. For me liquor did not exist, drugs did not exist."[2] Late in life, Arano admitted that he smoked too much and drank too much coffee.

The son of Efraín Arano Delfín and Amelia Bravo Bravo was born August 31, 1939. Ramón was one of eight brothers and sisters, four of each sex. Two of his male siblings became professional ballplayers and competed with and against Ramón in the Mexican League. None had nearly the success of their older brother.

Arano did not cast a big shadow on or away from the baseball diamond. He was 5'8" tall and weighed 160 pounds. The uniform number "10" he wore throughout his career probably did not help add any illusionary stature on the mound, either. He was a deliberate pitcher on the mound and a bit of a showman. His games regularly lasted three hours or more in an era when this was far from the norm. He was affectionately dubbed "Tres Patines" for his diminutive size and comportment. The nickname is a nod to the famous Cuban comic of similar build, Leopoldo Fernández, who broadcast a popular television show in Mexico in the 1960s and was known by that stage name.

Arano holds the Mexican League record for most wins, innings pitched, games, starts, complete games and shutouts. His 334–264 final mound tabulation, 4773⅓ innings, 811 games, 675 starts, 297 complete games and 57 shutouts in 32 seasons are all league standards that will not soon be challenged. His lifetime ERA was 3.26. Astoundingly, he won another 89 games in the Mexican Pacific League, throwing another 1,500-plus innings and notching 24 more shutouts.

The former pitcher was diagnosed with prostate cancer in 2002. Several times toward the end of his life, he was quoted as saying that he would like to die wearing his uniform on a baseball field. He nearly received his wish.

The 1959 Mexican League Rookie of the Year managed the 2011–2012 Boca del Rio Marlines of the Veracruz Winter League. Arano succumbed to cancer a few months after the season on May 5, 2012. He was survived by his wife of 50 years, Julia Tejada Arano, and four children, Julia de Jesús, Carolina, Ramón and Eloy, as well as six grandchildren.

More than deservedly, Ramón Arano was elected to the Mexican Baseball Hall of Fame in 1993.

Rubén Gómez

In an era when players were at the mercy of their major league owners, Rubén Gómez displayed the confidence and guile that would make him an outstanding pitcher, by employing an unorthodox business maneuver. In 1952, as a hireling of the New Yankees' Kansas City minor league club, Gómez bought out his contract for $3,000 and became a free agent. Convinced he was not being used properly, Gómez ponied up the cash he had originally received from the Yankees and gained his freedom from the organization that had signed him as an amateur in December 1951.

It turned out to be a great career move for Gómez, who was signed by the New York Giants in January 1953, for $10,000 and a $5,000 signing bonus. As a rookie for the big league club that season, Gómez became the Giants' top pitcher, winning 13 games while losing 11. A right-hander, Gómez also owned the best ERA among the club's starters with a 3.40 mark. He completed half of his 26 starts, also tops on the team. Gómez claimed a victory over every club in the league except Brooklyn.

His first major league victory came in an 11–1 cakewalk over the Chicago Cubs on June 5, at the Polo Grounds. Gómez went the distance, allowing eight hits, striking out 11—and walking seven. He also collected two hits and drove in two of the Giants' runs. Gómez recorded his first big league shutout on June 21 over the Milwaukee Braves at County Stadium in Milwaukee. The 5–0, two-hit, walk-free shutout was one of three spun by Gomez on the season.

After a second-place finish in 1952, the Giants underachieved strikingly in 1953, dropping into the second division of the National League. The club finished at 70–84, a whopping 35 games behind the powerhouse Brooklyn Dodgers, who won 105 games.

An incident late in the season helped shape a character trait of Gómez's that was sometimes slanted negatively by the North American press. When Sal Maglie of the Giants brushed back a player high and tight, he was characterized as a competitor. When a Hispanic pitcher like Gómez did the same thing, he tended to be labeled as temperamental. In a game at the Polo Grounds on September 6, Gómez struck the Dodgers outfielder Carl Furillo on the wrist with a pitched ball. After taking his base, Furillo, who was leading the National League in hitting, began pointing toward the Giants dugout at manager Leo Durocher, whom Furillo later accused of giving Gómez the order to hit him. Several pitches into the next hitter's at-bat, Furillo charged toward Durocher, and the skipper came out from the first base dugout to meet him. Punches were thrown by the two men and a melee ensued.

Both participants were ejected, and Furillo missed the remainder of the season due to a fracture in his hand. (With sufficient at-bats to secure the batting title, Furillo was able to return for the World Series.)

The Giants, with Durocher at the helm, rebounded dramatically the following season, winning the National League pennant by five games over their despised cross-borough rivals. Racking up 17 victories, Gómez was the second-winningest pitcher on the team, behind Johnny Antonelli and his 21 wins. Gómez's 32 starts (tied with Sal Maglie) trailed only Antonelli on the staff. Gómez posted an impressive 2.88 ERA in 221⅔ innings despite leading the league in bases on balls with 109.

The third of four shutouts recorded by Gómez on the campaign occurred on June 10. At Milwaukee, the right-hander hurled ten innings, allowing nine hits and four walks. Center fielder Willie Mays stopped a scoring bid by the Braves in the seventh inning when he threw out rookie Henry Aaron at home plate, trying to score on a tag play from third base. Gómez also waited out a 41-minute rain delay during the game. The win kept the Giants in a first place tie with Brooklyn, both teams sporting 31–20 records.

The Giants eventually pried first place away from the Dodgers, pulling out to a seven-game lead in mid July. At the time of Gómez's fourth shutout, August 19, the Dodgers had whittled the lead to two games. Gómez made sure the Dodgers drew no closer that day, blanking the Philadelphia Phillies at the Polo Grounds, 5–0. He surrendered seven hits and three walks.

The Giants clinched the pennant on September 20 with a 7–1 win, most rewardingly against the Dodgers in Brooklyn. Sal Maglie won his 14th game for Durocher's crew.

New York then pulled off one the most stunning upsets in World Series history. Facing the 111-win, American League champion Cleveland Indians, the Giants not only defeated the formidable team, but swept four games in a row to capture their final world championship in New York.

In Game 3 at Cleveland, on October 1, Puerto Rico's Rubén Gómez became the first Hispanic pitcher to start a World Series game. His mound opponent was Mexican-American Mike García, a prominent American League pitcher for several peak years with Cleveland during the 1950s.

Gómez had the better stuff on the day, downing the Indians and the burly Garcia, 6–2. Gomez pitched 7⅔ innings and permitted both runs on four hits and three walks. The next day, the Giants completed their improbable Series victory over the Al López–directed Indians.

The Giants never came close to duplicating that championship glory over their remaining three years in Manhattan. The team floundered during two of those three years, as did Gómez. The Puerto Rican won a combined 16 games and lost 27 in two seasons following the World Series campaign.

In one of those down years, 1956, Gómez was fined $250 and suspended for three games for an altercation with the Milwaukee Braves' Joe Adcock. On July 17, at County Stadium, Gómez fired an errant pitch which plunked the Braves' first baseman on the wrist. From first base, Adcock exchanged heated words with Gómez. Adcock snapped and the 6'4" 210-pound slugger charged Gómez, who threw the ball in his hand and hit Adcock, again, this time on the thigh. At this point, discretion overtook any sense of valor in the 6', 170-pound pitcher, and Gómez took off running into the Giants' dugout and club-

The starting pitchers of Game Three of the 1954 World Series, Mike García, left, and Rubén Gómez. The Giants pitcher came out on top of the Indians hurler, 6–2.

house, avoiding the field confrontation and wrath of Adcock. National League president Warren Giles fined Adcock $100 for his actions, but did not disqualify him from any future games.

In 1957, Gómez returned to form, winning 15 and losing 13, while becoming the ace of the Giants' staff. The Giants, under the direction of Bill Rigney, limped to a sixth-place finish with a record of 69–85, in what had to be the most melancholy of seasons for Giants rooters. Team owner Horace Stoneham had committed to moving his celebrated franchise to San Francisco at season's end.

On September 21, 1957, pitching into the seventh inning, Gómez recorded the last win for the New York Giants franchise, downing the Pittsburgh Pirates 9–5, in the second game of a doubleheader at Forbes Field. Gómez lost the next-to-last game played at the Polo Grounds, 1–0, to the same Pirates team on September 28. The Saturday afternoon game was the last Giants' Ladies Day held at the iconic ball yard, and Gómez hurled his 16th complete game, third in the league behind Warren Spahn's 18 and Bob Friend's 17.

At the start of the following season, Gómez's name was once again etched prominently into another historic game in franchise history. Opening the season on the mound for his relocated team on April 15, 1958, Gómez registered the first victory and first shutout for the

San Francisco Giants. At Seals Stadium, in front of a capacity 23,448 enamored fans, the 30-year-old pitcher whipped the other New York–abandoning franchise, formerly from Brooklyn. Gómez held the Los Angeles Dodgers to six hits, also walking as many, in the 8–0 win.

Gómez was in the middle of another rhubarb at Forbes Field on May 25. After winging Pittsburgh Pirates second baseman Bill Mazeroski on the arm in the previous half-inning, Gómez batted in the top of the fifth frame against Vern Law. The Bucs right-hander promptly low-bridged Gómez with a pitch. When the home plate umpire issued Law a warning, Danny Murtaugh, the Pirates manager, came out in apparent defense of his pitcher. But Murtaugh rushed Gómez, actually throwing a punch at the bat-holding opponent. The punch did not land. Gómez backed away from Murtaugh, "waving his bat menacingly," according to the *New York Times*, May 26, 1958. Order was quickly restored, and Gómez continued on to a 5–2 victory, his fifth. It was the first game of a doubleheader. The Giants, behind Venezuelan Ramón Monzant's nine-hitter, won the nightcap, 6–1, thoroughly disappointing a Steel City throng of 35,797.

The 1958 San Francisco Giants were a much improved team from 1957, gaining 80 wins on the campaign (11 more than the prior season). But the 1957 National League champion Milwaukee Braves proved to be the best team in the league once more, easily topping the runner-up teams of Pittsburgh and San Francisco, by eight and 12 games respectively.

Accepting 30 starts, Rubén concluded the 1958 season with a 10–12 record, including an 0–2 mark in 12 games as a reliever. Logging 207⅔ innings, the right-hander surpassed the 200 innings plateau for the fourth time in his six-year big league career.

Evidently, the Giants felt Gómez was declining, for the team shipped him, along with catcher Valmy Thomas, to the Philadelphia Phillies in December 1958. The team's assessment was correct, as the pitcher lost his major league stuff and won only five more games, playing for three teams over three more uneventful campaigns. He tried a comeback in 1967 with the Phillies, which lasted but seven relief games. A knee injury suffered in his first summer in Philadelphia was a contributing factor to the unfortunate descent.

LEGACY

Before he threw his first major league pitch in 1953, Rubén Gómez had become a star in the winter league of Puerto Rico. The youngster came up through the island's amateur ranks prior to inking his first pro contract. Patriarchal baseball owner Pedrín Zorilla signed Gomez for his Santurce Crabbers team as a 20-year-old in 1947. That year, Gómez commenced an unparalleled pitching tenure that lasted *29* winter league seasons. During his rookie season, he witnessed teammate Willard Brown's tremendous home run hitting exploit of socking 27 home runs in 60 winter league games. Gómez was an outstanding athlete who also played outfield early in his career.

It took the lanky right-hander two seasons to acclimate himself to Puerto Rico's high caliber of play. After a pair of campaigns with a composite 10–13 record, Gómez made a big splash in the winter of 1949, leading the league in victories with 14. He followed that up with 13 and 14-win excursions in 1950 and 1951 respectively. (Seasons were typically under 80 games during this period in Puerto Rico.)

The 1952–1953 season may have been the best in his fabulous, nearly three-decade-long career. Gómez won 13 games (second best in the circuit) and led the league in ERA (1.78) and strikeouts (123), in a remarkable 196⅔ innings of work. He won the opening game of the 1953 Havana-hosted Caribbean Series with a seven-inning complete game over the Chesterfield Smokers, 15–6. He also homered in the game, becoming the first Hispanic pitcher to hit a Caribbean Series home run.

Two days later, on February 22, Gómez culminated a historic comeback for his Santurce squad in a game against the Habana Lions. He pinch-ran for Willard Brown in the eighth inning and stayed in the game to play left field with his team down by two runs. In the bottom of the ninth inning, with two outs and no one on base, the Crabbers strung together five hits in a row to score three runs and snatch the victory from the dazed Cubans, 6–5. Gómez smacked the game-winning single.

Gómez, who played in multiple leagues in multiple countries over his long career, considered this Caribbean Series moment the greatest of his professional life. Santurce went on to win the Series without losing a game. (It was the only time a Cuban team did not win a Caribbean Series on its home field.)

As if those nearly 200 innings in four and a half months in Puerto Rico weren't enough, Gómez summoned another 204 innings from his arm, without much of a break, for the New York Giants in his 13-win rookie season. The excessive flinging may have forced Gómez to scale back on his pitching over the subsequent winter. He tossed under 100 innings in 1953–1954. His ERA of 2.86 indicated that his final 5–6 record may have been a little deceiving, however.

Gomez came back strong for the Giants in their stupendous 1954 championship run. Nine days after the Giants won the World Series, Gómez returned to Puerto Rico to a hero's welcome. "Despite a rainy afternoon, October 11," detailed a *Sporting News* snippet, "several thousand fans were on hand at Isla Grande Airport to acclaim hurler Ruben Gomez. A committee of senators and representatives tendered Gomez an official welcome, and then he headed a parade to City Hall, where he was received by Mayor Mrs. Felisa Rincon de Gautier and other government officials."[3]

An adept auto mechanic and expert fisherman away from the ballfield, Gómez was tagged with the nickname "el Divino Loco," translated as "the Divine Madman." It characterized, among his Latin American followers, an endearing quirkiness that Gómez possessed. Reflective of this peculiar charm, Gómez taught himself the screwball early in his career, a pitch that is more conducive to left-handed throwers because of its effectiveness against right-handed hitters. But that did not impede Gómez from mastering the pitch well enough to make it the most well-known weapon in his arsenal, and to impart valuable instruction later on how to throw the dipsy-do pitch to southpaw hurlers Luis Arroyo and Mike Cúellar.

The Divine Madman was a fan of race car driving. He enjoyed driving his flashy red Corvette on road trips in Puerto Rico, perhaps too much like the drivers in the sport he admired. There are tales of him ritually passing the Santurce team bus at some point along the travel route, with an engine-roaring flurry, to the encouraging hoots of his teammates on board the bus. "Ruben! Ruben!" they would shout out the windows as the sports car sped past.

"Gómez used to make the three-hour trip from San Juan to Mayagüez in two hours," attested one-time teammate José "Pantalones" Santiago. "I know. I rode with him. He'd race at 120 kilometers [70 mph], and on those terrible roads!"[4]

On at least one occasion, the recognizable Gomez was stopped by the police for excessive speed on a Puerto Rican roadway. His excuse to the officer was that he was "hurrying to see his wife." The officer answered that everyone knew that his wife had passed away several years earlier. "In that case," replied Gómez, "I'm rushing to the cemetery."[5]

The marriage to his first wife, Teresa, produced three children, two boys and a girl. After Teresa's death, Gómez remarried. He and his new bride adopted a child from the Dominican Republic.

Gómez had his cherished Corvette trashed by fans in Mayagüez during a playoff game in 1959. The destructive incident came as the result of a first-inning Gómez beaning of Joe Christopher, one of the Mayagüez players. Christopher, who had been feasting on Santurce pitching in the playoff series, had to be removed from the game. The entire Santurce team required a police escort out of town following the game.

Gómez was an undisputed competitor and was not afraid to "brush" any hitter off the plate to try and gain an advantage. "He had no friends on the diamond," recalled Pantalones Santiago. "He'd hit his own brother with a pitch if it would help him win a game."[6]

Gómez beaned Cincinnati Reds budding star Frank Robinson, who was known to crowd the plate, on July 16, 1957. It was the eighth inning; Gómez had a 4–1 lead and was heading for his 11th win on the season. Robinson, never losing consciousness, was carried off the field in a stretcher and played the following day. (Robinson later managed Gómez in the winter league as Santurce's skipper.) Gómez also beaned Pittsburgh's Vern Law in September, the prelude to the 1958 brushback incident with Law, involving manager Murtaugh and the bat-waving Gómez.

The amazing 29 Puerto Rican Winter League seasons (all but one with Santurce) Rubén Gómez participated in were more than Roberto Clemente (15) and Orlando Cepeda (13) had combined. It should be noted that in his last seasons as a starter, the 40-something pitcher was relegated to one trip through the opposing batting order before being relieved. As a result, he gained few decisions over his five final campaigns.

His lifetime pitching totals in Puerto Rico were 174–119, with an ERA of 2.97 in 2,486⅓ innings. His final big league mark was 76–86 in 1,454 innings with an ERA of 4.09. Gómez tied with Camilo Pascual and Venezuelan José Bracho as the winningest pitchers in Caribbean Series history with six victories.

In 1971, at age 43, with the Caribbean Series having restarted the prior year, Gómez participated in his 15th and 16th Caribbean Series games and seventh tournament overall, both records for a pitcher. Pitching in relief in the two games, Gómez absorbed his second Caribbean Series defeat on February 9, when he allowed two ninth-inning runs to the Hermosillo Orangegrowers, who beat the Frank Robinson-managed Santurce Crabbers, 7–5, at Hiram Bithorn Stadium. At the close of the competition two days later, the Dominican Republic's undefeated Licey Tigers were crowned champions.

According to Puerto Rican baseball historian Thomas Van Hyning, Gómez won another 88 games in the minor leagues of Canada, the U.S. and Mexico, and a handful more in the Dominican Republic.

Seventy-seven-year-old Rubén Gómez, whose number 22 was retired by Santurce, died July 26, 2004, in Carolina, Puerto Rico. He was buried in Guayama, near his birthplace.

Orlando Hernández

On the day after the first officially celebrated Christmas in Cuba in almost 30 years, Orlando Hernández and seven others clandestinely departed the Communist island by boat. A little more than a year earlier, Hernández had been banned for life from pitching in his home country for allegedly trying to defect.

Incredibly, six months later, one of the top pitchers in post-revolutionary Cuban baseball history was on the mound at Yankee Stadium, pitching for the team that most symbolized the anti-capitalistic dogma of his totalitarian nation.

The remarkable journey for Hernández began 32 years before his 1998 Yankee Stadium debut, as the second son born to Arnaldo Hernández Montero and his wife, Maria Julia Pedroso, in the central Cuban province of Villa Clara. The elder Hernández proved to be a distracted husband and a disinterested father, causing the family unit to splinter. Maria Julia and her two children resettled in a suburban district of Havana known as Wajay. Tragically, the couple's first child, Arnaldo, who was two years older than Orlando, later died of an aneurysm at age 30.

Arnaldo Senior had been a mediocre pitcher in the reinvented Cuban League of the 1960s and was nicknamed "El Duque." The sobriquet was eventually passed down to Orlando when the young hurler began showing baseball promise that would not only surpass his father's modest achievements but most other rival pitchers in Cuba.

Orlando's first serious pitching came for Ejército Occidental, an army team. At age 21, he was recruited by Industriales, based in Havana, and post-revolutionary Cuba's most recognized ball club. The team's mascot is a lion and their predominantly blue uniform color is stylized with white Olde English font lettering. The combination is an obvious, if not grudging, commingled acknowledgement to the two popular winter league teams of Habana and Almendares that co-habited the capital city before they were snuffed out by the Cuban Revolution. Only in recent years has Cuba begun to acknowledge the presence of professional baseball on the island before the Revolution. For decades, the government systematically erased from the collective minds of its populace the existence of the Cuban Winter League and its great players, especially those that fled to the United States beginning in the 1960s.

Hernández's debut for Industriales in 1986 was inauspicious and tied the pitcher's name to one of the most remembered games in league play. Placed into the difficult situation of not only having to relieve with the bases loaded, but also having to pitch against a legendary slugger named Luis Giraldo Casanova, the young Hernández ill-advisedly tried to slip a fastball past the home run hitter. Casanova, who hit more than 300 home runs and drove in over 1,000 runs in his 17-year career, redirected that first pitch over the left-center field wall.

In three future starts and eight total appearances as a rookie, Hernández notched a 2–1 mark. At the end of the season, Hernández and his team had the last laugh over Casanova's Pinar del Rio team, when Industriales captured the Cuban National Series.

The proverbial breakout season arrived for Hernández during the 1992–1993 campaign when he won 12 and lost only three in his 16 starts. For Hernández, it was a pivotal point in his career. The prior summer, he had been knocked out of the box in the first inning by team USA at the Olympics in Barcelona. (The Cuban team rallied to emerge from the hole their starter had placed them in and won the game 9–6, and eventually earned the gold medal.) If that season did not erase the memory of the bad Olympics outing, his next two seasons as an Industriales pitcher certainly did. Hernández posted 11–2 and 11–1 marks in successive campaigns. He "slipped" to a 7–2 record in 1995–1996 in 11 starting assignments.

Then Orlando Hernández, the pitching pride of Cuban baseball, team gold-medalist, team world amateur champion, was suspended from pitching for his beloved team.

"You Will Never Play Baseball Again"

The roster announcement for the Cuban national team that would defend its gold medal at the 1996 summer Olympic Games in Atlanta stunned every baseball fan on the island for its glaring omission of one name—Orlando Hernández. The pitcher, in his prime years, with the best winning percentage at the time (.733, 129–47) in reorganized Cuban baseball, was not selected.

In their delving biographical and socio-political study on Orlando Hernández and the Cuba of Fidel Castro, *The Duke of Havana*, Steve Fainaru and Ray Sánchez equated the news of El Duque's announced exclusion from the national team to that of the New York Yankees deciding before the World Series to waive Derek Jeter.

The Cuban government turned on Orlando Hernández, coldly forgetting the positive athletic reinforcement he had brought to Cuba on an international level. With the honed degree of cruelty acquired from decades of oppressive mistreatment toward its perceived non-conforming citizenry, the Cuban state punished Hernández in the manner that would most devastate him.

Hernández was not only not selected to the Cuban national team but was also banned from playing for Industriales or anyone else. In December 1996, a representative of INDER, the National Institute of Sports, Education and Recreation (the sports arm of the Cuban government), told Hernandez in a face-to-face meeting: "You will never play baseball again."[7]

Why had the government turned so mercilessly on this star athlete? That January, Orlando's 20-year-old half-brother, Livan, had signed a record multi-million dollar contract with the Florida Marlins. Livan had defected from a touring Cuban national team in Monterrey, Mexico, months earlier. The Cuban government blamed the older sibling for the loss of the young pitching talent. It also accused Orlando of wanting to follow his brother. The government also feared that he might convince Germán Mesa, an outstanding player and his best friend, to desert the island along with him. The recent trickle of defections, including those of other star pitchers Rolando Arrojo and Osvaldo Fernández, made it clear that INDER had misguidedly decided to make an example out of Hernández.

Hernández, indeed, had entertained thoughts of wanting to pitch at baseball's highest level, especially in the wake of his half-brother's previously unheard-of $4.5 million contract and record $2.5 million signing bonus. (Prior to the lifetime ban being handed down, Orlando had gone to work as a rehabilitation therapist with the monthly equivalent salary of $8.75.) The elder Hernández, in the past, had had contact with an expatriated Cuban turned sports agent named Juan Ignacio Hernández Nodar,[8] who had been involved in Livan's desertion.

But it was not until he was banned from Cuban baseball for life that the star pitcher seriously began contemplating escape from the living nightmare in which he had been wrongfully entangled. It was then, through the efforts initiated by a great-uncle living in Miami, that Orlando Hernández was eventually delivered from his island prison.

The uncle financed the perilous trip to freedom by arranging for a boat to take Hernández and his party out of Cuba under cover of darkness and drop them off on one of the small, uninhabited cays in the Bahamanian island chain called Anguilla Cay. The area was within a routinely patrolled sector of the U.S. Coast Guard and of the Miami-based Brothers to the Rescue. This humanitarian organization of volunteer flyers aided in the search and rescue of desperate Cubans who risked their lives attempting to cross the dangerous Florida Straights in makeshift flotation devices, in search of attaining a better life in the United States.

After reaching the deserted spit of land, and expecting to be picked up by a second boat that was to be sent by the great-uncle, Hernández and his group hid from a Brothers to the Rescue plane that flew over their location during their first 24 hours on the cay. They feared they would be repatriated to Cuba if the United States became involved in their rescue. But by the third day, when the expected second transport boat still had not arrived, the group prudently made their presence known to a passing Coast Guard cutter.

Hernández and company were taken to the Bahamas, under whose jurisdiction the fate of the freedom-seekers fell. From there, thanks to the rapid, mobilized efforts of three U.S. Senators and several U.S. congressional representatives,[9] Hernández, his girlfriend Noris Bosch and another ballplayer, Alberto Hernández (no relation), were extended a "humanitarian parole" to the United States. The other five people in the group were left in limbo.

With their issued invitation to the United States, Orlando, Alberto and Noris were freed from their detention facility on New Year's Day 1998. But Orlando stated he would not leave the Bahamas without the others. Enter Joe Cubas. The high-profile sports agent, who had negotiated the record deal for Livan Hernandez with the Marlins, secured visas from a third country for all of the hopeful aboard the original departure vessel.[10] On January 7, the happy group of eight left the Bahamas to fly into the sympathetically extended arms of Costa Rica.

Sixty-two major league scouts showed up in Costa Rica to watch the first open tryout of Orlando Hernández, who had not pitched in an elevated-level game in 14 months. Hernández displayed an average fastball that occasionally reached 90 miles per hour, with a seemingly disjointed, high leg kick that tucked his right knee under his jaw prior to delivering to the plate. Despite his fanciful delivery, the 6′ 2,″ 210-pound pitcher impressed few scouts. Some astute observers designated him as a major league middle reliever, at best.

One New York Yankees scout, however, named Gordon Blakely recognized El Duque's potential. Blakely had seen Hernández pitch previously, and put in a strong recommendation to his organizational bosses. The good word reached up through the Yankees' front office chain of command to George Steinbrenner himself. The Boss gave his subordinates the go-ahead to sign the pitcher.

The New York Yankees officially signed Orlando Hernández on March 23, nearly three months to the day since he had fled Cuba. It was a four-year, $6.6 million deal. In a story line that read like an Alexandre Dumas novel, Hernández, who had been discredited and buried by the Cuban government and stripped of his dignity with his banishment, now stood resurrected, about to return proudly to the baseball diamond with riches beyond his wildest expectations.

The Yankees were expecting the pitcher to spend the year in the minor leagues and then start making his contribution to the big club in 1999. But when his minor league appearances resulted in successively dominant performances and one of the starters in the Yankees rotation missed a start due to an injured finger, El Duque became the obvious "call-up" choice.

The incredible journey culminated on June 3, 1998, with El Duque's major league debut. Throwing seven innings of five-hit ball, with two walks and seven strikeouts, Hernández defeated the Tampa Bay Devil Rays, 7–1, at Yankee Stadium. Hernández struck out the first major league batter he faced (Quinton McCracken) and allowed a solo home run to Fred McGriff three innings later. The pitcher broke down at the end of a post-game interview. "I want to dedicate this game," he said, amid an onrush of tears, "to my mother and my two daughters in Cuba, and my family here in the United States. And to all the Hispanic community and all the Yankee fans."[11]

Hernández started again on June 9 at Montreal, and cruised to an 11–1 complete game victory. A one-out ninth inning single by the Expos' Vladimir Guerrero ruined his shutout bid. Hernández forced the Yankees to make room for him in their five-man pitching rotation, moving fifth starter Ramiro Mendoza to the bullpen.

The crowds at Yankees Stadium were used to winning, but in 1998, including post-season victories, the Yankees rewarded their home faithful more than any other year. A crowd of 42,735 came out to Yankee Stadium on September 14 and saw Hernández throw his first major league shutout. The affable hurler beat Pedro Martínez and the Boston Red Sox, 3–0. Hernandez yielded three hits and no walks and struck out nine. The New Yorkers rose to a superlative 60 games above .500 (104–44) and set a new attendance mark in the Bronx (2,657,785), with nine home dates remaining.

The predominant, 114-win New York Yankees would have run away with their division without Orlando Hernández in 1998. Whether the record-setting team would have reached the World Series without the Cuban defector is another thing. After sweeping the Texas Rangers in the Division Series, the Yankees fell behind two games to one to the Cleveland Indians in the ALCS.

In the pivotal Game 4, making his first post-season start, Hernández shut out the heavy-hitting Indians team over seven innings, on three hits. Hernández and the Yankees won, 4–0, at Jacobs Field, to even the series. Winning the next two games, the Yankees advanced to complete a one-sided World Series sweep over the San Diego Padres.

Hernández started Game 2 of the Fall Classic on October 18. The sight of the stylish pitcher on the mound in Yankees pinstripes, on baseball's biggest stage, had to give everyone familiar with his story head-shaking pause. Hernández, as he had done from his first major league pitch, exhibited a workmanlike ethic and charismatic delight, stemming from the drastic turnaround his life had taken on both a professional and personal level. The Yankees scored early and often, and the right-hander quelled the Padres over seven innings, on six hits, with one run allowed. The final score was 9–3.

As great as being part of the World Series-winning Yankees was, Hernández reaped his greatest joy from being reunited with his daughters, Yahumara and Steffi "from an earlier marriage" and his mother. The appeal for reunification came from New York Archbishop John Joseph O'Connor and was agreed to by the embarrassed Cuban government, which had received negative publicity from the high-profile case. As the Yankees were concluding a four-game sweep of the Padres, Hernández's mother and pre-teen girls arrived in the United States (along with their mother).

The contortionist-like leg kick of Orlando Hernández. The Cuban hurler enjoyed his greatest success with the New York Yankees, winning more post-season games, nine, than any other major league Hispanic pitcher.

Orlando Hernández, a man persecuted and branded as a traitor by his country's leaders, now had a gaudy World Series ring to waive under their despotic noses, and had the people he most loved at his side to share in his great triumph.

LEGACY

In 1999, the 33-year-old hurler followed up his 12–4, four-month campaign with New York by posting a 17–9 record, the best of his nine-year major league career. His ERA was a respectable (for the era) 4.12. He stretched out his arm to throw 214⅓ innings in 33 starts.

On June 22, Hernández tossed his second major league shutout (and surprisingly, the last of his big league career). Facing the team he had defeated for his first win, Hernández corralled the Tampa Bay Devil Rays on three hits, 6–0, at Tropicana Field. Hernández raised his record to 8–6.

The Yankees fought with the Boston Red Sox all season long for supremacy of the American League East Division. In the end, the Yankees were four games better than Boston. The teams eventually faced each other in the American League Championship Series. The Yankees, three games to one, went for the kill with El Duque on the mound on October 18 at Fenway Park.

Not even the daughter of Babe Ruth could beseech the baseball gods to reverse "the Curse." Julia Ruth Stevens threw out the ceremonial first pitch and affirmed her allegiance to the Red Sox, but Orlando Hernández, from the land of Santeria worship, had more hexes in store for the Sox and their long-suffering fans. Named MVP of the ALCS, Hernández pitched seven mystifying innings; he was reached for five hits and struck out nine with four walks thrown in. The Yankees eliminated Boston, 6–1, and advanced to a Fall Classic rendezvous with the Atlanta Braves.

The Yankees won the world championship again. Hernández contributed three postseason wins, saving his most masterful effort for World Series Game 1 in Atlanta. He tossed seven innings with one hit allowed, and struck out ten Braves. A four-run eighth-inning uprising by the Yankees provided El Duque with the 4–1 win, the only Braves run coming on a Chipper Jones home run in the fourth inning. Hernández improved his post-season record to 5–0 with his second World Series win.

In 2000, the Cuban pitcher's record slipped to 12–13 with an ERA of 4.51. In the play-offs that season, Hernández gave the Yankees a leg up in the ALDS against the Oakland A's, winning the third game of the series, 4–2. Hernández pitched seven innings, allowing two runs on four hits. Five walks on the evening probably played a role in manager Joe Torre bringing Mariano Rivera out of the bullpen to record a two-inning save.

Hernández won two more games in the ALCS after the Yankees defeated the A's in a hard-fought five-game series. Hernández pitched a fine 7–1, Game 2 victory over the Seattle Mariners at Yankee Stadium on October 11. The pitcher tossed eight innings of one-run ball, on six hits and seven strikeouts. The game was far from a "cruise control" victory for Hernández as suggested by the score. The Yankees did not dent the plate until the eighth inning. Rivera came on to spell Hernández in the ninth.

In perhaps his worst post-season outing, Hernández came away with a victory—a pennant winning victory, to boot—on October 17. In the sixth game of the ALCS, the Yankees scored nine runs and needed almost all of them to prevail, 9–7, over the Mariners. In seven innings, Hernández was charged with six runs, the last of which was an inherited runner let in by Rivera on a two-run double. The second run belonged to Rivera and ended a record 34⅓ scoreless innings put together in the post-season by the great New York closer.

The Yankees won the last of their three consecutive World Series titles by defeating the cross-town New York Mets. Hernández suffered his only World Series loss (Game 3, 4–2), and the only loss for the Bronx Bombers in the first Subway Series clash in 44 years.

Hernández won 12 games over the next two campaigns before a shoulder injury prevented him from pitching at all in 2003. The pitcher won only four games in 2001, relegated to only 16 starts because of injury. Hernández started Game 4 of the 2001 World Series, hurling 6⅓ innings and allowing one run to the Arizona Diamondbacks, in a game the Yankees won, 4–3, on a Derek Jeter home run in the tenth inning.

In 2002, Hernández made 22 starts for the 103-win Yankees, winning eight and losing five.

Working out of the bullpen, he was the losing pitcher in Game 2 of the ALDS to the Anaheim Angels. After hurling four scoreless innings in relief of Andy Pettitte, Hernández surrendered two eighth-inning solo home runs that gave up a 5–4 Yankees lead. The Angels won, 8–6, at Yankee Stadium, and two games later eliminated Joe Torre's squad from the playoffs.

In 2004, the right-hander eased back from his season-canceling injury with 15 starts and an 8–2 record, as a re-signed free agent with the division-winning Yankees. The Yankees did not use Hernández in their ALDS victory over the Minnesota Twins. In the ALCS, Hernández started Game 4 versus Boston at Fenway Park. He yielded three runs on three hits in five innings, with five walks. A more effective outing by Hernández would have buried the Red Sox in a four-game sweep by the Yankees. Instead, the foot-in-the-grave Red Sox rallied to win the game, 5–4, in 12 innings, to initiate the greatest series comeback in post-season history.

In 2005, El Duque appeared in his fifth World Series, albeit in a very limited role for the World Series-sweeping Chicago White Sox. Hernández, a bullpen reinforcement, tossed one scoreless inning for the Ozzie Guillén-managed championship team. The White Sox had signed the 39-year-old right-hander as pitching insurance prior to the season. Facing the Houston Astros in Game 3, El Duque relieved in the ninth inning of a tied game (5–5). He walked four batters in the inning, one intentionally, but did not permit a run. The White Sox eventually won the game in the 12th inning, 7–5. The White Sox won again the following evening, October 26, thanks in good part to the seven-inning shutout pitching of Venezuelan Freddy García, 1–0. Team member Hernández was fitted for his fourth World Series champions' ring.

On their way to the World Series victory over the Astros, the White Sox had taken three straight games from the Boston Red Sox in the American League Division Series. In the third game, played at Fenway Park, Hernández turned in one of the most dramatic relief exhibitions in post-season play. With the White Sox leading, 4–3, Hernández relieved in the bottom of the sixth inning with the bases loaded, no one out, and a run in. Hernández retired three straight Red Sox batters, on two popups and a strikeout, without permitting a run. After pitching two more scoreless innings, the pitcher, a few days shy of his 40th birthday, handed it off to closer Bobby Jenks for the save. With the momentum-shifting intentions of the Red Sox suppressed by Hernández, and the avoidance of a possible extension of the series, the White Sox held on to win, 5–3, to advance into the second playoff round.

Hernández called it a career after the 2007 campaign. He spent the full season with the New York Mets, having been traded to the club in May 2006 by the Arizona Diamond-backs, who had obtained the pitcher in an off-season trade with the White Sox. His major league record of 90–65, with an ERA of 4.13 in nine big league campaigns, was complemented by a shining 9–3 post season mark and sharp 2.55 ERA in 106 pressure-filled innings. He recorded 107 strikeouts and allowed only 77 hits.

While pitching in Cuba, his 129 victories were fortified by 75 complete games, against only 47 defeats, with a 3.05 ERA in an aluminum bat-dominant league.

Orlando Hernández recorded the most wins and second most strikeouts (107) by a Hispanic pitcher in post-season play. He won nine of his 14 post-season starts, with three setbacks and two no-decisions. He posted a 2–1 mark in the World Series, with one no-decision.

On April 28, 2013, El Mago (the Magician)—as he was known in Cuba—was honored with his induction into the Cuban Sports Hall of Fame.[12] The ceremony was held in Miami, Florida, where Hernández resides with wife Noris and five children.

Rubén Gómez's Career Statistics

G	GS	CG	SHO	SV	INN	HR	BB	SO	W	L	ERA	PCT	ERA+	WHIP	20*
289	205	63	15	5	1,454	154	574	677	76	86	4.09	.469	98	1.382	0

Juan Pizarro

Raw talent and a blazing fastball propelled Juan Pizarro to elevated heights as a winter league and major league pitcher.

Pizarro made his initial mark as an 18-year-old with the Santurce Crabbers, during the 1955–1956 winter campaign, pitching five games. On February 13, 1956, Crabbers owner Pedrín Zorilla sold Pizarro's contract to the Milwaukee Braves organization for $34,000. From that sum, Pizarro received a $2,000 bonus and a $2,000 salary to pitch for the Braves' South Atlantic League affiliate in Jacksonville.

The manager at Jacksonville was established Puerto Rican Winter League manager Ben Geraghty. The former big leaguer thought so highly of Pizarro that he gave the young pitcher the 1956 Opening Day assignment. Shining immediate light upon himself as a pitching prodigy, Pizarro fanned 14 Savannah Redlegs in six innings. He was removed in the seventh inning after loading the bases on two walks and a hit. Four days later, on April 21, Pizarro tossed a stupendous game, fanning *21* Charlotte Hornet batters in a 12-inning, 1–0, four-hit triumph.

In his first season in organized baseball, Pizarro won 23 games in 29 decisions, and hurled 26 complete games, not including a three-hit shutout in the playoffs. He finished with an ERA of 1.77 and 318 strikeouts, second all-time in South Atlantic League history.

That winter season, Pizarro was included in a quaking trade that sent him and team-mates Roberto Clemente and Ronnie Samford to the Caguas Criollos. The exchange was initiated by the new owner of Santurce, Ramón Cuevas.

In the spring of 1957, Pizarro found himself as a 20-year-old member of the Milwaukee Braves pitching corps. His initial major league assignment came in a start against the Pittsburgh Pirates on May 4. The young hurler allowed one run in seven innings and was defeated, 1–0, by Vern Law. The run was driven in by Gene Freese. Six days later, at Busch Stadium, his teammates supported him with ten runs in his second start. Defeating the St. Louis Cardinals, 10–5, for his first major league win, the svelte, 170-pound lefty surrendered nine hits in hurling the distance. Pizarro also cracked a home run, his first big league hit, victimizing Cardinals right-hander, and former Santurce Crabbers standout, Sam Jones. At 20 years old and three months, the Puerto Rican became the youngest Hispanic pitcher to hit a home run in the major leagues.

That was not the only laurel the youthful Pizarro achieved on the season. The Braves won the National League pennant and then the World Series, defeating the New York Yankees behind Lew Burdette's three victories. On October 5, in the first inning of Game 3 at County Stadium, Pizarro was called out of the bullpen to relieve ineffective starter Bob Buhl. The Yankees had scored three runs against Buhl before Pizarro secured the third out. Pizarro himself was excused from the game in the third inning, after allowing three singles, a walk and two runs. With his showing and recorded trip to the plate (0-for-1), Pizarro, at 20 years and eight months old, gained for himself the enduring designation as the youngest Hispanic pitcher to appear and bat in the World Series. It was the young left-hander's only appearance during the seven-game Series.

Pizarro returned to Puerto Rico over the winter as a world champion and established himself as the league's champion pitcher. (After two winter seasons, the young pitcher had a modest 9–9 record.) In 1957–1958, Pizarro captured the Triple Crown from the mound, winning 14 games, striking out 183 batters, and posting an ERA of 1.32. The Criollos hurler established a new league record with 19 strikeouts in a game, on November 20 against the Ponce Leones. Ten days after that 1–0 win, he tossed a no-hitter versus the Mayagüez Indios, walking four and striking out 11 in the 7–0 victory.

Caguas turned it on at season's end and won the island championship playoffs, earning a trip to the × Caribbean Series, which was held in San Juan that year. The sensation of the PRWL quickly established himself as the early sensation of the tournament. On February 8, the opening day of the Caribbean Classic and one day after his 21st birthday, the hard-throwing left-hander subjugated the Carta Vieja Yankees, 8–0, on two hits. He struck out 17 batters from Panama's championship squad, establishing a lasting Caribbean Series record.

It was, however, Pizarro's only victory in the competition, as Caguas fell on the final day of play to the Cuban champion Marianao Tigers and Bob Shaw, 2–0.

* * *

Over the next three summer seasons with Milwaukee, 1958–1960, Pizarro was held back in the bullpen and relegated to a part-time starter. He won 18 and lost 13 in the dual roles.

In December 1960, the left-hander was traded, with pitcher Joey Jay, to Cincinnati, for infielder Roy McMillan. Cincinnati immediately shipped Pizarro off to the Chicago White Sox with pitcher Cal McLish for third baseman Gene Freese.

While Pizarro was trying to reach his potential in the big leagues, in the winter leagues he remained a feared pitcher, although his record may not have indicated it. In the same three-season span, from 1958–1959 to 1960–1961, the pitcher, who been traded back to the Santurce Crabbers, achieved a 25–25 mark, but with full-season ERAs in the 2.09 to 2.77 range.

In his new Stateside league, in 1961, Pizarro finally came into his own, leading his new team in wins, though he was not given his first starting assignment until June 10—a no-decision against the Washington Senators, with no earned runs allowed in seven innings. Three days later, in a start on two days' rest, Pizarro won his first game of the season and his first for the White Sox. He defeated the Los Angeles Angels, 10–2, in the nightcap of a twi-night doubleheader at Comiskey Park. Pizarro pitched 7⅔ innings and struck out ten before being relieved. He also walked six batters.

In 39 appearances with the White Sox (25 starts), Pizarro won 14 and lost only 7, accumulating 188 strikeouts in 194⅔ innings. His ERA was 3.05. Pizarro nearly matched the league's winningest pitcher, Whitey Ford (25), win for win (14 to 16) from June 13 forward.

On August 20, Pizarro gained his first American League shutout, a 7–0 whitewash over the Kansas City Athletics in their home park. The victory, in the second game of a doubleheader swept by Chicago, placed the team three games above .500, in fourth place, 19 games behind the rampaging Yankees. The 86–76, fourth-place White Sox finished 23 games out of first.

White Sox manager Al López gave Pizarro the Opening Day start in 1962, and the 25-year-old did not disappoint. At Comiskey Park, Pizarro edged the Los Angeles Angels, 2–1. Catcher Sherm Lollar singled in the winning run in the bottom of the ninth inning, to the pleasure of Pizarro and the 18,124 in attendance.

Most of the rest of Pizarro's starts were not as good. The southpaw's record dropped to 12–14 at the conclusion of the season. His ERA swelled to 3.81, the result of inconsistent pitching. Except for a six-start stretch in July, of which he won five (the only loss, 1–0), he failed to display the brilliance from the prior season. Not helping matters, on August 19, the pitcher tried to knock down a hot smash off the bat of Al Kaline with his bare hand. The result was a dislocated ring finger and three weeks of inactivity. His record stood at 11–12 at that point. The White Sox disappointingly slipped, along with their projected top pitcher, to fifth place in the league.

* * *

In 1963, Pizarro bounced back strongly, winning 16 games for a 94-win Chicago White Sox squad that finished a distant second in the league to the last great Yankee team of the era.

In the left-hander's first start, on April 13, he threw nine shutout innings, allowing only two hits to the Los Angeles Angels. The game continued scoreless into the bottom of the 15th, when the Angels scored the only run of the contest. Pizarro's countryman Julio Navarro, with two innings of near-flawless relief for Los Angeles, was the winner. Pizarro's first win came six days later at the expense of the Minnesota Twins, 3–1. At Comiskey Park, the White Sox pitcher defeated Camilo Pascual on a five-hitter; he struck out nine and walked four.

Pizarro's initial shutout was registered on May 10. Continuing his success against the Angels, Pizarro blanked the men from the West Coast, 2–0. He permitted three hits and struck out six on a cold day in Chicago. The pitcher overcame his teammates' lack of offensive support and produced both runs himself with a home run (his first American League four-bagger) and a run-scoring single. The left-hander, apparently unperturbed by the 40-degree weather, did not allow a hit after the fourth inning and retired 15 straight batters entering the last inning.

On June 21, Pizarro thwarted Early Wynn's effort to win his 300th game. The hard thrower defeated Wynn and the Cleveland Indians, 2–0, at Cleveland Stadium. Pizarro improved to 8–3, while keeping the 39–28 White Sox in the hunt for the pennant, one game in back of the New York Yankees. (The 43-year old Wynn would require another three starts to reach the grandiose victory-mark.) Pizarro next defeated the Yankees on June 25, in his home ballpark, on a splendid five-hitter. The 2–1 victory was cheered by 46,177 fans, who undoubtedly reveled over the misfortune of the 11 Yankees strikeout victims. The win raised the White Sox to within percentage points of the Yankees' first place perch.

Pizarro was beaten in his next outing, but on July 4, he downed the Yankees again, at Yankee Stadium, for his tenth win. Pizarro required three innings of one-run relief help from Hoyt Wilhelm to earn the 4–2 win. The victory, in the second game of a holiday double-header, prevented a Yankees' four-game sweep and left the second-place Chicago team 4½ games behind New York.

Pizarro won four more games in August as the White Sox tried to keep the Yankees within their long-range sights. After winning his 16th game on August 28, Pizarro was shelved for the rest of the season with a lame arm. The White Sox were 12 games behind the now-cruising New York club. Pizarro's win total was achieved in 28 starts and four bullpen outings (214⅔ innings). A sterling ERA of 2.39 was good enough for second-best in the league, behind only teammate Gary Peters (2.33).

Chicago held on to the top consolation rung in the American League, 2½ games ahead of third-place Minnesota and 10½ behind the potent Yankees.

In Puerto Rico that winter, Pizarro continued to show how much of a polished pitcher he had become. He won ten games, bringing to 32 the number of victories he had earned over his last three winter campaigns (1961–1962 through 1963–1964).

* * *

The following season, 1964, the White Sox battled down to the wire with New York for the pennant and Pizarro enjoyed his finest major league campaign.

A fast start out of the gate for Pizarro helped the White Sox to the top of the league's standings. The 27-year-old pitcher started 5–0, with a 1.16 ERA (best in the American League) over 46⅔ innings. Pizarro himself could not account for the great record out of the starting block. "I don't know what it is," he said. "Usually I'm slow and sluggish at the beginning of the year. But this year I feel stronger. And better."[13]

The early success was more than likely attributable to the fact that the pea-thrower had fully matured and had reduced the number of walks he issued, something that had plagued him throughout his career. Manager Al López also cited in the press a new pitch—a "change-up curve"—that Pizarro had added to his repertoire, as helping the pitcher develop into his staff ace. During the string of initial successes, Pizarro downed the Washington Senators, 3–1, on May 22. He tied a career high in strikeouts with 13 and did not permit a single base on balls. Pizarro said afterward that he could not remember pitching a complete game without issuing a free pass.

After the perfect start, Pizarro split his next six decisions, with Orlando Peña of the Kansas City Athletics knocking the White Sox pitcher from the undefeated ranks on May 28. The score of the game was 4–1, with three of the runs surrendered by Pizarro unearned.

A six-game losing streak in mid–June, including five defeats in a row to the third-place New York Yankees, knocked the White Sox from their first place perch. Trying to scramble back to the top, Chicago beat the Baltimore Orioles for a second time in two days at Memorial Stadium, behind a Pizarro three-hitter. The 5–0 win came in the first game of a June 16 doubleheader. The Orioles won the nightcap to stay in a virtual first-place tie, eight percentage points behind the Chicagoans. It was Pizarro's first shutout and eighth win.

By the time of Pizarro's next shutout, July 5, the White Sox had slipped 4½ games behind the first-place Orioles. Retiring the last 13 men he faced, Pizarro completed a seven-hit, 2–0 victory over the Cleveland Indians at Comiskey Park. In the opener of the Sunday

Juan Pizarro was a 19-game winner with the Chicago White Sox in 1964. He won more than 300 games in his international career and is considered the best pitcher produced by Puerto Rico (photograph from Hall of Fame).

doubleheader, 18,675 fans witnessed Pizarro gain his 11th win, and a matching shutout in the nightcap (5–0) by teammate Joe Horlen brought the White Sox to within three games of first place.

On July 31, Pizarro became the American League's first 14-game winner, blanking the Washington Senators on four hits at Griffith Stadium, 6–0. The 5'11" hurler also struck out a personal best 14 batters, three times punching out the side in an inning. The White Sox inched to within one game of first-place Baltimore and New York with the win.

Pizarro equaled his win total from 1963, beating the slipped-to-third place Yankees, 2–1, on August 17, with relief help from Hoyt Wilhelm. It was Pizarro's second win over New York in less than a week, after losing his previous two decisions to the defending American League champions. Around this time, Pizarro was quoted as saying he would rather win a game from the Yankees than two from another team. Pizarro's lifetime record against the league's most resented team presently stood at 8–8. Two of the best known Yankees, Mickey Mantle and Roger Maris were both impressed by Pizarro's pitching speed.

After a no-decision against Baltimore, Pizarro pulled in his 17th victory with his fourth and final shutout of the campaign, on August 25. The five-hit, 1–0 blanking was achieved against the Minnesota Twins at Comiskey Park. The win edged the White Sox to within one game of first place, behind the Baltimore Orioles, and three games ahead of the still clawing New York Yankees.

Frustratingly, Pizarro won only twice more over the rest of the season. Over a stretch of 23⅓ innings, he surrendered 18 earned runs and was raked for 35 hits. Pizarro's ERA, rose to 2.56 at year's end. It was reported that the pitcher grew tired and his fastball lost its hop, and his winter ball pitching was the cited cause behind the apparent sapped strength. In spite of Pizarro's skid, which could not have occurred at a worse time, the White Sox stayed in the thick of a nip-and-tuck pennant race, between themselves, the Orioles and Yankees.

To their credit, the White Sox closed the season with a flourish, winning their final nine games. Pizarro claimed his 18th and 19th victories during the inspired stretch. His 19th win was 3–2 over the Kansas City Athletics on October 2, coming with only two days remaining in the season. Hoyt Wilhelm recorded a four-inning save.

The American League pennant was not decided until the last weekend of the campaign. The Yankees barely scaled past the other contenders to the summit of the American League's championship hill. Thanks largely to the September pickup of Pedro Ramos from the Cleveland Indians, the circuit's winningest franchise edged the 98–64 White Sox by one game in the final standings.

*   *   *

Back with the White Sox in 1965, Pizarro could not shake the arm problem that plagued him at the close of 1964. That he did not rest over the winter but won nine games and lost five for Santurce, pitching 127⅔ innings, was not only a testament to the pitcher's competitive spirit but his desire not to disappoint fans in his native country. In an attempt to bring his arm around, the White Sox limited the pitcher's spring workload and gave him extra rest between starts. Through his first seven big league starts of 1965, he did not pitch past the fifth inning. He had a record of 1–2, compared to 8–4 at the same point in the previous season.

The White Sox placed their beleaguered pitcher on the disabled list after a start on June 23, with a torn triceps tendon. He returned to action on July 30 and showed promise of a return to past form. He tossed eight innings with only one run allowed in a no-decision against the Detroit Tigers. Two starts afterward, on August 11, Pizarro spun his only shutout of the season, a dandy of an effort against Washington. A fifth-inning, leadoff single by Senators right fielder Woodie Held registered as the lone hit permitted by Pizarro. Allowing two walks, the left-hander struck out only two in the game, an indication that his fastball was still not quite back to its normal velocity.

Pizarro finished the season 6–3 in 18 starts, and Al López guided the White Sox to a third straight second-place finish, this time behind the upstart Minnesota Twins.

For the 1966 season, the White Sox decided to put Pizarro in the bullpen, and the pitcher performed more than respectably. In 34 appearances with nine spot starts, the ten-year veteran notched an 8–6 record, with a 3.76 ERA in 88⅔ innings. The White Sox, under new manager Eddie Stanky, dropped to fourth place, 15 games in back of the pennant-grabbing Baltimore Orioles.

Shortly after the season, Chicago obtained pitcher Wilbur Wood from the Pittsburgh Pirates for a White Sox player to be named later. That future arrived on November 28, and the player named was Juan Pizarro. The pitcher welcomed the trade notification, as he had not developed a strong bond with manager Stanky. Also, with the Pirates, he would find as teammates several Hispanic players, including fellow countrymen Roberto Clemente and José Pagan.

When Pizarro found out about the trade, he was in the middle of his second-best winter season on the mound. The left-hander eventually totaled 12 wins and lost only three games for his San Juan-based team; his ERA was 2.08 over 129⅔ innings. Pizarro was the winning pitcher in the sixth and final game of the Island Championship Series between Santurce and the Ponce Leones, 6–3. A five-run, ninth-inning rally by the Crabbers, managed by Earl Weaver, highlighted the climactic win at Paquito Montaner Stadium in Ponce.

As the 1967 major league season began, Pizarro had established himself as a pitcher, with a lifetime mark of 98–66, and he was only 30 years old. The Pirates were a .500 team (81–81) in 1967, and Pizarro was a couple of degrees worse than his mediocre sixth-place club, owning an 8–10 record and working the majority of his games out of the bullpen.

Back home over the winter, the devoted pitcher soared to an 11–2 record, throwing 148 innings and registering a 2.37 ERA. But the Crabbers fell short of defending their league championship with a six-game series loss to Caguas in the finals.

* * *

In June of 1968, the 1–1 Pizarro was sold by the Pirates to the pitching starved Boston Red Sox. The Santurce native won six games for the Red Sox, starting 12 contests. His combined record for the season was 7–9.

In 1969, Pizarro recorded the first official save by an American League pitcher for the baseball history books. The new statistic, implemented for the first time that year, was designed to measure a relief pitcher's worth over the critical last innings of a ball game with his team ahead. On Opening Day, April 8, Pizarro came in to nail down a 5–4, extra-inning victory over the Baltimore Orioles at Memorial Stadium. In the bottom of the 12th inning, Pizarro retired the three men he faced in order, including Frank Robinson and Brooks Robinson.

Eleven days later, the Red Sox sent Pizarro and two other players, including fan favorite Ken "Hawk" Harrelson, to the Cleveland Indians for three players. Pizarro then bounced around with four other major league clubs over the next six seasons, including a return stint with Pittsburgh, before hanging up his spikes in 1974.

One of the teams Pizarro hooked up with near the end of his career was the Chicago Cubs. In 1971, Pizarro had received an early-season demotion from Chicago. On August 5, in his fourth start since being recalled from the minors, the left-hander hurled a glittering one-hit, nine-strikeout shutout over the San Diego Padres at Wrigley Field. Ollie Brown's ground single between short and third prevented Pizarro from entering the record books with his 3–0 win.

On September 16, having earned a spot in the rotation with the one-hitter pitched six weeks earlier, the 34-year-old outdueled Tom Seaver of the New York Mets, 1–0, at Shea Stadium. Pizarro homered off Seaver, the National League's strikeout (282) and ERA champ-to-be (1.76) in the eighth inning, for the game's decisive blow.

Pizarro finished the season 7–6, his last winning campaign in the majors.

Legacy

The 1971 shutout versus Seaver was Pizarro's last big league whitewash. In all, he hurled 17, a number surpassed by only two other major league Latin American southpaws—Mike Cuéllar and Fernando Valenzuela. Pizarro's final big league ledger was 131–105, with a 3.43 ERA in 2,034⅓ innings. He appeared in 488 games over 18 seasons.

Pizarro also hurled a most impressive 17 shutouts in a brief, three-season career in the Mexican League between 1974 and 1976. In 1974, he tied a Mexican League record for shutouts in one season with nine. The lefty posted an outstanding record of 38–21, with 42 complete games in 63 starts south of the Rio Grande. He registered an ERA of 2.04 in nearly 500 innings with the Córdoba Coffeegrowers.

In Puerto Rico, Pizarro absolutely starred. He hurled in 22 consecutive winter campaigns, from 1955–1956 to 1976–1977, appearing in 351 games. Only Luis Arroyo participated in more games (364) as a left-hander on the Puerto Rican League mounds. Pizarro spent all but two full seasons with his hometown Santurce team. Tossing 2,403 innings, he logged 46 shutouts and a 2.51 ERA. His lifetime record was 157–110.

In the 1963 Inter–American Series, the short-lived tournament designed to replace the Caribbean Series, Pizarro pitched a no-hitter on the opening night of the Caribbean basin competition, February 8. On the fifth anniversary of his sensational 17-strikeout showing in the tenth Caribbean Series, Pizarro humbled the Valencia Industrialists, 5–0. He walked four and set down the last 16 opposing batters in a row.

With the recommencement of the Caribbean Series in 1970, Pizarro received three opportunities to accompany Puerto Rican teams to battle for the baseball championship of Latin America.

In 1971, he settled for a no decision in his only start for Santurce, in a competition won by the Licey Tigres on Pizarro's team's home soil. In 1973, at University Stadium in Caracas, Pizarro was the opening day starter for Santurce against Licey. The left-hander was defeated by Tigers starter Pedro Borbón, who tossed a complete game, 8–2 victory. Four days later, Pizarro pitched nine innings of his own in a 9–3 vanquishing of Mexico's Obregón Yaquis.

Licey, with a 5–1 record, won its second title in three years. On his 39th birthday, February 7, 1976, Pizarro recaptured his talented youth and tossed his second Caribbean Series shutout, in the second Caribbean Classic hosted by the Dominican Republic. As a roster supplement for the Puerto Rican titleists from Bayamón, Pizarro handcuffed the Venezuelan contingent, Aragua Tigers, on three hits. The Hermosillo Orangegrowers, with five wins in six games, took the championship trophy back home to Mexico.

"Juan Pizarro is the best pitcher Puerto Rico has ever produced. And he never head-hunted. " The words came from 85-year-old Pantalones Santiago, a 16-year veteran of the Puerto Rican Winter League, who has seen all of his island's great pitchers. "I tried to convince Hank Greenberg to sign Pizarro," stated the former Cleveland Indians pitcher. "I told him Pizarro was as fast as Herb Score. But Greenberg [Cleveland GM] let him get away."[14]

A year 2000 electee to the Caribbean Hall of Fame, the 75-year-old Pizarro shuns interviews and the limelight associated with his playing days. He is presently content to live as a private citizen in his homeland.

PART II
The Major Leagues

3

The 1920s and
1930s—Adolfo Luque

Adolfo Luque

"Pitching," Adolfo Luque wrote in 1927's *Secrets of Baseball Told by Big League Players,* "is the kind of work that is the finest sort of play."[1] What may sound like a convoluted Yogism by Luque, if extrapolated from the context of the writing, suggested that his profession, if practiced diligently and properly, yielded much satisfaction. Luque was the pitching voice in a how-to-*best*-play baseball book that included contributions from all-time greats Lou Gehrig, Rogers Hornsby, Tris Speaker, Pie Traynor and Gabby Hartnett. That Luque was chosen as the mound spokesman for the instructional book was testament to his status in baseball at the time as both a pitcher and pitching academic.

When the book was first printed, Luque had achieved his baseball acumen from 15 years of professional experience, beginning in his native Cuba in 1912 at age 22.

Luque was recruited to play in the United States in 1913 for the Long Branch Cubans,[2] an entry in the six-team, Class D New York–New Jersey League. In August of the same year, Luque was one of three Cuban players[3] on the team sold to the Boston Braves by Long Branch owner Antonio Hernández Henriquez. Luque joined the Braves, but not until spring camp in Macon, Georgia, the first week of March 1914. Luque was the only Hispanic on James E. Gaffney's team when it began the regular season on April 14, in Brooklyn, as his fellow cubanos failed to make the major league grade.

In May, Luque took the mound in the road uniform of the Boston Braves as the major leagues' first Hispanic pitcher. In that May 20 debut, Luque was defeated, 4–1, by the Pittsburgh Pirates; the home team scratched across their runs on five hits, two walks and a Boston error. Luque pitched two-thirds of an inning in relief in another game before being sent to the International League's Jersey City club in June. The Braves, incidentally, were 14 games under .500 after Luque's initial loss, but the team "miraculously" roared out from the National League's cellar and went on to win the pennant and World Series.

The next season was a near-repeat one for Luque, but not so for the Braves. The pitcher, who stood five-foot, seven inches in height (smallish even for the era), saw action again in only two games as a hurler for Boston—one as a starter, getting a no-decision, and the other as a reliever. Luque and another pitcher, Eugene Cocreham, were sent to the Toronto team of the International League in order to bring the Braves club to a required limit of players by May 1. Luque spent the summer pitching for the Maple Leafs and won 15 games for the Double-A team.

Two and one-half seasons passed before Luque returned to the majors; it came as a permanent return as property of the Cincinnati Reds. Luque was obtained by the Reds in July 1918, from Louisville of the American Association, which prematurely ceased operations that month in anticipation of impending war restrictions. It was a career break for Luque, who had spent the previous two summers with Louisville and who had not been given much of a major league opportunity with Boston. A national periodical's "wrap-up" column on the Louisville season told of the merited move in the following fashion: "Adolfo Luque left for Cincinnati, where he joined the Reds, the Colonels having sold him, just as he was about to pull out for Havana. Luque is about the best pitcher in the Association and will deliver in the majors. His winning of 12 games during the first half of the year, despite the fact that he had played infield and outfield for about three weeks, was a remarkable feat. Luque owns the distinction of being the only Louisville player to hit a home run on the local grounds this season."[4]

The Reds, facing the prospect of losing two pitchers to the draft and three doubleheaders in three days during the final week of July, were searching for additional pitching depth and found it in Luque.

The nearly 28-year-old rookie got his feet wet with the Reds with a scoreless inning of relief against his former team on July 24. Two days later, the Reds threw Luque into a twin fray in the same series with Boston at Braves Field, both games Reds' losses. The newest Reds pitcher took one for the team in the opener; he went the distance and suffered an 11–5 loss, allowing 14 hits. The score of the second game was 12–3, as Reds starter Larry Jacobus stunk up the place, with Luque coming back to pitch one scoreless relief inning.[5]

In his next start for the Reds, the Cuban pitcher obtained his inaugural major league win, beating the New York Giants at the Polo Grounds on a hot Thursday afternoon in early August. Luque threw a four-hitter, allowing two runs (one earned); he collected two hits himself and two runs scored in his special victory. No one could have known it then, but the Polo Grounds, its bleachers, and all of New York would come to know the name of Adolfo Luque very well in the decades that followed.

Just three days after beating the Giants in the grueling heat, Cincinnati manager Christy Mathewson assigned Luque another start on August 11. Though he lost, 5–3, to the St. Louis Cardinals, Mathewson, obviously liking the pitching habits he had seen so far from Luque, made a permanent spot for him in the rotation.

The 1918 baseball season was ended three weeks early, in cooperation with the "Work or Fight" order from the United States War Department. The mandate was passed with intentions of strengthening the country's industrial production and military ranks for a planned 1919 Allied trench-smashing "final push" into Germany, to bring a merciful end to the horrible slaughter that had decimated Europe. At the time of the sweeping order, no one expected an armistice to end World War I only two months following the earliest World Series, begun on September 5.

Luque had joined a fifth-place team, and by the time he pitched the final game of the season for the Reds on September 2—a 1–0, six-hit blanking of the Cardinals for his first major league shutout—the Reds had risen to third place. Luque's shutout, at Redland Field, was the first by a Latin American pitcher in the major leagues.

In just under six weeks, Adolofo Luque's first real big league pitching gambit produced a complete game in every one of his nine starts, for an admirable 6–3 record.

* * *

Over the course of the 1919 season, the New York Giants played ball at a .621-success rate, but even that could not stack up against the torrid .686 winning percentage sustained by the Cincinnati Reds. The Reds recruited a new manager, Pat Moran, and the team cruised to the pennant by nine games over the second-place Giants. Luque, pitching more than twice as often from the bullpen as in the starter's role, was one of six Reds pitchers with double-digit victories. Luque accrued a spiffy 10–3 mark and a 2.63 ERA in 30 appearances.

The Reds won their first seven games of the season, Luque winning the first and fourth games in the string, both over the St. Louis Cardinals at Redland Field. On April 26, three days after picking up the club's Opening Day victory in relief, Luque started and scattered nine hits, with three walks, in taking a 5–1 decision.

Not starting again until three weeks later, on May 16 at Brooklyn, Luque delivered a superb, 1–0 five-hitter over the Superbas and Rube Marquard. A week afterward, after gaining a victory over the New York Giants, also in relief, Luque beat the Boston Braves, 10–4, at Braves Field. Luque dispersed nine hits and allowed three earned runs. But then, after five unblemished victories, Luque suffered losses in consecutive starts. In his second setback as a Reds starter, on May 31, he permitted five earned runs in two innings to the Pittsburgh Pirates; it was the first time he had been hit hard on the season.

Luque was relegated to one start (a no-decision) and six relief appearances in the month following the second defeat. On July 31, Luque hurled the second of his two shutouts on the season, winning 2–0 and yielding four hits to the Boston Braves at Redland Field. That was, ironically, his last start of the campaign.

After that game, Moran decided to stick with a strong starting quintet of Hod Eller, Dutch Ruether, Slim Sallee, Jimmy Ring and Ray Fisher. Luque was first man out of the pen, finishing 15 games and throwing 106 innings on the season. The Reds had moved to 59–28 following Luque's second shutout, but still lagged percentage points behind the league-leading Giants. They posted a 37–16 mark in their remaining games to outsoar New York, with Moran understandably reluctant to change pitching cards during the sensational surge. The other four pitchers on the Reds' ten-man staff threw a grossly disproportionate 92 of the team's 1,274 innings on the season. Cincinnati took only *six* pitchers into the post-season; Luque was among them.

The Reds' World Series opponents were the Chicago White Sox, a team which was the odds-on favorite in the Series, even though Chicago was eight games weaker than Cincinnati based on team records. The 1919 World Series was one that pockmarked the game, stigmatizing several star White Sox players who, with lucre as their persuasion, allegedly did not pitch and play their best during the grand engagement. Cincinnati, with a team ERA of 2.23 during the season, more than three-quarters of a run better than the White Sox, would probably have beaten Charles Comiskey's team without collaborative aid from some of his players.

The Reds held their American League opponents to six runs in the first five games of the Series and won four of them. Then Moran's club weathered two losses before taking the championship in eight games, one of only a handful of World Series played that involved more than seven games.

Luque pitched twice in relief in the eight contests. Pitching one inning in Game 3 on October 3, Luque struck out the first batter to face him (Nemo Leibold) and retired Eddie Collins and Buck Weaver on ground outs to the right side of the infield. Four more games into the Series, on October 8, the pitcher threw four sharp innings. (Both of Luque's appearances were in Reds' losses.) In all, Luque hurled five scoreless innings, allowing only one hit and another base to a batter who reached on an error but was erased at second greedily trying to stretch his good fortune. Luque set down 15 of 16 batters faced, including Eddie Collins three times, Buck Weaver twice and Shoeless Joe Jackson once.

*   *   *

The Reds fell two places in the standings in their unsuccessful title defense of 1920. Luque worked as both a starter and reliever, with a greater emphasis on starting. Nineteen-twenty was a reputation-gaining year for Luque, one that would type-cast him for future generations as an oftentimes disorderly and tempestuous player.

Luque's inevitable and permanent placement into the Cincinnati starting rotation came at the end of May. Following the insertion, the right-hander won four straight starts, including an 11-inning, 3–1 triumph over the Philadelphia Phillies at the Baker Bowl on June 22. (In between, Luque suffered a defeat in relief, to the New York Giants on a late-inning unearned run.) Beginning on June 26, he lost four in a row, all of them by one run, and two 1–0, to the Chicago Cubs and Boston Braves, respectively. (The tough-luck loss to Boston was to Joe Oeschger, who earlier in the season had tangled with Brooklyn's Leon Cadore to produce baseball's most monumental pitching duel: a 26-inning, 1–1 tie).

Opening the quartet of defeats was a loss in Cincinnati in the nightcap of a doubleheader on June 26. After a first-game shutout at the hands of the St. Louis Cardinals, the Reds tried for the split with Luque on the mound. The Redbirds held a 3–2 lead in the sixth inning when, with a runner at third base, Luque bobbled a tapper and threw home late in an attempt to stop the aggressive runner from scoring.

The play at the plate was extremely close, but the call went against the Reds. The fans, having endured one defeat already, bristled virally from the arbitrator's perceived slight. Plate umpire Bill Klem was "showered with pop bottles" and Reds catcher Ivey Wingo was ejected for his protestations to Klem. The debris was eventually removed from the field and play continued with no other runs scored by St Louis. In the eighth inning, a sequence of events took place that led to a "fierce bodily assault on the judge of play" by Luque. A verbal exchange occurred between Klem and Luque as the pitcher was preparing to deliver a pitch to Cardinals first baseman Jack Fournier with two men out. Luque dropped the ball and bolted from the mound toward Klem, landing at least two punches on Klem's face and head before he could be pulled away. Ejected from the game, Luque was banished to the clubhouse and was forced to absorb a 4–3 defeat.[6]

Luque was not stringently castigated by the league,[7] and five days later, on July 1, made his next start. As happenstance would have it, Bill Klem was umpiring behind the dish. The Cubs and Grover Cleveland Alexander beat Luque, 1–0, the game's only run set up by a bad-hop triple. The game produced no flare-up between the prior combatants.

On July 5, allowing two runs in the bottom of the 11th inning, Luque absorbed his third straight loss, beaten by the Pittsburgh Pirates, 6–5. Luque permitted ten hits in the game and walked five. Five days later, Luque was defeated, 1–0, by Oeschger of the visiting Braves. The Reds starter wild-pitched home the only run of the game after surrendering a triple; each hurler allowed three hits, with Luque pinch-hit for in the eighth frame. Luque broke his losing slide, winning his next time out on July 14; the hurler corralled the Philadelphia Phillies, 3–2, in ten innings at Redland Field.

The Reds' battling pitcher beat Brooklyn four days later, 4–1, in the third contest of a five-game series in Cincinnati. The win lifted Luque's record to 6–5 and trimmed the difference in the standings to three games between the second-place Reds and the top-of-the-heap Brooklynites. The Reds split the next two games and lost the first two encounters of another five-game home series against the temporarily below-.500 New York Giants. In the second of those defeats, Luque lost bitterly, 2–1. The Giants scored once in the second inning when, with men on the corners, a potential inning-ending double play was not executed because shortstop Larry Kopf was called for missing second base prior to his relay throw to first. The second run scored against Luque following a single and two-base error by center fielder Edd Roush, who let the safety get passed him. A groundout plated the batter, who had ended up at third base.

Exactly a week later, on July 29, in his next trip to the mound, Luque edged Leon Cadore in Brooklyn, 3–2. Then, pitching with only two days' rest, Luque lost by the same score at the Polo Grounds. With two outs and no one on base in the final inning, Giants outfielder Ross Youngs beat out an infield hit to the second baseman. The call at first on the throw could have gone either way. It was reported that some in the field box crowd casually stepped onto the field heading for the outfield exits, thinking the third out had been recorded. They had to be ushered back into their seats. Then the Giants reached Luque for a single and double, plating Youngs, and with runners at second and third, a fourth consecutive hit by Vern Spencer brought the winning runs home.

The Reds went 8–10 against the teams from Gotham in their back-to-back, home-and-home series, but only lost one-half game in the standings. Luque followed the painful loss in New York with a 7–0 shutout of the Phillies at the Baker Bowl on August 5, which pulled the 53–42 Reds to within 1½ games of first-place Brooklyn.

Moran's men snatched the victory ring in ten of their next 14 games. The tenth, on August 20 against Brooklyn, was won by Luque by a score of 10–3. It was his third victory in the past five weeks against the former first-place team. The table-turning Reds had now moved two games ahead of the seemingly succumbing Robins. In that 10–3 win (his 11th), Luque came out after the eighth inning with a big lead, his arm bothering him. In what for many pitchers was common, but what was for him an extreme rarity, Adolfo Luque had been stricken with a sore arm. It would be 14 days before he made another start. The Reds fell out of first place during the interval.

The ailing arm rendered the pitcher inconsistent during the last month of the season, though he managed two wins. Luque's 13th—and final—victory of the campaign came in a 3–2 complete game on September 15 at the Baker Bowl, in which he struck out nine Phillies. The win kept the Reds five games behind Brooklyn, which had robustly returned to their previous place of league leadership. A week later, Babe Adams of the Pirates outdueled Luque, 2–0, handing the Reds pitcher his ninth defeat and final decision.

Over the final month of the season, Wilbert Robinson's Brooklyn team won 22 times and secured for themselves a place squarely at the head of the National League's ruling class table, with the Reds dislodged two places away in third position, 10½ games apart.

* * *

Nineteen twenty-one was another reputation-gaining year for Adolfo Luque, but not the kind to which a pitcher would necessarily aspire. Luque tied for the league lead in shutouts with three, but lost 19 games, ten more than in the previous season, against 17 wins. A starter from the beginning of the season, Luque's 25 complete games were third best in the circuit, as were his 102 strikeouts; his ERA was a reputable 3.38 and four-tenths of a run below the league's average.

For the season, it seemed, as far as Luque's teammates were concerned, it was all for one or nothing for one. When the right-hander pitched, when Cincinnati scored, it scored in bunches. Five times the Reds rang up ten runs or more in a game for Luque. At the contrasting end, in 18 of his 19 losses, the Reds scored 27 total runs, an average of 1.5 runs per game. Four times the Reds were shut out. The team provided one run of support in five separate starts and two runs in five others. The Reds owned the league's worst team batting average and scored the second-fewest runs in the circuit. The offensive deficiencies, combined with untimely bad breaks, instilled a spreading sentiment in pressbox circles. The Queen City hurler became known as the hard-luck pitcher of the National League.

During a late spring game, a seething response to an umpire's call led to an incident which, proved detrimental to the pitching ledger of the Reds' hurler. On May 28 at Forbes Field, protecting a one-run lead in the eighth inning with runners on first and third and one out, Luque induced a foul pop-up from the batter. The ball was caught by catcher Ivey Wingo against the stands behind home plate. Forbes Field during that period had a vast amount of ground separating first row seats from Wingo's position. The Pirates runner on third, Carson Bigbee, attempted to exploit the considerable foul territory, tagged up and tried to score after Wingo's difficult catch.

Luque covered the plate and applied the tag on Bigbee, but the brazen runner was called safe by home plate umpire Bill Brennan. Luque became infuriated and spiked the ball on the ground toward the Reds' dugout. Wingo scampered after the rolling ball and threw to third base, nailing the runner from first, who was trying to advance two bases. (Over the years, the play at the plate has often been omitted in the recount of Luque's actions, making it seem that Luque was overcome by an irrational nature on the mound when he "threw" the ball into the Reds' dugout.)

The Reds marched on to win the tied game (or so they thought) in ten innings, 4–3, with Luque not involved with the decision (or so he thought). But Pirates manager George Gibson protested the game on the grounds that the ball should have been dead once it had reached the dugout and his man should not have been called out at third, ending the eighth inning.

Although neither of the two field umpires had seen it, a player in the Reds' dugout, Eppa Rixey, had alertly intercepted the rolling ball and tossed it back to the pursuing Wingo, who turned and fired to third, nabbing the runner. But such a deceptive act could not proceed undetected in the home ballpark. The National League upheld the Pirates' protest, wiped out the last two innings, and ordered the May 28 game to be *re*-finished, picked up from the point of the successful protest in the bottom of the eighth inning.

A month later, in Cincinnati's next trip into Pittsburgh, the game continued from its contested point. As it turned out, it was Luque's rotation turn to pitch the opening game of the series so, prior to the regularly scheduled game, he was given the ball and a second opportunity to obtain a victory in the protested game that had stricken from the record books a game-winning hit by Edd Roush.

In modern baseball, Luque's act of displeasure with the umpire's call at the plate after the caught pop-up by Wingo would have earned him an immediate ejection from the game. It would have been better for Luque had Bill Brennan been a more sensitive person. When the game was resumed at the point of the decreed "dead ball" in the Reds' dugout, Luque achieved the third out of the eighth inning and the formerly-thrown-out runner was left stranded at third with the score tied, 3–3. But in the Pirates' ninth, after the Reds did not score in their half of the inning, first baseman Charlie Grimm lifted a Luque two-out offering into the right field bleachers to end the "brief" engagement. Then, in the game Luque was scheduled to start, he was done in by a three-run, seventh-inning uprising, and the eventual outcome saddled the Cuban with two losses on the day, 4–3 and 5–3.

The Reds were near the cellar at that point of the early summer and managed only a one-tier improvement, to sixth place in the standings, by the start of September. On September 4, with a record of 14–18, Luque made a home start against the first-place Pittsburgh Pirates. He lost, 2–1, in 12 innings. A triple and a single in the last frame, two of eight hits he allowed, beat him.

The pitcher won three of his remaining four starts. He had no decision against the New York Giants on September 13, at Redland Field. Luque took a 3–0 lead into the ninth inning. With one out, an error by shortstop Larry Kopf led to three runs. The Giants eventually won the game, 4–3, three innings later, and the first following Luque's removal.

The 70–83 Reds closed a disappointing year, one which Luque had opened promisingly with a 5–3, complete game win, in front of the largest Opening Day crowd, 30,444, in franchise history.

PERVERSITY OF FATE

No man is an island except Adolfo Luque on the pitching mound for the Reds in 1922. Cincinnati improved to a fourth-best league ranking in team batting average. Yet when it was Luque's turn on the hill, the team inexplicably lost its hitting eye. The tone was set early on as the Reds pushed across a grand total of two runs in Luque's first three starts, all losses. Luque slid to a 4–11 record through the first two months of the season. One of the wins was a 2–1, 12-inning triumph over the Philadelphia Phillies at Redland Field on May 20. In the eight-hit, nine-strikeout performance, the lone run allowed by Luque was unearned.

Led by 25-game winner Eppa Rixey, the Rhinelanders climbed to second place in the National League. Luque chipped in with 13 wins, but they were harshly overridden by 23 losses. An exonerating breakdown of some of the losses reveals that Luque was defeated four times by 2–1 scores, three more by 3–1 counts and two others by shutouts. Luque held opponents to a .268 batting average, second best among National League pitchers, but he could not overcome the paltry run support and a damaging *27 unearned* runs.

Three of those 2–1 losses were to John McGraw's Giants. Two were home losses and the other was in New York. The defeat at the Polo Grounds, on June 11, featured a game-winning home run by Charles Dillon "Casey" Stengel. Luque allowed four hits in the game, two on the infield. The Giants scored their other run thanks to an error by the usually sure-fielding Luque.

Baseball Magazine ran an article on Luque's season the following May. It was titled, "The Strange Case of Adolfo Luque ... Explain, If You Can, How a Pitcher with a Powerful Club, Ranked Sixth in Earned-Run Effectiveness, and Yet Lost More Games Than Any Other Big League Hurler." Comparing Luque's 3.31 ERA with teammate Rixey's 3.53

(11th-best in the league), the article concluded "that Adolfo Luque was about the unluckiest pitcher of the season. And in the face of such a run of tough luck all mathematics and science and statistics and baseball dope take a back seat."[8]

The story concluded, "The player with an alibi is not very popular in baseball. But for all of that we think that Adolfo Luque has a just right to kick at the strange perversity of fate which, in spite of his good work, made his season's record one of the biggest flivvers in recent history."[9]

THE NERVE OF A GRIZZLY BEAR

The year Adolfo Luque compiled in 1923 should not be called a "career year" because few careers boast years with the numbers Luque posted. It should rightfully be referred to as one of the greatest pitching seasons in post–Deadball baseball history.

Interestingly, Luque began the season at the rear of the Reds' four-man rotation, and as such received only three starts in April. He won two of them while getting a no-decision on April 28 after his shortest outing of the season, 2⅓ innings with three runs and seven hits allowed against the St Louis Cardinals.

It appeared the right-hander would begin May in auspicious fashion as he took a 1–0 lead into the last inning against the Chicago Cubs. But a fielding lapse altered the positive outcome. On a potential game-ending double play, Reds second baseman Sam Bohne threw so wildly passed shortstop Ike Cavey that both runners on base scored. The unearned runs provided Chicago a ninth-inning, 2–1 road victory over Cincinnati.

Luque had two no-decisions in subsequent starts. In the middle game of a three-game set at the Polo Grounds, he defeated the Giants, 7–0, showing what made him the elite pitcher of both leagues that season. A New York newspaper account elaborated on the May 18 game as follows:

> The shutout was the first of the season for McGraw's doughty men, a fact for which Adolfo Luque of Havana ought to be held responsible. Luque pitched exceedingly well. He generally does, but the Reds are not always appreciative. When they don't give him weak batting support, they field terribly or indulge in what are known technically in the trade as "boners." Luque has earned the reputation of being the "hard luck" pitcher in baseball and there is a saying in dear old Havana that if it were raining gold Adolfo would be equipped with a sieve.[10]

The five-hit win by Luque evened the Reds' record through 26 games.

On May 22, Pat Moran used Luque questionably in relief of Pete Donohue against Brooklyn. Luque pitched five scoreless innings in a game he entered with the Reds behind, 9–6, and which ended by the same score. Both Eppa Rixey and Donohue received multiple starts ahead of Luque during the eight-day span before he started again. Cincinnati lost all six of the games. Luque ended the losing streak by defeating the Cardinals, 2–1, on May 27. Two ninth-inning errors deprived Luque of a shutout and snapped a 24-scoreless innings streak he had in place. On the last day of May, Luque won for the fifth time with a 3–2 complete game victory over the Chicago Cubs at Redland Field.

The pitcher promptly took off in June, winning five of six starts, including two by shutout. He missed a third blanking in that stretch on an unearned run, settling for a 2–1 win over the Philadelphia Phillies. His only loss came 2–0 to the Cubs' Grover Cleveland Alexander.

Luque and Brooklyn Robins teammate Dazzy Vance (right) sit atop the dugout steps in 1930. Traded to the Robins that February, Lugue would spend two seasons with the team before finishing his career with the New York Giants.

On the first of July, two days after recording his tenth win of the season with his fourth shutout, Luque saved a 3–2 win for Donohue by setting down the six Pittsburgh Pirates to face him over the game's final two innings. The Reds, who had entered June two games under .500, were now ten games over and in third place.

Luque started on the Fourth of July and won, 6–3, over the Cubs at Cubs Park. Four days later, he beat the world champion New York Giants for the third time in as many tries, 6–3. In his next time out to the mound, on July 12 against the Phillies, the pitcher reclaimed the shutout his defense had cost him the previous month. The 2–0 road win bumped the Reds into second place, a full game ahead of the third-place Pittsburgh Pirates.

In mid–July, the Reds faced three doubleheaders in one week and four in 11 days. Luque offered his manager double-duty labor. In the third twin bill, on July 17, the gritty pitcher started both games, winning decisions in each against the Boston Braves and pitching 15 total innings on the day. "Dolf Luque caused torch-light parades in Havana the other day," wrote one Cincinnati writer, "when he won both halves of a doubleheader at Boston. Pat Moran was surprised when the Cuban volunteered to pitch the second game, but sent him in, and nobly the Senor did his duty."[11] The victories, 4–3 and 9–5, were his 14th and 15th against only two losses. (The defeats: 2–1 and 2–0.)

Luque improved to 16–2 prior to Brooklyn and Dazzy Vance besting him, 6–3, on July 25, to end a seven-game win streak. The loss, coupled with two Pittsburgh wins on the day, dropped the Reds into a second-place tie with the Bucs in the National League, 4½ games in back of New York.

As July was nearing expiration and nearly halfway through a 19-game homestand, Luque rung up his 17th victory; it came as a 2–1 triumph over the Braves, Luque himself scoring the winning run after tripling in the eighth inning. The Reds played doubleheaders over the next two days, July 30 and 31, against the Philadelphia Phillies, sweeping a pair and dropping a pair. Moran called on Luque in relief on August 1, three days after his 2–1, complete game win over the Braves. The right-hander saved his second game of the season, with 1⅔ accomplished innings in the 5–3 Reds win over Philadelphia.

As the Phillies and Reds wrapped up their series, the first-place Giants came into Cincinnati for a five-game set. The Reds were now in sole possession of second, trailing McGraw's New Yorkers by three games. Peter T. Toot's 2004 book on Cuban outfielder Armando Marsans gave an insight into a strategic deployment that surfaced at that junction of Luque's and the Reds' season. Toot stated that Luque "volunteered to pitch out of turn to face the Giants as many times in the remaining twelve games against the Reds' main rivals." Toot offered the following presumably paraphrased quote attributed to Luque, taken from the *Cincinnati Times-Star,* supporting Luque's desires as a pitcher on a roll: "A lucky pitcher should press his luck. Send me in four or five games of the 12 if my luck holds good."[12] Luque had not missed a "pass" against the Giants all year, winning all three of his starts against the New York team, two by shutouts.

Given this, and the season Luque was compiling to this point, it might be difficult to fault Moran's quick acceptance of the pitcher's grand offer. However, in a broader view, there were two full months of the season left. With the advantage of hindsight, it can be queried now—was it necessary for Moran to appease Luque with so many games remaining (55), to rearrange the rotation in the thick of a pennant race? Changing things to suit Luque's well-intentioned desires required disrupting the routine of the other starters as well.

With the Luque vs. Giants plan settled upon, and in order to give Luque two starts over four days in the extended series against the McGrawmen, August 4 through 7, Moran reshuffled his pitching staff. (This was a departure from the Moran of 1919 who would not alter his starting pitching scheme over the final two months of the season.) The manager did not start Luque in his regular turn, which would have been two days prior to the Giants series. Eppa Rixey was also held back a day from beginning the series against the Giants in what would have been his normal turn, and Pete Donohue, the other of the Reds' terrific threesome of pitchers, was pushed up to pitch on two days' rest to take Luque's place in the Phils series finale (August 2).

Enter the Giants. In the opener against the Empire State front-runners, which was also his 33rd birthday, Luque responded with his worst showing of the season. He was knocked from the box by McGraw's team after allowing ten hits, unable to finish the fifth inning. The Giants crushed the Reds, 14–4, and took three more contests, including a doubleheader on August 6. (Rixey and Donohue lost their starts.) Trying desperately to avoid a pennant-deflating home series sweep, Moran, as planned, threw Luque back at the Manhattan sluggers in the fifth game on August 7, three days after the opening loss.

Luque took his lumps again and then tried to give some back—literally. Behind three runs in the eighth inning, with derisive chortles spewing forth from the Giants' bench, which was openly extended along the grandstand, and certainly frustrated by the imminent prospect of a second successive loss stemming from another sub-par performance, the unpleasantly mounting circumstances were apparently too much for Luque to stand. In the course of pitching, Luque deserted the mound, ambled directly into the picket line of Giants players on the sidelines and picked a fight with one goading Gothamite in particular: Casey Stengel.

The retelling of the occurrence, from the perspective of one home team newspaperman, appeared as follows:

> The big climax, of course, was the scrap between the fiery Luque and as many of the valiant Giants as could get near him. Right or wrong, Luque has the nerve of a grizzly bear and showed it when he walked straight into the crowd of Giants to soak Casey Stengel. Luque says that Stengel called him names of a kind no real man should have to endure, and John McGraw says that Luque overestimated the language—also that it wasn't Stengel at all. However this may be, Luque laid down the ball, drew off his glove, marched right into the Giant roost.... then the bench boiled over and half a dozen Giants were attacking Luque before the Reds could hurry into the mixup. Edd Roush put on the warpaint and got as busy as a wolf in a sheepfold. Fans began to fall out of the stands and run for the field of action. As it was the cops were just in time to stop Luque, returning with a bat and slaughter in his eye.[13]

From Toot's book, the pitcher's side of the story was presented in this quote attributed to Luque: "I was called a name that no man has to take, and I am positive that Stengel called it—I think I ought to know his voice by this time. I am sorry for the row, but I could do nothing else."[14]

A week's suspension was handed down to Luque by National League President John Heydler. As haphazard scheduling would have it, the first eligible game back for the castigated pitcher came against the Giants. Starting with a doubleheader, the two teams initiated a repeat five-game series eight days after their last encounter.

Allowing one earned run in the series opener on August 15, Luque avenged his recent setbacks to the New Yorkers with a 6–3 decision; it was his third Polo Grounds win on the season. Luque homered in the game. The blast, coming in his second at-bat, made a statement powerful enough to elicit a turnabout from much of the expectedly hostile crowd. Luque's defiant determination during the game was no more strongly displayed than with that particular at-bat, which motivated the crowd to level a subjective pardon upon the enemy pitcher for his previous belligerent actions. "Luque advanced to the plate amid groans and swung such a wicked bat that he splashed a homer into the upper tier in left, scoring Pinelli ahead of him," read one on-the-scene news source. "After he had hit the homer, the jeers changed to cheers and all was forgiven, even the attempted braining of Mr. Stengel."[15]

More than likely sensitive to the recent eruption of hostilities between the clubs, or perhaps still queasy over having to swallow the disruptive results to the rotation that the Luque pitching scheme had caused, Moran deviated from his plan to pitch Luque as often as possible against the Giants and did not use Luque again in the four-day set. Instead, Moran called on Eppa Rixey, the opening twin bill's second-game starter, for a second start in the August 18th finale. Rixey, with good run support, won both times out, and the Reds, taking four out of five, left New York with renewed pennant hopes, having shaved their deficit to 5½ games.

Two more wins were reaped by Luque after his unbending outing in upper Manhattan, including his 20th. In a style befitting its significance, Luque four-hit the Robins, 4–0, at Ebbets Field. Luque recorded his 21st win and the Reds' 12th victory on the 15-game road trip August 28, at Boston. In the 4–1 triumph, Luque allowed the Braves three hits; shortstop Ike Caveney's 41st error cost Luque a shutout in the ninth inning.

A fifth straight victory for Luque opened September, as he beat a personal nemesis in Grover Cleveland Alexander, 4–3, at Redland Field, for victory number 22. The Reds' star pitcher registered a 5–3 mark through the remainder of the month, one of the losses, 2–0, coming against the Phillies. One of the wins came in his fourth and final relief session of the season, against Boston, on September 16; Luque hurled four innings with one run allowed. The relief effort came just two days after he tossed a complete game four-hitter (9–1) over the same Braves, which kept the Reds four games behind the first-place Giants.

The third loss of the month occurred on September 25, as the Giants defeated Luque for a third time in Cincinnati, 3–2. It was the last game of the season between the rival teams. Scheduled starter Rixey complained of a sore arm during pre-game warm-up and was scratched. Luque volunteered to start, and Moran allowed it. The Giants' Mule Watson out-pitched the courageous Luque in the pitchers' duel. Pitching with only one day's rest, Luque battled for eight innings, surrendering 12 hits, before being lifted for a pinch-hitter. Casey Stengel drove in one of New York's runs with a single.

It was a difficult loss to take for both Luque and the Reds. Had Cincinnati won, the club could have drawn to within two games of the Giants and made the last week of the season very interesting. Instead, with the loss, the two remaining series of the season for both teams were converted into arithmetical speculation heavily favoring McGraw's team.

Reprisal for the Luque vs. Giants stratagem was quite deserved, as the Reds placed 4½ games behind the pennant-winning Giants when the final curtain descended. In the best case scenario, had the burdened Luque reversed his three out-of-turn pitching losses to New York, he would have won 30 games and *possibly* led the Reds to the pennant (adjusting for a different last-week scenario). Nevertheless, the continuity of keeping Luque (and the others) pitching *in turn*—at least until later in the season when more of the pennant cards were on the table—would have done more for the Reds' pennant chances, and Luque, with more "normal" rest, would almost certainly have won 30 games.

Though the Reds came back to win four games from the Giants eight days after the series fiasco in Cincinnati and stayed in the pennant battle to the near end, it can be submitted that Moran needlessly and unduly hampered the team with his pitching decisions, especially involving the manly Luque. The incident involving Stengel would not have happened, and Luque would not have lost a subsequent start due to the week's suspension. It was quite in Luque's character to have sought the challenge, but the final decision ultimately rested with the manager. The 47-year-old Moran, who had three thoroughbred pitchers that year (Rixey and Donohue were both 20-game winners), could easily be called to task for *not* winning the pennant. Glaringly, in late May, Moran called on Luque for five pointless innings of relief in a game the Reds were losing.

Luque's 27th and final victory came against the St. Louis Cardinals with three games left on the schedule. Everyone in Cincinnati knew it was Luque's final appearance of the season. The pitcher's bags were all but packed in anticipation of his annual repatriation. At Redland Field, Luque started his third game in seven days and defeated the Cardinals, 11–1, permitting four hits. After a disappointing road loss to the Pittsburgh Pirates on September 5, 6–2, Luque had publicly abandoned all hope of winning 30 games. He set for himself a goal of 28 wins. The 3–2 loss to the Giants made him settle for one fewer.

Luque's monumental season encompassed 322 innings pitched with a major-league-leading ERA of 1.93, 2.06 runs lower than the National League average. His .771 winning percentage (27–8) and six shutouts topped all big league pitchers. Luque completed 28 of the 37 games he started. Injecting a modern statistical evaluation measure, Luque's Wins Above Replacement player rating of 10.8 was second only to the incomparable Babe Ruth (14.0) in all of baseball.

In a departure from the norm, preceding the pitcher's final success against St. Louis, the Reds signed Luque for the 1924 season prior to his return to Cuba, where he was received like royalty by his island compatriots. The 1924 contract Luque left Cincinnati with called for $12,000 and made him, behind hitting champion Edd Roush, the highest paid member of the team.

*   *   *

The first Hispanic pitcher to win 20 games in the major leagues sailed for Cuba on October 3. The Associated Press relayed his arrival with this report:

> No conquering hero returning to his native land could have received a more hearty welcome than did Adolfo Luque, the premier pitcher of the National League, when he arrived in Havana late today.
> Long before the steamer Governor Cobb came to her pier the wharves and nearby streets were jammed with thousands of admirers.
> The army, navy and city, and the professional and amateur baseball leagues were represented in the parade that escorted the Cincinnati pitcher up to the offices of *El Diario de La Marina,* where toasts were drunk to his health. Several people brought out every conceivable noise-making instrument to add to the din raised by the shouts of "Viva Luque!"
> He was showered with flowers along the route from the pier to the newspaper office.[16]

Luque was the toast of the town the entire winter in Havana, and the increased celebrity may have taken a toll on his personal life, which took a negative turn. His wife, Eugenia Valdés de Luque, filed for divorce in December. The couple had an eight-year-old daughter, Olga.

As he always did, Luque stayed busy with off-season baseball that winter. He managed and pitched for the Habana Leones,[17] which finished second in the circuit to Santa Clara and was considered one of the best single-season teams in the long history of Cuban professional baseball. Luque pitched in 11 games and won seven for Habana. The inexhaustible hurler also pitched in a handful of other games for Habana in a one-of-a kind, post-winter league mini-season. The end of that six-week "novelty" campaign brought him to the eve of spring training with the Reds.

Three days after Luque received an honorary send-off by the Havana city council, with the presentation of a gold medal on March 18, he reported to Reds' camp in Orlando, Florida. It was 11 days after the passing of Pat Moran; the manager had died of liver and kidney failure.

The Reds' new skipper was Jack Hendricks, who began the first of six years at the helm. The Illinois-born Hendricks guided a club that in 1924 feebly supported their National League ERA-topping staff with the second fewest runs in the league.

Surprisingly, Luque did not get the starting nod on Opening Day; it was given to Pete Donohue, who was starting his fourth year with the club. Luque started the second game and was beaten, 1–0. That loss to Pittsburgh was one of four games Luque lost by shutout on the season.

Another example of the Reds' deficient offense was a home doubleheader on July 8, which saw extra innings for each game and the home team scoring only three times in 26 innings. Starting the first game against the Philadelphia Phillies, Luque lost in ten innings, 3–1, allowing one earned run. An error by second baseman Hughie Critz and three hits lead to two Philadelphians crossing the plate in the tenth. Luque, an excellent fielding pitcher, notched five assists in the loss.

The second game became a towering pitching duel between Eppa Rixey and the Phils' Hal Carlson. Although the Philadelphia pitcher was quite hittable throughout the season, winning only eight games and losing 17, that day was an exception. Carlson threw 15 innings of one-run ball before the Reds pushed across a run in the 16th to win the game, 2–1, Carlson was unable to retire a batter in the frame. Cincinnati used three catchers in the nightcap game, which lasted until darkness, but only one pitcher—Eppa Rixey. The Reds' lustrous left-hander permitted only eight hits and four walks in the laborious 16-inning competition. All four of the day's starters pitched complete games.

Halfway through the season, Luque had more losses than wins and, given his pitching from the prior year, was naturally subject to criticism. A syndicated columnist in mid–July penned the following reproof:

> Senor Luque, who was the greatest pitcher in the National League last season, is having a difficult time winning this year. It is an "old saw" in baseball that pitchers seldom have two great seasons in succession. This may be the trouble with Luque but his winter playing in Cuba is probably the real cause of his ineffectiveness. Luque was the uncrowned king of the island last winter. His great work with the Cincinnati Reds made him the idol of the Cuban fans, and he was wined and dined and feted so much that he lost all sense of condition. He also pitched two or three games a week. This and the gay life he was forced to follow was enough to take the edge off any pitching arm.[18]

(For the benefit of younger readers, the word "gay" connoted frivolity.)

Luque did pitch in his usual heap of games over the winter, but that appeared not to impair his pitching with the Reds. Luque posted the second-best ERA among regular starters on the team and virtually the same mark as teammate Carl Mays (3.16 to Mays' 3.15), but won half as many games (ten) as did Mays, while losing 15.

Again, as in 1922, Luque had the right to kick up dirt at the lot of unkind fates handed down to him by unsmiling baseball gods.

* * *

The Cincinnati Reds of 1925 reproduced the 83–70 record of the preceding season and climbed up one rung from their fourth-place finish of 1924, but Luque, despite leading the league in ERA and shutouts for the second and third times, respectively, could again not ascend the break-even mark in wins and losses.

The right-hander auspiciously won four out of his first five decisions. During a Flatbush foray against the Robins on May 10, neutrality presided over Luque's record—but not his conduct. It was a wet, overcast day in Brooklyn, but the Robins and their fans chirped with the sunshine of victory on their lips at the end, thanks to a 12th-inning, game-winning hit by Zach Taylor. Midway through the game, angrily responding to pitched ball drilled into his ribs, Luque threw his bat at the pitcher and charged the mound. The pitcher was Ernest Preston "Tiny" Osborne, six-foot, four-and-a-half inches tall, who outweighed Luque by 55 pounds or more. That apparently meant nothing to the 160-pound Adolfo Luque, a man who simply would not be intimidated, no matter the type of intimidation or the size of the intimidator. Home plate umpire Cy Rigler, himself of measure and proportion to Osborne, quickly interceded, and physically halted Osborne (throwing him to the ground) until order was restored. Luque was ejected from the game (and later fined $50) for his actions and was long departed at the time of Taylor's electric hit.

In his next start, four days later, in New York's chief island borough, Luque seemed destined for his fifth win. He took a 4–1 lead into the bottom of the ninth inning, when, on the potential final out of the game, shortstop Ike Caveney threw wildly to first base, permitting a run to score and the game to continue. Billy Southworth followed with an inside-the-park home run. Travis Jackson, who had been safe on Caveney's error, scored along with Southworth to tie the ball game.

The game went into extra innings with the Reds taking three batting turns and showing no aptitude, while Luque kept the Giants muzzled. In the bottom of the 12th inning, with one out, Frankie Frisch "poked a double off [third baseman] Babe Pinelli's feet." Two batters later, George "High Pockets" Kelly drove a Luque offering beyond the reach of anyone in left field and Frisch came home with the Giants' victory run. The Reds and Luque lost, 5–4. Had he tripled in the game, Luque would have hit for the cycle.[19]

Over June and July, Luque twirled his season's complement of shutouts—four, two against the Giants. The first blanking of the New Yorkers came on June 17, a 1–0 five-hitter in Cincinnati; it was the Reds' 11th victory in 12 games. That raised the team, with a record of 30–24, into third place and three games behind the top-seated Manhattanites. But by the time of Luque's next shutout over McGraw's gang on July 18 (3–0), the Reds had slipped back a place in the standings, a game below .500 and 9½ games away from first place.

Receiving a decision in seven of eight August starts, Luque won three times. One of the victories was a 13-inning, 2–1 Polo Grounds judgment over the Giants on August 26. In the final inning, the Reds provided sparkling defensive support for their embattled pitcher. Edd Roush turned in a galloping catch in center to rob Billy Southworth of extra bases. The next batter, Frankie Frisch, was retired. Then Luque's 39th—and the Giants' last—out of the game was recorded by a leaping Elmer Smith at the left field wall on a smash by Irish Meusel. Giants hurler Jack Scott and Luque allowed first-inning runs and then kept the opposition scoreless for 11 innings until the Reds scored. Luque followed with a 12th scoreless frame for the win.

Entering September, Luque's record stood at 15–14. (Luque had only two no-decisions in 36 starts on the season, indicating consistent and purposeful pitching.) In his first outing of the month, Chicago defeated the 35-year-old pitcher at Cubs Park, 3–2, in 11 innings. On September 12, Luque evened the score against the Cubs with a 5–2 win in Cincinnati. It was his last win of the campaign.

Luque concluded the season with losses of 2–1, 3–0, and 4–3 in a rain-shortened five-inning finale against Pittsburgh. It had been against the Pirates, on May 3, that Adolfo Luque had become the first Hispanic pitcher to register 100 major league victories. In that game, at Redland Field, Luque had the Bucs shut out through eight innings, but the visitors mounted a rally as he apparently tired in the ninth. Eppa Rixey relieved his mound associate with two outs and the tying run at second and saved the historic 5–4 win for Luque with a game-ending strikeout.

The workhorse efforts of Luque, who fell one complete game shy of throwing 300 innings for the third time in five years, was recognized by someone in a position to best appreciate them—catcher Ivey Wingo. The Reds backstop, as the season was winding down, declared, "Give Luque as much a rest between starts as Vance gets and no team will score more than a run or two against him."[20] The association of Luque with Dazzy Vance, the league's best pitcher in 1924 and a 22-game winner in 1925, was warranted. Vance pitched 26 fewer innings than Luque in 1925 but gave up six more runs, and 19 more *earned* runs. The pitchers tied for the league lead in shutouts (four) but Luque's ERA was nearly a full run lower, 2.63 to 3.53. Yet the Brooklyn strikeout artist led the league in wins and had half the number of losses (nine) as Luque.

* * *

The Pittsburgh Pirates had gained the supremacy of the National League from the New York Giants in 1925, and the succeeding year, the St. Louis Cardinals engaged the Reds in a battle for the National League's championship that went down to the season's final few games.

There was some doubt during the months leading up to the start of the 1926 season whether Adolfo Luque would be ready to pitch for the Reds by Opening Day. Luque had undergone surgery for removal of his appendix in January. In the first part of the twentieth century, this was not considered the minor operation it is today. The pitcher's Cuban physician, however, was not concerned with Luque's recovery and publicly implied that his work had improved his famous patient's athletic prowess. "Luque's doctor has said since the operation that Luque would be able to pitch better ball as a result of going under the knife," reported *The Cincinnati Post's* Tom Swope, adding his own evaluation. "This we seriously doubt. It's hardly possible for any one to pitch better ball than Luque hurled last year. He may have better luck, but he is not likely to have better skill."[21]

Luque made the Reds' April 13 opener all right—as a reliever—putting down a five-run, eighth-inning uprising by the Chicago Cubs against starter Pete Donohue. The Reds won in ten innings, 7–6, with Luque not involved in the decision. Luque's first start of the new season came five days after his first appearance. PINELLI'S WIDE THROW LETS IN TWO RUNS IN NINTH THAT DEFEAT REDS, 3–1, read the headline over the boxscore in the April 19 edition of one newspaper.

Four days after Luque's 3–1 defeat on Babe Pinelli's error, the pitcher missed a chance at his first win in a game against the Chicago Cubs. He was lifted after eight innings with a 5–4 lead, in favor of Donohue. The tall right-hander permitted a game-tying run in the ninth by the Cubs, and the game was called after two more innings because of darkness.

That same Cubs team, two months later, made their second trip into the Queen City, to play a four-day, five-game series. The last act, on June 23, matched Luque against second-year pitcher Charlie Root. A former Pacific Coast League hurler in his first full big league season, Root beaned Luque during the game's midpoint, with the Cubs ahead, 1–0. Sportswriter Tom Swope's description of the incident and consequences follows:

> Wednesday, Charlie Root hit Adolfo Luque above the left temple with a wild pitch in the fifth inning and flattened him.
>   Luque refused to leave the game and when Root led off for the Cubs in the sixth the Cuban's first pitch went right at Charlie's head. The latter threw up his arms and saved his head. There came near being a scrap between the two clubs but no blows were struck. This hit batsman paved the way for two Cubs runs and kept Luque from winning the game in nine innings and cost him the game in the tenth when he collapsed from the effects of the blow he received on the head and lost his grip on the game.[22]

Luque left the game with two outs in the tenth inning and one man on base. Eppa Rixey then came in and surrendered a two run home run to pitch-hitter Chick Tolson. The Reds did not score against Root in the bottom of the tenth and lost, 5–3.

A national baseball periodical provided a supplemental recap of the game that read: "Luque was hit in the head by a pitched ball in the fifth and had to retire in the tenth when he developed severe nose bleeding. In the sixth inning, Luque hit Root with a pitched ball. There followed an argument by Luque and McCarthy, the Cub manager, but the umpire acted as peacemaker and quiet soon was restored."[23]

Examination of Luque's physical state is in order. Luque was not an infielder or outfielder; he could not relax the remainder of the game, periodically uninvolved in the events of each inning, as other field positions often allow. He, from the center of the diamond, had to exactingly initiate, pitch after pitch, every progressive aspect of the contest. Let us then, with this in mind, contemplate the game's second-half effort on the part of the Reds' redoubtable pitcher. Image the plight endured by Luque from the beaning as he pitched for five-plus innings *after* the explosion to his temple, which was covered only by the band cloth of his cap. Add the debilitating effects of such a furious blow: bells ringing in ears? clouded depth-perception? blurred vision? Add the surely blood-stained uniform from his bloodletting nose, and the montage has to make one's lips tighten with marveling approval and lasting regard for this braveheart of a pitcher named Luque.

Exactly one week later, on June 30, Luque came back at the Cubs and beat them, 3–2, in a complete game at Cubs Park. The game, the first of a doubleheader, opened a six-game series to be played over a four-day Chicago encampment by the Reds. An additional game had been added to the scheduled five, the result of the 5–5 tie played in April. Twin bills bookended the series and on the fourth day, July 3, with Jack Hendricks having used up his complement of starters, Luque, with only two days' rest, took the mound in the second doubleheader's nightcap. The Reds scored two runs all day and both came in the first challenge. Luque was beaten, 3–0, pitching his second complete game in four days.

Charlie Root, having last pitched on June 28, making him well rested enough to start any of the last three games, did not make a start in the series. Joe McCarthy, it seemed, was intent on not using Root in the series. However, extra innings on the second day forced McCarthy to call on Root for 1⅔ relief innings. Root picked up the win, holding the Reds scoreless while the Cubs took a 2–1 decision in 11 innings. (Root did make two other starts against the Reds later in the season and beat the Ohioans both times, once by shutout. In neither game was Luque his pitching opponent.)

After a 17-game homestand took up the better part of July, over which the Reds won only seven contests, Cincinnati headed East in a fortuitous tie for first place with the Pittsburgh Pirates, considering the just-concluded poor showing at Redland Field. Luque's pitching produced a scorecard rarity in Brooklyn on July 28. In his defeat of the Robins and Doug "Buzz" McWeeny, 4–3, not one Cincinnati outfielder recorded a putout, assist, or error.

Although four teams had a shot at the pennant entering September, the race was geared around two—the Reds and Cardinals. The Reds won 18 games in August, including ten in a row, to reach their contending position. St. Louis had won 22 games during the same month to take over first place by one-half game over the Reds as the final month of the season began. Unable to keep up its torrid pace, and compiling a 14–11 mark in September, the Redbirds appeared ripe for the taking. But the Reds, with their vaunted pitching, floundered, and the team finished the month with a 13–13 ledger. In six September starts, Luque was less than mediocre, losing three of five decisions.

Cincinnati did have one surge when it won eight in a row. When it appeared Luque was going to stretch the Reds' winning streak to nine games, the pitcher failed to protect a 3–1 eighth-inning lead against the Giants, on September 17 in New York. Frankie Frisch delivered a bases-loaded single in a three-run eighth-inning uprising for the home team, and the Reds went on to lose, 5–4, in ten innings. Rixey was the pitcher of record, in relief of Luque. The loss was especially discouraging because it cost the Reds a chance to tie the Cardinals in the standings with fewer than ten days left in the season, and because Luque had pitched exceptionally well for most of the game. New York had solved Luque for only two hits entering the eighth inning. One was a double by Travis Jackson and the other stayed on the infield. After Jackson's hit, a passed ball and a boot by shortstop Hod Ford allowed Jackson to score the only run for the Giants until the eighth. The pivotal setback sent the Reds into a six-game losing spell that erased any practical chance at a title.

A crushing blow was dealt to the Reds three days following the ten-inning loss to the Giants. The Ohio team had another opportunity to tie an idle Cardinals team for first place with a doubleheader sweep over Boston. But the seventh-place Braves grabbed both games from Cincinnati, 4–3 and 3–0, with Rixey and Luque, respectively, on the losing side. Cincinnati fell two games short of the flag, and Luque, with 13 wins, fell three games short of a .500 record.

* * *

Adolfo Luque, in the past half-dozen baseball seasons, had persevered through five of them with more losses than victories. For anyone who had watched him pitch, it was hard to comprehend how. In Luque's five losing seasons, his record was 69–91 with an ERA of 3.17, compared to the league's ERA average over the same five-year span of 3.97.

In 1925, Luque's circuit-leading 2.63 ERA had been more than a run and a half better than the 4.27 league composite, and Luque had held National League hitters to the lowest opponents' batting average (.239) for the third time in his career. Yet that season he ended up with a 16–18 record. Luque's 1926 record of 13–16 produces more repetitive head-scratching when juxtaposed against Eppa Rixey's pitching ledger of 14–8 with an ERA (3.40) almost identical to Luque's (3.43) in a nearly equal number of innings pitched (233 to 233⅔).

It was thought the Reds' front office would move Luque during the winter meetings of 1926, as much for his benefit as for the team.

> "That Adolfo Luque will be placed on the market when the Red bosses invade New York for the February meeting of the National League seems certain," wrote Tom Swope. "He may be traded before that time. It is becoming apparent that Luque's family troubles make it advisable that he will not play ball with the Reds this year. The Cuban is still a great pitcher and there is every reason to believe he will thrive in new surroundings."[24]

The "family troubles" had arisen from an estrangement between Luque and his wife of less than a year. Luque had married a Cincinnati native prior to the 1926 season, and the marriage was now disintegrating. The woman, the former Mae Dennison, had stayed with her parents in Ohio and had not accompanied her husband on his winter pilgrimage to Cuba.

The time was perhaps no more opportune for John McGraw to acquire the pitcher he had long coveted. But no deal was struck for Luque; instead, the Reds traded Edd Roush back to the Giants. The busy McGraw no longer seemed interested in the 37-year-old Luque, or he was too content with having acquired the three years-younger Burleigh Grimes from Brooklyn, a deal which came not long after McGraw had secured Rogers Hornsby in a block-buster trade with St Louis.

And so, the 1927 season began with Adolfo Luque still wearing the crimson trim of the Cincinnati Reds uniform. In the spring, one familiar beat writer wrote of the return of the longest-tenured Reds' pitcher and of the pitch that became most associated with Luque for the rest of his career and that characterized him in biographical sketches. "Adolfo Luque is again with the team," penned Tom Swope, "apparently satisfied to remain a Red all season and is planning to take Roush's old locker in the Redland Field clubhouse. And he's getting that famous curve of his to looking better each day."[25]

Three straight years with a losing record came to an end for Luque in 1927, and curiously a reversal of fortune occurred with the Reds at the same time. Luque, for his part, still managed to lose his share of close games, but gained one more scale-tipping credit for a final 13–12 record, while the Reds dipped to 75–78 and a fifth-place showing in the National League. Luque's best efforts of the season came in two August shutouts against the Giants and the Braves, the latter a sparkling 1–0 triumph at Braves Field.

The first meeting between Luque and Charlie Root since last season's beaning occurred August 11, at Chicago. The game was played without incident and Root outdueled Luque, 2–0. Luque allowed only five hits to Root's six, but three came in the third inning when the Cubs scored both of their runs. It was Root's 21st win of the season, with five more awaiting him to complete the best season of his pitching career.

Topping his shutout efforts on the season, at least in terms of valor, Luque pitched two 13-inning complete games. The first was a 2–1 triumph over the Brooklyn Robins at Ebbets Field on July 21. Luque tripled in the game's first run in the top of the tenth inning, but the

Robins tied the game in the bottom of the frame. Three innings later, the Reds pushed across a run and Luque retired the Robins in order for the win.

Two months afterward, on September 26 at Redland Field, Jesse Haines of the Cardinals outlasted his Reds counterpart for a 3–1 victory. Luque permitted two earned runs, while Haines masterfully held the Reds without an earned tally. Luque struck out 11 in the extra-inning affair, a career high.

In October, Swope closed out the matter of Luque's home-life dilemma, glossing over some perturbing testimony from the pitcher's wife in the following manner:

> Adolfo Luque ... hasn't been heard from since his wife, a Cincinnati woman, was granted divorce and $2,500 alimony in the local court of domestic relations last week, but Red officials expect Luque to be back on the squad pitching just as ably as yore.
>
> Luque expected to be hit with the alimony award and did not contest the suit. His wife charged cruelty and desertion and told under oath that he was very cross after losing tough games and laid hands on her. That Luque doesn't go around singing after a defeat is no news to the fans, a majority of whom wish that every pitcher was as anxious to win as the Cuban.[26]

* * *

The bad marriage behind him, Luque arrived at the Reds training camp in Orlando, Florida, the following spring a new man, and the positive residuals may have helped him pitch himself to the front of the Reds' staff. His manager, as much for recognizing Luque's pitching in Florida as for what he had meant to the organization, selected the pitcher in 1928—his 11th year with the club—for his second inaugural undertaking.

The Governor of Ohio, A. Victor Donahey, and Commissioner Kenesaw Mountain Landis were present to witness Luque confirm his manager's faith in him. On April 11, the 13-year major leaguer pitched a seven-hit complete game and beat the Chicago Cubs and old adversary Charlie Root, 5–1.

The Reds played well in April and May, and three weeks and a day into the latter month, the team wrestled first place away from the Cubs. A week later, Luque was stricken with tonsillitis and missed nearly three weeks of service time. Upon his return on June 18, Luque's pitching helped the Reds gain back a slice of the ground the club had lost to the St. Louis Cardinals, a team which had overrun the Reds for the league lead during Luque's absence. Twenty days after his last start, the right-hander took the mound against St. Louis and pitched ten innings, holding the Redbirds to two runs. He missed out on a 2–1 victory by allowing a game-tying home run to Jim Bottomley in the ninth inning. With Luque retired from the game, the Reds went on to win, 3–2, in 14 innings, and pulled to within two games of first place.

Sometimes it may have appeared that even a higher power was against Luque. On July 12, in his only shutout of the season, Luque blanked the Brooklyn Robins for nine innings on six hits. Then an afternoon downpour over Redland Field in the bottom of the ninth called the game a 0–0 tie; the Reds had two men on base and one out when the heavens opened up.

Luque beat the New York Giants, 5–4, in his next start five days later, to kick off 12 wins in 14 games by the Reds. Luque won three starts and absorbed one of the two losses. On July 25, three days after tossing a complete game win over the Boston Braves (5–4), Luque allowed an unearned run in his fourth inning of relief, in the second game of a doubleheader against the Philadelphia Phillies; it came in the bottom of the ninth inning and handed Luque and the Reds a 7–6 defeat. The pitcher won his eighth game and third during the hot streak on July 28, with a 7–3 decision at Brooklyn.

The second-place Reds won again the next day to climb to 59–40, their best record all season. The team was 4½ games behind the Cardinals. Then the Reds dropped eight in a row. Cincinnati played respectably for the remainder of the campaign, but mired themselves in middle-of-the-pack ways for a second year in a row.

By the time of Luque's 11th win, on September 16 against Brooklyn, Cincinnati had dropped 11 games behind the first-place pace of St. Louis. Luque hooked up against Dazzy Vance and held a 2–0 lead going into the ninth inning, but Brooklyn tied the game. Vance was removed for a pinch-hitter in the ninth, and in the tenth the Reds scored twice and the Robins came up empty against Luque and reliever Rixey. The final score was 4–3 in ten innings.

The finest labor of the season by Luque came in his final start and went by the boards. Hendricks' team, with nothing but their pride on the line, met the New York Giants on September 23. McGraw's team, on the other hand, was battling the Cardinals for the pennant as the Reds paid their final visit to the Polo Grounds to open a three-game series. Joe Genewich of the Giants engaged Luque for 14 innings before prevailing over him, 2–1. Genewich allowed only five hits to the 12 dispersed by Luque. The Reds reached Genewich for their run in the seventh inning. Luque allowed a second-inning tally and then held the Giants scoreless until the 14th. A Sunday gathering of approximately 40,000 went home pleased after the contest, played in exactly two hours and 30 minutes in spite of the five additional innings.

Apart from Travis Jackson's game-winning single, the game's biggest thrill for the large crowd took place on a defensive play in the visitors' half of the ninth. The first batter, first baseman Wally Pipp, tripled to deep left-center. He tried to score on a potential sacrifice fly, but center fielder Jimmy Welsh threw out Pipp at the plate "by an eyelash," bringing extra frames after the Giants failed to score in their turn.

The Giants' Hall of Fame-bound middle of the batting order reached Luque in the end. The pitcher had retired Mel Ott to close the 13th inning, but the future Cooperstown trio of Freddie Lindstrom, Bill Terry and Travis Jackson all singled in succession in their sixth go-around against the stalwart Cincinnati pitcher. Luque suffered his tenth loss of the season against the 11 wins, which stood as his final record.

The Giants missed out on the pennant by one game, although the fifth-place Reds played a part in helping the rival club stay close at the end by losing the remaining two games of the series.

* * *

In 1928, as the number two pitcher on the Reds staff behind Eppa Rixey, Adolfo Luque, for the ninth straight season, threw over 200 major league innings, and for the tenth consecutive season reached double figures in wins.

In 1929, for the first time, all the innings that his right arm had thrown over close to two decades of virtually year-round pitching appeared to catch up to him. Luque's ERA bounced nearly a full run higher than the prior season (though still below the league average), from 3.57 to 4.50. A couple of breaks here and there, though, could have gone a long way in softening his final ledger.

In his five most difficult losses, the battler gave up all the runs in one 3–1 defeat, one run in a shutout loss, two runs in a 4–1 setback, zero earned runs in a 3–2, complete game defeat, and both runs in an 11-inning, 2–1 crusher to the Cardinals. When the unlucky fall, they fall the hardest. Luque's won-loss record fell to a distasteful 5–16, playing for the worst Reds team of the decade, a team 22 games under .500.

A game played in May in which Luque shut out the Giants, 7–0—one of the bright spots in an otherwise dismal campaign for both pitcher and team—may spark some speculative interest about Luque's place in the game and the respect he commanded from his peers. The Giants had cause to protest the game because Luque was not properly attired. The pitcher, for an unspecified reason, donned white stockings instead of the usual red worn by Cincinnati players. One can wistfully imagine John McGraw asking his Cooperstown cadre of Lindstrom, Ott, Terry, Jackson, Roush, one by one, if they had a problem with Luque's uniform or wanted to make a grandstand issue of it, and each of them answering that he did not.

Luque flashed his improper white stockings around the bases, as well, as he homered in the game, his fifth and final big league blast.

* * *

The Reds, with and without proper uniforms, had sunk to near the bottom of the league and looked to make some changes for the new season. One of them involved trading their elder statesman pitcher, who had shown for them, at all times, nothing but courage and an unquenchable competitive fire for winning. Adolfo Luque took his leave of "*el querido Cinci*" in an even-up trade for another, younger starting pitcher, Buzz McWeeny of the Brooklyn Robins.

The February 1930, trade ended up being heavily one-sided, in Brooklyn's favor. The six years-younger McWeeny made only two starts for the Reds and threw a total of 25⅔ innings, pitching in what was his final major league season in 1930. Luque started 24 games for Brooklyn and missed the 200 innings-pitched mark for a tenth time by one frame.

Turning 40 over the summer, Luque turned in a rejuvenated 14–8 record. The "Lively Ball Era" reached its peak in 1930 and Luque benefited residually, as he nearly received more supporting runs in his first season of starting assignments in Brooklyn than he had in several combined seasons with Cincinnati.

An example of the welcomed support came in Luque's first game on the mound for Brooklyn, on April 21. At Ebetts Field, the pitcher tossed eight-plus innings against the Boston Braves, permitting four runs, three earned. The Robins put the game away, scoring eight runs in the bottom of the seventh inning. Luque started the ninth, but was excused after allowing a run without recording an out. Two Brooklyn relievers followed before sealing the 15–8 victory. Incidentally, with his initial appearance, Luque became the first Hispanic player in Brooklyn franchise history.

Ironically, Luque's first loss of the season—after six wins—came on June 13 to the Reds. (Luque had beaten longtime comrade-in-arms Eppa Rixey a month earlier at Redland Field, 7–4.) The loss was marked by some of the hexed ruin that marred Luque in Cincinnati. The visiting Reds put up five runs before most of the Robins rooters were comfortably in their seats. In the first inning, with two outs and the bases loaded, George Kelly popped a ball to short right. Robins second baseman Neal Finn misplayed the catchable ball (ruled a hit), allowing two runs to score. Tony Cuccinello followed with a three-run home run. The Reds used the five-run opening inning to gain an 8–5 win.

Brooklyn topped the league for the first two and a half months of the season before the Chicago Cubs, last year's champions, challenged and briefly overtook Wilbert Robinson's club, only to lose back their hold on first place to the Robins one week into July. A little over a week later, Joe McCarthy's Cubs, now three games behind in the standings, crossed into Brooklyn for a five-game series, beginning with a July 16 doubleheader. More than 30,000 fans crammed into Ebbets Field and another 15,000 were turned away, it was reported. Brooklyn had contended for the pennant only once since 1920, and the turnout for the Wednesday afternoon duet reflected the renewed baseball zeal pouring out from the borough of bedrooms and churches.

The air of excitement that surrounded the pair of games, though, turned acrimonious late in the first contest. A thrown bottle from the stands nearly struck Cubs catcher Gabby Hartnett, who was heading into the dugout after tagging out a Brooklyn runner at the plate, in the eighth inning of the initial game. The Robins' Del Bissonette, trying for an inside-the-park home run, hit his head on the plate as he slid into Hartnett's tag and was knocked unconscious. Hartnett was targeted after Bissonette, out cold, had to be carried off the field.

Also taking umbrage was Brooklyn third base coach Ivy Olsen, who got into it with McCarthy and one of his coaches, so much so that Olsen, McCarthy and his coach were all ejected. The agitated atmosphere extended into the second game, featuring starters Charlie Root and Adolfo Luque. A bottle was heaved in the direction of umpire Bill Klem after he called Brooklyn's Wally Gilbert out at third base on a close play in the second inning. Adding to the intensity, Root drilled Luque with a pitch in the fifth. Luque charged after Root, but the *New York Times* (6/17/1930) reported the two were impeded "before threatened blows could be struck." Earlier, Luque had tripled in two runs. Trailing 5–1, Root was pinch-hit for his next time up and was spared indubitable retribution. Luque, pitching shutout ball until Riggs Stephenson bounced a home run into the bleachers in left field, continued on to a 5–3 victory, avenging Brooklyn's first game 6–4 setback. Chicago won the next three games, however, and left Brooklyn tied for first place.

A month later, the teams met again in Chicago, in a four-game series, with first place hanging in the balance. The Cubs took three of the games, the third win belonging to Root, over Luque, in the series' concluding contest. The four games, which drew 160,000 fans, 140,000 paid, set a National League attendance record for a four-day series. More people than Wrigley Field could hold were admitted to see the Friday, August 15 finale involving the two pitchers with no love lost between them. A crowd of more than 45,000, including 17,500 women who were admitted free of charge, witnessed the defending NL champion Cubs defeat Brooklyn, 4–3, in ten innings. The surplus crowd for the Luque-Root showdown was redistributed into the outfield, cordoned off and made part of the park's revised ground rules. The latter day's *cozy* confines became the present day's *cramped* confines as both teams played in front of a ringed outfield of standing fans. For the Robins and Luque, the teeming conditions led to their undoing. In three separate innings, the Cubs hit four balls into the outfield revelers, all ruled doubles; two of the four drove in runs and a third came around to score. Chicago outfielder Danny Taylor's second "ground rule" double of the game, brought in the winning run all the way from from first base.

A Brooklyn writer wrote about the deciding play:

The winning hit was Danny Taylor's double into the crowd with two out in the last half of the tenth. On a clear field that fly ball would have been easy picking for any right fielder in the league. Babe Herman had the ball gauged perfectly. He leaped high in the air as he approached the rope restraining the eager customers, and the ball stuck in the web of his glove. But as the Babe descended to earth, some Chicago fan, male or female, gave Herman the shoulder. He dropped the ball and the cause of the Robins became desperate indeed.[27]

The first-place Cubs could not shake the Robins, however. McCarthy's club also had other teams to worry about at the time Luque came back to blank Chicago, and Root, at Ebbets Field, ten days into September. Luque's 6–0 victory helped elevate three teams to within three games of the Midway men in the tightly bunched standings. The Robins, in the middle of their longest winning streak of the season (11 games), and the St Louis Cardinals were both 1½ games off the lead, with the New York Giants the same distance behind both of the trailing clubs.

With the string of consecutive wins, Brooklyn swept into first place by one game over the Cardinals, coinciding with a St. Louis visit to Ebbets Field starting on September 16. Gabby Street's Redbirds sent the Robins into a pennant-race fade with a three-game sweep. The second game was lost by Luque, 5–3, when a pinch-hit, two-run double in the ninth inning by Andy High brought down the pitcher and team.

The scorching Cardinals won 21 out of 25 games in September and claimed the pennant by two games over Chicago and five over the Giants. The Robins, losers of eight of their final ten games, slid to fourth place, a game worse than the Polo Grounders.

* * *

Following a second consecutive fourth-place finish in 1931, 68-year-old Wilbert Robinson ended 18 years of guiding Brooklyn's baseball team. The Flatbush boys gave Uncle Robbie one last winning season (79–73), but the team finished well back of league-topping St. Louis. Brooklyn did not offer the 7–6 Luque—reduced to a spot starter in 1931—a contract for 1932, but another New York team did.

"Adolfo Luque, the veteran Cuban pitcher recently cut loose by the Brooklyn club, has been snapped up by the New York Giants," revealed a press release in February of 1932. "John McGraw has been after Luque for years and this seems an illustration that patience as a virtue does not always go unrewarded."[28]

McGraw did not get to manage his long-time adversary for long. The baseball world was stunned by McGraw's announced retirement in June 1932. The long-entrenched manager of the Giants, whose health was failing, handed over the reins of his ball club to first baseman Bill Terry. The Giants were not doing well when McGraw called it quits. The club persisted in its deterioration under its new player-manager and dropped to an unaccustomed seventh place in the National League.

Terry used the 42-year-old Luque the same way McGraw had—out of the bullpen and as a second starter in doubleheaders. In 1931, Luque had made 19 appearances, all but four as a starter. In 1932, the veteran pitcher made twice as many appearances for McGraw and Terry, but only five as a starter. One of those times was in the second game of a July 6 doubleheader at Forbes Field. On the same hill from which he had thrown his first major league pitch 18 years earlier, Adolfo Luque threw his final complete game—his 206th lifetime (one of only two Hispanic pitchers to top 200 complete games in the major leagues). Luque absorbed a 3–1 loss.

Luque's start on July 29 was the penultimate of his major-league career. Pittsburgh was again the opponent at the Polo Grounds. The game contained a disheartening outcome for Giants fans. Luque took the loss, 4–3, with the Pirates scoring all their runs in the eighth inning. Holding a 3–2 lead, with two men in scoring position, Luque appeared to have thrown his needed "out" pitch. But the batted ground ball scooted between the legs of third baseman Gil English for an error, allowing the final two runs to score. There were two outs at the time.

Adolfo Luque made his last major start, his 366th lifetime,[29] on August 6, in the night-cap of a Polo Grounds twin bill against the St. Louis Cardinals. Rookie Cardinals pitcher Dizzy Dean was his opponent. Luque pitched three scoreless innings, then was bounced from the box in the fourth inning by a battery of hits. The Giants lost badly, and Luque, with the detectable apparition of Father Time tugging portentously on his uniform sleeve, retreated from the terrain of some of his greatest and most valorous battles, never to throw a baseball game's first pitch again.

* * *

The New York Giants surprised everyone and regained the top spot in the National League in 1933. Luque, working exclusively in relief, won eight games against two losses, and had a solid 2.69 ERA in 80⅓ innings. He and fellow Giants reliever Hi Bell (6–5) combined to form the best relief tandem in the National League.

New York played well from the start of the season and climbed into a first-place tie with the St. Louis Cardinals on June 4, after sweeping a doubleheader from Brooklyn. Six days later, following a one-day drop into second place, the men from Manhattan recouped first place with a win over the Philadelphia Phillies and a loss by the Cardinals to Chicago. By month's end, the Giants, with a fine arrangement of starting pitchers, had a 2½-game advantage over St. Louis.

Nobody in manager Bill Terry's starting rotation was finer than Carl Hubbell. On the first Sunday of July, Hubbell defined his season as the best pitcher in the National League and simultaneously redefined for the Giants, as a team, their potential for ultimate accomplishment. Eighteen innings of baseball were scheduled for the Polo Grounds, July 2, against the St. Louis Cardinals. Twenty-seven innings were played instead, and Hubbell pitched two-thirds of them. In the opening contest, Hubbell threw *18 shutout innings* and won the game, 1–0. The left-hander overcame the combined brilliance of the Cardinals' Tex Carleton (16 innings) and Jesse Haines (1⅔ innings), who took the loss after Hughie Critz singled home Jo-Jo Moore with the winning run.

In the second game, the Giants' Roy Parmelee defeated Dizzy Dean by the same score, Johnny Vergez providing the game's only run with a fourth-inning four-bagger. The double-header victory stretched the front-running Giants' lead to 5½ games over the Cardinals and firmly positioned Terry's troops on the path to the pennant. It was a trail the team steadily traversed without much detour throughout the summertime months and into September.

The eighth game Luque won at the summons of Terry was a 4–3 decision with 4⅔ innings of scoreless relief at Sportsman's Park on September 17. The win that day over the Cardinals put the Terrymen nine games ahead of the competition. The New York Giants, expected by many baseball experts not to crack the first division, sauntered from there to the pennant and a tenth World Series appearance.

Earlier that September, Washington pitcher Alvin "General" Crowder and three other Senators had watched a game at Braves Field that featured the Giants. In town ahead of their team, which was scheduled to play the Red Sox in two days, Crowder and company watched Adolfo Luque throw eight innings in relief as the Giants beat the Braves in 14 innings in game one of a doubleheader. The Senators were doing some advanced scouting in anticipation of a World Series engagement between themselves, 8½ games in front of the American League pack at the time, and the Giants, ahead by a similar margin in their league.

The Fall Classic appointment materialized for both clubs against the other, beginning October 3.

In Game 5 at Griffith Stadium, with the Senators down in the Series three games to one, Crowder made the start, hoping to fend off elimination for his team. His Giants opponent was Hal Schumacher. It was a pitching rematch of Game 2, won by Schumacher, 6–1.

The Giants led 3–0 in the sixth inning when the Senators staged a two-out comeback capped by a three-run home run by Fred Schulte. Two singles followed the timely home run, and Schumacher was replaced. Making his first appearance in the Series, Luque prevented further damage by enticing catcher Luke Sewell to ground out to second.

The game stayed tied at 3–3 for four more innings until the tenth. Then Mel Ott delivered a debated home run to center field. Luque went out to pitch in his fifth inning of relief, with a one-run lead and the world championship in his hands.

The 18-year veteran obtained outs from the tenth inning's first two batters, but Joe Cronin singled—the second hit allowed by the pitcher. A carefully-pitched-to Schulte walked, and left-handed Joe Kuhel, a 100-RBI man and .322 hitter for the season, was the next hitter to face the "grizzled, gray-haired old campaigner," as the New York Times described Luque on October 8, 1933. Luque struck Kuhel out swinging on a 1–2 pitch. Luque asked for the ball from catcher Gus Mancuso as both triumphantly left the field.

In a city where topical opinions were habitually divided, Adolfo Luque had crushed all partisan hopes prevailing for the Senators.

*　*　*

Unlike the unbridled happiness that reigned over the team at the close of the 1933 season, reproachable despair fell upon the New York Giants 12 months later.

Terry's club possessed a 2½-game lead over the St. Louis Cardinals with one week to play in the 1934 season. The Giants lost their last five games of the season, and the Cardinals, with Dizzy Dean starting three games in six days and winning all three, including his 30th victory, vaulted past the afflicted New Yorkers to win the pennant by two games. Two season-ending losses to Brooklyn, whose very existence Terry had openly and sardonically questioned earlier in the season, compounded the collapse and gave the Cardinals the title.

Luque suffered one of the team's eviscerating five losses in a row on September 26, 5–4 to the Phillies. The decisive run scored in the top of the ninth inning on a passed ball by catcher Gus Mancuso, after the Phillies had loaded the bases on three hits. It was Luque's third loss of the season against four victories, his campaign's final ledger.

It was during the winter of 1934 that the 44-year-old Luque's name surfaced for the role that was so suited to him—pitching coach. It was assumed that Luque was through pitching during this speculative period. Luque was not through, however, and he earned a 1935 roster spot as the team broke spring training in Miami Beach and headed north. It was an extended spot on the 25-man team, though, as all teams were required to reach a 23-man player limit by May 15. Fighting the numbers game, Terry reluctantly dropped Luque as a player and optioned infielder Joe Malay to the minors to trim down to the required number.

The 20-year major league career of Adolfo Luque ended with his appearance at the Polo Grounds on April 26, 1935.[30] Luque provided one hitless inning of relief against the Philadelphia Phillies, the final frame of a 13-inning game called by darkness, tied 5–5.

Bill Terry, as previously speculated, designated his old warhorse as pitching coach of the Giants, a position Luque accepted and held under two Giants managers.

LEGACY

Adolfo Luque was one of the greatest Latin American pitchers who ever lived. Not beginning his big league career in earnest until he was 28-years-old, Luque won 194 major league games plus a career-crowning World Series triumph in 1933 at an age when most players have long since quit competing.

The Cuban hurler earned a litany of ethnic achievements in his major league career. He became the first Hispanic pitcher to win a game and to author a shutout, the first Hispanic pitcher to appear in and record a World Series victory. As the first Hispanic 20-game winner, Luque was also the first Hispanic pitcher to start an Opening Day game and belt a big league a home run. Into the second decade of the 21st century, Luque's single-season victory mark of 27 in 1923 had not been topped by any Spanish brethren.

Luque's 1923 campaign was the greatest produced by a Hispanic pitcher, unmatched in terms of sheer brilliance in the complete craft of pitching. He tossed six shutouts and, incredibly, was denied *seven* more solely due to unearned runs. Luque permitted a solitary unearned run in five separate complete game wins during the season and two unearned runs in two other complete game endeavors, which he lost, 2–1 and 2–0. He threw 322 innings and posted an ERA of 1.93—one of only two starting pitchers in the entire decade of the 1920s to register an ERA under 2.00. (Pete Alexander, the other.)

Second only to Martín Dihigo in lifetime Cuban Winter League wins, Luque won 106 games from the pitching mounds of Cuba, with 71 losses. (Remarkably, Luque pitched three innings in a Cuban Winter League game at the age of 54.[31]) Toss in another 65 Class D & AA wins and Luque is one of the few Latin American pitchers to have won 350 games. Luque pitched for more than two decades, and his right arm wrought more than 5,000 innings, pitching at various professional baseball levels.

Luque had a short-arm delivery to the plate, stiff-legged with little follow through. That kind of delivery puts a great deal of strain on the arm and shoulder. It was a miracle he was able to pitch as long and as often as he did. As a major leaguer, Luque gave up slightly more hits than innings pitched, a dangerous ratio for a pitcher. Placed against his lifetime era of 3.24, though, it reaffirms what a tough pitcher he was in the clinches. Through 2013, there were 17 starting pitchers in the National Baseball Hall of Fame with higher lifetime ERAs.

Adding acclaim to Luque for his hitting, the athletic hurler compiled a lifetime major league batting average of .227 and on-base and slugging percentages of .283 and .291, respectively, numbers exceeded by only the best of "good-hitting pitchers." In slightly over 1,100 trips to the plate, Luque had a more than a 1:9 ratio of strikeouts to at-bats, a figure bettered only by baseball's so-called "contact hitters." Luque owns the most hits by a Hispanic major league pitcher with 237. (Only Livan Hernández and Juan Marichal collected as many as 200.) Luque's all-around athleticism was apparent in other career offensive areas as well. His RBI (90), runs scored (96), triples (10), walks (70), and stolen base (7) totals are unmatched among his Hispanic big league colleagues.

* * *

All great pitchers lose close, low-scoring games, but Adolfo Luque lost more than his fair share. Luque lost 22 games in which he threw nine or more innings and allowed three runs or fewer. Averaging 9⅔ innings in those 22 complete games, his ERA was 1.68.

The unsympathetic fan might say that Luque was simply outpitched. Nonetheless, it was clearly apparent that unfortunate happenstance cost Luque a chance at accumulating over 200 wins, which for many decades was the defining Hall of Fame criterion for a starting pitcher. By pitching to the end of close games, Luque obtrusively swallowed more defeats than he deserved, defeats caused by the increased tendency of a fatigued pitch or fielder's miscue. The tenacious pitcher didn't receive the no-decisions that spare recent starters from defeat. Luque completed a phenomenal 56 percent of the big league games he started (and had an astounding 89 percent decision rate in his career starts).

Was Luque's incendiary temperament a detrimental factor in his lack of Hall of Fame consideration? Relying on the reports of the day, which are objectively best for getting a sense of the general feeling of the times, there was no negative press associated with any of the "highly-charged incidents" that have become anecdotally attached to Luque's baseball biography. Though that can be skirted around by saying that writers of the day were more "forgiving" of ballplayers' indiscretions—on and off the field—that Luque did not have dominion over more winning campaigns is the much more valid reason for his lack of Cooperstown attention. It was years after Luque had died that his career *retroactively* engendered a stereotype of the hot-tempered Latin ball player that was portrayed through the eyes of mostly disconnected North American sportswriters.

Luque the Cuban was no doubt subjected to bigoted taunts on the field from fans and players. But this should not be presented as a particular badge of honor, for many players were targets and victims of their own nationalities in the great North American "melting-pot." In Luque's case, any endured racial slurs can be mitigated because his light skin tone gained him entry into the separatist major leagues. That said, Adolfo Luque, as has been presented, was not the type to turn the other cheek either.

In his grand book on the long history of Cuban baseball, Roberto González Echeverria wrote the following about Adolfo Luque: "He was a snarling, vulgar, cursing, aggressive pug, who though small at five-seven, was always ready to fight."[32] González Echevarria separated his view of Luque the man from Luque the baseballer in this manner: "If, in addition to his accomplishments as a player, one considers Luque's impact as a manager in Cuba and Mexico, it is an injustice that he is not in the Hall of Fame in Cooperstown. There are worse ballplayers and characters enshrined in that American temple."[33]

Luque piloted teams in 30 winter seasons in Cuba. He headed squads during nine other summer campaigns in Mexico and one in the Florida International League. He managed a total of 2,438 games, winning 1,310. Indeed, if the Hall can one day broaden its player résumés to recognize the hemispheric achievements of its major leaguers into perhaps an "Interna-

Clasping hands in a show of managerial fraternity are the four pilots of the 1955–1956 Cuban Winter League Adolfo Luque's last season as a manager in Cuba. Left to right: Napoleón Reyes, Marianao; Conrado Marrero, Almendares; a smiling Luque, Habana; Oscar Rodríguez, Cienfuegos.

tional Wing," then Adolfo Luque deserves recognition as the first "International Inductee." (Luque is in the Cincinnati Reds Hall of Fame, installed on July 14, 1967. He was also posthumously inducted into the Mexican Hall of Fame in 1985.)

The square-jawed, middle-aged Cuban whose mottled and weather-worn complexion conformed well to the characterization "grizzled veteran" given him in many a story late in his career, also had a playful side, at least with teammates. There are hints of it from the rough and tumble right-hander in photographs. A 1920s team photo of the Reds pitching staff, standing in a row, shows Luque with his hands playfully wrapped around the waist of Carl Mays, directly in front of him. A 1933 group shot of the Giants has Luque standing in the back row with his hands on the shoulders of Carl Hubbell, who is standing directly below and in front of him. In both photographs, Luque's posture is conspicuously different from most of the other stiffly-posed players.

It would seem that Luque the pug, if he was one, was also an inescapable charmer. He was able to woo into marriage one of the most admired Mexican women of her day. Making their 1947 wedding most eyebrow-raising was the fact that Luque, nearly 57 years of age, was 30 years his bride's senior. It was the charming pug's fourth marriage, and the nuptials did not interfere with his life's vocation. Released in the usual public manner, the partial record of the May day in which the beauty and baseball lifer tied the knot read as follows: "Adolfo Luque, former big league pitcher and coach and now managing Puebla in

Adolfo Luque's wedding day in Puebla, Mexico, in 1947. Luque's young wife, the former Ivonne Recek Saade, stayed married to Luque for the remaining years of his life. She, along with Luque's daughters, were at the former pitcher's hospital bedside when he passed away, in Havana, on July 3, 1957 (photograph from Charles Monfort).

the Mexican League, married Miss Ivonne Recek Saade, well known society girl of Puebla recently. Luque's team helped Dolf celebrate the occasion by providing a doubleheader win against Monterrey, May 8."[34]

In this author's humble opinion of him, Adolfo Luque was the no-nonsense type who cared only about winning and who, with ire provoked or dignity injured, could be ignited into a human torch of anger. In comparative size and temperament, one Alfred Manuel "Billy" Martin was cut from the same incendiary baseball cloth.

Luque the pitcher may be best described as a pint-sized Don Drysdale. Both were workhorse performers; both were exceptionally good hitters; and both were fiercely competitive on the rubber. It must have been much easier to stand in against the ten inch-smaller Luque than the 6'5" Drysdale.[35] While Luque was not nearly the same model of aggression that Drysdale was on the mound, Luque did, when deemed necessary, use the mound to its intimidating and retaliating fullest.

Adolfo Luque's other baseball personage was that of manager. In this, inviting the closest comparison is Leo Durocher. An inflammatory figure as both a player and manager, Durocher could be as mean-spirited and viciously combative in order to achieve victory as anyone who ever donned a pair of spikes. "The Lip" would do anything he could to gain an edge over his opponent. He believed genteel sportsmanship only brought genteel losses. As field generals, Luque and Durocher ascribed to the same win-at-all-costs doctrine, though Luque was more coarse or gruff than he was mean-spirited.

Carlos Pascual pitched for Luque with the Havana Cubans of the Florida International League in 1951. His comments to me several years ago reinforced Luque's turbulent traits as a manager who never wanted to lose any game in which he was involved. Defeat clearly was not something to which Luque wished any connection, as Pascual recalled with this punitive, season-ending episode under the 61-year-old manager: "We lost the [playoff] series against Tampa and returned to Cuba the next day. Luque made the team leave for the airport at 6:00 a.m. even though our flight for Havana was not scheduled to depart until three in the afternoon."[36] Asked about the generally intolerant temperament attributed to Luque, Pascual responded: "The players respected him. Some feared him. Because of his character. He was an extremely aggressive manager. I played with him when he was getting on in age. I always respected him, and before I played professional baseball, I was a great fan of Adolfo Luque."[37]

"Irascible" was Luque's temperament as described by Jorge S. Figueredo. When questioned about Luque's personality the Cuban baseball historian passed along the following on the person who, along with Mike González, Figueredo considers as the two most important men in the history of Cuban baseball: "In truth, his character was irascible, and in my book I trace several incidents that demonstrate his ferocity with umpires and players who did not perform up to their jobs."[38]

"El Pitcher"

What is most redeeming about Luque was that he was a well-respected pitcher in his day and became a well-respected pitching coach after he permanently left the mound. His 1957 *New York Times* obituary made direct reference to the second point. "His ability as a coach was unquestioned in the league," read the death release. "He was a superb tutor of young pitchers, possessing the ability to spot and correct a fault quickly."[39] The same notice of his passing stated that Luque was one of the game's finest curve ball pitchers.

After nearly three seasons as pitching instructor, a falling-out occurred between the pitching sage and boss Terry prior to the 1938 campaign, and Luque informed "Memphis Bill" via cable from Havana that he had better find someone else to tutor his twirlers.

As soon as Terry left the Giants a few years later and Mel Ott became manager, Ott sought out Luque for a return to Gotham in his previous capacity. George Hausmann was a player on Ott's Giants of the early 1940s. His recall of Luque's second term with the Giants was similar to that of today's bench coach—50 years before the post became applicable in baseball. "Dolf was pitching coach and very good at working with pitchers," offered Hausmann. "He was so knowledgeable about the game that he was able to help Ott in a lot of ways. Dolf was almost an assistant manager to Mel."[40]

New York Giants pitcher Sal "the Barber" Maglie notably credited Luque with teaching him to perfect his hard-breaking curveball, while pitching in the Mexican League. The pitch became the consternation of National League hitters for years. The Pascual brothers, Carlos and Camilo, were two Cuban Winter League pitchers who were early pupils of Luque's teaching and went on to achieve significant pitching success, especially the younger Camilo.

The second coaching go-around for Luque with the Giants ended following the 1945 season. That December, Luque telegrammed Giants owner Horace Stoneham with news of his acceptance of a managerial job with the Puebla team in Jorge Pasquel's reanimated Mexican League.

Luque remained loyal to Mexican baseball in the face of the punishing banishment organized baseball dealt out to him and all those who affiliated themselves with Pasquel's rogue league. He may have been greatly influenced in the matter from changes arising in his personal life. In December of 1946, Luque filed for divorce from his wife of eight years and the same month announced his intentions to sell his ranch house outside of Havana. Shortly thereafter, a reinstatement request to organized baseball was denied, and Luque, in 1948, relocated to Mexico.

Parting with his home must have been most difficult for Luque. In October 1946, former teammate Charlie Dressen had brought a group of major league barnstormers to Cuba, and many of them called upon Luque's hospitality. Writer Arturo Flores, accompanying them, painted a picture of a sultan-like Luque inside his "palatial home" and described some of the more striking and stirring elements of the visit:

> We were at the Luque hacienda 20 miles outside of Havana, and the grizzled old man was dishing out baseball wisdom while a dozen big leaguers, some of them no youngsters in the game themselves, hung on every word emitted by the former star right-hander.
>
> The name on the gate of Dolf's estate was "El Pitcher," and for miles around the countryside they could direct you to the house of their idol, this little battler who wanted to win every game he pitched as badly as any man alive ever wanted to win. Now he was here, surrounded by his hundreds of fighting cocks, his family, his memories.[41]

After organized baseball reinstated all of its previously banished players, Luque returned to Havana and managed several years for different clubs in the Cuban Winter League. His last winter season came at the helm of the Habana Leones in 1955–1956.

Adolfo Luque died on July 3, 1957, at the age of 66. He had been hospitalized after suffering a heart attack a few weeks earlier. According to Jorge Figueredo, his condition had improved to the point that he was looking forward to being discharged and managing again. "I have to die fighting on the ball field,"[42] Luque characteristically said. But he suffered a fatal cardiac arrest; his wife Ivonne and daughters Gladys (believed to be from Luque's third marriage) and Olga were at his hospital bedside.

Luque's widow used her cultured upbringing and became a writer, actress and women's activist in the arts and theatre in Mexico. She passed away at age 92, on March 23, 2012. One of her obituaries stated that she continued to sign her name "Ivonne Recek de Luque" until the day she died.

At his wake and burial, Luque's coffin was draped in the Almendares Scorpions banner, the team Luque most identified with in Cuba.

The following year, Adolfo Luque was posthumously elected to the Cuban Hall of Fame in Havana.

4

The 1950s—Camilo Pascual

Camilo Pascual

The artistry that belonged to Camilo Pascual on the pitching mound lies in vivid remembrance of the crescent beauty of one pitch—his curveball. Inflicting cringing paralysis on major league hitters, it was, at its best, a pitch of elegance. It spun forth from Pascual's right hand in an accelerated, compressed whirl toward an oblique rendezvous with the catcher's mitt, defiant of nature's laws and awkward Louisville Slugger swings.

Pascual began throwing what became his signature pitch at a young age in the parks of San Miguel del Padrón, the Havana neighborhood in which he and his siblings, an older brother and younger sister, were raised. The Pascual boys had their love of baseball instilled in them by their father, Camilo, Sr. "He would take us to the ballgames. He was a *fanatico* of club Almendares,"[1] said Carlos Pascual, the eldest son. Camilo Pascual, Sr. probably did not imagine in any of those outings to La Tropical or Gran Stadium in Havana that *both* of his sons would one day become big league pitchers, and that the youngest, Camilo Jr., would complete a distinguished 18-year residency in the major leagues.

Camilo Pascual was signed by Joe Cambria and, ironically, did his first professional pitching in the United States before he did so in his own homeland. In 1951, at the tender age of 17, Camilo (three years his brother's junior) pitched with three different farm teams of the Washington Senators that summer: Big Spring (Class C), Geneva (Class C), and Chickasha (Class D). Pascual won five of nine decisions on the three teams.

More than a decade later, the established pitcher reminisced about the considerable bus travel associated with his first year in North American baseball.

> I arrived in the United States at Key West, then rode a bus for three and one-half days to Big Spring [Texas]. They didn't have an opening for me, but because they liked Carlos, they sent me to Geneva [New York]. I couldn't speak English, so they pinned a tag on me to let the bus driver know where I was going. That was another three days on the bus. Then I went back to Big Spring for a couple of weeks and they sent me to Chickasha [Oklahoma]. Another day on the bus. When I got there the season was almost over. Then I rode the bus another three and one-half days back to Key West. When I got there ... all I had was $40. And needed $20 of that for plane fare. But I made it [home].[2]

Two winters after his professional debut in the States, Pascual took his first turn in the Cuban professional arena, performing for the Marianao Tigers. He won his only decision, appearing in ten games. The manager for Marianao was Cuban pitching legend Adolfo Luque. A better teacher a young pitcher could not have had.[3] Luque had a key role in the development of the pitch that would become synonymous with Pascual's name. "When I started pitching," Pascual said in 1962, "I threw with a three quarter motion. Luque changed my delivery to overhand when I played for him."[4] The change in motion made his curveball more effective, with a higher release point allowing for a more pronounced drop. Simple enough on the surface to understand and see, but not so simple for most pitchers to execute consistently.

As Camilo Pascual entered his third decade of life, to all who had seen him it was clear he was destined to be a big league pitcher. He met his major league destiny, in 1954 at the young age of 20, partly because of his raw talent and partly because he was property of the Washington Senators. The club averaged 95 losses (in a 154-game schedule) during the pitcher's first five seasons and finished, on average, 40 games out of first place from 1954 to 1958. A better team may not have had room for Pascual and he might have spent a few more "grooming" years in the minors. It was, for the pitcher, a mixed blessing.

Senators manager Bucky Harris had noticed Pascual pitching for Chattanooga, a Senators farm club, and was responsible for getting the young hurler onto the Washington roster. Pascual debuted on April 15, 1954, at Fenway Park, in relief of Bunky Stewart, who had come in for starter Bob Porterfield. Pascual pitched three scoreless innings in a 6–1 Senators loss.

Exactly three weeks later, on May 6, Pascual made his first big league start. He was one out away from his second major league win (his first having come in a two-inning scoreless relief stint against the Philadelphia Athletics four days after his debut). But the pitcher gave up a two-out double to Nellie Fox and a game-tying single to countryman Minnie Miñoso. Third baseman Eddie Yost then booted what would have been the inning's third out, and the next batter singled to score Miñoso with the winning run; the Senators failed to score in their half of the ninth as Pascual lost to the Chicago White Sox, 5–4.

The discouraging loss earned Pascual another start six days later. Pascual lost again, 4–2, to the Detroit Tigers, their players reaching him for all of their runs and eight hits in five innings. Pascual did not receive another start until June 6, a start he lost by shutout. On the last day of the same month, the pitcher accepted his fourth and final starting assignment of the season; he escaped a loss to the Philadelphia Athletics when his teammates tied the encounter with a late rally before losing the game, 8–7. Pascual finished the season out of the bullpen with a 4–7 record and a 4.22 ERA.

* * *

In Pascual's first start of 1955 he received a no-decision, allowing one run in 8⅓ innings of work, in a 2–1 Washington loss to the Baltimore Orioles that took ten innings to decide. Three days later, on April 27, Pascual chipped in with a pair of scoreless relief innings during a much more protracted engagement versus the Cleveland Indians, in which he was not involved in the decision. Bobby Ávila's sacrifice fly in the bottom of the 17th inning against the fourth Washington pitcher of the day ended the four hour and 46-minute game, 6–5, in Cleveland's favor. Only two days hence, on April 29, Pascual started and lost, 3–2, to the Detroit Tigers, after two fielders collided chasing a sixth-inning pop-up that fell in for a two-out, game-tying double and the next batter followed with a run-scoring single.

On May 8, Pascual was victorious for the initial time in 1955, giving up five runs in seven innings, as the Senators brought their hitting shoes to the ballpark and throttled the Orioles, 15–7. The right-hander threw seven shutout innings the next time he started, on May 21, before he had to withdraw due to a blister. The Senators went on to defeat the

Boston Red Sox, 1–0, in a 12-inning contest in which rookie teammate Pedro Ramos gained his first major league win. After another no-decision, the New York Yankees defeated Pascual, 5–3, in a relief role on May 30.

In the first game of a twi-night doubleheader in Kansas City on June 7, Pascual downed the relocated Athletics, 3–2, when the Senators scored three times in their half of the ninth inning. It was the pitcher's last win of the campaign.

Though he made four times as many starts (16) as in his rookie season, Pascual was still pitching primarily in relief for Charlie Dressen, managerial replacement in 1955 for Bucky Harris. In 43 appearances, Pascual compiled a 2–12 record with a distressing ERA of 6.14. He lost his last nine decisions. The worst was yet to come.

* * *

The major leagues is not the best place for a pitcher to develop his skills, and playing for a basement team makes the task increasingly daunting, as Pascual deflatingly found out. In 80 starts and 19 relief outings over the next three seasons, Pascual endured a combined record of 22 wins and 47 losses and 4.37 composite ERA.

In 1956, the 22-year-old hurler simply hung too many curves, led the league in home runs allowed, and permitted over 100 earned runs (for the only time in his career). Two of the league-leading 33 homers yielded came on Opening Day to Mickey Mantle. On April 17, the Yankees' star became the first player to hit two home runs over Griffith Stadium's gigantic center field wall in the same game. (The young pitcher gave up another tape-measure home run to Mantle the following month at Yankee Stadium.) The Yankees solved Pascual for six runs on ten hits in six innings and took care of business, 10–4. The inaugural was attended by U.S. President Dwight D. Eisenhower, who took part in the traditional first ball tossing and stayed until the final out.

After winning twice in April, Pascual did not win a game in May. One victory in June, another the following month, and two in August were all the pleasant results for Pascual, who started the second-most games (27) on the Senators' staff. The developing strikeout artist fanned 162 hitters, the most by a Washington hurler in 38 years.

Purgatory on the Potomac

It was a tribute to Pascual's own mettle that he did not lose his confidence during his indentured time with the Senators in Washington, D.C.—his pitching purgatory on the Potomac.

> I can't figure out why Pascual isn't one of the game's winning pitchers," Phil Rizzuto wondered out loud to his listeners, as he was starting out on a new career as New York Yankees broadcaster. "He has a curve as good as anybody in the business and his fast ball sings. And he's not that wild. Sometimes he forgets to pitch with his head, sometimes he tends to take a little off a pitch and puts it right over the middle. And every time he makes a mistake like that, it has been his luck to get murdered.[5]

Al Cicotte of Rizzuto's Yankees, in the sixth inning of a game on May 30, 1957, batted a ball that struck Pascual on the right arm below the shoulder, forcing his withdrawal. The line shot could have been sarcastically looked upon by observers as a literal example of the damage usually inflicted upon American League pitchers by the hard-hitting Yankees. Along similar lines, the Senators' pitchers had been some of the league's most heavily battered by the Yankees, including their youthful curveballing apprentice. Ahead in the contest at the time of the hit to Pascual's biceps, the Senators held on and won the game, 5–1; it was Pascual's first victory, after ten losses in a row, over New York.

But the liner hurt Pascual for the rest of the season. He continued to pitch with an aggrieved arm and it was a contributing factor in a lack of success again—an 8–17 record, but with a slashed ERA of 4.10 from 5.87 in 1956. The pitcher eventually had to be removed from the rotation for the better part of August because of the injury and did not win a game after August 2.

Based on Pascual's outstanding record in the 1956–1957 Cuban Winter League (15–5), Washington had raised expectations coming into the 1957 season for their declared star-in-the-making. When those expectations were not met during the major league campaign, the team tried to prevent Pascual from pitching again over the winter in Cuba. Parent clubs now were not able to prohibit Caribbean basin-born players from participating in their countries' winter leagues, but the Senators appealed to the Commissioner's Office with the argument that Pascual had not recovered from his arm ailment and might re-injure his arm and thereby jeopardize his future worth to the Washington ball club.

The Senators did have Pascual's best interest in mind. They wanted to make sure his arm was in tip-top shape for the 1958 season. The team even hiked Pascual's pay as an inducement to skip winter ball. During the first week of November, Ford Frick sided with the Senators, prohibiting Cienfuegos—Pascual's winter league team—from using their popular pitcher "until further orders."

Two weeks later, Frick, sticking to a previous accord organized baseball had reached with the Caribbean Professional Baseball Federation, made a final ruling—against the Senators—and gave Cienfuegos permission to reinstate the right-hander. However, this subsequent report from Cuba snipped away further potential acrimony: "Pascual announced he would rest [over the remainder of the season], due to his physical condition. He is said to be suffering from high-blood pressure and liver troubles."[6]

* * *

Whether Pascual had been the subject of a seemingly exaggerated medical condition or not, the pitcher's health appeared to be fully restored in his final spring tune-up before the 1958 regular season. Pascual was defeated by the Cincinnati Reds and Harvey Haddix, 2–0, in an exhibition game at Portsmouth, Ohio. Both hurlers went the distance. In the third inning, Pascual hit the Reds' Frank Robinson with a pitch on the side of the head that sent the 1956 National League Rookie of the Year to the hospital.

Pascual himself met with an out-of-sorts opening to the season, as he did not make it past the second inning versus the Baltimore Orioles on April 15. Pascual allowed two runs and four hits in taking the 6–1 loss to the Orioles. In his next start, on April 20, he was equally unimpressive: three innings, five walks, with a pair of hits and two runs allowed, in a no-decision versus the Boston Red Sox. In his third start, two days into May, the pitcher was back on the beam. The right-hander defeated the Chicago White Sox, 3–2, in ten innings, for his first win; Julio Bécquer singled home the game-winner with two outs in the tenth, pinch-hitting for Pascual, who struck out 13.

On the cultural assimilation front, in an earnest effort to improve his English skills, Camilo Pascual requested to change roommates from Pedro Ramos to Dick Hyde that season.

The experiment had a merry inverse effect as Hyde ended up learning more Spanish than Pascual did English.

On May 11, Pascual's pitching required no translation. The hurler baffled New York, 4–0, in his first Yankee Stadium win. The five-hitter's most tense moment played out in the eighth inning when the Yankees put two men on base and Mickey Mantle stepped to the plate. Jim Lemon bailed out his pitcher with a leaping catch of a Mantle line drive in front of the low retaining wall in right field.

Pitching for the 1958 Washington Senators, Pascual was repeatedly reminded that the margin for error was very fine. The right-hander lost four games by the score of 2–0 (one in 13 innings); he lost two others, 3–1, and another 2–1.

Only nine regular starters in the American League posted a better ERA than Pascual's 3.15 (in 27 starts and 4 relief appearances), yet he concluded the season 8–12, his fifth consecutive losing season.

* * *

In February of 1959, Camilo Pascual received the only involuntary shower during his professional baseball life that he did not mind—the traditional "rice shower" after he left the bachelor ranks and married sweetheart Rachel Ferrero.

Nothing changed much for the Washington Senators as a team that year. The club was betrothed to last place for the third time in the last four campaigns, but the newlywed Pascual honed his craft to a new level and rose well above the surrounding sludge. The 25-year-old, in 30 starts, won 17 decisions against ten losses—for a team that lost 91 games. Pascual led both leagues in shutouts, paced the American League in complete games and posted the circuit's second-best ERA at 2.64.

His first start came in Boston on April 14, in the Red Sox' home opener. He was reached for four runs, two earned, in six innings. The final score was 7–3. The second outing for Pascual evolved into the season's second-worst start for the pitcher. Holding a 4–1 lead in the seventh inning of a twin bill opener against the Baltimore Orioles on April 19, he gave up three singles and a double, and was removed in favor of Dick Hyde. His roommate obtained the second out of the inning as the tying run scored. Then Hyde hit the Orioles' Chico Carrasquel in the helmet with the bases loaded, forcing in the go-ahead tally. Pascual was eventually charged with five runs in the 7–4 setback.

The 0–2 Pascual tweaked a muscle in his back and missed his next turn to the mound, and as a result his first win of the season did not come until May 1. Pascual defeated Detroit and Jim Bunning at Tiger Stadium, 4–3, in ten innings. Twenty-three-year-old Harmon Killebrew's second home run of the game staked the victory. Another impressive young Washington player, Bob Allison, pounded a grand slam home run off Early Wynn at Chicago on May 6. The blow was instrumental in Pascual evening his record to 2–2, by way of a 6–4 victory over the White Sox. Hyde and Tex Clevenger relieved Pascual in the game after he allowed two earned runs in six innings.

Two earned runs—one of them gift-wrapped—were all Pascual yielded four days later in New York, in a 3–2 extra-inning loss. The second game of a Mother's Day doubleheader went the way of the home team (as the first game had, 6–3) when right fielder Lemon came up short this time in another rescue attempt. In the tenth frame, Lemon attempted a shoestring catch that failed, with Mickey Mantle on first base. The Yankees' center fielder raced around the bases to score the winning run. Taking a no-hitter into the eighth inning of his next outing, on May 16, Pascual gave up an inning-opening double to Bob Cerv and ended up settling for a 7–2, four-hit victory over Kansas City, his first win of the season at Griffith Stadium. He followed that up with a 4–3, complete game loss to the Boston Red Sox. He threw his first shutout of the season, a two-hit, 2–0 triumph over the Orioles in Baltimore, on May 27. The win leveled Pascual's record at 4–4.

On the last day of May, Pascual tried to get over the .500 mark but could not. A fatal pitch, thrown at the end of a game at Griffith Stadium, foiled him. Pascual dueled the Yankees' Bob Turley into the ninth inning of a scoreless contest. After a double with two outs by Mickey Mantle, manager Cookie Lavagetto decided to walk Yogi Berra intentionally. Moose Skowron belted a three-run home run, and Turley completed a two-hit, 3–0 decision.

Another ninth-inning hit, this time a single by Al Kaline, dropped Pascual to 4–6 in his next start. Kaline's RBI safety beat the Senators, 7–6. Four of the runs yielded by Pascual in the June 5 game were unearned. Six days later, for the third start in a row and fourth time on the season, the right-hander was pinned with a last-inning loss. A day after moving into sole possession of first place, the Chicago White Sox beat the Senators, 3–1, in Washington. A two-run double in the ninth inning by Jim Landis rewarded the one-hit pitching of Pascual's opponent, Billy Pierce.

Pascual fired his eighth complete game in succession on June 17 to defeat the Kansas City Athletics for a second time at Griffith Stadium, 7–2. Four days hence, a second matchup with Bunning ended the complete game streak, and resulted in a no-decision for both pitchers. Pascual pitched eight innings and Bunning seven-plus, as the Senators, with a run in the ninth, eked out a 4–3 win. Falling short of another route-going effort by two outs, the Senators' hurler beat the Athletics for the third time, 8–4, in his next trip to the hill on June 26. He then mounted the nine-inning bronco again on July 1, with a four-hit complete game against Boston. An error in the ninth cost him a shutout in the 4–1 home triumph.

In the clubhouse, Camilo Pascual was said to crack up his teammates with his impressions of film star James Cagney. In a real "Yankee Doodle Dandy" performance, on the day after the Fourth of July, Pascual shut down the Bronx Bombers on four hits in New York. In the last game prior to the season's first All-Star Game, Pascual struck out ten and walked one in the 7–0 victory, as the clubs entered the mid-season break surprisingly on opposite trends. The Senators had won seven out of their last ten; the Yankees had been victorious only four times in the same span of games played.

Following the shutout and three-day All-Star Game respite, Pascual permitted the most runs in any one start on the season—six—and still came out on top by one run over the Baltimore Orioles, thanks to four Senators home runs, including Harmon Killebrew's 29th. Efficient relief pitching by Chuck Stobbs helped Pascual gain the 7–6 home win on July 10.

Pascual gained his tenth and 11th victories with successive shutouts over Detroit and Kansas City, on July 15 and 19 respectively. The former was a five-inning, rain-shortened endeavor. The Senators played a pair of games on July 19. Starting with the second game of the doubleheader that day, the team proceeded to lose 18 games in a row and sank like a brick in the American League standings.

As August opened, it appeared Pascual was going to end the suffering at 13 straight losses. He had a 1–0 lead at Comiskey Park but strained an elbow muscle and had to be relieved after seven innings, having allowed just one hit. The White Sox rallied for two runs in the ninth inning against Dick Hyde to pull out a 2–1 victory.

The sore elbow forced Pascual to miss his first earned All-Star Game berth and an additional three weeks' worth of starts. (Teammate Pedro Ramos was chosen to replace him in that season's second All-Star Game.) Pascual returned to the hill on August 23 for a Washington team that had lost 27 out of its past 33 games. Pascual beat the Athletics at Kansas City, 7–3. He threw six shutout innings and was removed following a flare-up in his elbow. In his next outing, on August 28, he suffered a 4–0 setback to Art Ditmar of the Yankees. Pascual's record stood at 12–10 at that point.

Pascual won five of his last six starts, missing an 18th win on the penultimate day of the season when he could not close out a 4–1 lead in the ninth inning against the Red Sox. He did not figure in the decision in the game won by Boston in extra innings. Two of the flurry of five wins were shutouts. The second one, 5–0 over the Orioles on September 20, inspired the following praise in a Shirley Povich column: "There is doubt now that there is a finer pitcher in the league than the Cuban-right-hander whose feat of winning 17 games for a last-place team borders on the heroic."[7]

Pascual's accolades were earned not only from the mound during the season. He batted out 26 hits for a .302 average, not only the highest among regular American League pitchers, but the highest average on his *team*. Pascual also fielded his position flawlessly, accepting more chances (73) without a miscue than any other pitcher in the majors.

A single Cy Young Award had been instituted three years earlier as a "most valuable pitcher" prize. The previous years' winners were all members of first-place clubs. Voters in 1959 followed the same criteria as Early Wynn of the pennant-winning Chicago White Sox was named the winner. Thirteen of the 16 writers cast votes for Wynn, the veteran stalwart who won 20 games for the fifth time in his career.

Pascual's slow start (4–7) and 12–10 record entering September hurt him considerably. Wynn's quantity of wins (22–10) for a first place team outweighed Pascual's overall pitching superiority, however. Pascual was better than Wynn in every significant pitching category except wins and innings pitched. Wynn, with seven more starts (37 to 30), could not match Pascual's

Camilo Pascual's best season with the Washington Senators came in 1959. The right-hander led all of baseball in shutouts with six and starter's ERA with 2.64.

complete games (17), shutouts (6) and strikeouts (185), and Wynn had an ERA more than one-half run higher than the Senators ace. (Wynn, with his advantage in starts, rather insignificantly topped Pascual in innings, 255 to 238⅔.) Utilizing more modern statistical measures, Pascual's WAR pitching metric was 7.8; Wynn's was 2.8. Including hitting, the Cuban ranked highest in WAR in the *entire* American League with an 8.6 rating (8.0 or above is considered MVP-caliber). And for overkill purposes, Pascual's WHIP was 1.135 compared to Wynn's 1.256.

It may have gone too much against the spirit of the still relatively new award to have named Pascual—whose 2.64 ERA was the lowest of any starting pitcher in both leagues—yet there was undoubtedly no better pitcher in baseball in 1959 than Camilo Alberto Pascual.[8]

PITCHING PEARL OF THE ANTILLES

In late December 1959, it was widely published that Senators owner Calvin Griffith "had looked one million dollars in the eye and expressed no interest." It was an offer not for his Washington franchise but merely for two of his ballplayers. One of those published reports further explained the matter: "The bidder was Gabe Paul, vice president of the Cincinnati Reds. 'I offered Griffith $500,000 each for Killebrew and Pascual and it was a firm offer,' Paul said. 'I consider Pascual the best pitcher in the majors.'"[9]

With Paul's offer declined, Pascual, on Opening Day 1960, showed why he was such a prized commodity by his owner and such a coveted one by other baseball executives.

> Camilo Pascual, the pitching Pearl of the Antilles, read a *Washington Post* sportswriter's lead the next day, "made the 60th opening day for the Senators a memorable one yesterday when he tossed a three-hitter and set a new club record of 15 strikeouts backed by four Washington home runs, which humiliated the Boston Red Sox, 10–1.
>
> Never was a pearl in a more glittering setting. An appreciative crowd of 28,327, including President Eisenhower and a host of notables, gave the sturdy Cuban an ovation when he struck out Gene Stephens in the ninth to erase the mark first set by the incomparable Walter Johnson.[10]

The club mark established a still-current major league opening day record for strikeouts by a pitcher. Pascual won five of his first eight decisions and was leading the league in strikeouts when a setback occurred that hampered his season. Leading up to it, the pitcher had rung up his first shutouts, in back-to-back starts, on May 14 and 18. The former game, a 4–0, 11-strikeout, four-hitter against New York at Griffith Stadium, snapped a Senators' three-game losing spell. Pascual topped that effort in the second whitewash—an 11-inning, 3–0 victory over the Tigers at Briggs Stadium.

Then in late May, a heated incident in a game against the Boston Red Sox physically derailed Pascual. The pitcher struck out Pete Runnels in the fifth inning, and Runnels, rankled and still fuming over being knocked down by a previous pitch, made a detour as he headed back to the dugout and ran out to the mound to get a piece of Pascual.

As both benches obligatorily emptied in the triggered melee, Pascual badly wrenched his shoulder as he wildly tried to free himself from the grips of restraining teammates. Though he completed the game, it was 11 days before Pascual could pitch again.

Pascual made two subsequent home starts and beat Kansas City and Detroit, though he was still hurting. Against the Athletics, Pascual pitched into the seventh inning, and versus the Tigers he hurled only five innings. Pascual tested his arm for a third time since the injury with a road start against the Athletics on June 17. In the third inning, the pitcher aggravated the shoulder he had hurt in the Runnels brawl, throwing a third strike past Harry Chiti. A game report indicated Pascual was in so much pain, following the pitch, that he bent over and had to sit down on the mound. He was out another two weeks.

Splitting two decisions after returning to the mound on July 2, Pascual's 8–5 record on July 7 earned him selection to the American League's All-Star squad, but he had to be replaced for the game because of the shoulder. (He was also selected for the second game that season but was not called upon to pitch.)

In August, it was pretty clear that Pascual had stemmed, if not turned, the tide against his previous hardship club, the New York Yankees. The hurler beat the Bronx Bombers for the second of three times (without a loss) on the season, on August 14, and made history while doing it. Using his bat as well as his arm to achieve a 5–4 victory, the pitcher, batting in the sixth inning with the bases loaded, sliced a ball to the opposite field that struck Yankee Stadium's short-distanced right field foul pole for a grand slam. The hit capped an inning in which the Senators scored all of their runs. Until that moment, no Hispanic pitcher had ever homered with the bases loaded in the major leagues.

The shoulder, though, proved too much of a burden. Pascual did not pitch at all over the final month of the season. His last start came on August 29; he lost his second straight game in which he surrendered only two earned runs.

In an injury-hindered season similar to 1958, Pascual finished the year winning 12 games with 8 losses. In 22 starts and four bullpen outings, his ERA barely nudged over three (3.03).

Unlike previous winters, Pascual did not pitch again until the following January in Cuba, getting in only a few "rehab" innings prior to spring training.

* * *

A uniform change was in store for Pascual in 1961—but not because Calvin Griffith had a change of heart about trading his premium pitcher, but because the Washington Senators relocated to Minnesota. The new "Twins" team was nicknamed for the "Twin Cities" of Minneapolis and St. Paul that loomed over the south suburb of Bloomington, where the team's new home ballpark was located. The relocated club maintained the Senators' pinstriped home white flannels with scripted team lettering across the chest for their new home in Minnesota. As far as American League hitters were concerned, the sight of Pascual's slightly varied attire with the same number 17 on the back remained all too familiar.

Change was also prominently imposed on the Antillean pitcher in his personal life. The United States and Cuba had dissolved diplomatic ties in January. Following the 1960–1961 winter campaign, when a promised re-entry into the United States from the Cuban Foreign Ministry failed to materialize, Pascual and several Cuban Winter League teammates were forced to travel to a third country (Mexico) to obtain the U.S. visas they required to enter the United States and continue their major league careers.

Pascual was the starting pitcher for the Twins in their initial home game in Minnesota. The Twin Cities had warmly welcomed their first-place boys (by virtue of five wins in their first six road games) to their new home. City officials held a breakfast for the team in St. Paul, then treated the team members to a parade into Minneapolis and also a luncheon there. The next day, April 21, a non-capacity crowd of 24,606 at "revamped Metropolitan Stadium" came out to see the Twins take on the expansion franchise from Washington, D.C. Trailing in the bottom of the eighth inning, 3–2, Pascual was pulled for a pinch-hitter. In the same frame, a Lenny Green home run tied the score to get Pascual off the hook, but the Senators scored twice in the top of the ninth inning to win, 5–3.

Pascual hurled a pair of shutouts in May and one each in June and July. The fourth whitewash (6–0) was in Los Angeles on July 19, against the American League's other expansion franchise, the Angels. Pascual, who had spoiled the Angels' first home game with a 4–2 victory back in late April, equaled his career high in strikeouts with 15, in the five-hit, one-walk gem.

In his first year in the "Land of 10,000 Lakes," Pascual was pitching as well as ever, but he was also as erratic as his final won-lost record indicated. Pascual led the league in shutouts (8) and strikeouts (221), worked 252⅓ innings and had a respectable 3.46 ERA. But his won-lost mark came in at 15–16. He was chiefly prevented from a better mark due to 17 unearned runs accrued to his pitching ledger, though 100 walks did not help his cause either. In retrospect, 15–16 might have been the best any pitcher could have hoped for on a team 20 games under .500. But even so, the record seemed beneath the acknowledged best right-hander in baseball. The hurler tied Christy Matthewson and Rube Waddell for most shutouts recorded in a season while posting a losing record.

Following a selection to the second All-Star Game of the year, Pascual made his first Midsummer Classic appearance at Fenway Park on July 31. The 27-year-old held the National League hitless over the final three innings of a 1–1 game called after nine innings due to rain.

During the 1961 season, Pascual contributed to the great Roger Maris-Mickey Mantle home run chase. He yielded a game-winning grand slam to Mantle in the tenth inning of a game in Bloomington on May 2. It was Mantle's eighth round-tripper. Three months later, at Yankee Stadium, Maris registered his 41st four-base wallop of the season against Pascual, who made four starts versus the 1961 Yankees and won two of three decisions. The games Pascual didn't win were the ones in which the M & M boys connected for home runs; in the other two starts, Pascual shut out the Bronx Bombers.[11]

The athletic pitcher lengthened a flawless defensive record he had attained until September 3. An errorless streak Pascual had begun on September 19, 1958, spanning 88 games and 150 chances, ended that day against the Red Sox, on a throwing error following a sacrifice bunt.

* * *

Both the Minnesota Twins and Camilo Pascual made a correction for the better with their records the following season. In 1962, the Twins completely turned around their 1961 campaign and finished 20 games *over* .500, good enough for second place in the American League. Pascual entered pitching's charmed circle, as the curveballer led the league in shutouts for the third time in four years.

Pascual could hardly have started the season better. In the Twins' second game, on April 11, he shut out the Kansas City Athletics on four hits, 8–0. The right-hander won three out of his next four starts, throwing complete games in each of the victories.

On May 21, RBI singles by Pascual himself in the seventh and eighth innings produced the Twins' final two runs in a 5–3 road wins versus Washington. Five days later, Pascual improved to 7–2 with a 4–1 complete game win over the Chicago White Sox.

His second shutout of the season, coming on June 26, delivered his fourth victory of the month. At Yankee Stadium, in a 5–0 win, Pascual permitted nine hits and overcame three Twins errors by not walking a batter and striking out a dozen. The last came in the form of MVP-to-be Mickey Mantle, pinch-hitting with the bases loaded in the ninth inning. The triumph put the Twins ten games above .500, at 42–32, a game behind the first-place Cleveland Indians and two ahead of third-place New York.

The only pitcher on his team with a double-figure victory total, Pascual, on July 1, notched win number 12 with an easy 9–0, five-hit blanking of the Senators at D.C. Stadium. Maris and Mantle (two) then cuffed Camilo for three home runs as the pitcher took his fifth loss of the campaign on July 6, to the visiting Yankees. The score was 7–5.

On July 13, in his first start after the first All-Star Game, Pascual blanked the Senators again, this time at Metropolitan Stadium, 4–0, on four hits and ten strikeouts. Two weeks later, in his final start before the second All-Star Game, Pascual showed why he had been a selectee for each of the games. Pascual was the losing pitcher in the first All-Star Game, July 10, allowing two of the National League's three runs in its 3–1 triumph. The right-hander registered a 2–1 decision over the Cleveland Indians. A Bob Allison ninth-inning home run provided the 15th win against six losses for Pascual, who seemed headed for an exceptionally illustrious season.

But in the game versus Cleveland, an arm ailment spiked up. Pascual, it turned out, had strained a tendon in his pitching arm, which did not dissuade him from completing the game, but which affected him enough to miss two starts afterward. A too-soon return to the mound on August 7, against the Yankees, proved ill-fated as well as short-lived. Pascual could not pitch more than two innings because of the inflammation in his elbow; he gave up five runs in the first frame and was tagged with his seventh loss. A form of tendinitis called epicondylitis had afflicted the elbow.

Pascual made only two other starts in August, the second one coming toward the end of the month, a 5–3 win on the road over the Chicago White Sox. It came on August 29, and with the victory the surprising 76–59 Twins had moved to within two games of the now catbird-seated New York.

Pascual resumed pitching with regularity after that. He defeated Washington and Detroit in successive starts for his 17th and 18th wins. On September 12, four days following his 9–2, complete game win over the Tigers, Pascual was beaten at home, 2–1 in 12 innings, by the White Sox.[12] It was an extraordinary effort, especially considering Pascual's recent elbow problems. In today's arm-protective and pitch count-sensitive game, there certainly would have been widespread calls for the manager's head for letting Pascual pitch so long. But the Twins were fighting to stay in the pennant race, and in that era of baseball, whenever they could, teams fought to the end with their best starting pitchers.

The Twins' fight for the pennant was as gallant as it was unexpected. Pascual hurled nine more innings against Cleveland on September 16 for his 19th victory. The home win moved Minnesota to within three games of the Yankees with ten games to play. The 12-strikeout, 4–3 decision over the Indians was followed by Pascual with a 3–2 loss to Baltimore and a 5–1 defeat at the hands of the Cleveland Indians and Pedro Ramos. The former game's loss virtually cinched the pennant for the Yankees.

The Twins split their last ten games and finished five games (91–71) behind pennant-winning New York. The Twins also placed second to the Yankees in team hitting.

On the final day of the campaign, September 30, Pascual won his 20th game in grand and efficient style, shutting out the Baltimore Orioles, 1–0, in one hour and 49 minutes. Harmon Killebrew's first inning single drove in the run which made a 20-game winner out of the "Cuban cutie" for the first time.

Pascual was a terror with the timber in 1962, hitting .268 (eight points higher than the Twins' team average) and knocking in 19 runs in 97 at bats. (His RBI number was equal to or greater than the *entire* pitching staff totals of four other American League teams.) In 103 plate appearances, Pascual received six walks and fanned only *eight* times; not surprisingly, he was called upon to sacrifice not once during the entire season. As a hitter, Pascual choked up slightly and stood hunched forward with feet spread far apart at the plate (a Joe DiMaggio-type stance). He had a six-game hitting-streak, with RBI each game, no easy feat for a pitcher.

For the second time in four years, and boosted by his hitting, Pascual earned the highest overall WAR ranking in the American League—6.2

* * *

Summing up his first 20-win season the following spring, Pascual could not help comparing the improvement in his current pitching environs to his difficult formative years in Washington. "It use to be that when the ball was hit on the ground I'd close my eyes and try to figure if it would be a single, a double or a home run," he said, in an exaggerated point about the importance of a sound defense behind a pitcher. "But last year when the ball was hit on the ground, I'd be happy because I knew that we had some players who could catch the ball."[13]

In 1962, Pascual had been the last major leaguer to sign on the dotted line, delaying his arrival at spring training by a month; in 1963, Calvin Griffith avoided any potential contract wrangling with his star pitcher and increased Pascual's salary $10,000 to $37,500, making him the highest-paid pitcher in franchise history. A statistic Griffith probably knew going into 1963 was that only four active pitchers had more lifetime shutouts than Camilo Pascual—and all them, Early Wynn, Whitey Ford, Warren Spahn and Robin Roberts, were eventual Hall of Famers.

Pascual's 26 shutouts had tied him with Adolfo Luque for most by a Hispanic pitcher, and he improved on the career numbers of his former manager by three in what was probably his finest pitching season in the major leagues. The right-hander won 21 games, though the bothersome arm trouble that seemed to plague him annually, in one form or another, returned.

Receiving his first Opening Day start as a Twin, Pascual did not fare well, losing to the Indians and Mudcat Grant, 5–4, on April 9. He started 0–3, then won four in a row, before New York defeated him in mid–May, 4–3, avenging an earlier 4–1 loss.

Three more triumphs, including a 3–2 decision over Washington on May 30, fluffed the pitcher's record to 7–4. The good news for the Twins was that the victory was the team's tenth win in a row; the not so good news was that the team was only two games over .500 through 44 games played.

Three starts later, Pascual improved to 9–5, but then was limited to one appearance over the next five weeks. From June 12, the day he won his ninth game (8–1 over Kansas City) and strained a muscle near his right shoulder blade, until July 18, Pascual was virtually lost to the club. In his only appearance during the period, on June 30, he retired after three innings due to a pain in his right arm. On July 18, with their returning ace pitching 5⅓ innings in a 9–3 win over New York, the fourth-place Twins won their 50th game of the season and climbed eight games over .500.

Following his victory over the Yankees on July 23, Pascual again threw caution to the wind shortly after a return from an arm injury and pitched into the bottom of the 13th inning at Cleveland. The Indians' Tito Francona homered with two outs in the inning against Pascual to give Mudcat Grant—who had previously been a Washington killer and who now seemed to be continuing the dominance over the Twins—a complete game 3–2 victory. (It was the second extraordinary extra-inning pitching duel of the month in baseball. In the National League, three weeks earlier, Warren Spahn and Juan Marichal had engaged in a towering 16-inning struggle.)

Minnesota eased into New York for a four-game series from July 26–28, 8½ games out of reach of the top rung of the American League standings. The Twins lost the first two games and turned to their ace to prevent a further disastrous series outcome. Pascual responded with a 5–1 route-going victory over Whitey Ford. Nicked for a run in the first inning, Pascual cruised to his 11th win. The Twins, though, lost the nightcap, and never were a challenge after that to a very strong New York Yankees squad.

Pascual challenged the league's best pitchers by winning his next seven starts. The streak was snuffed on September 3 by visiting Kansas City by a score of 3–2. Pascual then dropped his next two starts, 5–2 to Chicago, and 2–0 at home to New York. Second-year Yankees hurler Jim Bouton won not only his 20th game in besting Pascual, but clinched the Yankees' 28th American League pennant, on September 13.

With second place left to the Twins or Chicago White Sox, Pascual needed to win two of his remaining three starts to reach 20 victories. He won all three by complete games. In the final victory, Pascual subdued the Yankees for the fourth time on the season, 4–3, on September 27 at Yankee Stadium.

For a third time, Pascual topped the league in complete games (18), and led the circuit in strikeouts (202) for a third year running. His ERA, at 2.46 (third-best in the league behind Juan Pizarro and Gary Peters), was as

Pascual became the first Hispanic two-time 20-game winner in the major leagues with the Minnesota Twins in the early 1960s.

bitingly sharp as his curve. The hurler registered the highest WAR ranking for an AL pitcher at 6.2 and tied (with Peters) for second-best composite WAR at 7.0, behind AL leader Bob Allison (7.4). Pascual had now won 85 games in his last five seasons, after winning only 28 in the five prior.

From the day Pascual rejoined the rotation, Minnesota won 42 of its remaining 70 games. Their 91–70 record was third best in the American League, trailing only the White Sox (94–68) and New York, which won 104 games.

"It's a dream come true"

The Twins of 1964 took what can only be described as backward steps following two 91-win campaigns. Pascual, left-hander Jim "Kitty" Kaat, and Mudcat Grant, acquired during 1964 in a mid-season trade with the Indians, were the only pitchers on the staff with appreciable win totals. Pascual did not miss a start all year and had 15 wins, second to Kaat's 17. Grant contributed 11 (for a combined 14 on the season). No other Twins pitcher won more than seven games, however, and the team won a dozen fewer games than in each of the two previous seasons, finishing 20 games behind the aging American League champion Yankees. Twins fans, however, by no means sat on their hands during the course of the campaign. They had much to cheer with Harmon Killebrew's 49 home runs and the appearance of a once-in-a-generation hitter from Pascual's home country named Tony Oliva.

Pascual could have easily had a third 20-game-win season had his defense and relievers pulled their combined weight. The pitcher allowed two earned runs or fewer in 15 starts but won only seven of them. He also was heavily burdened by shoddy defense; a damaging 23 unearned runs were scored on Pascual, ten more than the last two seasons combined. The 30-year-old tossed the most innings of his career, 267⅓, compiling a 15–12 mark with a 3.30 ERA. In his final start of the season, Pascual pitched 12 innings, only to lose to Kansas City on a solo home run, the first earned run he allowed in the game; the final score was 5–4.

Yet, on the personal side of his life, 1964 was a most gratifying year for the pitcher. Working mechanisms had been in place for arranging the emigration of his parents and sister from Cuba. Their release was secured in August through the efforts of Minnesota Senator Hubert H. Humphrey.

"I have been working with Senator Humphrey's office for a year to get my parents out of Cuba," Pascual happily stated, after learning his family had left the Communist island and were in Mexico City, awaiting clearance for the last leg of their journey to the U.S. "I thought I might not ever see them again. This is terrific, a wonderful thing. It's a dream come true."[14]

Coincidentally, at that same time, the Twins were in Washington to play a short series with the Senators. The team paid a visit to Lyndon Johnson's White House (also facilitated through Humphrey's office). "The Twins became the first major league club ever to be greeted by a President in the State Dining Room,"[15] a Twin Cities sportswriter wrote of the occurrence. President Johnson personally welcomed the team and shook every player's hand. Later, on the evening of the team's August 18 White House call, with the euphoric knowledge that an imminent reunion with his family was at hand, Pascual pitched a 6–1, complete game victory over the baseball Senators. The eight-hitter was Pascual's 13th win. But it was only the Twins' 60th victory in 120 games. The club won 19 more times over the next six weeks and limped to the finish line in seventh place.

Upon their arrival, Camilo Sr. and Maria Pascual were soon able to meet for the first time their three grandchildren, Camilo III, Maria Isabel and Adalberto. Later in the year, they were present when daughter-in-law Rachel gave birth to a fourth child, Sandra.

The Pascuals, who had been wintering in Miami for the past few off-seasons, stayed in Minneapolis after the 1964 campaign and bought a home for everyone to live in. The head of the household and two-time major league 20-game winner took a job at a Bloomington car dealership during the off-season to make ends better meet for his happily reunited family.

*   *   *

Sometimes, in order to take a substantive step forward one must take one or two steps back. The Twins, having taken their "steps back" in 1964, made a grand leap forward in 1965, all the way to the top of the American League. Led by Mudcat Grant's 21 wins and Jim Kaat's 18, and the hitting of repeat batting champion Tony Oliva, and solidified by the MVP season of shortstop Zoilo Versalles, the Minnesota Twins were the team that derailed the New York Yankees' decades-long dynasty.

Pascual moved out to a terrific start at 8–0—then went nine starts without a win, losing three. In his second win, April 27, Pascual pitched a two-hit victory over the Indians. He hit a grand slam and drove in five runs in the Cleveland Stadium 11–1 triumph.

The Twins had used the impetus of their veteran starter's early string of wins, plus five each from Grant and Kaat, to rise above the American League pack. At 32–16, following Pascual's eighth win—a 6–2 complete game over Cleveland on June 8 at Metropolitan Stadium—the team was 2½ games in the lead.

During the dearth of victories for Pascual in June and July, on two occasions the pitcher had to withdraw after a few innings of work because of tightness in his shoulder. On July 28, a lump was detected beneath Pascual's pitching arm by Washington team physician George Resta. The Twins were in Washington during a road trip and Pascual had gone to see Resta, a friendly acquaintance of the right-hander from his original Senators days.

Initially thought to be a benign tumor, the lump turned out to be a knot of sheared shoulder muscle tissue that had rolled up under Pascual's armpit. Pascual was scheduled to pitch while he was in Washington and did so. His team was in first place by four games, and the pitcher felt compelled to take his regular turn. The Twins staked Pascual to three runs early but the hurler's arm gave out. Pitching in extreme pain and not having given up a run, Pascual was forced to leave the game in the fourth inning in mid-count on a batter. The Twins went on to win, 8–1.

Harmon Killebrew had gone to the same doctor the day Pascual found out about his condition. The following spring, Killebrew revealed in an interview what Pascual had been through for the sake of the team. "I played first base that night," Killebrew said. "I was one of the few who knew what was wrong with him. I watched his face grimace with pain on every pitch. But he kept on as long as he could. Anyone who could have seen that would know what a competitor this man is."[16]

Pascual went under the knife on August 2 and, amazingly, was able to return and pitch again before the end of the season. After what can be described as a miraculously quick recovery, Pascual was back on the mound on September 6, and did not miss any of the Twins' pennant celebrations. Minnesota, five games up on the rest of the league at the time of Pasucal's surgery, lost no ground during the pitcher's absence and grabbed the title by seven full games over the second-place Chicago White Sox. Pascual won once more (with five no-decisions) and contributed nine of the Twins' 102 wins.

After 12 major league seasons, many with wretchedly poor teams, Camilo Pascual arrived at the cherished place all ballplayers dream of reaching the moment they are first old enough to associate competition with professional baseball desires. Pascual was going to compete in the World Series. Opposing the American League champs were the Los Angeles Dodgers.

Mudcat Grant beat Don Drysdale, 8–2, in the World Series opener. Jim Kaat, who hurled the Twins' pennant-clinching victory, beat Sandy Koufax in Game 2, 5–1.

Pascual made his only Fall Classic start in Game 3 against Claude Osteen on October 9. And on the day he needed her the most, pitching in the biggest game of his life, Camilo Pascual's curvaceous companion of many years ... deserted him. Left him standing alone on the mound at Dodger Stadium in front of 55,934 people like a man jilted in public by his beautiful lover. As much as he summoned, she was nowhere to be found. The betrayal left Pascual numb. "It was as if I didn't know what I was doing out on the mound," the dejected hurler said after the Twins' 4–0 defeat. "When I realized that my curve was not doing what I wanted it to do, I tried to overpower them with my fastball. But unless you have one more pitch to keep them guessing, you don't have a chance to overpower anybody."[17] Pascual took some responsibility for the abandonment. "I just didn't get enough work in after the operation to get my curve ball sharp,"[18] he lamented. Bandied about for eight hits, Pascual gave up three runs in five innings. The Dodgers treated owner Walter O'Malley to a Series-turning victory on his 62nd birthday. The game was the first of three shutouts the heavy-hitting Minnesotans suffered in the Series (two to Koufax).

The Twins, after having won the first two games, batted a puny .195 for the Series and lost to the Dodgers in seven games.

* * *

In 1966, Pascual, the number two man in the rotation behind Grant, opened the season similarly to 1965. The pitcher won six of his first seven decisions. But again, in a repeat of the prior season, he was beset with a winless spell and arm troubles after the initial successes.

The Twins were thankful for Pascual's early standout performances. The hurler was responsible for six of the team's first 13 wins. The Twins team, though, struggled in May and June, as Pascual also struggled through a six-start winless phase. Pascual snapped a personal four-game losing stupor on June 24, with a 9–2 win at Detroit. He picked up his eighth win four days hence with seven scoreless innings in a home start against Cleveland with a 4–0 final score.

It was, unexpectedly, Pascual's last victory of the season. The right-hander injured his shoulder in the win against the Indians and was placed on the disabled list on July 7 with a combination sore arm and tendinitis outbreak around his elbow. Pascual made only two more starts the remainder of the campaign. Over the summer, he did not pitch for a span of 46 days.

More than a bit of contentiousness arose between Pascual and manager Sam Mele over the pitcher's lack of use. The Twins skipper had relegated Pascual to the bullpen and would not use him during a time when Pascual claimed he had recovered and was ready to pitch. The year ended disappointingly for Pascual, with an 8–6 final record and only 103 innings pitched, the fewest in his 13 major league seasons.

Minnesota, despite a strong second half showing, did not successfully defend their American League title, finishing second, nine games behind the Baltimore Orioles.

* * *

Calvin Griffith was not going to pay an eight-game winner $40,000-plus again, the salary he was shelling out to Pascual, so he traded the man he had once refused to part with for a small fortune, to the Washington Senators in December 1966. The Twins received reliever Ron Kline and the Senators also acquired infielder Bernie Allen in the deal.

Professional baseball players, especially the better ones, year after year, in a rite of passage as customary as spring training itself, had to haggle with their bosses for equitable salaries. It had taken Pascual many years and many lengthy haggles to attain the salary level he currently governed. His new team, the Senators, wanted the veteran pitcher to take a pay cut of as much as $10,000 from a reported $44,500 he had received the prior season from the Twins. As a result, the pitcher failed to report to spring camp.

Capitulations by both sides finally ended a 28-day holdout, with the acquired pitcher signing for $40,000 and, although not his primary focus, becoming the highest paid player on the Senators team.

The holdout may have been an underlying reason why Senators manager Gil Hodges did not give Pascual his first start until April 24, two full weeks into the season. The veteran hurler was charged with four earned runs in 6⅔ innings of work against the Boston Red Sox and was not involved in the game's final outcome. Six days later, Pascual recorded his first win, defeating the Twins, at home, in his first encounter against his former team. The score was 7–3; Pascual pitched six innings, giving up all of the visitors' runs.

In two subsequent starts, Pascual bested the California Angels in a complete game, 4–1, and was defeated by the Cleveland Indians, 2–1, pulled after eight innings for a pinch-hitter.

Any previous concerns over Pascual's health, after four outings, seemed to have been put to rest. Set in the rotation, Pascual won four out of six more starts, including a four-hit, 1–0 sparkler at D.C. Stadium against the California Angels on June 1. Pascual was 5–2 with a 2.66 ERA at that point. Pascual then defeated Boston and Baltimore and lost twice to the Yankees. He dropped to 7–5 when his ex-mates beat him, 4–1, in his return to Minnesota as a Senator on July 2.

On July 27, in their 100th game, the sixth-place Senators registered their 48th victory when Pascual (10–7) defeated Kansas City, 6–4. He lost three out of four decisions in August, including a 1–0, two-hit heartbreaker to Cleveland's Steve Hargan.

After defeating the Red Sox, 5–2, on September 4, for his 12th win against ten losses, Pascual had his sights set on at least 15 campaign wins. But in his next start, on September 9 versus the Angels in Washington, he fractured his ankle on a freak base-running play. After reaching on a hit, Pascual took a wide turn around first base and thought better about trying to advance. As he pivoted to get back to the first base bag, he caught his spikes in the dirt and twisted awkwardly; his fibula cracked right above the ankle. Pascual pleaded with his manager to let him remain in the game, but quickly sensing the futility of the case, limped off the field. Pascual's season was finished.

* * *

The 1967 Washington Senators were not quite as terrible a club as some of the ones in Washington that Pascual had toiled for in the 1950s. The team's 76–85 record installed Hodges' squad into seventh position in the ten-team league, and two slots above the fallen New York Yankees. Pascual led the staff in wins with his 12.

The 1968 Washington Senators *were* as terrible a club as some of the ones in Washington that Pascual had toiled for in the 1950s. The team's 65–96 record dragged new manager Jim Lemon's squad to a dead last finish. Pascual outstandingly accounted for one-fifth of the terrible team's total wins.

The Senators opened the season at home against Minnesota and were shut out, 2–0, Pascual taking the loss. The American League's winningest active pitcher then won three straight starts. The first was a 7–0, seven-hit whitewash of the California Angels on April 15. Pascual struck out nine and topped 2,000 strikeouts for his career—the first Hispanic major league pitcher to record as many. The 2,000th sacrificial strikeout offering tendered by Pascual was the Angels' Chuck Hinton, who succumbed to a called strike three, knee-buckling curveball.

Four days after Pascual's third victory—2–1 over the Indians (eight innings, rain) on April 27—the Senators fell into a tailspin, losing 20 out of 25 games. During a portion of the awful stretch, Senators left fielder Frank Howard put on a home run display unequaled in baseball history. The behemoth, right-handed hitter belted ten home runs over six consecutive games, from May 12 through 18.

Pascual did not start any of the games, but started the day after Howard's blasting ended; Pascual lost, giving up four runs to Detroit in a 7–0 defeat. Pascual was 3–3 with a 1.91 ERA at that point (the Senators had scored a combined two runs in his three losses). Pascual slowed the team's freefall on May 30, with a 6–2 triumph over the New York Yankees; the win ended the 25-game stretch of embarrassing play.

The Senators used Pascual's triumph as a starting point for seven more victories in the next ten games. But then, just as suddenly, the Senators dropped eight games in row. Pascual stopped the slide, hurling the distance to defeat the Oakland Athletics on June 21, 7–3. It was the pitcher's sixth victory.

On the first of July, Pascual defeated the Yankees, 3–1, at D.C. Stadium, for his eighth victory. Pascual's ninth win of the season (against five losses) came two and a half weeks later, in a similarly close game against the same team. The second victory over the Yankees on the season also ended another extended Senators' losing skein of nine games. The game fell on an intensely hot day in New York, where the afternoon field temperature was reported to have reached over 100 degrees. Under such conditions, the right-hander could not duplicate his previous July 1 complete game endeavor against the New York team, but still managed a 2–1 triumph with relief help.

Over the next two months, Pascual won only four more games. The reason can best be attributed to the Senators' lack of hitting that had been present since Opening Day. In the 12 losses suffered by Pascual, his team scored 20 runs for him. The classy pitcher still won 13 games and had a sterling 2.69 ERA. The "Year of the Pitcher" curve notwithstanding, it was, given the composition of Pascual's team, a standout season by anyone's standard.

* * *

But there was no carryover to 1969. Pascual received his fifth career Opening Day assignment on April 7. He lost to the Yankees, 8–4, ousted in the third inning by two home runs and a double. In his next start, Pascual lacked command of his pitches. The pitcher walked four and yielded four hits, and was charged with four runs in two innings of work in a 9–0 loss to the Baltimore Orioles.

Over the first three months of the 1969 season, Pascual was victorious in only two of seven decisions. Through his first 13 starts, the Senators hurler accrued an unacceptable ERA of 6.83. The Washington club decided to move him. On July 7, four days after Pascual had suffered his fifth loss of the campaign, to the Cleveland Indians and Luis Tiant, 7–2, the Senators sold the 35-year-old pitcher to the Cincinnati Reds for considerably less than the price the Reds had offered ten years earlier.

LEGACY

In May 1959 the New York Yankees had packaged pitcher Tom Sturdivant in a multi-player deal to the Kansas City Athletics. A newsprint report stated that the Yankees had previously been "within an inch" of trading Sturdivant in 1956, to Washington, for Camilo Pascual, but called off the deal at the last minute. The 1956 potential exchange of Sturdivant for Pascual will always be one on which the Yankees regret not pulling the trigger. It would be a rich "what if" scenario, indeed, to speculate about Camilo Pascual having pitched in the pinstripes of New York for most of his career instead of more than half of it in the pinstripes of the Washington Senators.[19]

Pascual won a total of 174 games and lost 170. He completed nearly one-third of his 404 career starts. Pascual appeared in another 125 games in relief, amassing just under 3,000 major league innings (2,930⅔). His major league ERA was 3.63.

His credentials in the Cuban Winter League and the national pride brought to Cuba from his pitching in the Caribbean Series opened for Pascual the doors of the Cuban Hall of Fame. Pascual's formal induction was made in Miami in 1983.

In his homeland, the 5'11" right-hander twice led the Cuban League in victories, complete games, winning percentage and ERA. In seven full seasons and three games of another, he threw a total of 751 innings and struck out 612, with a magnificent ERA of 2.04. His record was 58–32.

Pascual also pitched for the minor league Havana Cubans for two seasons and pitched one in the Venezuelan Winter League, where he won a combined 25 games.

The winter league standout's eminent pitching in the Caribbean theatre also brought Pascual elite recognition in 1996, from the newly inaugurated Caribbean Hall of Fame. The initial class from that year included the Cuban pitcher, along with Rico Carty, Hector Espino, and Willard Brown, representing the Dominican Republic, Mexico and Puerto Rico, respectively. The honored placement was earned from a 6–0 Caribbean Series record, with five complete games and a 1.73 ERA, forming part of three separate Cuban Caribbean Series championship teams. Included in the victory total was a one-hit triumph over the Santurce Crabbers in 1960.

The Havana native was also part of a larger inaugural class of inductees into the Latino Hall of Fame in the Dominican Republic in 2010. The Minnesota Twins ushered their well-remembered pitcher into the team's Hall of Fame with a ceremony July 14, 2012.

How good was Pascual's curve? Since Pascual's time—circa six decades, now—only two pitchers *throughout* their careers, Bert Blyleven and Doc Gooden, consistently commanded a curve ball as comparably crisp, pristine and devastating.

But did throwing this taxing pitch contribute to the nagging arm problems Pascual seemed to develop annually? "Everyone thinks I put a big strain on my arm with my curve," Pascual said not long after his speedy return from his 1965 shoulder surgery. "But I don't. I put 100 percent effort into my fastball. But I only throw 80 percent as hard on my big curve."[20]

From 1956 to 1965, Pascual averaged 29 starts per season, on the surface a tad low for a regular starter. But the first three of those seasons also included 19 relief outings. Over the second half of that ten-year period, and beginning with the advent of a 162-game schedule in 1961, Pascual averaged 32 starts per year, a better average for a frontline starter. Although periodically sidelined with arm issues, Pascual's overall number of big league appearances (529) confirmed his dependability.

It was actually the right-hander's contention that inactivity was a detriment to his effectiveness, especially when it came to his curve. He made a comment along those lines in the mid–1960s. "Since I quit pitching in winter baseball," Pascual said, "and started resting all winter, it has taken me quite a while to get really sharp with my curve. The last few years, I have not started striking out a lot of batters every game until July."[21]

Pascual's 1969 tenure with the Reds was short-lived. He appeared in only five games for Cincinnati. He hung on for two more seasons, pitching for the Los Angeles Dodgers and Cleveland Indians, mostly out of the bullpen and mostly poorly. In June of 1972, he was released by the Indians, ending his major league career.

Washington sports dean Shirley Povich bade farewell to the former Senators moundsman in the following manner, the day after the pitcher's trade to Cincinnati was announced:

> Pascual served a generation of Washington fans with the finest pitching they ever saw on a Washington team.... He was as complete a pitcher who ever strode to the mound, and probably the finest fielding pitcher of his time.
>
> Obviously the Reds believe that Pascual can reach back for some of the pitches that once made him the American League's most-feared pitcher.
>
> The Reds, in fourth place, are yet only four games out of it in the West Division, and will be quick to give Pascual a shot at winning some games for them. And thus, among the Washington people, they have created a new sentiment for Cincinnati in the National League race.[22]

And thus, with this writing, a new, broader sentiment for now the now octogenarian Camilo Pascual, who lives in Miami and is a scout for the Dodgers organization, can also be created.

5

The 1960s—Juan Marichal, Luis Tiant

Juan Marichal

Hispanidad's most brilliant pitcher was born October 20, 1937, in Laguna Verde, Dominican Republic. Juan Marichal and his two older brothers and sister were raised on a modest vegetable farm. The farm was carved on a plot of land outside of their small northeastern town, located a few miles south of the port city of Monte Cristi and bordering the mountainous divide separating the Dominican Republic from Haiti.

The Marichals lived in an ample-sized wood frame house that had no electricity but had three bedrooms and indoor plumbing, provided by water tanks in their bathroom that had to be hand-filled. Juan and his brothers shared one bedroom, and his mother and sister, named María, used the other two. Juan Marichal's father died when Juan was only three years old. The cause of death was liver failure.[1]

At the age of 12, Juan gave his family a terrific scare, resulting from a near-fatal experience. Juan's body literally shut down after he went swimming in an irrigation canal to cool off following a hard day of rice planting. The young Marichal had already cooled off in the ditch once, then headed home and gorged on a mid-day meal. Right afterward, he returned to the same place for another swim. Juan collapsed as he emerged the second time from the ditch and fell unconscious.

For six days and five nights his family kept a prayerful vigil as Juan lay motionless in his bed. The doctor who had been called did not hold out much hope as Juan's comatose state stretched on for nearly a week. But late in the evening of the sixth day, with his anxious mother and siblings hovering nearby, Juan awoke suddenly with a cry, and regained consciousness. Marichal delivered this brief recollection of the ordeal in his autobiography, *A Pitcher's Story:* "I swam and ate—but after eating, I went back to swimming again. The next thing I knew it was six days later."[2]

That Juan took to baseball was no surprise, as his two older brothers played the sport. One of them, Gonzalo, was a pitcher for a team in Monte Cristi. On horseback, a young Juan often accompanied his brother, 11 years his senior, to watch him pitch in the nearby town. Juan balanced his chores on the farm with school and playing baseball. As a pre-teen, he could snap off a curve sharply enough that Gonzalo knew there was to be another pitcher in the Marichal family. Gonzalo helped his brother develop the bending pitch. By the time Juan was 15, Laguna Verde had a team, sandlot tantamount, and Juan was the pitcher. Two years later, the younger Marichal brother was hurling off the same mound in Monte Cristi as his older sibling had.

In 1956, at 19, Juan was "drafted" from the Dominican Junior World Championship team into the Air Force. The draft order came directly from the son of the country's ruling potentate, Ramfis Trujillo. It was really a baseball round-up, in the guise of conscription, in order to place Marichal and some of the Dominican's best young players on Trujillo's Air Force baseball team. Trujillo did not digest defeat well, and after one doubleheader loss threw his entire team—players and manager included—in jail, believing his men had not given an all-out effort for him. (Marichal fell, 1–0, in the second game, an unearned run the victimizer.)

Young Marichal did not stay long in jail, and soon received a permanent reprieve from Trujillo and the Dominican military. A month prior to his 20th birthday, the San Francisco Giants inked Marichal to his first professional contract. The Giants arranged for him to pitch for Escogido, one of the Dominican Winter League teams. The first professional uniform Marichal wore was that of the capital city Leones.

Several months later, Marichal was wearing the uniform of the San Francisco Giants, at their Sanford, Florida, minor league spring camp. Marichal, the rookie recruit, received the customary Class-D assignment. It was to the Midwest League in Indiana. On the bus route out of Florida, he and other non–Caucasian teammates had to remain sequestered in their bus seats, while "acceptable" team members brought out their meals from restaurants catering to "white only" Floridians or visitors.

Upon his Indiana arrival, Marichal showed right away that he was no ordinary recruit. The 20-year-old right-hander became a 20-game winner in his first year of stateside professional ball. In 35 appearances for the Michigan City White Caps, Marichal won 21 times with only eight losses. The pitcher then returned to Escogido over the winter, where he sported an 8–3 record.

Marichal's performance for Michigan City earned him a three-rung promotion in 1959, all the way to Class A ball for the Giants' Springfield, Massachusetts affiliate. Springfield's manager, Andy Gilbert, suggested a change in Marichal's pitching delivery, one that would lead to great success and establish a signature throwing motion. Marichal had always thrown side-arm. But Gilbert thought the motion exacted too much stress on the young pitcher's arm, so he persuaded him to throw overhand to the plate. But this new arm motion caused Marichal's pitches to sail and end up high over the plate.

"Kick higher with your leg," Gilbert instructed Marichal. "That will bring the ball down, because the body force will be coming down as you release it."[3] The technique worked, and the distinctive, leg kick that raised one foot higher than his head as he wound back his baseball-gripping hand to the calf of his rubber-straddling foot, was born. The pinwheel delivery allowed Marichal to moderate, on occasion, the delivery and use different arm angles to consternate batters.

Andy Gilbert also instilled in Marichal the importance of hustling all the time. Gilbert fined a player one dollar for not touching first base on a routine out. Even though Marichal was a pitcher, he learned to run out every batted ball through the first base bag. That discipline, along with his own pure joy in pitching, started the young pitcher off on a routine of running to the mound between innings. "I run to the mound to make the game faster,"[4] Marichal further reasoned.

Marichal wanted to be more than a thrower. He wanted to learn the art of pitching by acquiring and mastering different types of pitches. His dedication to his craft led him to perfect five different pitches, and he was able to throw all of them for strikes. Gilbert helped him with his changeup and slider, and Marichal taught himself a screwball in his last year of minor league ball. The pitches became part of an intimidating repertory that hitters facing Marichal had to overcome.

Frank Robinson commented in a video documentary on what it was like to face the varied-angled, multi-pitch pitcher. "Marichal had 15 pitches," the Hall of Famer said. "Five pitches he could throw from three different angles—over the top, three-quarters and side-arm. Once in a while," added, not altogether in jest, the great home run hitter and two-time MVP, "I thought he threw a couple between his legs."[5]

Marichal, sharpening his English skills along the way, won 18 games, with eight shutouts, and threw 271 innings for Gilbert at Springfield. The performance paid his transport, in the first spring of a new decade, to Phoenix, Arizona, to the Giants' new big league training camp. As the end of training neared, there was a good probability that Marichal would accompany the team west, but while throwing batting practice, he was struck in the groin by a line drive. Marichal was painfully sidelined for a week and subsequently optioned to the Giants' Triple-A team in Tacoma, Washington.

Tom Sheehan was the head of scouting for the San Francisco Giants and became their interim manager in July of 1960 when the team fired Bill Rigney. Sheehan's first move as Giants manager was to recall Juan Marichal from Tacoma, where the right-hander had won 11 games. Immediately after his recall, the debut of the first Dominican pitcher in the major leagues was made in spectacular style. Marichal presided over a one-hit victory (2–0) against the Philadelphia Phillies, at Candlestick Park on July 19. The young, hard thrower, who had never seen a live major league game except on television, pitched no-hit ball for 7⅔ innings, retiring the first 19 big league batters he faced. The string was broken on an error by shortstop Eddie Bressoud. An inning later, Clay Dalrymple singled to center field. Marichal struck out 12 and walked one, facing 30 batters.

The pitcher made his second start for the Giants on July 23, and nearly as easily defeated the Pittsburgh Pirates, 3–1. The two complete game victories were assessed by the Giants' farm director, Carl Hubbell. "Most youngsters, starting out, copy some pitcher," said the former pitching great. "Marichal doesn't look like anybody I've seen, except Marichal."[6] Hubbell summarized Marichal as a player about whom it could be said the proverbial mold had broken after casting.

In his third start, 22-year-old Juan Marichal faced Warren Spahn and vanquished the pre-eminent left-hander of the Milwaukee Braves, 3–2, in ten innings. Felipe Alou singled against Spahn with the bases loaded to drive home the winning run for his fellow Dominican. The right-hander then received two no-decisions in his first road starts. In a third outing away from Candlestick Park, on August 16, Marichal downed the St. Louis Cardinals and second-year pitcher Bob Gibson, 7–3.

The next time toeing the rubber for Marichal came on September 5, against the Dodgers at the Los Angeles Memorial Coliseum. The rookie suffered his first defeat, 4–3. Marichal won two out his next three decisions to complete a 6–2 record in 11 starts for the second-division Giants.

*   *   *

In 1961, the San Francisco Giants, under first-year manager Alvin Dark, improved into a first-division club. Earning a position as the team's fourth starter, Marichal received 27

The signature leg kick of the inimitable Juan Marichal. In a 16-season career, Marichal won 243 games and completed 244, an all-time record for a Hispanic major league pitcher.

starts and won 12, with an additional victory gained in one of two relief appearances on the season. Coming out of the bullpen, Stu Miller led the third-place Giants in wins with 14, and two other hurlers on the club besides Marichal had one fewer.

Marichal received his initial start on April 15, and lost, 2–0, to the Philadelphia Phillies.

The pitcher won his next two starts, then, following three no decisions, lost, 6–4, to the Cincinnati Reds on May 30.

In his next start, on June 3, Marichal faced the Dodgers, with the largest crowd of the National League season, 51,853, turning out at the Los Angeles Memorial Coliseum. On the mound for the Dodgers was a left-hander nearing bountiful maturation by the name of Sandy Koufax. An unearned run had Marichal trailing 3–2, heading into the ninth inning. The Giants tied the game on a two-out single and double, but in the bottom of the inning, Dodgers third baseman Daryl Spencer lofted a home run over the Coliseum's high, short left field screen to win the game for Koufax, 4–3. The defeat dropped Marichal's record to 2–3.

A similarly unimpressive 6–7 mark belonged to Marichal when he took the mound on July 27 at Forbes Field. In the contest, Marichal spun his first shutout of the season, five-hitting the Pirates, 2–0. He followed that with a one-hit masterpiece over the Dodgers at the Coliseum on August 2. A Tommy Davis fifth-inning single and two walks permitted the only three Dodgers baserunners in the 6–0 outcome. A third blanking was achieved by Marichal on August 23, against the Cincinnati Reds at Crosley Field. The score was 14–0, expanded by a 12-run ninth-inning by the Giants in which five players hit home runs. It was Marichal's seventh win in a row.

In September, in a game against the Los Angeles Dodgers, Marichal was spiked on his left heel by Duke Snider on a play at first base, and the resulting tendon damage caused him to missed the last three weeks of the season. The sophomore hurler's record was 13–10 with a 3.89 ERA.

* * *

The following season, 1962, the San Francisco Giants gelled into a pennant-winning club. Alvin Dark chose Marichal as the pitcher to open what became a dramatic 165-game National League championship campaign. In the first of ten Opening Day assignments Marichal accrued, the newlywed pitcher hurled a three-hit, home shutout over the Milwaukee Braves on April 10. Marichal had taken five days away from the Giants' Casa Grande training facility in March to marry his Dominican sweetheart. The requested leave came with a rather sentimental blessing from Alvin Dark. "I think everybody should be married, and Juan's in love,"[7] said Dark, himself a devoted family man.

San Francisco leapt off to a fast start. The team was 20–6 when the 4–2 Marichal accepted his seventh mound mission on May 8. On the road, facing the team trailing the Giants in second place, Marichal defeated the St. Louis Cardinals, 4–3, striking out Curt Flood to end the game with the tying run on base. Marichal won two of his next three starts and entered June with a 7–3 record.

In the spacious expanse of a baseball season, all teams encounter peaks and valleys. The Giants wandered into their biggest valley mid-month in June, losing nine of 11 games. Marichal, with four victories overall in the month, used two of them to snap losing streaks of six and three games during the hurtful string. In only his second full season, Marichal seemed to have established himself as the type of pitcher that all managers love, dependable and determined—not to mention one who can interrupt deflating team losing streaks.

The Giants had entered July with a slight half-game lead on the new second-place team, the Los Angeles Dodgers. The Dodgers, gaining 20 wins in July, moved a handful of games into first place ahead of Dark's team at the conclusion of the month.

In a crucial series over the second weekend of August, the Giants swept a home three-game set from Los Angeles. Marichal won the third game, 5–1, on August 12 (his 15th win versus eight defeats). Entering the series, the Dodgers had a chance to inflict serious damage on the pennant hopes of the Giants; instead, the Southern California team left Candlestick Park with its first-place lead trimmed to 2½ games.

When the clubs met again in L.A., three weeks later, the margin of separation had not changed. The Giants won three out of four contests. Marichal was a 3–0 winner on September 5, in the series' third game. The right-hander was forced out of the game after twisting an ankle while covering first base for the last out of the sixth inning. Bobby Bolin kept the shutout intact for the Giants and Marichal received credit for his 18th victory—all but this one by complete game.

Although x-rays did not reveal a break, the pitcher suffered what could best be described as a hairline fracture. His instep swelled, and 16 days passed before he took the mound again. Dark, with suspicious looks, silently questioned the severity of Marichal's foot injury because x-rays had shown no damage. Not only did the play cost Marichal a 20-win season, but when the pitcher returned he was ineffective; hampered by the foot, Marichal was winless in his last two starts of the season.

San Francisco and Los Angeles concluded the campaign in a 101–61 dead heat and engaged in a three-game pennant playoff to decide the National League title.

On October 3, the 11th anniversary of the Giants' miraculous playoff win versus the Dodgers in New York, the West Coast Giants pulled off nearly as breathless a finish by rallying for four runs in the top on the ninth inning of the deciding third playoff game of 1962. Marichal started the game; the right-hander hurled seven innings and left the contest trailing, 4–2. At Dodger Stadium, the battling Giants rallied against Dodgers reliever Ed Roebuck, who had tossed three scoreless relief innings up until the fateful ninth frame. With the 6–4 win, the Giants reaped their first Fall Classic appearance as San Franciscans. Don Larsen, in relief, was the Giants' victorious pitcher in game 165.

The Bay City team squared off against the New York Yankees for the championship of the baseball world. Jack Sanford, the Giants' top winner with 24, Billy O'Dell and Billy Pierce, the teams other frontline hurlers, all made starts ahead of Marichal in the World Series.

In Game 4 at Yankee Stadium, October 8, Marichal made his only Fall Classic appearance. Ahead by two runs, Marichal had the Bronx Bombers shut out for four innings when bad luck struck him again. In the top of the fifth inning, a Whitey Ford fastball careened off Marichal's right index finger on a squeeze bunt attempt. The resulting injury knocked the pitcher out of the game and the remainder of the Series, although he was not scheduled to make another start.

The Giants lost a hard-fought, back-and-forth World Series, whose outcome hung in the balance down to the final out of the final inning of the seventh game.

*   *   *

The year after the Giants lost the World Series, Juan Marichal figured exponentially in his manager's plans. Alvin Dark sensed that he had a thoroughbred in the Dominican pitcher, and the manager turned him loose on the National League in 1963.

Dark gave his right-hander the most starts of his 16-year career, 40. Marichal's response was to tie for the most victories in baseball (25) and lead the league in innings pitched (321⅓). Sandy Koufax also won as many as Marichal, 11 by shutout, led the league in strikeouts, and had an ERA one-half run better than Marichal's 2.41 mark. Koufax, with the lowest ERA in the National League in 20 years, won the Cy Young and Most Valuable Player awards for the world champions Dodgers.

Marichal faced Koufax twice that season and split two decisions. Juan beat Sandy, 7–1, in a Candlestick Park complete game effort on May 24, 13 days after Koufax had, at Marichal's and the Giants' expense at Dodger Stadium, thrown his second career no-hitter.

The two most memorable starts for Marichal in 1963 (and of his career) came within six weeks of the second Koufax meeting. Marichal hurled a no-hit, no-run game against the Houston Colt .45s on June 15. A bit over two weeks later, the pitcher engaged in one of the greatest pitching duels in baseball history, one that will never be seen again as long as the contemporary "pitch-count culture" of baseball endures. In his 1–0 gem against the Colt .45s, Marichal walked two, the only batters to reach base in the game. At only one point in the game was his no-hitter threatened. "The nearest approach to a legitimate hit," wrote San Francisco sportswriter Bob Stevens, "came in the seventh when Carl Warwick ripped a wind-twisted drive close to the left field screen. Willie McCovey grabbed it awkwardly because of the changing flight of the ball."[8]

> "Magnificent," said Carl Hubbell, offering greater scope to the feat because the game was up for grabs almost all of the way through. "You know, I had one myself. But mine wouldn't compare with this one. The difference was that Marichal had to do it the hard way. The first thing in a pitcher's mind is to win, but Juan couldn't even think of a no-hitter until we scored that run in the eighth.
>
> "So it wasn't until the ninth that he could bear down. Up to that time, he didn't know how many innings he'd have to pitch."[9]

"This was the first no-hitter I ever pitched,"[10] revealed Marichal, who ranked the feat second as far as career-level excitement, behind the start he made against the Dodgers in the decisive pennant playoff game.

In June, Marichal posted a 5–0 mark and a 1.57 earned run average. It would have been 6–0 had his manager not decided to remove his top-notch thrower prematurely from a game on June 28, against the Cincinnati Reds. Heading toward his ninth victory in a row and holding a 3–2 lead, Marichal was removed with two outs in the eighth inning and two runners on base. Marichal, who had allowed no earned runs and only two hits (one a two-run home run) and struck out 13, was livid.

The previous season, Dark had removed his young pitcher from a game against the Dodgers with the Giants three runs ahead and one out in the eighth inning. Dark had convinced himself that Marichal was tiring, even though the pitcher had opened and closed his two most recent innings with strikeouts and had 12 for the game. As it happened, the Dodgers rallied against Marichal's replacement and won the game. And now against the Reds, Marichal thought, Dark had stubbornly refused to learn from that decision, and unnecessarily removed him from the mound again. In the June 28 contest, Cincinnati tied the score against Dark's reliever, Billy Hoeft, but the Giants managed to fight right back for the win. A steaming Marichal refused to speak to the press after the game.

As it did in 1962, the pitching change cost Marichal a potential win, but in Dark's defense, this time, Marichal had uncharacteristically walked six Reds, and Dark was a manager known to worry about over-extending his pitchers. Dark reinforced this sentiment a few weeks later when, as National League All-Star Game skipper, he held out the league's top hurlers from the early weekday game. Warren Spahn, Sandy Koufax and Marichal had all made starts on the Sunday prior to the showcase game and were not used by Dark during the National League's 5–3 victory at Cleveland Stadium. Additionally, Marichal and Spahn had participated in a particularly taxing game, to say the least, against each other, two starts and exactly one week prior to the July 9 Mid-Summer Classic.

As the baseball season moved into its fourth month, the Milwaukee Braves visited San Francisco for the second time. Twenty-five-year-old Juan Marichal matched up against 42-year-old Warren Spahn, in the opening game of a three-game set on July 2. Marichal was looking to avenge a 3–1, early season loss to the antediluvian left-hander, who was pitching in his 19th major league campaign. The Giants were in third place, 1½ games behind the top-seeded St. Louis Cardinals, while the Braves were a .500 ball club, in sixth place, 6½ games in arrears of St. Louis. Marichal had won 12 games in 15 decisions for his team, and Spahn was sporting an 11–3 record for the 38–38 Milwaukee team.

At slightly past eight o'clock, Marichal stormed the mound from which he had been unceremoniously removed by Dark four days earlier. After allowing a one-out hit to Braves second baseman Frank Bolling, Marichal made quick work of the next two men to set the side down in the first inning. The Braves left another runner on base to end the second, as Marichal worked past a two-out throwing error by third baseman Harvey Kuenn and retired the next man, Roy McMillan.

Orlando Cepeda, the Giants' fifth-place hitter, obtained the Giants' first hit of the game in the second inning, following the failures of the four preceding teammates against Spahn. Cepeda stole second and advanced to third on catcher Ed Bailey's fly out to right. But José Pagan popped up to Bailey's opposite number, Del Crandall, to end the threat.

Three hitters traipsed to the plate in each half of the third inning and all six fell by the wayside, goaded into four benign bouncers and two aerial outs by the teams' mound adversaries.

In the top of the fourth, Marichal made quick work of the first two batters, but a two-out transgression threatened the pitcher. Marichal walked Norm Larker, and Mack "The Knife" Jones followed with a single to left, moving Larker to second. Crandall followed with a soft single to center that Willie Mays charged, fielded, and threw a strike to the plate to nail Larker trying to score. It had been a charmed half-inning for the Dominican pitcher. Henry Aaron had led off the frame with a drive to deep left field that Marichal said, the next day, he thought was gone. Willie McCovey hauled the ball in a few feet from the fence, as Candlestick Point's strong westerly winds stonewalled the ball's impetus.

McCovey made his only (official) hit of the night in the lower half of the fourth inning with one out, but was forced at second by the next batter, Felipe Alou, who was left stranded at first when the next hitter, Cepeda, popped out.

In the Braves' fifth, Marichal issued his second walk, and as far as walks were concerned, the most tolerable kind—with two down. It was received by Lee Maye; the left fielder then stole second but had no place farther to run after Kuenn snared Frank Bolling's line smash for the third out. Three Giants batters failed to get the ball out of the infield against Spahn in the home half of the fifth, and through five innings of the scoreless contest, Marichal had allowed three hits and two walks, to Spahn's two safeties with no free passes.

Henry Aaron, as he had in the fourth inning, led off in the sixth, but this time only mustered a pop-up to Ed Bailey in foul ground. Denis Menke, who had replaced the less-than–100-per cent Eddie Mathews at third base two innings earlier, batted for the first time. Menke singled, the Braves' fourth hit. The third baseman stole second but died there when the next two hitters lifted elevator-shaft outs on the infield.

Spahn kept his corner outfielders in the game by inducing Marichal to pull a fly out to Lee Maye in left and then by coaxing two opposite-field fly outs from both Kuenn and Mays to Aaron in right field.

In the seventh inning, both pitchers were touched for two hits. Crandall notched his second single but was thrown out at second on a failed hit-and-run attempt by McMillan. The Braves, having already successfully stolen two bases in the game, may have been trying to exploit a perceived weakness in the Marichal-Bailey battery. But this time their aggressiveness cost the club a potential breakthrough. The next hitter, Spahn, doubled deep to right field. He was left anchored to second when Maye grounded out to Cepeda at first.

In the lower half of the stanza, Cepeda and Bailey dented Spahn with consecutive two-out singles. But Spahnie, who had retired ten straight batters before the hits, set down Jim Davenport, pinch-hitting for shortstop José Pagan, on a fly to center fielder Jones.

A one-out walk to Aaron was all Marichal allowed in the eighth inning; Spahn put the Giants down in order in his turn.

In the ninth, Marichal duplicated Spahn's efficiency from the previous half-inning. Willie Mays led off the Giants' hopeful inning and grounded out to shortstop McMillan, Spahn getting an assist when his glove nicked the bouncer. Willie McCovey then stepped to the plate. The Giants' left fielder smoked a pitch deep to right field, just missing a home run—or so said the first base umpire. This was *San Francisco Examiner* sportswriter Curly Grieve's account of the call and the commotion that it set off: "McCovey was so enraged when Chris Pelekoudas called the blast a foul that momentarily it appeared he would push the arbiter around the outfield and wind up ejected in the clubhouse. McCovey, Alvin Dark and [first base coach] Larry Jansen surrounded Pelekoudas, claiming the ball left Candlestick fair. Pelekoudas stuck to his call, which took courage."[11]

McCovey said the following in post-game remarks: "I followed the ball all the way out but evidently the umpire didn't. It was at least three feet fair when it left the park. I think the umpire was watching where it landed and made his call on that. As hard as I hit the ball it didn't have a chance to curve before leaving the ball park."[12] When he stepped back into the batter's box, a disconsolate McCovey grounded out to first base, with Spahn covering. Cepeda popped up to Menke at third, and the game moved into extra innings, scoreless.

Spahn led off the tenth for the Braves, sending a message that he had no immediate plans for leaving the game. He struck out, and Marichal retired the next two batters on ground balls to the infield. In the Giants' half-inning turn, Marichal batted with two outs and a runner at first, making it clear that he also aimed on sticking around if the inning proved fruitless. It did, as Marichal forced the runner at second on a grounder to short.

Into the 11th inning the game advanced. Marichal struck out Aaron, solicited a fly to left from Menke, and induced Larker to ground out to second. Spahn matched his rival's orderly work in the lower part of the frame against the Giants' top three hitters in the order.

Marichal had been uninterruptedly disposing of Braves batters since the eighth, and remarkably, four innings later, nothing had altered. The right-hander recorded his fourth 1–2–3 inning in a row in the 12th, striking out Jones, detouring Crandall on an outfield fly, and retiring McMillan with a roller to third. Spahn, as if he and Marichal were engaged in a diamond-construed game of H-O-R-S-E, sallied forth to face the Giants and promptly induced a fly out and two ground outs in succession, to send the game to the 13th inning.

Beyond the center field fence at Candlestick Park loomed the largest scoreboard in the National League. The innings line score tabulation had turned over and the sparse set of zeros now showing could have misled an unaware eye as to the game's elongated plight. The leadoff batter for the Braves in the 13th was none other than Warren Spahn. For the second time in a row, Marichal struck him out. Maye followed and flied to Felipe Alou in right. The third batter, right-handed hitting Frank Bolling, gained his second hit of the night, a single to the opposite field. The hit ended a streak of 16 consecutive batters retired by Marichal. The Braves had their first baserunner since the eighth inning, and Henry Aaron was coming to the plate.

As the game wore on, Marichal began using a double-rocker windup "to get more speed on my fastball," the pitcher explained. Marichal did not use the double-rocker windup on Aaron with a runner on first, but that he dropped down with a fastball or curve is likely as he made Aaron swing late, which yielded from the dangerous hitter an inning-ending pop-up to first baseman Orlando Cepeda in foul ground.

Spahn had a modest (in comparison to Marichal) streak of eight batters in a row retired abruptly ended with a base hit by the first hitter he faced in the 13th, Ernie Bowman, Pagan's replacement. It was the first time in the entire game that a Giants leadoff batter had reached base against Spahn. The success, however, was short-lived. The left-hander hung Bowman out to dry with a pickoff move to first, Larker to McMillan covering second base for the putout. Then second baseman Chuck Hiller beat a ball into the ground to his infield counterpart, Frank Bolling, who tossed to first for the second out. Marichal was due up next, and Dark considered pulling his burgeoning star pitcher.

Orlando Cepeda, in his co-authored 1998 autobiography, *Baby Bull, From Hardball to Hard Time and Back,* recalled that night and the encounter between pitcher and manager at that point. Dark asked Marichal if he had had enough. Cepeda remembered Marichal barking at Dark, "A 42-year-old man is still pitching. I can't come out!"[13] Marichal, his machismo bruised, could have easily crystallized these or similar thoughts at Dark's proposal for removal. *How could he face his countrymen if he came out of the game before Spahn? Returning to the Dominican Republic having yielded to Spahn would be a thousand times worse than losing to him. "There goes Juan Marichal," his people would say disdainfully when he walked past, "outlasted by an North American pitcher* 17 years *his senior!"* No, Marichal would not come out, he could not come out!

Dark, certainly with the game four days ago weighing somewhat on him, the game in which he yanked Marichal to the pitcher's great displeasure, accepted—or was startled into acceptance by Marichal's ardor—and let him bat and continue in the game. Marichal flied out to complete the inning, and the game pushed forward, zero to zero.

It was five innings past regulation as Marichal toed the far left side of the rubber, his positioning angle to batters that season, to deliver a pitch to leadoff batter Denis Menke. Marichal disposed of Menke via strikeout and then walked Norm Larker. Pinch-hitter Don Dillard followed and was Marichal's tenth and final strikeout victim. Larker was left stranded when Del Crandall tapped back to the box.

The Giants mounted their biggest scoring opportunity against Spahn in the lower half of the 14th. Harvey Kuenn's short, twisting fly fell in between shortstop McMillan and two outfielders for a double. Spahn walked Willie Mays intentionally (his only free pass on the night) to set up the double play. The sagacious left-hander made a money pitch to the next hitter, McCovey, who skyrocketed the offering directly upward, tailing behind home where Crandall cradled it on its downward descent for the first out. Alou, who had solved Spahn for a hit in the ninth, could not do so again and flied out, the runners holding. That brought up Cepeda. The first baseman grounded to third, but Menke booted it, and all runners were safe. That raised the excitement to a level the crowd had not experienced since McCovey's near home run in the ninth. Ed Bailey stepped to the plate with the bases loaded, with every Braves fielder knowing any bobble or late jump on the ball would cost the team and Spahn the game. The loudest, prolonged noise of the tense night was now heard throughout the stadium.

Few, if any of the 15,921 in attendance had left the game, and those watching boisterously cheered with the dual objective of rooting on Bailey and rattling Spahn. But there was no rattling of the World War II combat veteran, and Spahn provoked Bailey to fly to center, deflating the house majority.

Marichal shook off his catcher's failure and assailed the mound for the 15th time. As if he had gained strength against his team's impotency, Marichal overtly restated his unimpeachable position and resolutely retired the side in order. *I will not yield to you, Mr. Spahn. The best you can hope for is a tie.*

Coming off the field after the top of the 15th inning, Marichal or one of his Hispanic teammates might have glanced into the Braves' dugout and spied Spahn peeling off his jacket in order to resume his duties. Above the scratching sounds of returning cleats on the concrete dugout steps and over the slapping noises of a glove or two whacked down in frustration, Marichal or Cepeda or Alou could have easily blurted out in abject frustration, *"Ese maldito viejo no se cansa?"* "Isn't that damned old man tired?" That old man, for the eighth time in the game, set the Giants down in order in the bottom of the 15th inning, Marichal the third out on a strikeout (one of only two whiffs notched by the Braves' starter).

Juan Marichal and Warren Spahn had recorded 90 outs, equally divided through 15 innings of pitching grandeur. Had it been a championship prize fight, a draw could have been declared to no one's contention. Had they been two enslaved gladiators fighting for their lives in an ancient Roman arena, the reigning Caesar would have been compelled to free both of them. Such magnificence from the hill had rarely been displayed in baseball annals by two pitchers in the same game.

As was his custom and as he had done in each of the 15 prior innings, Juan Marichal sprinted to the mound in the top of the 16th with all the appearance and enthusiasm of a schoolboy released from classes for the summer, except that he clutched a baseball glove instead of a glowing report card. Inning after inning after inning, Juan Antonio Marichal had scaled the hilly sandbox that acted as his playground and disposed of batters with a brimming confidence that bordered on nonchalance. How much longer could the bravado of youth sustain him?

Marichal retired the first two batters of the inning on fly outs to right and center fields, respectively. He gave up a two-out hit to Menke, the eighth and final hit he allowed in the game and only the second by the Braves since the seventh inning. Marichal then registered, on a comebacker, his *48th* out, on his *227th* pitch of what was now, according to the scoreboard clock, a new day.

As was his custom and as he had done in each of the 15 prior innings, Warren Spahn strolled to the mound in the bottom of the 16th with all the appearance and enthusiasm of a factory worker walking to his next shift, except that he toted a baseball glove instead of a lunch pail. Inning after inning after inning, Warren Edward Spahn had reached his elevated, dirt-compressed work station and methodically doled out reject-tags to an assembly line of hitters. How much longer before the albatross of advanced age claimed him?

Braves outfielder Don Dillard nestled under a fly ball hit by leadoff batter Harvey Keunn, and with the catch Spahn recorded the first out of the bottom of 16th inning. The left-hander received the thrown-in ball from an infielder and prepared to pitch to the next armed challenger, Willie Mays. The cruelty of baseball for a starting pitcher is that one bad pitch can often ruin the cumulative effort of a hundred good ones. In Spahn's case, at a few minutes past midnight, it was 200 good ones. The same ball Keunn had swung under and lifted to Dillard in center field, Spahn threw as his 201st pitch to Mays.

Mays' bat met Spahn's first pitch with a crackling fury that sent the ball shooting high and far into the heavy San Francisco night, soaring on a shimmering arc of triumph not even the treacherous Candlestick Park winds could betray. And just like that, the dramatically pitched game dramatically ended—Marichal, the exhausted victor, Spahn, the valiantly defeated. The home run was the ninth hit allowed by Spahn.

After the game, Marichal informed all those who were not aware that he had been involved in a similar game in Class A ball. In that effort, Marichal was the losing pitcher of

A true pitching maestro on the mound, a sometimes sidearm-slinging Marichal made it that much more difficult on National League hitters.

a 1–0 game, in 17 innings. He was quick to add that this game had a much happier outcome for him, "thanks to Willie."

One of Alvin Dark's post-game quotes sounded a bit camouflaged. "I hate to see a pitcher go that long," the manager said. "I wanted to take Juan out, but he said he was strong enough to go on. Naturally, I left him in."[14]

"I've been around a long time and that's the finest exhibition of throwing I've ever seen," Henry Aaron asserted. "It may be 10 years or even 20 before you see another its equal."[15]

The game would not be complete without returning to that baseball savant known as Willie Mays. In the fourth inning, Mays threw a runner out at the plate from center field, which allowed this game for the pitching ages to develop, and then won the game in the 16th inning with a home run. That was Willie Mays, every day.

It had been nine years since two pitchers had locked up in a scoreless duel the length of Marichal and Spahn's game. Only once in the more than half-century since has one pitcher thrown as many innings in one baseball game as thrown by Marichal against Spahn.[16]

Both Marichal and Spahn made their appointed starts five days later with no ill after-effects (the Sunday before the All-Star Game). Spahn complained of a sore elbow, which apparently flared up on him enough to land him twice on the disabled list. He still went on to lead the league in complete games with 22 at season's end.[17]

In his second start following the spectacular confrontation with Spahn, and the first following the All-Star Game, Marichal defeated the Philadelphia Phillies, 4–3, on July 11. Bobby Bolin came on in the ninth for the save after Marichal allowed a two-run home run. Marichal then suffered his toughest loss of the season on July 15. He took a 1–0 lead into the ninth inning at Forbes Field, but could not get anyone out as the Pirates rallied for two runs and the win on a bases-loaded single by Willie Stargell. Marichal won twice more in July as the Giants, in the middle of the National League pack, ten games off the pace, reeled off nine wins in a row to get back into contention. During the win streak, the team picked up 6½ games on the first-place Dodgers in only ten days. At the close of July, Dark found himself guiding a second-place team, 4½ games from the top spot.

But in August, the 17–5 Marichal was a mediocre 2–3 and fell to 19–8. The Giants also played .500 baseball at 14–14, and should have considered themselves fortunate to have fallen only two games further back in the standings.

Three days into September, Marichal became a 20-game winner for the initial time, with an easy 16–3 home win over the Chicago Cubs. Of his six remaining starts, Marichal won five with one no-decision. All five victories were complete games. Marichal finished the season with a sterling 25–8 record.

The Dodgers, though, in the month were as hot as Marichal, and the Los Angelinos won the pennant by a comfortable six games over St. Louis. Dark's Giants lagged in third, 11 games in the distance.

* * *

After returning to the Dominican after the major league season as a 25-game winner, inexplicably the pitcher's own people turned on him. It had been a laborious campaign for Marichal with over 300 innings pitched, and with little respite, he was back pitching for the Escogido Leones in late October.

Soon after, the fans in the pitcher's home country accused Marichal of virtual treason for wanting to rest over a portion of the winter, instead of continuing to pitch for Escogido. Marichal compromised and pitched 60 winter league innings (including a 13-inning loss against Valencia in an interleague mini-series played by Escogido in Venezuela). Then, with spring training less than two months away, Marichal decided to give his arm a rest. For those Dominicans devoted to the game, the pitcher's decision was an affront to their national identity. The Marichal name was smeared in the sporting press, and at one game, with the Marichals in attendance as spectators, the couple required a police escort from the stadium when fans around them became abusive. "Everywhere I went people would call me names," Marichal was quoted in *Sports Illustrated.* "One day at the ballpark a bunch of guys sitting around me threatened to kill me. My wife and I couldn't get out without a policeman. There must have been 50 cops to get us out. We were really scared."[18]

Marichal abided the scare but was so disenchanted by his countrymen's actions that he decided to make San Francisco his year-round residence. The pitcher filed for the required U.S. residency papers. The move caused an uproar at home, as the press and populace there misinterpreted the residency documents as citizenship papers and accused Marichal of renouncing his country. Things had cooled somewhat by the time Marichal reported to the Giants' training facility in Casa Grande.

As the start of the 1964 season rolled around for the Giants, Marichal was named the Opening Day starter for the second time in three years. The right-hander opened the season with six consecutive victories, stretching to 12 his streak of decisions without a loss, dating to last season.

On Opening Day, Marichal downed the Milwaukee Braves and Warren Spahn, 8–4. The pitcher received a no-decision against the Cincinnati Reds in his second start, five days later on April 19. In his first road start, Marichal coasted to a 15–5 win over the same team five days afterward. Then a 4–0 combined-shutout win over the Chicago Cubs, April 29, was followed by back-to-back wins over the Los Angeles Dodgers.

The second victory over the Dodgers came as a 5–0, five-hit victory at Candlestick Park on May 8. Four days later, Marichal followed with another five-hit shutout, this time over the Houston Colt .45s at Colt Stadium. Following a no-decision against the New York Mets, Marichal absorbed his first loss, 7–2, to the Philadelphia Phillies on May 20, as he allowed six earned runs. In St. Louis on May 27, the Giants, behind Marichal, handed a 4–0 Bob Gibson his first defeat of the season, 2–1. The first two batters of the game for San Francisco, Chuck Hiller and Duke Snider—playing in his last major league campaign—homered against the Cardinals' right-hander. Marichal allowed seven hits, struck out 11 and walked none.

St. Louis gained more than a measure of revenge when it came back to beat Marichal twice during the following month, by 7–6 and 1–0 scores. On June 23, Marichal improved to 9–3, tossing his third shutout of the year, 4–0, over Cincinnati at Crosley Field. In his next start, June 27, Marichal became a ten-game winner with an easy 9–1 home triumph over the rival Dodgers. The win gave the Giants a record of 43–27 and put the team in a virtual tie for first place with the Philadelphia Phillies.

Marichal won four of his next six decisions. In between, he was the winning pitcher for the National League in the All-Star Game on July 7, played at baseball's newest outdoor venue, New York's Shea Stadium. Johnny Callison's home run with two men on base in the Nationals' last turn at bat thrillingly delivered the 7–4 victory. On July 29, in a ten-inning,

6–3 road win over the Phillies, Marichal won his 15th game with his 15th complete game. The last 23 batters failed to hit a ball out of the infield as Marichal set down the final 19 hitters in succession. The victory pushed the 58–43 Giants to within one-half game of first place.

Two days later, the pitcher awoke with a back pain so debilitating that he could not bend over to tie his shoes. The pain and recovery period prevented Marichal from making six starts. Dark publicly questioned his pitcher's fortitude.[19] Marichal, not fully healed, made a road start against the Dodgers on August 25, and was beaten by a 3–1 count. Eight days later, Marichal returned to the mound and shut out the Mets, 4–0, at New York. On September 6, Marichal beat the first-place Phillies at Connie Mack Stadium, 4–3. He struck out 13 hitters, including seven in a row from the third to fifth innings.

The Giants stayed in contention for most of September, then fell off the pennant path and eventually dropped behind three teams involved in a hotly-contested pennant race. As a result of the late September implosion of the Phillies, San Francisco was able to crawl to within three games of the pennant-winning Cardinals, in fourth place, on the final day of the season.

Marichal won five of his last seven starts, and one of the two losses he suffered came as his second 1–0 defeat of the season. On September 23, the pitcher collected his 20th win, 4–1, over the Colt .45s in Houston. His final record was 21–8, his ERA 2.48.

* * *

The frustration Marichal felt, at times, with Alvin Dark's handling was no longer a cause for concern in 1965, as the manager was dismissed by the team after his fourth season at the Giants helm. Herman Franks was named new Giants manager. It took some time for Franks to put his squad in gear, and the early season drudgery cost the Giants the pennant. After 50 games, San Francisco was 27–23; over the remainder of campaign, the team produced a 68–44 record fell just short of the Los Angeles Dodgers at the top of the standings.

A ten-inning, 1–0 Opening Day loss to Bob Veale and the Pittsburgh Pirates did little to discourage Marichal from his appointed role as staff ace. Marichal confirmed the position by spinning a career-high ten shutouts over his next 36 starts, from which he gleaned 22 wins and shrank his ERA to the lowest mark he had yet attained, 2.13.

The special year took shape early for Marichal, and the New York Mets formed a discontented part of it. In New York's season-inaugurating homestand, Marichal bounced back from the tough loss to Veale and vanquished the Mets, 4–0, on April 17. Marichal improved his lifetime record against the lambkin New York team to 10–0 with a 1.10 ERA in 98⅓ innings. During the Giants' first homestand of the season the following week, Marichal avenged his loss to the Pirates (3–2) and blanked the Mets again, 5–0, for his third win.

Early in May, Marichal defeated, as a reliever, Sandy Koufax. Marichal had not been able to make his scheduled start in the May 9 home game against the Dodgers' left-hander due to a sinus affliction. Manager Franks turned to Marichal later in the game and summoned the pitcher in the eighth inning with the Dodgers threatening to untie a 2–2 contest. Marichal could not prevent the Dodgers from taking the lead, but the Giants scored four runs (three against Koufax) in their subsequent at-bat, with Marichal singling in the final run of the inning against Koufax's reliever Bob Miller. Marichal recorded three additional outs in the ninth to gain credit for the 6–3 win.

The San Francisco starter won four games in May and was a respectable 7–5 when he faced Cincinnati at Crosley Field on June 5. Marichal outdueled Jim Maloney, 1–0, allowing five hits, with no walks, and striking out nine. Five days later, Marichal blanked Casey Stengel's men again, 3–0, at Shea Stadium. Nine days afterward, on June 19, the Dominican raised his career mark to 13–0 against the cellar-dwellers from Queens, when he defeated the Mets again, 2–1. Jack Fisher was the tough-luck loser.

It was not only the second division teams that Juan Marichal triumphed over with regularity, as manifested on June 28, with the Giants pitcher's tenth Candlestick Park victory over the Dodgers without a loss. The 5–0, six-hitter was Marichal's third career home whitewash of the men from Los Angeles. Marichal topped Don Drysdale, who was undone by three costly errors, two by his own hand. It was Marichal's second victory over Drysdale, having defeated the reliable Dodgers pitcher, 2–1, earlier in the month.

Including the second win over Drysdale, Marichal pitched a trio of shutouts in five starts, mixed in with a pair of losses. The other whitewashes were in road starts against the Chicago Cubs (4–0; five hits, no walks, nine Ks), and the Philadelphia Phillies (a 7–0, two-hitter). His two defeats were by the scores of 3–1, at Candlestick Park, to the Phillies' Jim Bunning (Marichal allowed two runs in eight innings) and 3–2, to the St. Louis Cardinals at Busch Stadium.

Marichal had seven shutouts and a record of 14–7 at the All-Star Game pause. At Minnesota's Metropolitan Stadium on July 13, the pitcher made the first of his two All-Star Game starts, hurling three scoreless innings for his league, which nosed out a 6–5 win. For the one hit-allowed effort, Marichal was named MVP, the first Hispanic player so recognized in the fan-popular game. In his first start after the mid-season break, on July 17, Marichal blanked, on five hits, the "Astros," the nickname-changed team from Houston now residing in a new "space-age" stadium called the Astrodome. Four more wins followed, the last on Marichal's ninth shutout.

The ninth whitewash was muraled at home on August 18, by the score of 5–0, over, yes, the Mets. Poised for his third 20-win campaign following the suppression of the Mets, Marichal was hoping to reach the plateau in his next start, which was scheduled against the Dodgers. The National League had five teams within five games of first place on the day of Marichal's 19th win, and two of the top three teams were the Giants and Dodgers. The archrivals met for four games over an extended weekend, starting Thursday, August 19. The final game of the series resulted in a malicious brawl in which Marichal and Dodgers catcher John Roseboro were the main event antagonists.

The Scene: Sunday afternoon at clear and breezy Candlestick Park. Squaring off on the mound: the two best pitchers in baseball, Juan Marichal and Sandy Koufax. The Rivalry: long-running and hateful. The Stakes: an intensely close pennant chase. The Game: culminating contest of a hotly contested four-game series. The Episode: a nefarious incident with Juan Marichal, at the plate, striking John Roseboro over the head with his bat in a fit of anger. The Rage: triggered by Roseboro's return throw to the pitcher which nearly hit Marichal. The Result: Marichal was suspended for ten days and fined for his violent action, which opened a blood-letting gash in the Dodgers' catcher's cranium. (Roseboro was fortunately not seriously hurt.)

In Marichal's *Pitcher's Story* autobiography, he explained his side of the incident: "I was looking at Koufax. Then I felt the ball tick my right ear. If I had turned my head it would have hit me in the face. Nobody has to throw a ball that close and that hard."[20] Marichal then confronted Roseboro for an explanation. The catcher replied with an expletive, Marichal wrote. Marichal also felt intimidated by Roseboro's catching gear, construed in Marichal's boiling rage as armor. "He's got the mask, the chest protector," explained the pitcher. "I don't think I can fight with a guy like that. I know from the way he was coming toward me, he was coming to fight. I hit him one time—the first time. I was sorry about what had happened. I was sorry [I was out of the game]. I don't like to fight, but I don't like anyone to hit me."[21] Marichal also apologized publicly for his actions and, later, to Roseboro.

Roseboro, a hard-nosed catcher, aware of prior Dodgers-Giants beanball wars, initially wanted to put the incident behind him, but later sued the man he called "a coward" for damages amounting to $110,000 (the suit was eventually settled in 1970 for $7,500).

In today's multiple media sports scene, the negative saturation wrought from the incident would have probably left Juan Marichal with a more permanent stain than it ultimately did. Not that there was not a great deal of outrage over the incident at the time. Many in the print-dominated media felt the suspension and fine Marichal drew were not severe enough. (The fine was $1,750, the largest fine ever handed down by a league to a major league player.) Marichal, for his part, was regretful and showed immediate remorse.

The pitcher's eligible return to the mound came on September 2, in Philadelphia. Marichal's appearance was met with expected derision. He was booed at every opportunity by most of the 30,410 fans in attendance, and was defeated by Chris Short, 4–3.

The president of the National League, Warren Giles, prohibited the scorned pitcher from accompanying the Giants to Los Angeles, the final leg of their road trip. With the Giants right on the first-place Dodgers' tail and in order to avoid another pitching "layoff" because of the Giles edict, Marichal volunteered to pitch on two days' rest on September 5, the game prior to the two-game mini-series in L.A. Franks agreed, and Marichal beat the Cubs at Wrigley Field, 4–2, yielding two solo homers to Billy Williams, while striking out ten.

The repeat 20-game winner won his next two starts, both against Houston, to improve to 22–10, but then suffered three straight defeats, in two of which he was hit hard. In his last start of the season, on September 30, Marichal received a no-decision, allowing two runs in seven innings against the Cincinnati Reds. The Giants won the game, 5–3. In relief, Masanori Murakami, the first Japanese major league player, picked up the last of his five career wins.

San Francisco, with three games to play, trailed the Dodgers by two games, and were unable to make up any more ground on the eventual pennant-winners.

*   *   *

The San Francisco Giants criticized Marichal during contract negotiations the following spring because he had lost three of four decisions to close the season, noting that the Giants lost the 1965 pennant by two games to the Los Angeles Dodgers. A 23-day hold-out ensued before the three-time 20-game winner agreed to terms on a contract calling for $70,000.

In a late spring training game between the Dodgers and Giants, Marichal batted with Roseboro behind the plate without incident. No verbal exchanges were made between the two men before or during the game. Roseboro had batted against Marichal first, in their initial diamond encounter since the previous summer's bloody incident. Roseboro hit a three-run inside-the-park home run (the ball took a high hop over charging outfielder Jesús Alou, allowing the burly catcher to circle the bases standing up). "I didn't feel any tension," Roseboro said after the game, probably not altogether truthfully but professionally spoken. "It was just another game as far as I was concerned."[22] Marichal himself would not address the topic. It seemed clear both men wanted to move on.

Marichal cracked the 300-innings barrier for a second time in 1966 and, in early June, was featured on the cover of *Time* with the title, "Best Right Arm in Baseball." As such, Marichal became the first Hispanic athlete to grace the cover of what is considered North America's most prestigious magazine.[23] That right arm won for Marichal his first seven starts, six of them by complete games. Manager Herman Franks pulled the pitcher after five innings on May 7 because the Giants had broken the contest open with a 13-run third inning. Marichal's pitching, along with an 11-game team win streak, propelled the Giants to a 22–7 start.

In his eighth starting assignment, on May 17, Marichal pitched ten innings against the Dodgers, allowing one run, in a game the Giants lost in 13 innings, 2–1. It had appeared Marichal would obtain his third shutout of the campaign, but the Dodgers scratched across a run in the ninth frame to tie the contest. It was Marichal's first start at Dodger Stadium since the Roseboro bat incident (the Dodgers catcher was 0-for-5 in the game). Marichal received the expected boos, but surprisingly, the still-sensitized fandom within the packed house also jeered Don Drysdale when he came inside with hard pitches to Willie Mays.

Marichal tossed his third and fourth shutouts in consecutive starts on May 22 and 26. The latter one was exceptional as it took 14 innings to defeat the Philadelphia Phillies, 1–0. Jim Bunning threw the first ten stanzas for the Philadelphia team. Marichal allowed six hits, walked one, and struck out ten in the exhibition of prime pitching played at Candlestick Park. On the last day of May, Marichal beat the Cincinnati Reds, 5–3, to run his record to a perfect 10–0.

Quickly, talk began to circulate about Marichal winning 30 games. The buzz lessened considerably after Marichal lost his next two games. The Phillies' Chris Short and Houston's Mike Cuéllar beat the previously undefeated pitcher with identical 6–1 complete games. Marichal straightened himself out with three victories in succession. He defeated the Dodgers and Drysdale, 3–2, and avenged his recent defeat to Houston, 2–1. Marichal's 13th win came against the Chicago Cubs on June 21. As indicated by the final score of 9–7, the complete game victory was not achieved in his usual dominating manner. A *Chicago Tribune* writer confirmed as much in the following account of the encounter:

Juan Marichal was more devastating as a hitter and baserunner yesterday than he was as a pitcher. In one of the most bitterly-contested struggles of the season in Wrigley Field, Marichal seemed to be in the middle of everything.

Until Marichal slid hard into third base in the seventh inning and sent Ron Santo writhing to the turf in pain, there was firm belief among most of the 11,483 witnesses that the Cubs were destined to whip him. Marichal stayed to watch the ministrations to his fallen victim at third base and heard a chorus of boos as he trotted to the dugout.[24]

The two teams combined for seven runs in the ninth inning, with the Giants accounting for four of them. Marichal drove in his second run of the game with his second base hit. Santo, who had been removed from the field on a stretcher following the spiking from Marichal, was taken to the hospital to receive a precautionary tetanus shot. The next day, Santo played every inning of a doubleheader loss to the Giants.

With the victory over the Cubs, Marichal re-established a 30-win pace that was ahead of baseball's last 30-game winner, Dizzy Dean. But another NL pitcher, Sandy Koufax, became the first pitcher to reach 14 wins on June 26. Marichal matched Koufax's win total in early July. The Giants hurler then gained his 15th win—halfway to the ethereal pitching mark—in the Giants' 89th game; victimized in the 8–1 victory were the Philadelphia Phillies, on July 15 on their home ground.

But perhaps an indication that it was not meant to be came in Marichal's next outing on July 20. Marichal was nearly beaten by the New York Mets for the first time in his career. Trailing 2–1, entering the ninth inning, his teammates tied the game and spared Marichal a loss; by the same token, their weak support had prevented a potential win by their starter. The Giants lost the home game in the next inning, 3–2. Hurling the extra-inning distance, Jack Fisher outpitched the Giants right-hander, who had been removed for a pinch-hitter in the bottom of the eighth inning.

Following a 2–1 home win over the Pittsburgh Pirates on July 25, for win number 16, Marichal suffered an accidental injury to his right middle finger when a car door slammed shut on it. Marichal had to miss one start. He then made a relief appearance against the Mets in New York. The call from the bullpen, 1⅓ innings in duration, was a test for the bruised finger, which responded well enough for Marichal to take the mound two days later, on August 4, to start the final game of the Giants-Mets' four-game series. Marichal took a 6–4 lead into the ninth inning and was relieved when he allowed a lead-off homer to Ken Boyer. Teammate Ron Swoboda later hit a three-run home run, giving the Mets an exciting 8–6 home win in front of more than 41,000 fans who showed up for the Thursday afternoon engagement. (A Swoboda round-tripper had also provided the winning run in Fisher's 3–2, ten-inning win in San Francisco two weeks earlier.) The Giants bullpen denied Marichal, who gave up three earned runs in the game, a chance at his 18th win, setting back further the 30-win pace for the ace pitcher.

The 30-win hope faded for good when nearly three weeks passed before Marichal picked up his next win. The seemingly jinxed hurler was forced to miss another start after jamming his ankle by inadvertently stepping on a baseball while running in the outfield. He lost, 3–0, to the Astros on August 13. In his next start, on August 17, Marichal was removed after only two innings, having surrendered three runs to the St. Louis Cardinals. The pitcher won his subsequent two starts, beating Cincinnati and Los Angeles.

On August 31, Marichal won his 20th game, over his favorite team, the Mets. It was a close game, 2–1; dual four-hitters were tossed by the superlative Dominican and Jack Fisher, who allowed only one earned run. It was a Wednesday evening, and in excess of 50,000 fans turned out at Shea Stadium—one day after 50,000-plus fans had clicked through the turnstiles to watch astonishingly as the ninth-place Mets soundly defeat Sandy Koufax. It might have been too great a leap of faith for even the quixotic fans of the young and predisposed-with-losing New York Mets franchise to hope to conquer Koufax and Marichal, *back-to-back*. It would have been a "Homeric"—as the *New York Times'* Joseph Durso termed it— achievement, *if* it had come to pass. Marichal, with his tight victory, spoiled what would have been the grandest two days in Flushing, Queens, since the opening of 1939 and 1964 World's Fairs.

Marichal won five more games in his six remaining starts. A particularly pulsating triumph was gained on September 21, against the Pittsburgh Pirates. In a 3–3 deadlock at Candlestick Park, the mound wizard permitted two ninth-inning runs (one unearned) to the hard-hitting Bucs. But in the lower half-inning, catcher Tom Haller cracked a two-run home run to tie the game. Then, becoming the first Hispanic pitcher to hit a walk-off home run, Marichal followed Haller with his second career homer to give himself a 6–5 win.

Four games separated the first-place Dodgers and third-place Giants in the National League standings after Marichal stepped to the mound on September 26 and downed the Braves, 8–2, in the franchise's relocated city of Atlanta. With six days remaining in the season, the Giants, who were also 1½ games behind the second-place Pittsburgh Pirates, seemed out of the race. But the Pirates lost five of their final seven games and the Dodgers also stumbled a bit coming down to the wire.

The Giants, after sweeping a doubleheader from the Pirates on October 1—Marichal winning his 25th game in the opener—actually had an outside chance to tie for the pennant. The Giants trailed the Dodgers by two games entering the last day of the campaign, October 2. The San Francisco team needed to win its final game that day and required the Dodgers to lose both games of their scheduled doubleheader against the Philadelphia Phillies. That scenario would force a makeup game of an earlier rained-out contest to be played by the Giants that, if they won, would force yet another pennant-deciding playoff between the Dodgers and Giants. The Dodgers, however, split their doubleheader and won the National League crown by 1½ games over their archrivals.

On a personal note, 1966 was Marichal's greatest season to date, and arguably his greatest ever (though in other seasons he would have more wins and shutouts, and have a slightly better ERA in another). Baseball's only 20-game winner four years running was defeated only six times in 36 starts. Excluding his one relief victory, Marichal won 24 games, completing all of them except the one in which the Giants' offense exploded early and handed him a big lead, prompting his manager to remove him. Only 11 times during the entire season did Marichal fail to finish a game that he started. Opposing teams hit a National League-low .202 against him. The redoubtable right-hander allowed only 36 walks in 307⅓ innings. Marichal held batters to a .230 on-base percentage, the best in both circuits.

No pitcher in baseball, except Koufax, had recorded more wins and shutouts over the past four seasons. (Koufax won 27 games for the repeat National League champions and soon won his third Cy Young Award.)

That winter, Marichal traveled home and was ceremoniously honored with other returning major league Dominican ball-playing heroes by President Joaquín Balaguer.

* * *

The surprise retirement of Sandy Koufax left Juan Marichal as the game's premier pitcher in 1967. Koufax, after a much-publicized and protracted dual holdout with Don Drysdale, had earned $120,000 in 1966. Marichal asked for the same amount for 1967. It was not about the money for the 29-year-old hurler. He was prospering elsewhere, through the agricultural expansion of his family farm, which he had now grown to more than 1,000 acres. Marichal's lifetime record was 130 wins and 58 losses. He was an athlete at the top of his profession and he simply wanted to be paid accordingly.

After another holdout, Marichal settled for $100,000, the first Hispanic pitcher to reach this monetary plateau. Marichal had the satisfaction of knowing that he had reached the symbolic compensation mark in his seventh full season, while it had taken Koufax 12

As if to indicate more good things are ahead, Marichal shows his pitching grip to team owner Horace Stoneham on March 27, 1967. The now amiable pair had just come to terms on a new contract, ending an extended holdout by the sensational San Francisco pitcher. By signing on the dotted line, Marichal became the first Hispanic pitcher to earn $100,000 in the major leagues.

years and Don Drysdale, baseball's only other $100,000 pitcher, 11 years, to achieve a six-figure salary.

The repeat contract stalemate left Marichal barely two weeks to prepare for the season's opener. The short spring had not hurt him in 1966, but it was a different story in 1967. Marichal lost his first three outings. His control, which was normally impeccable, was off, and he admitted the limited time in training camp had caught up with him this time around.

But beginning on April 25, Marichal reeled off eight victories in a row. The high-kicking right-hander mowed down the Reds, Dodgers, Mets, Cubs, Astros, Cubs, Astros and Dodgers, all in complete-game succession. The Philadelphia Phillies and Jim Bunning snapped the string on May 30, with a 5–4 decision at Candlestick Park.

Marichal copped his ninth win four days afterward at home over the Mets, 11–2. It was Marichal 19th straight victory over his favorite patsies. But he suffered a no-decision to the Cincinnati Reds and a ten-inning loss (4–3) to the Atlanta Braves in two subsequent trips to the mound. On June 20, Marichal won for the tenth time, five-hitting the Reds in San Francisco, 5–1. Bill Singer of the Dodgers shut out the Giants and Marichal, 2–0, but Marichal turned around and defeated the Phillies, 12–3, on June 30.

During the same Eastern road swing, a three-game series with the occupants of Shea Stadium was scheduled, during which the maestro finally lost his touch. This artful lead by sportswriter Leonard Koppett captured the civic sentiment surrounding the occurrence:

> Always sensitive to the symbolic, the New York Mets used July 4 for a modest declaration of independence of their own yesterday by beating Juan Marichal of the Giants for the first time, 8–7.
>
> King Juan, who has clear claim to the rank of baseball's most distinguished pitcher now that Sandy Koufax has taken his arthritic elbow to a broadcasting booth, had beaten the Mets 19 times in succession. Not even Koufax was that tyrannical in the years since 1962, when the Mets were created decidedly unequal.[25]

The Mets' revolt against King Juan consisted of 14 hits and eight runs (five earned), while running Marichal off in the sixth inning. Jack Fisher was the well-supported deposer.

Marichal split his next four decisions. Earning his 14th victory on August 1, against the Pittsburgh Pirates, 3–1, the pitcher was on target for a fifth straight 20-win campaign. But running in between starts, Marichal pulled his right hamstring muscle and was not able to pitch again until August 25. Obviously rusty upon his return, he was knocked around for 11 hits in under five innings by the Atlanta Braves. In suffering his tenth loss, 5–1, Marichal re-aggravated the hamstring injury.

Marichal could not push off the mound without enormous pain, and the injury prevented Marichal from any further pitching during the remaining five weeks of the season.

* * *

In the National League, the St. Louis Cardinals had coasted to the 1967 pennant and an eventual World Series title. The Giants finished a distant second, an outcome that would not have changed even with Marichal pitching in September. Still, negative whispers had circulated around the seriousness of Marichal's hamstring injury.

In 1968, Marichal completely suppressed any remnants of those detracting soft voices and left no doubt about his desire to pitch. He high-kicked his way to *30* complete games in 38 starts and set a personal high in wins with 26, one short of matching his, by now, well-known uniform number.

On Opening Day, April 10, the Giants saved the removed Marichal from a loss against the New York Mets, when they rallied for three ninth-inning runs against Tom Seaver and reliever Danny Frisella, to pull out a 5–4 Candlestick Park win. Four days following the no-decision, the Giants team continued its early charitable treatment toward Marichal by scoring 13 runs against the Philadelphia Phillies in the pitcher's return to the hill. Marichal allowed two runs in recording his first win of the campaign. He won two more games in April and five more in May, while suffering only two setbacks.

The nine-year veteran registered his eighth win on May 29 against the world champion Cardinals, 2–1. The victory nudged the first-place Giants into a slightly firmer 1½-game lead over the Atlanta Braves. Six more victories in as many decisions hiked Marichal's record to 14–2, three-quarters of the way through June. Then on June 27, the pitcher absorbed his third loss of the campaign. This defeat, to the visiting Dodgers, ended two lengthy winning streaks Marichal had perpetuated. The Dodgers' Zoilo Versalles homered in the 11th inning to send Marichal and the Giants to a 6–5 defeat. The loss snapped Marichal's personal ten-game winning streak and marked his first-ever reversal at Candlestick Park to the hated Dodgers in 15 decisions.

Also at Candlestick Park, the 30-year-old hurler won his 15th game on July 2, a 5–0 five-hitter over the Braves. At this point, the Giants and Braves had fallen 7½ games behind a blistering St. Louis squad, which had assumed the chief position in the National League standings. Four days later, on July 6, Marichal engaged that season's eventual Cy Young Award winner, Bob Gibson. At Candlestick Park, the Cardinals' right-hander, tossing one of an incredible 13 shutouts on the season, bested Marichal and the Giants, 3–0. It was the 30th win in 39 games for the streaking Redbirds. The loss dropped the sagging, fourth-place Giants to 42–41, 10 ½ games off the pace.

Marichal next pitched as the first pitcher out of the National League bullpen in the All-Star Game in the Astrodome. He hurled two perfect innings. The game's only run had already been scored for starter and winner Don Drysdale.

It was against Drysdale, who himself threw eight shutouts that season and set a record for consecutive scoreless innings pitched, that Marichal secured his 20th win, on August 1. Three singles were all Marichal allowed to the Dodgers in the 2–0 road victory. But with eight weeks to play in the season and the 53–52 Giants 17 games out of first place, only Marichal's pitching and the swatting of Willie McCovey (the league's home run and RBI champion) appeared to be reasons for Giants fans to remain interested in the rest of the campaign.

It bears mentioning that in eight All-Star Game appearances, Marichal allowed only one earned run, and seven hits, in 18 innings pitched for an ERA of 0.50. Among starting pitchers with at least nine innings of work, only Mel Harder bettered Marichal's effectiveness, with 13 innings and no runs allowed, in his four All-Star selections. Marichal tied with Lefty Gómez and Jim Bunning for the second most All-Star innings thrown, behind Drysdale's 19⅓ frames.

While the Giants would play better ball than anyone but the Cardinals over the last two months, two teams Marichal was accustomed to beating—the Mets and Dodgers—turned the tables on him and handed him losses in August to prevent a stronger pass at greater glory.

The home defeat to the Mets came in an especially disenchanting manner. In the game on August 9, Marichal held a 4–2 lead, entering the ninth inning. The right-hander secured two outs, but also gave up three singles and a run. Down to the their last out, with runners on first and third base, the Mets' Cleon Jones hit a high pop-up between home and the mound. The entire Giants infield surrounded the ball, fighting the swirling Candlestick Park winds. Finally, third baseman Jim Davenport called for the crazily descending ball; he lunged, but could not make the grab, as the ball carried away from him at the last moment. Both baserunners scored on the error, providing the tying and winning runs of the game after the Giants failed to answer in their last at-bat. (Marichal probably could not have complained too loudly. His team *had* bailed him out of the apparent Opening Day loss to the same Mets at the same locale by scoring three runs in the ninth inning.)

Marichal then won three straight starts, over the Pirates, Phillies and Mets. The Los Angeles Dodgers, temporarily in last place, scratched out a 5–4 win over the 23-game winner on August 25, scoring a run in the ninth inning, set up by Marichal's own error. A third second-division team (and eventual National League basement tenants), the Houston Astros, defeated Marichal on August 29, by the count of 6–1.

The marvelous pitcher won his next two starts over Chicago and St. Louis, giving him a 25–7 record, but lost on September 11 to the Braves, 3–1. Marichal did not start again for nine days. When he returned to the mound, the staff ace downed Atlanta, 8–1. His 26 wins were the most by a Giants pitcher since Carl Hubbell attained as many in 1936.

On September 25, with a chance to tie Adolfo Luque for most wins by a Hispanic pitcher in a season, Marichal, in his last outing of the campaign, went down to a 3–2 defeat, in the Astrodome to the Astros and Dave Guisti.

* * *

The Giants had clawed into second place, nine games behind the Cardinals in 1968; it was the team's fourth second-place finish in a row under Herman Franks. In team management's eyes, it was a commendable but unsatisfactory accounting for the manager. The Bay Area franchise replaced Franks and chose Clyde King as its manager for the 1969 season. All National League clubs now had to focus on a different path to the pennant, in baseball's first year of divisional alignment. As one of six teams in the newly created National League West Division, the Giants opened the season, on April 7, against co-division inhabitants, the Atlanta Braves.

Marichal made his seventh Opening Day start, and was ordinary, giving up three runs in six innings and receiving a no-decision in Atlanta's 5–4 home win.

By anyone's standards, the first six weeks of the season were good for Marichal. He had a 5–2 record, with two shutouts and five complete games in ten starts. The Giants were pressing for the division lead, two games behind Atlanta in second place. The Giants' best pitcher was then derailed by a groin pull and a "sore side muscle." The afflictions caused him to miss three starts.

By June 7, he was all better. Marichal spun a three-hit victory over the Philadelphia Phillies, 3–1; Cookie Rojas spoiled the shutout with a two-out, ninth-inning single. Including that start, the workhorse right-hander threw 22 complete games in his final 26 starts, winning 16 of them. Marichal recorded his seventh win and third shutout on June 17, by a 4–0 count against the Cincinnati Reds at Candlestick Park.

Three starts later, on July 2, with a 6–3 decision over the San Diego Padres, Marichal notched his tenth triumph. It was the expansion Padres that handed Marichal his fourth setback on July 15, by the score of 10–3. Marichal gave up seven runs but only one was earned. Marichal retired the first two batters in the Padres' fifth inning. Giants shortstop Tito Fuentes bobbled a grounder for an error, allowing the inning to continue. In one of those unexplainable sequential baseball happenings, Marichal was unable to retire another batter, as eight more Padre hitters batted and six runs scored before the inning's final out was registered by a Giants reliever.

The same day, the All-Star team was announced and Marichal received his eighth nomination. Marichal did not receive an opportunity to pitch in the star-studded classic, the National League's seventh win in a row over the junior circuit. But he pitched the day after the game, on July 24, and lost to the St. Louis Cardinals and Nelson Briles, 2–1. It was the first of four straight losses incurred by the right-hander.

Four days later, Marichal, who was usually money in the bank with any kind of lead in the late innings, lost a game against the Chicago Cubs that seemed to have been put away except for one remaining formality out. Scoring a run in the tenth frame at Wrigley Field, the Giants gave their grand pitching master a 3–2 lead and stimulus for victory. The incomparable hurler promptly retired the first two batters of the home half-inning, but then issued his only walk of the game to pinch-hitter Willie Smith. Lead-off hitter Don Kessinger followed with a single, and Glenn Beckert also singled to tie the game. Third-place hitter Billy Williams swatted a pitch just beyond first baseman Willie McCovey's reach, giving the Cubs a 4–3 win. It was only the sixth time in 22 decisions that the Cubs had beaten Marichal. Things that season seemed to be going the way of the Wrigley men, who nudged out to a five-game, first-place lead in their division with the come-from-behind win.

Two more losses, in which the pitcher did not display his sharpest skills, followed and reduced Marichal's pitching ledger to 13–8. On August 15, Marichal stepped back on the right track with a 4–0, four-hit shutout of Chicago at Candlestick Park. His next assignment came four days later in New York against the Mets. These were no longer Casey Stengel's Mets, mind you. The Mets team Marichal faced belonged to Gil Hodges, and this squad was greatly improved. Already, the Mets had accumulated 66 wins (two more than the Giants), with 45 games left to play.

Just under 49,000 fans filled Shea Stadium for the Tuesday night game, pitting Marichal against Gary Gentry, a slim rookie right-hander. Gentry kept the Giants from scoring through nine innings, as did Marichal with the Mets. Gentry racked up a scoreless tenth inning, pitching around a Marichal single. Marichal matched his counterpart but not without a tussle. Mets outfielder Cleon Jones singled to lead off the inning, only the third hit surrendered by the Giants' pitcher. Jones was sacrificed to second by the next batter. Jones then bravely stole third base, forcing the Giants to bring the infield in. Wayne Garrett grounded to second baseman Ron Hunt on the edge of the infield grass for the second out, the runner unable to advance. Marichal intentionally passed the next hitter, Ed Kranepool, to pitch to light-hitting Bud Harrelson. The Mets shortstop struck out to end the inning.

Gentry was pulled after the tenth frame, changing the game's complexion from pitchers' duel to pitcher vs. team. Tug McGraw was the new Mets hurler and he kept away any Giants' scoring proclivities for the next three stanzas, getting a big assist in the 13th inning from his left fielder with Willie McCovey at the plate. McCovey drove a ball to the 371-foot sign in deep left center field. Cleon Jones made a leaping a catch against the wall, the impact knocking him down on the warning track.

In the 11th, the Giants ran themselves out of a possible breakthrough when left fielder Bob Burda tried to stretch a single into a double but was thrown out by counterpart Jones. The next batter walked, with two outs, but shortstop Don Mason popped up to end the Giants' hitting turn. In the bottom of the 11th inning, Marichal struck out the side.

In the 12th inning, the Giants had been set down quietly by McGraw, including Marichal, who owned one of the Giants' five hits in the game. In the Mets' turn at-bat, Jones reached on a one-out infield topper, but was thrown out at the plate, trying to score all the way from first base when Marichal threw errantly past first base on a sacrifice attempt by McGraw, ruled a hit and an error. Hustling second baseman Ron Hunt recovered the loose ball and threw home in time to nail Jones, whose daring dash around the bases ended in vain. Marichal induced Garrett to fly out with McGraw on third, leaving the winning run there for the second time in three innings.

In the bottom of the 13th, Marichal retired the Mets in order, the ninth time in the game he had done so. Marichal had walked only one—and that had been purposely, in the tenth inning.

The Giants went out weakly in the 14th inning; then the Giants' seasoned ace charged the mound for the 14th time, to offer his team another chance at victory. Unbeknownst to Marichal, unbeknownst to anyone, the New York Mets had embarked on a baseball journey equal in size, scope and wonder to that of man landing on the moon—which had been accomplished only a month earlier—and no pitcher or team was going to impede their fate. Marichal recorded his 40th out, eliciting a tap-back to the mound from Rod Gaspar. The magnificent hurler then delivered his 150th pitch of the evening—an economical number considering the game's duration—to Tommie Agee. Agee did not swing. A ball was called. Agee did swing at the next pitch and parked it over the wall in left field. Marichal bowed his head and quickly left the field.

It was not the era of over-the-top, wasteful jersey-tearing celebrations at home plate that have become the vogue in modern day baseball. A sports page photo showed only two Mets greeting Agee at home plate following his dramatic circular jog—on-deck batter Bobby Pfeil and, for an unknown reason, pitcher Jim McAndrew. Also in the photo are the Mets batboy and home plate umpire Stan Landes. Jack Hiatt, the Giants catcher, was prominently visible, holding his ground waiting for Agee to step on the dish.

Marichal won his next start five days hence, against the East Division's expansion franchise from Montreal, the Expos; the score was 6–4. On August 29, in a rematch against Gentry in San Francisco, the Giants scored four runs in the first inning and Marichal took it from there, four-hitting the Mets, 5–0. The Giants had moved into first place by a game and a half over the Atlanta Braves. The Mets, meanwhile, despite the loss, were in second place, four games behind the division-leading Cubs.

The Expos came to town next and Marchial defeated them, 2–1, for his 17th win. The Giants, still holding a slim lead in the West, traveled to Cincinnati for Marichal's next start on September 8. Marichal opened the first game of a doubleheader and lost, 5–4, to the Reds, two of the runs scored against him unearned. In a cross-country scheduling zig-zag, the Reds faced Marichal at Candlestick Park in his next starting assignment on September 12. Marichal was never better, and said so himself. "I have never pitched a better game than that,"[26] declared the pitcher after tossing a one-hitter, with one walk permitted. Marichal faced only 28 batters, as one of the two baserunners was thrown out attempting to steal; he struck out six and threw 108 pitches. "Where does he dress?" wondered Reds manager Dave Bristol. "In a phone booth?"[27]

Four days later, the peerless pitcher threw his eighth shutout of the year, beating Atlanta and regaining for the Giants the precarious foothold on first place the team had lost on its recent road swing East. Marichal crowned his sixth 20-win campaign a quartet of days later on September 20, defeating the Dodgers, 5–4. It was his ninth straight complete game and 26th in 34 starts. The victory maintained for the Giants a scant half-game first-place advantage over the Braves.

On September 24, a poor beginning and a poor fielding play cost Marichal and his team a game against the Padres at San Diego. The home team's first three hitters reached the Dominican hurler for two singles and a double, plating a run and placing two men in scoring position. Marichal struck out the next two hitters before left fielder Jim Ray Hart misplayed a routine fly hit by Ivan Murrell for an error, allowing both runners to cross home plate. It was the end of the scoring for the Padres. The Giants and Marichal lost, 3–2. In the seventh inning, King lifted his starter for a pinch-hitter. Although he could not be blamed, Marichal lost for the second time on the season to the lowly Friars.

Atlanta won ten games in a row, September 19 through 30, to win the West Division title. Marichal's 21st and final win (8–1) on September 28, against the Dodgers, came two days prior to the Braves' clinching the West. As a result of Atlanta's late winning surge, its final margin of victory over the Giants was three games. As a consolation to Marichal, when it seemed he could not get any better, the 31-year-old right-hander, with the subsidy of eight shutouts, posted the best ERA of his ten major league seasons, 2.10, the lowest in both leagues.

*   *   *

Juan Marichal completed his nearly full ten-year run over the 1960s with a record of 191–88. The new decade, however, did not commence favorably for him. He experienced a physical ailment that drained him physically and depleted his efforts on the field.

It was all brought on by a 13-day good will tour to Japan made by the San Francisco Giants in February 1970. Marichal was stricken with an ear infection on the trip. Prescribed penicillin shots upon returning to San Francisco caused an allergic reaction that put Marichal in the hospital. The staff ace missed his first Opening Day assignment in six years as a result.

Trying to prepare for the start of the season, Marichal pushed himself beyond the parameters of his convalescence and returned to the team to make two exhibition starts in late March. He threw five scoreless innings in the first outing, but suffered a relapse following the other. He not only missed the season's opener but failed for the first time to win a game in April. Marichal did not win his initial game until May 10.

Through the malaise of his recovery period, Marichal continued to pitch, and that he wound up with 33 starts, even though he did not get off the starting blocks until three weeks into the season, says much about the pitcher's competitive desires. Marichal pitched in a weakened state, deprived of speed and sharpness from the debilitating effect of the penicillin, which also caused him to lose weight. Giants team physician E. C. Sailer diagnosed the pitcher's situation at the time. "The kind of reaction to penicillin made Marichal a very sick man," stated Sailer. "It takes a long time to regain strength after that kind of a thing."[28]

Marichal gave up 100 earned runs (111 total) on the season for the first time in his career; his ERA expanded into a previously unknown region, the four-run plateau (4.12). Marichal had only two wins through May 30, and was a disbelieving 3–9 after a July 21st loss to the Philadelphia Phillies and Rick Wise.

Starting to feel like himself again, from July 26 to September 7 Marichal won seven out of eight decisions to even his record. Marichal ended the year 12–10 and picked up his 200th lifetime win in the process. Achieving the grand victory mark on August 28, Marichal downed the NL East-leading Pittsburgh Pirates, 5–1, at Candlestick Park. Not walking a batter, Marichal allowed eight hits and struck out five.

The recuperated pitcher's only shutout of the season came on September 21 against the Dodgers, a six-hitter. In the 7–0 win at Dodger Stadium, 39-year-old Willie Mays drove in four runs and hit the 628th home run of his unparalleled career.

The Giants, a team that had switched managers a quarter of the way through the season, ended a half-decade run of second-place finishes in 1970—by placing third.

*   *   *

Finally, in 1971, the San Francisco Giants took hold of the elusive top spot in the standings at the time of baseball's appointed October reckoning. Last year's dugout replacement, Charlie Fox, in his first full season as a major league manager, guided the team to the top.

The Marichal of old pitched the Giants to a five-hit, 4–0 win over the San Diego Padres on Opening Day, April 6. A month away from turning 40, Mays contributed his 629th home run and a double. Two starts later, on April 16, Marichal blanked the Chicago Cubs, 9–0. The win boosted him to a 3–0 record, but he lost his next two starts, one of them 2–1.

Marichal was pitching in a five-man rotation for the first time in his career, and in the year of his 34th birthday the pitcher advocated its use. "If we have five starters, as they plan, it will help a lot in the hot weather," Marichal said prior to the season. "If I pitch every fifth day, and maybe win 21 or 22 games, it will be better for the club, I think, than if I start more often and have a record like 26–11 instead of 21–5."[29]

On May 15, Marichal blanked the Dodgers, 1–0, improving his record to a sensational 21–1 at Candlestick Park over the Giants' arch-enemies. (Marichal lost only four games at home in his entire career to the Dodgers, and overall amassed a 37–18 lifetime record over his club's greatest adversary.) The shutout provided Marichal's team with its 27th win in 36 games played; Fox's Giants had sailed out to a nine-game lead in the division.

On June 23, the great pitcher won his tenth game, 5–2, over the Cubs. Marichal accounted for the last two runs of the game with his fourth and final career home run. The Giants' big lead in the division had been pared slightly to 8½ games. But Marichal then endured eight starts without a win. Four of the starts resulted in losses, dropping his record to 10–8. The Giants maintained a comfortable six-game lead with fewer than 50 games to play.

Over the season's final two months, there was a return to normalcy in Marichal's pitching ledger despite a near-costly downturn by the Giants. The right-hander notched seven more victories against three defeats, to register his second 18-win campaign. Marichal led the staff in victories and pitched the division-clincher on the last day of the season. After a torrid first two months, the Giants had swooned in June but recovered enough to live up to their early promise. A Memorial Day lead of 10½ games had been cut by more than half by the Dodgers in August. At the start of September, the advantage regenerated to eight games. The Giants, however, won only eight of their final 24 games and were nearly knocked off their first-place steed, as the Dodgers closed with a hard gallop. The Giants' lead had dissipated to one game on the last day of the season.

A Giants loss and a Dodgers win on the final day, September 30, would have caused a tie between the two teams. In that Giants' finale, Marichal won his fourth decision in a row, 5–1, over the Padres in San Diego. It was vintage Marichal; the pitcher used only 81 pitches to record 27 outs.

The League Championship Series started two days later in San Francisco, between the 90–72 Giants and the 97–65 East Division champion Pittsburgh Pirates. The clubs divided a pair of games, with the Giants winning the first contest behind Gaylord Perry, 5–4.

Marichal opened Game 3 of the best-of-five series at Three Rivers Stadium on October 5. He pitched a four-hitter, but two of the hits were solo home runs, one to Bob Robertson in the second inning, and the other to Richie Hebner in the eighth. Marichal suffered a 2–1 loss. The West Coast club lost its next game and was ousted by the better Pirates team.

It was the last time the San Francisco Giants made the post-season until 1987, and the last refulgent season for Juan Marichal Sánchez.

LEGACY

In the Cy Young Award races, Juan Marichal was often beaten in photo finishes by another pitcher's career year. In 1964, 1968 and 1969, Marichal ran as Alydar to Dean Chance, Bob Gibson and Tom Seaver's Affirmed. Then there was the Cy Young Award sweeper Sandy Koufax, who kept reinventing career years. But anyone who saw Juan Marichal pitch, or had to hit against him, knows no engraved trophy from the league was needed to validate his superb abilities.

Marichal was one of the half-dozen greatest pitchers of baseball's pitching renaissance period of the 1960s and 1970s. Two of the master pitchers from baseball's Florentine Age, Gibson and Seaver, fell one short of Marichal's six seasons in pitching's charmed 20-win circle. (Gibson, besides his five 20-game seasons, won 19 games twice, and 18 in another year, while Seaver won 19 and 18 in other seasons to go with his five 20-win campaigns.) Marichal's lone ERA title came in 1969, edging out 25-game winner Seaver. Marichal won 25 games in three different seasons, equaled by Koufax, but more than Seaver, Gibson, and the era's two other great pitching artists, seven-time 20-game winner Ferguson Jenkins and eight-time 20-win titleist Jim Palmer, combined.

Juan Marichal won 51.6 percent of the games in which he appeared. Through 2013, only *six* modern era pitchers with more than 200 wins had won a greater percentage of their games. Marichal was one of baseball's all-time elite pitchers, one of only 19 six-time 20-game winners. He completed 244 games, ranking among the top 90 pitchers all-time.

No Hispanic pitcher has registered more 20-win seasons than Marichal. No Hispanic pitcher has equaled Marichal's three seasons of 300 innings (and he missed two others by a combined five innings). Marichal stands alone among Hispanic pitchers with 11 seasons of at least 200 innings. No other Hispanic pitcher completed more games or tossed more shutouts. Only Dennis Martínez indexed more major league innings and more wins. Some bad luck with freak injuries and a chronic bad back in the latter years of his career derailed Marichal's chance at winning 300 games. (Marichal exerted a great deal of force upon his body with his high-leg-kick-induced-follow-through finish to the plate.)

In the Dominican Winter League, Marichal pitched eight seasons and posted a record of 36–22, with an ERA of 1.87 in 557⅓ innings.[30]

"The pain in my back last season was so intense I had to fight hard not to cry,"[31] Marichal said, expounding on what the 1972 season had been like for him. He started 24 games and pitched with excruciating pain in his back, caused by a protruding spinal disc that was surgically removed after the season.

On the field, Marichal's teammates did little to alleviate the discomfort in his back. He suffered six losses by shutout; in seven other defeats the Giants scored two runs or fewer for him. That support thinly added up to a 6–16 record, pitching for a next-to-last place and well-below .500 San Francisco Giants team.

Marichal followed with another sub-par season in 1973. Though the Giants drastically improved their record, it was not enough to suit Marichal, who ended up with an 11–15 record in 32 starts. In Marichal's last two seasons with the Giants, he endured 11 shutout losses, including four by a 1–0 score. (Marichal, in his career, lost eight 1–0 games, a high number. Three came against the Mets, against whom he finished with a 26–8 lifetime record. Marichal also threw seven 1–0 victories, including two extra-inning masterpieces.)

The sub-.500 marks of 1972 and 1973 and two seasons with an ERA in the high 3s signaled an end to the Juan Marichal pitching era in San Francisco. The aging hurler was unceremoniously sold to the Boston Red Sox in December of 1973. Marichal pitched sparingly for Boston in 1974, winning five games with one loss. The last of his 243 career wins came against the A's in Oakland on August 11, 1974. Marichal tossed eight scoreless innings and garnered a 2–1 victory.

It was for those same Oakland A's that Marichal became a Caribbean scout for almost a decade after his 1975 retirement as an active player. (Marichal attempted a final comeback try in April of that year with his former foes, the Los Angeles Dodgers. After two poor starts, he retired.)

Showing no regrets on the day of his announced retirement, April 17, 1975, Juan Marichal displays for the last time his Los Angeles Dodgers uniform. Marichal had signed in March with the once archrival team for one last comeback attempt. Note the psychedelic 1970s pants.

In the mid-eighties, the A's sponsored a baseball academy in the Dominican Republic, in which Marichal was deeply involved. It always falls upon those who go first to try and make it easier for those who follow, and for Marichal that became an accepted credo with his involvement in the school. The school taught English for two hours a day to its student athletes. Marichal stressed how important it was to have a fundamental knowledge of the language in order to help ease a player's transitional assimilation.

Marichal left the A's after 13 years and soon thereafter was appointed his country's Sports Minister by Dominican President Leonel Fernández. He was instrumental in the nation's behind-the-scenes preparation for the 2003 Pan American Games. The 66-year-old Marichal was accorded a prominent part in the Opening Ceremonies, along with Pedro Martínez, as the shining examples of the nation's past and present baseball pitching glory.

Since then, the pitching legend has been seen in the broadcast booth, on occasion, for ESPN Deportes, and has been a regular returnee for the annual Hall of Fame ceremonies in Cooperstown. Away from the baseball spotlight, Marichal, now in his seventies, still spends time actively involved in his farming business back in the Dominican Republic.

It was in his third year of eligibility that Juan Marichal—who became only the second pitcher in Giants franchise history to have his uniform number retired, the pitcher who had a better than 3-to-1 strikeout-to-walk ratio, who won 53 percent of his starts, and who is one of fewer than 20 pitchers in history with more than 100 more career wins than losses—was elected to the National Baseball Hall of Fame.

The "treasonous incident" of 1963 long forgotten and buried by his people, as it was hoped, too, the nefarious Roseboro encounter, Marichal received the selective news with joyous gratitude. On the latter issue, immediately following his 1983 Hall of Fame election, Marichal made public a letter John Roseboro had written to him. It read: "My hope now is that the U.S. press and writers will remove any stigma attached to the Juan Marichal name and vote you into the Hall of Fame as you most certainly deserve it.... I hope we can now be 'amigos' for the rest of our lives."[32]

"It is all forgotten, especially with me and John," said Marichal. "We are very good friends. He came to the Dominican Republic last October and played in my golf tournament. He was also my house guest. Later, John sent me the letter."[33] That Marichal did not reveal the letter's contents until after his election to the Hall showed it was important for him to get in on his own deserving pitching merits, and not on what may have been perceived as a self-orchestrated, sympathetic appeal.

Roseboro and Marichal were amigos for the rest of Roseboro's life, which ended at age 69, from a stroke, in August of 2002.

Marichal eulogized his fallen former adversary in this manner: "Roseboro forgiving me was one of the best things that happened in my life,"[34] said the man who was one of the best things to happen to baseball.

Luis Tiant

A month into the Habana Leones' 1940 season, the wife of one the starting pitchers on the team gave birth to a healthy baby boy. Isabel Rovina Vega de Tiant presented a son to her husband, Luis, on November 23. The child, an only child, was named after his father.

As a youngster growing up in the Marianao district of Havana where he was born, it became evident that Luis Tiant, Jr. had been blessed with the same baseball-throwing ability as his father, a well-respected pitcher for decades in U.S. black baseball and throughout the Caribbean.

By the time Luis Jr. was a teen, the elder Tiant had long since retired from pitching and had taken to working as a furniture mover. It was not the only blue-collar job Luis Tiant, Sr. knew over the course of his post-baseball life. He did not stay in baseball after his mound days were finished (he may not have been asked), yet he remained one of the most remembered pitchers in the baseball history of Cuba. One can speculate that Tiant Sr. had ultimately been disillusioned by the sport to which he had wholeheartedly given the best years of his life. "I think my father still had bad feelings about his own career," Luis Tiant stated in *El Tiante,* a 1976 autobiography he co-wrote with Boston sportswriter Joe Fitzgerald. "The colored leagues never paid him much money, and the major leagues didn't want him because he was black."[35] The wife of the man who pitched against Satchel Paige and struck out Babe Ruth in barnstorming competition also worked as a cook.[36]

The long-term goal, as with any loving, married couple, was to give their child a better life. It was hoped that a better life would be achieved through education. But after Luis Jr. developed the strongest arm among his adolescent playmates, there was no deterring him from playing the game of his father. While the father never pushed his son toward the game, he was always there to offer Luis Jr. a few technical pointers. The father was a left-hander; the son threw with his right arm.

At 18, Luis Tiant, Jr. was rejected in a tryout with the Cuban Sugar Kings held at Gran Stadium. Luis Sr. had accompanied his son to the tryout. The disappointment over the rejection was soon forgotten when a former major league player recommended Tiant to the owner of the Mexico City Tigers. Bobby Ávila, scouting for the organization that had brought him to the major leagues, the Cleveland Indians, arranged for the teenage Tiant to sign his first professional contract. The baseball job in Mexico with the Tigers paid $150 a month. Tiant was overwhelmed by the batters of the Mexican League in his first season. He won only five games and lost nearly four times as many. It did not help that Tiant was a member of the worst team in Mexican League history.

Upon his return the next spring to los Tigres, Tiant provided a dramatic improvement. The Mexico City Tigers of 1960 were a classic "from worst to first" team. The team's record in 1959 was a dismal 39–104. The following season, the club made a complete reversal and won the Mexican League pennant with a 77–66 mark. Luis Tiant's 17–7 record mirrored the team's incredibly quick turnaround.

A personally gratifying achievement followed Tiant's first professional championship. In the winter of 1960, he donned the white with red trim uniform that his father had been most renowned for wearing: the uniform of the Habana Leones. Still carrying the zealous umbrage of youth, Tiant initially refused to pitch for his country's capital city team because he had been previously snubbed by the club. (A year earlier, Tiant had been "passed on," in another tryout, by both Habana and its biggest Cuban Winter League rival, Almendares.) But Tiant eventually was convinced by his father to accept the opportunity with Habana, which enhanced his career. The right-hander accrued a 10–8 pitching mark for Habana and was named Rookie of the Year, in what was the last season of professional baseball in Cuba in the 20th century.

Tiant was eager to return to Mexico City after the Cuban Winter League season, as much to resume pitching for a title defense as to resume pitching woo. He had met a young Mexican girl the previous summer and they had dated until he departed at the end of the season for Cuba. Luis Clemente Tiant knew this was the girl for him, for he asked for the hand in marriage of Maria del Refugio Navarro upon his spring return to Mexico in 1961. The pair completed the proposal with an August wedding in Mexico City.

It was the young couple's intent to honeymoon after the summer season on Isla de Pinos, or Isle of Pines, a small island off the southwest coastline of Cuba. But the Cuban Revolution of 1959 had by then completed its Marxist-Leninist conversion. In September 1961, Tiant was told bluntly by his father not to attempt to return to Cuba. "Luis, stay in Mexico," the father told his son by phone. "Don't come home. There's nothing for you here now. Stay where you are and make a good life for your family."[37] This was, in microcosm, through one family's heartrending separation, the most damaging and damning backlash of the ruinous socio-political reform that convulsed the island of Cuba in the early 1960s.

"That's why you have to love your parents," Tiant expressed in later years. "No matter how much it hurts them, all they want is the best for you. That's their only consideration. From the time you are a baby, they always watch out for you. You will never find two other people like them in the world."[38] Tiant sidestepped Cuba and did his winter hurling in Puerto Rico with the Caguas Criollos.

Tiant's Mexico City contract had been purchased for $25,000 by the Cleveland Indians at the close the 1961 Mexican campaign. Though the excitement of that had undoubtedly been tempered by the forced separation from his parents, Tiant, with his assignment to the U.S. minor leagues in 1962, had a chance to reach the baseball level that had been denied his father.

It did not take Luis Tiant long to reach the baseball echelon to which so many aspire and so few make valid. In July 1964, at 23 years of age, Tiant found himself on a plane, soaring across the continental United States, from Portland, Oregon—where he had been pitching (and how! 15–1, his only loss, 2–0)—to New York, baseball capital of the world. After two and a half minor league seasons, Tiant was en route to join the parent Cleveland club. The pitcher immediately validated his recall from the Indians' Pacific Coast League team.

In his first major league game, on July 19, Luis Tiant beat the New York Yankees and Whitey Ford, 3–0, in the second game of a doubleheader. The Yankees did not reach Tiant for a hit until the sixth inning, on a push bunt by Tom Tresh, and managed only three singles the rest of the game. Leonard Koppett wrote in his game report that Tiant reminded him of former Brooklyn Dodgers pitcher Don Newcombe in appearance and tenacity on the mound.

Four starts later, on August 11, Tiant blanked the Los Angeles Angels at Dodger Stadium, 3–0. It was Tiant's fifth win in six decisions (one win had come in relief). Over the last two-plus months of the season, Tiant won ten games in 16 starts and three relief appearances, with nine complete games for the sixth-place Indians. He posted an ERA of 2.83 and tossed three shutouts. The third whitewash came in Boston on September 30; it was Tiant's first time setting foot on the Fenway Park mound. Tiant allowed the Red Sox four hits in a 5–0, first-game-of-a-doubleheader win. Sam McDowell also shut out the home team (3–0) in the Wednesday afternoon twin bill attended by fewer than 1,000 fans.

* * *

As a Cleveland Indians rookie in 1964, Tiant tossed shutouts the first time he stepped on the mounds of Yankee Stadium, Dodger Stadium and Fenway Park (photograph from Hall of Fame).

Counting his PCL victories, Tiant was a 25-game winner in 1964. Yet Tiant started the 1965 season in the Indians' bullpen. Rookies in the major leagues had to wait their turn.

After four relief appearances to open the season, Cleveland manager Birdie Tebbetts gave Tiant his first start on May 1, against the Washington Senators. It was a clunker. The pitcher allowed two runs, on four hits and five walks, in less than four innings of work. He received a no decision in the game won by the Indians, 7–2. On May 7, Tiant defeated the Red Sox, 5–1, on May 7, at Fenway Park. Tiant then lost consecutive games against the Baltimore Orioles, one as starter and the other as a reliever. In a forgettable start, Tiant surrendered a home run and three other hits to the first four Baltimore batters he faced and was removed. The next day, May 13, he relieved; in the seventh inning, the Orioles' Boog Powell reached him for a solo home run, the deciding run in a 3–2 Cleveland loss.

Over the next month, Tiant won four games. On June 16, he tossed a one-hit gem against the Washington Senators. Woodie Held's leadoff single in the top of the seventh inning was the only Senators safety in the 5–0 final. Tiant's seventh win (in ten decisions) came on the road against the Red Sox, 9–2, on June 28.

The Indians swept a doubleheader from the Chicago White Sox on July 7, to move 19 games over .500; through 77 games played, Cleveland was a second-place contender, 1½ games behind the league-leading Minnesota Twins. It was the watershed mark for the team, however. From that point, the Cleveland club's pace stalled to a fifth-place landing, 12 games behind league champion Minnesota.

In 30 starts and 11 relief showings on the season, Tiant managed a break-even 11–11 record and 3.53 ERA, with ten complete games and two shutouts.

* * *

Tiant opened the 1966 campaign as the American League's most dominating starter. The pitcher tossed three shutouts in his first three starts, including a 1–0 dazzler at Yankee Stadium on May 3.

An earlier Tiant shutout had come against the Kansas City Athletics. Tiant allowed three hits and struck out 12; the 4–0 final was also the Indians' ninth consecutive win to begin the season, tying an American League record. Two days later, on April 28, Cleveland tied the season-opening record for wins with ten, held by two National League teams, with a 2–1 victory over the California Angels. Beaten in its next game, the Indians won again before Tiant improved the club's mark to 12–1 with the 1–0 shutout of the New York Yankees. The Tribe followed that with two more triumphs.

On the impetus of its 14–1 slingshot start, Cleveland, played over .600 ball for the first 66 games of the season. Birdie Tebbetts, in early June, displaced Tiant from the rotation, preferring to use 23-year-old Steve Hargan as the team's fourth starter. Tiant had lost three out of four decisions since his shutout over the Yankees. The manager's decision followed not long after a 1–0 loss suffered by Tiant to Mudcat Grant and the Minnesota Twins on May 29, and ten innings of one-run relief by Hargan, two days later, in a marathon 17-inning, 7–5 Indians win over the Angels (in which Tiant earned a save by retiring the final batter of the game).

In July, the Indians began to fade and quickly dropped out of contention. On August 6, Tiant lost a game in relief to New York, 5–4, surrendering a game-deciding homer to Horace Clarke in the eighth inning. On August 20, George Strickland replaced an ailing

Tebbetts at the helm and eventually released Tiant from the bullpen. But it was late in the season when he did so.

Exactly one month after taking over, Strickland gave Tiant his first start since the second game of a doubleheader on July 3; Tiant downed the Twins at Cleveland Stadium, 4–1, striking out 12 and walking one. Four days later, Tiant defeated the Kansas City Athletics, 3–1, with two innings of relief aid from Dick Radatz. Against the Twins again, in their ballpark this time, Tiant hurled his fifth shutout of the season, 4–0, on September 28. Tiant defeated 25-game winner Jim Kaat.

Over a 13-day closing stretch, culminating on the 2nd of October, Tiant made four starts in the Indians' final ten games. He won three of the four, losing the season's finale in Anaheim, 2–0, to Angels right-hander Jorge Rubio, who threw the only shutout of his ten-game major league career.

Cleveland, with an 81–81 record, held on to a first division finish, in fifth place. Tiant, 12–11, tied for the league lead in shutouts with five—in only 16 starts. His 2.79 ERA was second-best on the team to Hargan, who was 13–10 on the season with a 2.48 earned runs mark.

* * *

Cleveland hired a new manager in 1967, Joe Adcock. The former first baseman placed Tiant in the role that best suited him, that of permanent starter. Tiant tied with Steve Hargan for second-most starts (29) on the team behind Sam McDowell (37).

Tiant lost his opening assignment, in the Indians' second game on April 14. It was a poor outing. Tiant surrendered seven runs on eight hits in four innings to the California Angels. Perhaps as a result, and due to scheduled off days and rainouts, Tiant became the odd man out in the rotation and received one other start before May 13 on April 23—a short, no-decision outing against the Angels, in which Tiant was betrayed early by a sloppy defense. At Griffith Stadium, the right-hander bested the Washington Senators, 3–1, the last inning pitched by Orlando Peña. After a no-decision, Tiant defeated the Senators again on May 24, this time going all the way and striking out 12 in the 9–1 final.

Tiant followed that with 9–0 shutout of the Detroit Tigers, May 31, at Tiger Stadium. In his next start, six days later, neither Tiant nor his relief were able to close out a three-run, ninth-inning lead against the Minnesota Twins. Harmon Killebrew crashed a home run leading off the inning. Tony Oliva followed with a single, ending Tiant's night. Sonny Seibert came in and was tagged with a tying two-run round tripper by Bob Allison. That was all the scoring in the inning for the Twins. The Indians scored twice in the top of the tenth for a 6–4 win; Seibert was the winner.

Tiant sported a 7–2 record following a 5–3 road victory over the Detroit Tigers on June 29; Cleveland moved a game over .500 with its 36th win. Respectability slipped away from the club from there. Tiant's showing during the same deteriorating seven-week stretch was anything but impressive. The pitcher failed to gain a win in nine starts.

Tiant broke the spell with a scintillating 3–2 victory in which he struck out 16 California Angels on August 22, and evened his record at 8–8. Tiant racked up 16 strikeouts through 7⅓ innings and seemed headed toward a new single-game strikeout mark. But after fanning Don Mincher to open the eighth inning, the right-hander, who was engaged in a tight contest the whole way, lost his whiff ball. It took a solo home run from batterymate Joe Azcue in the bottom of the ninth inning to reward the overpowering effort.

Tiant's record on the season was a more than respectable 12–9 for eighth-place Cleveland, a team that won 75 games and lost 87. For the third time in four years, Tiant finished with an ERA under 3.00 (2.74), and he cracked 200 innings pitched in a big league season for the first time.

*   *   *

At the close of 1967, Luis Tiant, already the proud father of a five-year-old boy (named Luis), welcomed a baby girl into the family, christened Isabel, after Tiant's mother. Tiant pitched in Venezuela over that winter and fashioned a 1.34 ERA, in 87 innings, for the Caracas Leones. Amazingly, that was only a little better than the ERA he posted for Cleveland in three times as many innings during the upcoming major league season.

There were several major league pitchers at one point or another during the 1968 season that were virtually unhittable. The American League had its share, but one of them, Luis Tiant, set the most unprecedented stringency standards from the mound. For the first time in 50 years, the ERA averages of both leagues were under 3.00. Tiant's ERA was well under 2.00 at 1.60. Tiant lost nine games the same way Bob Gibson lost nine games that season while posting the all-time ERA record of 1.12—his team mounted very limited scoring for him in the majority of the defeats.

One of the nine losses for Tiant came out of the bullpen, in the second game of the season. In an age when only elite starters were exempt from relieving, Tiant's initial setback was suffered during a 3⅓-inning relief stint against the California Angels. He was nicked for two decisive runs in the 7–5 loss. A second loss, 3–2, the result of a three-run home run by the Red Sox's Reggie Smith, occurred in starting assignment number two, on April 20. Four days earlier, the pitcher had chalked up his first win in his first start, 3–1, over the visiting Chicago White Sox.

Tiant evened his record with the first of four consecutive shutouts that masterfully emanated from his right arm. Tiant blanked the Washington Senators on two singles (2–0), in the second game of a Griffith Stadium doubleheader, after the Tribe had been shut out in the opener. Five days later, on May 3, Tiant also prevented the Minnesota Twins from scoring any runs at Cleveland Stadium; he allowed one additional hit than in the previous start. The Yankees were next, set down for nine innings without scoring in their home ballpark, and managing only four singles and a double against Tiant's dominant offerings. Tiant struck out ten in the 8–0 final. In the pitcher's next start, May 12, he blanked the Birds of Baltimore, 2–0, in a twin bill opener at Memorial Stadium. Nine-strikeouts in the game gave Tiant 35 strikeouts in his last 36 innings during which he was reached for only one extra-base hit and 14 hits in total. His ERA for the season dropped to 1.03.

The fifth-year hurler was within one of the American League record for consecutive shutouts, held by Doc White of the 1904 Chicago White Sox, when he took the mound on May 17, against the Orioles in a return match at Cleveland. For five innings, Tiant nursed a 1–0 lead. In the top of the sixth inning, he walked Curt Blefary with one out. Frank Robinson, hit a grounder to shortstop Larry Brown, who flipped to keystone cohort Chico Salmon. At the bag, the second baseman lost control of the ball during his pivot, which was disrupted by the sliding runner. Salmon missed not only a chance at an inning-ending double play, but by dropping the ball made the umpire reverse his initial "out" call on the apparent forced runner at second.

The runners moved up on a wild pitch during Boog Powell's at-bat. Tiant extended the confrontation against Powell to a 3–2 count. Powell homered on the payoff pitch, and the blow snapped the pitcher's consecutive scoreless streak of 41⅓ innings. The Orioles won the game, 6–2, scoring three other runs against the Cleveland bullpen following Tiant's removal for a pinch-hitter in the seventh inning.

The start following that one resulted in another loss, to the former Kansas City franchise, now relocated to northern California. On May 21, in the second game of a twi-night doubleheader, the Oakland Athletics, behind John "Blue Moon" Odom, defeated Tiant, 2–0, managing but one earned run. Sam McDowell had defeated Odom's A's in the opener, 1–0, in 11 innings.

Tiant won his next four outings. The fourth triumph in the string came on June 9, at Tiger Stadium. Tiant bested Denny McLain, 2–0, tying the Tigers' right-hander for the league lead in wins with nine. Tiant's poorest start of the season immediately followed; he gave up five runs (two earned) and walked seven, losing 7–2 to the Boston Red Sox in Cleveland. Tiant rebounded from that off night by producing three straight wins to complete June with a record of 12–5.

Tiant always utilized a deceptive pitching motion, and in 1968 he added another element. "The first time I do it [swivel his head an instant before delivering his pitch] was against California," Tiant explained to Cleveland sportswriter Russell Schneider. "I forget who is batting but I know it bothered him."[39] During the same interview session, different sides to Tiant's personality were fleshed out by the reporter.

> "Before a game—even one that he's scheduled to pitch—Tiant is the center of attraction with his clubhouse hijinks," Schneider revealed. "When Garry Bell was with the Indians, they formed a team that would rival Abbott and Costello. But once the game starts, he becomes deadly serious."
>
> Another facet of Tiant that is not often seen by the public is his devotion to his family in Cuba—Looie's parents and his father's three brothers and six sisters. "I'm always thinking how much I would like to go back and see them, and for them to meet my wife and my two children. My mother write to me and say do not come because maybe I cannot leave if I go there," Tiant related sadly.[40]

The best game of Tiant's season occurred a few days into July. It was a ten-inning, 1–0 masterpiece, in which he struck out *19* Minnesota Twins. At Cleveland Stadium, in a memorable battle with opposing starter Jim Merritt, Tiant was the victor when Joe Azcue singled home the winning run. Merritt was permitted to hit in the top of the tenth inning with runners on the corners and no one out. The pitcher struck out; Tiant then fanned John Roseboro and pinch-hitter Rich Rollins.

Tiant's All-Star status was all but a formality. When the official news of his selection to the American League squad was received, he felt especially rewarded, but not for himself. "My father will be proud because he never got a chance to play in the big leagues," Tiant said. "He was a better pitcher than me."[41] Tiant started the All-Star Game and took the loss, allowing the only run of the game (on his own throwing error) in the first inning. Tiant won four additional starts during the month of July. His only loss was, 1–0 on July 24, to the Baltimore Orioles and Dave McNally.

On the night of August 1, with a record of 17–6 record, Tiant faced McNally again and the shrewd Orioles left-hander defeated his counterpart once more, 5–1. The game was tied going into the ninth inning when the Birds reached Tiant for four runs on a walk and three hits. Tiant did not receive a decision in his next start, on August 6, hurling nine innings of one-run ball in a game that took eight more innings for the Indians to lose, 2–1. Four days later, Tiant emerged victorious, 3–2, in a complete game over the Chicago White Sox at Comiskey Park.

Then the pitcher was shut out in successive starts, losing both decisions by 3–0 counts. One of them was to the first-place Tigers and Mickey Lolich. Detroit, at that point of the season, had scored nearly 100 more runs than the Indians. The run differential stood out to one of Lolich's teammates. Denny McLain was a 20-game winner before the end of *July*. After two starts by Tiant in the course of eight days against the Tigers, in which the Indians had scored a combined one run, McLain remarked, "Luis and I would each be fighting for 30 wins if he had our kind of hitting to go with his kind of pitching."[42] Tiant closed out August making two starts lasting only five innings each. He left both games ahead, but the slim leads did not hold up.

In his initial September start, Tiant received the most run support in a game all season. It was appreciated, as the Cleveland pitcher allowed four runs in 5⅔ innings of work. The 9–5 road victory over the California Angels was the 19th win of the season for the staff ace. It was only the third win of the campaign he had not completed. Tiant's next start produced another complete game and win number 20. At Bloomington, Minnesota, on September 9, Tiant gained a 6–1 victory over the Twins, with a decorative 16 strikeouts adding to the benchmark occurrence.

Arm soreness, which had abbreviated two earlier outings, caused Tiant to miss his next three starts. Possibly to test his mechanics, the righthander made his second showing out of the bullpen, on September 21, tossing two innings of scoreless relief against the Angels. Tiant's final start of the season was delivered four days hence. He painted his league-best ninth whitewash, one-hitting the New York Yankees in New York. The only New York hit was a first-inning single by Mickey Mantle: the final hit of his celebrated career.

Tiant's incredible 1.60 ERA, in 258⅓ innings, was the lowest by a starting pitcher in the American League in 49 years. Only Denny McLain (31) of the 103-win Tigers and Dave McNally (22) of second-place Baltimore recorded more wins.

The Indians finished third in the American League, the team's best placement in nine years. Cleveland increased their 21-game winner's $20,000 salary 150 percent and forbade him from pitching over the winter. According to Tiant, the dictum was the worst order he could have received.

*   *   *

Except for the winter of 1965, Luis Tiant had not stopped pitching for any extended period since he had become a professional. Multiple summers in Mexico and the U.S. minor leagues, followed by consecutive winters in Cuba, Puerto Rico, Nicaragua and Venezuela had all escorted him to his fabulous 1968 campaign.

"When I arrived at spring training [in 1969] I had a stiff shoulder," Tiant explained in his book. "Then a muscle in my back tightened and I couldn't get rid of it. It bothered me all year long."[43] The theory subscribed to by Tiant was that he had to pitch to keep his arm muscles loose and to stay sharp with his control, and that meant pitching year-round with little interruption.

Tiant was derailed, and derailed badly in 1969, the year baseball put new franchises into four cities and apportioned its major leagues into divisions. Tiant was befallen with a mysterious "weakness" in his arm. The zip was gone on his fastball. Even so, Tiant gritted through 37 starts, the most he had ever made in the big leagues.

It took Tiant nine starts to win his first game. By that time, May 30, the Indians had made themselves at home in the East Division's cellar. After the season of a lifetime, Tiant came back and lost 20 games, brokered against only nine wins. His ERA was nowhere near as atrocious, at 3.71. With 19 losses, Tiant did not shirk his final pitching turn, which fell on the last day of the season. He was defeated 4–3, by the Yankees in New York. Throughout the season, the right-hander was plagued by walks and home runs, allowing more of each than any pitcher in the league.

Cleveland's manager in 1968 and 1969 was Alvin Dark. The manager disapproved of Tiant's exaggerated manner of pitching. In the midst of Tiant's poor encore season, Dark openly and pointedly criticized the unorthodox gesticulations that Tiant incorporated into his delivery. "You've got to keep your eye on the target. You can't throw your head up in the air, then look over at the scoreboard and then pitch a baseball,"[44] said Dark about the pitcher who had won 21 games for him the prior season using the same technique.

Tiant, an "untouchable" player after the 1968 campaign, suddenly became expendable at the close of the 1969 season. In December, he was shipped off with Stan Williams to the Minnesota Twins for four players in return.

*   *   *

Cleveland's quick disavowal of their 29-year-old moundsman seemed a hasty and regrettable decision as Tiant won his first six decisions for the Twins in 1970.

In the sixth victory, on May 28, the pitcher suffered what was diagnosed as a cracked shoulder blade. It happened as he threw a fastball to Milwaukee's Mike Hegan. Tiant finished the inning and then took himself out of the game. He initially thought he had popped an adhesion. He considered it a positive occurrence, thinking the knotted tissue mass had been what was causing his arm to stiffen during starts. But it was not the case. Tiant was placed on the disabled list, and the defending West Division champions called up 19-year-old right-hander Bert Blyleven to take the injured starter's place in the rotation.

Tiant returned in August but his velocity did not accompany him. The pitcher gained one victory in four decisions, as the Twins wrapped up a second straight division title. Minnesota repeated its League Championship Series defeat to the Baltimore Orioles from 1969, bowing out in three straight games to the East Division champions. Tiant was a non-factor in the series, pitching only two-thirds of an inning in one of the losses.

*   *   *

Tiant arrived at the Twins' spring camp in 1971 weighing 195 pounds, having lost 30 pounds over the winter thanks to a strict exercise regimen. The hurler with the self-described "funny-shaped body" had gained weight over the years and had not pitched at under 200 pounds since his initial seasons in Cleveland. He was listed as being six feet in height, but was probably closer to 5'10". His was a stocky, roly-poly build.

Tiant that season was also at an important crossroads. He had turned 30 the past November. He came to spring training with an arm that had been labeled "suspect" at the end of last season. He pitched in Venezuela over the winter, starting off slowly but improving as the season moved along. He was intent on proving to everyone that Luis Tiant had a lot more mileage remaining in his tank.

The Twins, though, with a front line pitching corps of 1970 Cy Young Award-winner Jim Perry, veteran Jim Kaat and young marvel Blyleven, decided to cut Tiant the day before heading north from Florida. Tiant had pitched only eight innings during the whole exhibition month and had not made an impact (an inopportune muscle pull in his rib cage curtailed his ability to throw for two weeks). The release was a blow to Tiant, who had worked hard over the past six months with the goal of proving to everyone he could still be a productive major league pitcher. Instead, with the release, the label of pitcher with a suspect arm was downgraded to "washed up."

The Atlanta Braves offered Tiant a 30-day minor league contract with their Triple-A team less than three weeks after his Twins release. But the Braves never gave Tiant a fair shake, using him sporadically. The organization let him go at the end of the trial period. Tiant seemed branded for good.

But just as quickly as aspersions can be cast, so too can word of mouth dole out positive results. Pedro Ramos, a 16-year veteran hurler, mostly in the American League, had latched on with the Richmond Braves after *his* recent expulsion from the Washington Senators. Ramos mentioned Tiant to José Santiago, another former major league hurler who, like Ramos, was trying to resurrect a career that had nothing but memories left. Santiago, the Opening Game starter for the Boston Red Sox in the 1967 World Series, was pitching for the Louisville Colonels in the same International League as Richmond. Santiago was told by Ramos, Tiant's teammate, that the Cuban pitcher had regained his fastball, and that all he needed was more of an opportunity to pitch. Santiago had the ear of his manager, Darrell Johnson, who disregarded the poor numbers Tiant had racked up with Richmond and publicized the pitcher to his bosses in New England. Two days after the Braves had given up on him, on May 17, Tiant signed with the Johnson-managed Colonels. Just three weeks afterward, Luis Tiant was promoted to the Red Sox.

Eddie Kasko was a New Jersey-born infielder who had spent the last season of a decade-long major league career as a utility player for the 1966 Boston Red Sox. Four years later, the 38-year-old Kasko had become manager of his former team. In 1971, the Red Sox, as well as the rest of clubs in the American League East, were unable to contend with the Baltimore Orioles and the team's *four* 20-game winners, so Kasko was not adverse to give the promoted Tiant several starts over that summer. Tiant failed in all of them. He lost seven decisions before winning once, the final composition of his won-lost record for Boston in 1971.

The Red Sox, eight games better than .500, finished two places below and 18 games behind the high-flying Orioles in the standings.

* * *

The following year, Tiant started the season where he had finished it in 1971—in the Red Sox bullpen. The 1972 major league season was the first one ever to be snipped of scheduled games due to labor strife. An accord was reached between management and players that allowed the season to begin April 15, ten days after the planned traditional opening in Cincinnati. The schedule was picked up as if there had not been a strike, and no lost games were made up by any of the 24 teams.

The only pennant races that season were both in the American League. In the West Division, the Chicago White Sox put up a moderately good challenge against Charley Finley's Oakland A's, before being counted out in late September. In the East, it was a dog-fight between the Detroit Tigers and Boston Red Sox. And that was due to Luis Tiant.

As of the morning of August 5, Tiant had notched three wins in relief and one as a starter, a complete game. Kasko, who could have easily soured on Tiant after the pitcher's sub-par performances of a season ago, had not discarded the veteran as a potential contributor to his 1972 team, even this deep into the season. Kasko had called upon the right-hander to substitute for Sonny Siebert when Siebert came up with a sore shoulder prior to a start. Tiant, the emergency starter, hurled the distance and defeated the Minnesota Twins, 8–2. That occurred on July 3. Tiant, however, did not receive another start until the second game of a doubleheader on July 30; he was humbled by the Detroit Tigers, 7–2, and his record slipped to 4–4.

Six days later, Tiant defeated the Orioles, 6–3, for his fifth win. That was the evening of August 5, and the fourth-place Red Sox climbed three games over .500, 4½ games behind the division-leading Detroit squad. A week later, in Baltimore, Tiant defeated the Birds again, 5–3, salvaging a twin bill split for the Sox. Seven days after the second conquest of the Orioles, on August 19, Tiant shut out the White Sox, 3–0, on two hits. That effort earned Tiant a permanent spot in the Red Sox's starting rotation. Tiant celebrated the elevated rank with a second shutout in his next start on August 25. The four-hit victims were the Texas Rangers, the former Washington Senators franchise that had abandoned the nation's capital for a fresh start in a new state with a new identity. The victory was Tiant's eighth against four defeats. In his last start of the month, on August 29, Tiant blanked the White Sox by the same earlier score of 3–0, this go-around at Fenway Park.

Boston won five games in a row, bookended by Tiant victories. The fifth win—and Tiant's fourth consecutive shutout—came on a 2–0 whitewash of the Brewers in Milwaukee, in the first game of a Labor Day doubleheader on September 4. Tiant earned the distinction of becoming the first pitcher in big league history to *twice* toss four consecutive shutouts. The 67–59 Red Sox closed to within one-half game of the division lead despite a loss in the second game.

The New York Yankees ended Tiant's cipher string at 40⅓ innings when the club pushed across a run in the fifth inning of his subsequent start on September 8. Tiant prevailed, 4–2, for his seventh win in a row, all by complete games. His record stood at 11–4. In a quick turnaround rematch at Yankee Stadium on September 12, Fritz Peterson, with three innings of relief help from Sparky Lyle, combined to defeat Tiant, 3–2, breaking the pitcher's winning and complete game streaks at seven.

Tiant brushed off the loss to the Yankees and delivered, in back-to-back outings, his fifth and sixth shutouts in his last eight starts. The sixth whitewash on September 20 against Baltimore, was one to remember as much for the pitching effort as for the way the Boston fans hailed Tiant. The resurrected pitcher was showered with standing ovations to open and close the game he pitched against the Orioles, a collective acknowledgement to the man who had become an unexpected savior in a season that had been thought unsalvageable only a two months earlier. With Tiant batting in the eighth inning and the Red Sox leading, 4–0, long-time New England sportswriter Larry Claflin described the exalting sentiment of the evening and the untiring applause it inspired from Fenway fans at that moment.

"When Tiant walked to the plate for his last time at bat," wrote Claflin, "the entire crowd, even some of the paid ushers, stood and cheered. For as long as he was in the batter's box, Tiant was given a standing ovation. In all the years I have been watching baseball in Boston I have never heard anything like it, except for perhaps the day Joe DiMaggio made his final appearance at Fenway Park."[45]

Separated by three games, four American League East teams were in the division hunt on September 24, ten days before the end of the season. The Red Sox moved in front of the pack that day, breaking a tie with the Tigers, after Tiant defeated Detroit and Woodie Fryman, 7–2, in front of a packed house at Fenway. Boston ended the fourth-place Orioles' three-year hold on the division on September 29, when Tiant topped Jim Palmer, 4–2, in ten innings. It was Tiant's ninth complete game victory in his last ten starts. The Red Sox clung to a 1½-game lead with five games remaining. But the baseball winds of fate blew cruelly across Massachusetts over the next few days.

The Red Sox split their next two games. The team arrived in Detroit for the last three games of the season with a one-half game lead and promptly let the division title slip from their clutches. Mickey Lolich, gaining his 22nd win, downed the Sox in the series opener on October 2. The next day, a do-or-die game for Boston, the pitcher the Red Sox most wanted to have on the mound took his turn. But Tiant was out-pitched by Fryman. The Tigers' left-hander, with late-inning relief help, defeated the Red Sox, 3–1. It was only Tiant's second loss in two months; he was removed in the seventh inning, only the second time in 13 starts that he had not registered the game's final out.

The Red Sox had needed two wins in the series, but gained only one, which arrived inconsequentially on the final day. The Tigers' 4–1 loss to Marty Pattin placed the Tigers' record even with the Red Sox in the loss column. The Red Sox finished the season 85–70; the Tigers completed their schedule 86–70. By incidental virtue of winning a surplus game not wiped out by the players' strike, the Tigers won the division.

Luis Tiant, the pitcher who had been cast aside and counted out by many, who had started only three games before the All-Star break, finished the campaign with a record of 15–6 (10–1 at Fenway), with a league-leading 1.91 ERA, and had nearly single-handedly pitched the Red Sox to the division title.

* * *

Luis Tiant—who else?—was the 1973 Opening Day starter for the Red Sox, and for the first time in his career, Tiant and other American League pitchers had to worry only about pitching during games. The Designated Hitter rule, the third big schematic change in the game in five years, was adopted for use in 1973 by the Junior Circuit. Tiant kicked off a second 20-win campaign by cruising past the Yankees, 15–5, on April 6.

Many in baseball, Tiant included, thought the new rule, giving American League teams nine regular batters per lineup, might lead to more pitching inside and possibly an increased number of beanball wars. Tiant also thought the "DH" would allow pitchers to throw more innings, the result of staying in close ballgames longer. Tiant predicted he would throw between 250 and 275 innings. He was off by only three, on the high side.

The 1972 American League "Comeback Player of the Year" did not get off to a great start; Tiant split his first 12 decisions. The Red Sox were also stuck in neutral during that time. When Tiant earned his seventh win on June 12, it nudged the Sox's record to 27–26. His ninth victory, three weeks later, buoyed mediocre Boston back to sea level through

72 games; Tiant handcuffed the visiting Milwaukee Brewers, 4–2, on eight hits, for the team's 36th win.

On July 10, Tiant earned his 11th win, tying Bill Lee for most on the team. The 2–1 victory over the Minnesota Twins was the Red Sox's tenth in 12 games, and moved the squad into first place, percentage points ahead of the New York Yankees. Since their 36–36 record on July 1, Eddie Kasko's fifth-place team, spurred by its noise-making run in early July, made a steady climb up the American League East Division ladder. The club won 54 games of the remaining 90. Tiant won 12 of the 54, including five in September.

An early fall game at Fenway Park saw Tiant outduel the Orioles' Jim Palmer—winner in 1973 of the first of his three Cy Young Awards—2–1, in 12 innings. Ben Oglivie homered leading off the 12th against Palmer to give Tiant his 16th victory. It was one of the few losses for the Orioles in September, however. After slipping in 1972, Baltimore rebounded, with strong pitching again, to the top of the division, outdistancing the second-place Red Sox by eight games.

In his last start of the season, on September 28, Tiant tossed his 23rd complete game, gaining his 20th win, 11–2, versus the Milwaukee Brewers.

* * *

As brilliant as Luis Tiant was in 1968 and in the second half of 1972, his most outstanding season in the major leagues may have been 1974. Tiant tossed seven shutouts, completed 25 of 38 starts, and accumulated a career-best 311⅓ innings pitched. His record was 22–13. It could have been even better.

Tiant was battered on Opening Day, April 5, for seven earned runs in under six innings, but he and the team were not overly pained by the outing as the Red Sox outscored the Milwaukee Brewers, 9–8. In his second start and first at home, Tiant received a no-decision. The Baltimore Orioles outlasted the home team, 7–6, in 11 innings, as neither Tiant nor Orioles starter Jim Palmer brought their best stuff to the ballpark. On April 16, Tiant came out on the short end of a pitcher's duel, 2–1, to the Yankees and Mel Stottlemyre at Shea Stadium, both starters hurling complete games. The author attended the game with his father. The memory of that clear, breezy spring afternoon is quite appreciable to the present day.

My father and I sat in the mezzanine at Shea Stadium, almost directly behind home plate. It was a weekday game and I must have been off from high school on Easter break. I can still see Tiant, pirouetting on the mound, displaying the "23" on his back prior to every pitch to the plate ... the Yankees putting men on bases seemingly in every inning, but they could not break through significantly.... Graig Nettles hit Tiant well all game long.... Most of all I remember Tiant, paunchy and squat—the antithesis of a ballplayer, yet mesmerizing and entertaining in the way he pitched, and without any hint of showmanship. He would come set on the rubber with his hands together, his glove chest-high. And then, as if to tease the hitter, his hands would slowly lower to his belt, shaking as if he had a palsy affliction, before beginning his wind-up.

Tiant started 1–4, before straightening things out against the same Yankees on May 9, at Fenway Park. He three-hit the Bill Virdon-led club, 2–0. Four days afterward, in another complete-game effort, he lost, 4–1, to the Cleveland Indians. After that, Tiant's tosses bore through the bats of American League hitters for four months.

Commencing with a 10–2 win over Baltimore on May 18, Tiant won six straight starts, all by complete game. A game at Anaheim in June, ended the winning streak, but not without a championship effort on Tiant's part. Tiant's third win of the campaign, the 10–2 triumph over the Orioles, kicked off a Red Sox's winning run of 17 victories in 23 games that lifted the team from three games under .500 to eight over and a first-place perch (by three games) in the American League East. Boston hoped to maintain or improve its top position as the team flew cross-country to play the California clubs in mid–June.

In his first start on the West Coast swing, Tiant, riding his six-game winning streak, stepped into the ring of battle with Nolan Ryan of the California Angels. And battle is what it was. Ryan, 27, had emerged as one of the fastest-throwing pitchers in baseball history. As with most speedballers, Ryan was known for double-digit strikeout totals. A year earlier, the boyish-looking Texan had broken Sandy Koufax's record for strikeouts in a single season. Ryan was vexed by bases on balls, but indefatigably pitched around them.

Ryan opened the June 14th Friday night game by striking out the side, wedged around a walk and a single, then pitched two more scoreless innings, allowing one free pass. Tiant retired the first nine Angel's batters in the game.

In the fourth, Ryan walked the bases full, struck out Dick McAuliffe, forced in a run on another walk, and struck out the next two batters. In the bottom of the inning, Tiant ran afoul. Leadoff hitter Mickey Rivers singled, then was picked off by Tiant, but the pitcher threw wildly to first base and Rivers scampered safely into second. Denny Doyle doubled Rivers home. A walk, a single and a groundout plated two more California runs before the frame's final out was recorded by Tiant.

The Angels threatened again in the fifth inning, but Tiant struck out Leroy Stanton with runners on second and third to end the inning and prevent any scoring. In the sixth, the Angels went down quietly against Tiant's offerings. Ryan had struck out two Red Sox hitters in the fifth and whiffed two more in the sixth, twice more keeping the visitors off the scoreboard.

Back-to-back singles by Boston with one out in the seventh did not lead to any runs, as Ryan struck out Bernie Carbo and coaxed a fly to center field from Rico Petrocelli. The Red Sox went down without much of fight in their next go-around against Ryan. A two-out single by shortstop Mario Guererro was forgotten when Cecil Cooper struck out to complete the half-inning. In the lower half of the seventh and eighth innings, Tiant set down the home team again, 1–2–3.

Down by two runs in the ninth inning, the Red Sox tied the game against Ryan. Rick Miller walked. Carlton Fisk flied out to right field for the first out, but Carl Yastrzemski smashed a home run to give Boston new life. The clutch blow rattled Ryan, for he walked the next two batters. But the fastballer regrouped and prevented further damage by fanning McAuliffe and inducing a ground ball out from rookie Rick Burleson, who had entered the game in a prior lineup switch. DH Frank Robinson snapped Tiant's streak of batters consecutively retired at ten when he singled to open the bottom of the ninth. Robinson was forced at second on a unsuccessful sacrifice attempt, and then Al Oliver bounced into a double play to snuff out any further notions of a game-winning score.

In the tenth inning, Boston put runners on first and third with two outs. Yastrzemski batted with a chance to be more of a hero. This time, though, the "Ryan Express" left Yaz standing at the whiff station. The Angels put the leadoff man on again in their turn at bat.

The next hitter, catcher Ellie Rodríguez bunted back to the mound; Tiant fielded and forced John Doherty, who had singled, at second base. Rodríguez complicated things more for the home team when he attempted to steal and was gunned down by his counterpart Fisk. Pinch-hitter Tommy McCraw popped up to complete the first extra stanza.

Ryan registered a three-up, three-down inning in the 11th without striking out batter, his first such inning since the second. Tiant did not have it quite as easy in his opposite half-inning. Leroy Stanton drew a two-out walk, stole second and continued to third on a throwing error by Fisk. Tiant stayed tough and induced Robinson to pop up to the infield.

Two more strikeouts from Ryan emphasized the scoreless top of the 12th for the Red Sox; the whiffs were the 18th and 19th of Ryan's evening. The Angels, in their half-inning, appeared that they would reward their pitcher's blazing efforts when they loaded the bases with one out against Ryan's unremitting opponent. Bobby Valentine, who had entered the game in the 11th inning, lofted a ball to short left field—not deep enough for a tag play from third—for the second out. The next batter, Mickey Rivers, grounded out, keeping the game stalemated at 3–3.

Angels manager Bobby Winkles wanted to take Ryan out after the 12th inning, but the pitcher talked his manager into pitching one more inning. It would have been fine with the Red Sox had Winkles exerted more authority. In the 13th inning, Ryan retired the heart of the Red Sox order on two ground outs and a fly out. The third out was a bounce out to second base by the man who had forced the additional innings—Yastrzemski; it came on Ryan's 235th—and last—pitch of the night.

Intent on giving his mates another chance at victory, the intrepid Tiant took his turn on the mound in the bottom of 13th frame. Doyle greeted the gutsy right-hander with a hit to left field. The Angels executed a sacrifice bunt successfully. Stanton deadened the ball toward third, the play made by McAuliffe, now playing at the left infield corner position. Frank Robinson and Joe Lahoud were afforded opportunities to bring home the winning run from second. Tiant struck both of them out, swinging.

After retiring the last ten men he faced, Ryan was now out of the game. Opening the fifth surplus inning, Ryan's replacement, Barry Raziano, picked up where Ryan had left off and set down a trio of Red Sox batters in order. In bottom half of the 14th inning, the Angels' sixth, seventh, and eighth hitters could not get the ball out of the infield against the magnificently stubborn Tiant.

In the top of the 15th inning, the Red Sox were retired for the fifth inning in a row without putting a man on a base.

Darrell Johnson had been appointed manager of the Red Sox that season, and he must have had his reservations about letting Tiant continue, well aware of Tiant's full curriculum over the past five weeks, including *eight* straight complete games, coming into this one. But, no doubt, after checking with his ace, Johnson allowed Tiant to come out for a sixth additional inning.

As the hour neared midnight in Anaheim, with most of New England and much of the country sleeping soundly, and with Ryan showered and dressed, the 33-year-old Tiant began his attempt at an 11th scoreless inning since the Angels had reached him for their three runs in the fourth.

The pertinacious pitcher obtained his 43rd out on a Bobby Valentine fly out to center. Mickey Rivers batted for a seventh time and singled to the same field. The next batter, Doyle, with two previous hits against Tiant, poked a fastball inside the line in left. Yastrzemski, shading the slap-hitter that way, sprinted over to cut off the ball in the corner. Rivers, who walked around the diamond like his shoes were two sizes too small but ran the bases like he had rockets around his ankles, raced around second and third, and scored.

Tiant, backing up home, silently walked off the field as Rivers was congratulated by teammates. For however many fans remained from the 11,083 that had bought tickets for the game, the applause they provided could have been equally showered upon the bulldog performance of the paunchy, squat pitcher disappearing into the visitors' dugout.

Boston, as a consolation, took the next two games of the series, and headed to Oakland, where the team also won two out of three contests against the A's. The second win belonged to Tiant, 2–1, in 11 innings. The right-hander pitched ten innings and received help in the 11th from Diego Seguí to win his ninth game. The Red Sox flew home from the left coast having gained one-half game on the division.

Tiant himself gained, in two successive starts, his 10th and 11th wins, before losing on the Fourth of July to Baltimore. The Red Sox held on to first place as Tiant won three more starts, allowing one earned run in 27 innings. Tiant won his 15th and 16th games in his final two July starts, prevailing over New York and Detroit by identical 5–4 scores. The hurler moved to 17–7 with a 7–3 road win over the Yankees on August 4.

Over his next four outings, Tiant pulled in three more victories. On August 23, the largest crowd at Lansdowne Street and Brookline Avenue in 18 years (35,866 paid) observed Tiant become the first pitcher in either league to reach 20 wins. It was a gaudy time in Beantown for Sox supporters after Tiant pitched his fifth Fenway shutout of the season, disabling the Oakland A's, 3–0, on six hits. Five straight Red Sox wins, including Tiant's victory this day, created a seven-game advantage over the rest of the division, making for delightful dispositions throughout New England. After starting 1–4, Tiant had won 19 and lost four, with six shutouts.

But over the next five and a half weeks, the Red Sox lost two-thirds of their games. The team's offense became enfeebled, most often when Tiant was on the mound. Following his 20th victory, over the course of four starts made by Tiant, the Red Sox scored one solitary run. Tiant lost three games by shutout, 3–0, 1–0, and 2–0, and received a no-decision in the fourth game, which the Red Sox lost, 2–1, to the New York Yankees in 12 innings.

In the extra-inning game, Tiant departed under frustrating circumstances, after nine innings of a tie game. At Fenway Park on September 10, Tiant was ahead 1–0 entering the ninth. With one out, Lou Piniella walked. Chris Chambliss hit a fair ball down the right field line which was touched by a fan for a ground-rule double. But the umpires, in an infrequently invoked summary judgment, allowed the tying run to score, ruling that the slow-footed Piniella would have scored all the way from first base had the ball not met with interference. Manager Johnson blew his stack and was ejected. With all appeals exhausted, Tiant walked Thurman Munson intentionally to play for two; he retired the next two batters to end the inning, and was then removed from the contest. The Yankees' Pat Dobson pitched a terrific game, spinning 11 innings without allowing an earned run. Alex Johnson hit a home run in the top of the 12th inning, and Sparky Lyle came in to record the save. After that loss, which was Boston's 13th in 17 games, the reeling team found itself in a second-place tie with the Baltimore Orioles, two games behind Bill Virdon's first-place squad.

Boston scored five runs for Tiant on September 15, but Tiant showed up with his worst pitched game of the season, yielding a first-inning grand slam and allowing nine earned runs to the Milwaukee Brewers. The Red Sox were beaten, 9–5. Tiant tossed his 24th complete game in his next start, on September 19, losing, 3–1, to the Detroit Tigers. Five days later, the pitcher recorded his second win of the season at Shea Stadium, 4–0, over the Yankees, in the first game of a twi-night doubleheader. Boston also won the second game. At the end of the two-win day, the 80–74 Red Sox were 3½ games out of first place with eight games to play. A non-champion-like split of those remaining games followed. On September 28, Tiant closed out his 22–13 season with a 7–2 road win over the Tigers.

The Red Sox, who were riding so high in late summer, were left grasping at the tail feathers of the Baltimore Orioles, who put on an absolutely sensational stretch drive and won the division, edging out the second-place Yankees by two games. Boston, 84–78, finished five games further behind.

* * *

In 1975, Luis Tiant won 18 games and lost 14, but his ERA edged over four to 4.02. The swelled earned run ledger was of little consequence because the wiley veteran did his best pitching when the American League champion Red Sox needed it the most.

The Red Sox received fine pitching from their other frontline hurlers. Rick Wise led the staff with 19 wins, Bill Lee added 17, and Reggie Cleveland and Roger Moret combined for 27 victories, split nearly evenly between them. Darrell Johnson also had a potent group of offensive players in the championship mix, including two spectacular rookie outfielders, Fred Lynn and Jim Rice.

Johnson took a more determined Red Sox team into summer's hottest month that season, sitting on a nine-game cushion over the rest of the division. The 1975 club voyaged through a choppy month of August with 16 wins and 12 losses and saw its lead over the second-place Baltimore Orioles recede to five games.

Tiant made a start on August 26 and lost to the California Angels, surrendering five runs. Except for another ineffective start four days later, he did not pitch again until September 11. His back was ailing him, and the Red Sox took extended precautionary measures and rested their stalwart pitcher until the problem had completely dissipated. Tiant returned on September 11 and made sure the first-place lead—still five games—would not change for the worse. He defeated the Detroit Tigers, 3–1, permitting three hits and one walk, while striking out ten.

Tiant followed that start with a 2–0 triumph over Baltimore on September 16, putting the Red Sox 29 games over .500 with their 90th win. The Tigers and Mickey Lolich defeated Tiant four days later, 5–1. Eight days were left in the season, and Boston held a 3½-game lead. Tiant's next start was rained out in New York, and so was the make-up doubleheader the next day, September 24. Tiant had to wait until Friday, September 26, to pitch again, the start of the season's final weekend of games. The magic number for the Red Sox was cut to two that evening as Tiant and Reggie Cleveland befuddled the Cleveland Indians, throwing doubleheader shutouts with four and five hits allowed, respectively. The dual 4–0 Fenway Park wins lifted the Red Sox 4½ games over next-closest Baltimore. Potential make-up games from rain-outs for both the Orioles and Red Sox were not played after the Yankees swept two games from the Orioles the following day, presenting the Red Sox with the American League East title.

With his son watching approvingly, Luis Tiant, Sr., throws the ceremonial first pitch prior to a game at Fenway Park in the late summer of 1975 (photograph from Hall of Fame).

Alvin Dark's Oakland A's were the 95–65 Red Sox's opponents in the playoff series for the American League pennant. In the first game, Tiant showed his former manager the pitching form with which he had closed the season; Tiant shut down the hard-hitting A's on three hits and won, 7–1. Shortstop Rick Burleson's eighth-inning error cost him a shutout. Boston ousted the five-time West Division champions in three straight games. After three consecutive world championships, Charley Finley's Oakland dynasty came to an end on its own home turf, on October 7. Kenny Holtzman, making his second start of the series on two days' rest, was defeated, 5–3, by Rick Wise.

Three games was all it had taken the Cincinnati Reds to dispatch the Pittsburgh Pirates in the National League Championship Series and claim their league's World Series berth. Cincinnati, with a host of offensive and defensive specialists in its lineup and with its 108-win regular-season résumé, was the big favorite to gain possession of the ultimate crown.

In Game 1 of the Fall Classic, October 11, Tiant ground to a screeching halt the "Big Red Machine" that had steamrolled its way to a 20-win margin over its nearest division competitor. Scoreless through the first six and a half innings, Tiant, who had batted once all season, started the Boston rally with a leadoff single in the seventh. Four hits, a walk, a sacrifice

Following his 160-plus-pitch performance in Game 4 of the 1975 World Series versus the Cincinnati Reds, a paunchy Luis Tiant ices his right elbow while puffing on a victory cigar.

fly and three outs later, the Red Sox had batted around for six runs to break the game open. Having allowed five hits through seven innings, Tiant retired the Reds' formidable lineup of Rose, Morgan, Bench, Pérez, Foster and Concepción, in order, in the eighth and ninth innings to record the first World Series shutout by a Hispanic pitcher, 6–0.

The Reds won the next two games but in Game 4, in a jockstrap-test of pitching fortitude, Luis the Lionhearted countered the gauntlet of Reds stars for nine steadfast innings. Without his best stuff, Tiant utilized 163 pitches, making a five-run fourth inning by the Red Sox, in which Tiant himself scored the fifth run after singling, stand up for a 5–4 complete game win. Tiant labored for most of the game. Cincinnati scored twice in the first and fourth frames. Only the second, third and seventh innings were easy on the pitcher as he set down the Reds without a baserunner. In their final crack at Tiant, the Reds put two men on base with one out. Ken Griffey drove a shot into deep left center. Center fielder Fred Lynn, on his horse, made a reaching, two-hand catch of the ball in full stride as he fringed the outfield warning track. The next batter was Joe Morgan. Tiant prodded the National League's Most Valuable Player to pop up to Carl Yaztremski at first base to end the game.

Tony Pérez broke loose from a batting slump and hit two home runs that drove in four runs in Game 5. Pérez, who had been 0-for-15 in the Series, was the primary thrust behind Don Gullett's 6–2 win.

Mother Nature played an intrusive role as the Series moved back to New England. The Red Sox plane arriving from Cincinnati was greeted by a boisterous throng of supportive fans at the airport. The disembarking player gaining the longest and loudest cheers was Luis Tiant. Persistent rains caused three postponements of the sixth game. During the evening of one of the rained-out games, Tiant attended a Bruins hockey game at the Boston Garden. Upon his being identified in the crowd on the arena's scoreboard, the entire audience broke out in the same devotional and exalting chant that had greeted Tiant at the airport a few days earlier: "Loo-ie! Loo-ie! Loo-ie!"

The postponements altered Darrell Johnson's starting pitching scheme. Tiant, slated to pitch Game 7, was redesignated to pitch Game 6. It was difficult to argue with Johnson's decision. Facing elimination, the Red Sox had to win, and if the team lost, it was not going to be with their rested, best pitcher on the bench. Tiant's mound opponent for the October 21 Game 6, which was replete with exciting and suspenseful moments and one frozen-in-time ending, was Gary Nolan.

Fred Lynn gave the Red Sox an early lead with a first-inning, three-run home run. Tiant held the Reds scoreless for four innings. In the fifth, Cincinnati reached the Red Sox pitcher for three runs on a walk and three hits, one a two-run triple by Ken Griffey. Tying the game, the Reds ended Tiant's streak of 40⅓ consecutive innings without yielding an earned run at Fenway Park, begun during the season. Tiant's opposite number, Nolan, had received an early hook from "Captain Hook," the nickname of Reds manager Sparky Anderson. Following Nolan, four other Reds pitchers kept the Red Sox off the board for five more innings.

Tiant retired the Reds in the sixth inning without any damage, coaxing Pete Rose to ground out with men on first and second. In the top of the seventh, George Foster doubled home two runs with two outs to give the Reds a 5–3 lead. César Geronimo then deposited Tiant's first pitch of the eighth inning into the right field bleachers for the Reds' sixth run; the blast triggered Tiant's removal. He had given it his best. Perhaps Tiant was too well-rested, with six days having elapsed since his tenacious start in Cincinnati. Or perhaps the great Reds team had finally risen to his challenges.

Tiant was removed to a standing ovation. He walked back to the dugout, the close-fitting double-knit uniform clinging unflatteringly to his bulging body, a chewing tobacco tin clearly delineated in his back pocket. Tiant was enveloped in the dugout by consoling teammates. One of the first was Bill Lee, who had originally been scheduled to pitch Game 6 and had voiced his disapproval at being passed over in favor of the dumpy pitching master.

Held without scoring since the first, in the bottom of the eighth inning, the Red Sox eliminated their three-run deficit with one swing of the bat. Lynn opened with a single and advanced to second when Rico Petrocelli walked. Two outs later, the players had not advanced. Johnson called on Bernie Carbo to pinch-hit for pitcher Roger Moret. Carbo, a left-handed hitter who had pinch-hit a home run earlier in the Series, took the count to two balls and two strikes against Reds right-hander Rawley Eastwick. Carbo then fought off an inside offering from Eastwick, looking bad on the swinging foul. Eastwick's next pitch was swung at by Carbo and lifted high and deep to straight-away center field. The ball carried and carried and landed, with a few rows to spare, in the elevated bleacher seats. An explosion of cheers, shouts and screams after the electrifying blow shook the tectonic limits of Fenway Park. The deafening noise within the venerable structure pumped new life into the faintly breathing Red Sox.

In the ninth inning, after the Reds did not score, the Red Sox nearly snatched away the victory, loading the bases with no outs. Denny Doyle was thrown out at the plate by left fielder Foster on a 7–7–2, inning-crushing double play. Amid the park's din, single-syllable barked halts from third base coach Don Zimmer were misinterpreted by lead runner Doyle, who ran the Red Sox out of potential victory. ("No! No! No!" *not* "Go! Go! Go!") The next hitter, Rico Petrocelli, grounded out.

In the tenth inning, the Reds stranded a man on second without scoring and the Red Sox sent only three men to the plate, each coming up empty.

Pete Rose was hit by a pitch leading off the 11th inning and was forced at second by Ken Griffey. Joe Morgan turned on a 2–2 pitch from Dick Drago (who pitched three relief innings of one-hit ball) and drove a screecher into right field that seemed ticketed for extra bases. Dwight Evans, arguably the best defensive right fielder of his era, raced back in front of the low outfield wall and made a sensational, twisting, game-saving catch of Morgan's drive—and threw back to the infield to double off Griffey at first base.

After Boston was retired again in order in their half-inning, the Reds put two men on base with one out in the 12th stanza. Rick Wise, Drago's reliever, held firm and prevented the Reds from scoring.

Carlton Fisk was the first batter in the bottom of the 12th inning. With a slightly out-in-front upper-cut swing, the Red Sox catcher whacked at the second pitch from Reds pitcher Pat Darcy. Fisk connected, and the ball sailed high in the air down the line toward the narrow foul pole in left. The ball was headed out of the park, and the only question was whether it would do so as a fair or foul ball. Loitering attentively at the plate, with animated, arm-waving gestures, Fisk implored the flight of the ball to remain true and fair. Within seconds, Fisk reacted with exultant hand-claps and upward arm thrusts at the sight of the ball clunking off the Green Monster's yellow antenna. The sequence of Fisk's energetic appeal has become part of the temporal mural of baseball's greatest moments.

The Red Sox won, 7–6, one of baseball's greatest World Series games. The victory was an integral part of a World Series credited with reawakening a slumbering game in the consciousness of the North American fan.

Nothing—not even the seven-game World Series loss to the Reds that followed the next night—could have spoiled Luis Tiant's year in 1975. Tiant had been joyously reunited with his parents in August. The experience was a very emotional one for Tiant, to finally embrace the father he had unexpectedly been forced to separate from 14 long years ago.

The reunion had been made possible through the combined political efforts of two United States Senators, Edward W. Brooke of Massachusetts and George McGovern of South Dakota. Brooke arranged for McGovern, who was making an unsanctioned trip to Cuba, to hand deliver a letter to Fidel Castro requesting that Tiant's parents be allowed out of Cuba to visit their son. The dictator acceded to the request.

The son met the father at Logan International Airport on August 21, 1975, and broke down in tears in front of a scrutinizing contingent of press and media. The first moments of the meeting were retold this way by Tiant in his book: "As soon as I saw my father step off that plane, I put my hand over my eyes and cried. I wasn't going to do that, but I couldn't help it."[46]

The son and father embraced.

"Don't cry," spoke the father softly. "The cameras will see you."

"I don't care," answered the son. "That's the way I feel."[47]

Isabel Tiant had managed a rendezvous trip to Mexico City to see her son and his fledgling family in October of 1968, so the reunion with her son, while emotional, was not quite as poignant as her husband's. Isabel Tiant watched happily as her son introduced to her husband the daughter-in-law and three grandchildren he had never met.

Luis Tiant called the reunion with his father and mother at Logan Airport the greatest day of his life.

He had wanted more than anything in his baseball career to pitch in a World Series and to have his father present during it, and it had happened. The arrival of his parents had turned Luis Tiant, the complete pitcher, into Luis Tiant, the completed man.

*　*　*

The Red Sox failed miserably in the defense of their American League title in 1976. Tiant was one of the few bright spots on the team, winning 21 games.

The pitcher won his first three starts in April, but following the third victory, on April 23, the Red Sox lost ten games in a row. Tiant was stained with two of the losses. The Red Sox never recovered; the team barely played above .500 ball over the entire season.

The "Gold Dust Twins" of Lynn and Rice were more like dust in the wind as sophomores in 1976. Rice did lead the team with 25 home runs; he also led the league in strikeouts with 123. The unique 1975 Rookie of the Year and MVP Lynn hit .314, but clubbed only ten homers and drove in a meager 65 runs in 132 games. The team that had led the majors in hitting in 1975 was a shadow of its former self, dropping a dozen points in team batting average. Darrell Johnson was fired a little more than halfway through the schedule and replaced by Don Zimmer.

Tiant himself produced a mediocre first half. As a by-product, questions increased in frequency, all pointing to his age as the reason for his "decline." But the 35-year-old resoundingly answered those who wanted to put him prematurely out to pasture. Following a loss to the New York Yankees and Ed Figueroa on July 30, that left his record at 10–10, Tiant won 11 out of his final 13 decisions. He was named the American League "Pitcher of the Month" for August, winning six games. One of the wins was a 2–1, ten-inning duel against Nolan Ryan and the California Angels in Anaheim. Left fielder Rice threw out the potential tying run at the plate to end the game.

Defeating the Milwaukee Brewers, 7–1, on three hits, one walk and 12 strikeouts on September 21, earned Tiant his fourth 20-win season and third with Boston. (Only Cy Young claimed more 20-win campaigns for the Red Sox.) In his next start, on September 25, Tiant vanquished the Baltimore Orioles and Ross Grimsley, 1–0, permitting but two singles at Memorial Stadium.

That 1–0 loss by the second-place Orioles, coupled with a win by the New York Yankees on the same day, gave the Yankees their first title of any kind in 12 years. The 83–79 Red Sox finished well back in third place.

In December, 71-year-old Luis Tiant, Sr., died. After attending his wake, Isabel Tiant suffered a heart attack and slipped away to join her husband, two days later.

* * *

In November 1976, the Red Sox dipped into the free-agent pool and signed reliever Bill Campbell to a million-dollar deal. Recently, the team had also locked up Lynn, Fisk and Burleson to individually lucrative contracts. Tiant wanted his contract, which had a year remaining at $180,000, extended. He thought he should be rewarded for the exceptional work of the past, and the multi-year contracts doled out by the Red Sox fueled discontent on his part when he did not receive further commitment from management. Tiant was not asking for millions like the other players—"just what I earned," he told the press, as the leading pitcher of the Red Sox staff the past five seasons. Tiant only wanted to be treated fairly.

Tiant's position led to a late 1977 arrival to spring camp. The end result was that Tiant did not receive his first start until the season's fifth game. He pitched the five-inning foundation to the Red Sox's first win, 8–4, on April 16.

The Red Sox were inconsistent early on, and so was Tiant. But in May, the Red Sox gained momentum, and they caught fire in June, winning 16 out of 18 games during a three-week stretch. The 14th win, on June 21, was provided by Tiant with a 7–0, two-hit, road shutout of the Orioles and rookie Dennis Martínez. Jim Rice and George Scott slugged home runs in the game, giving the team 24 long balls in seven games. (The next night, four Red Sox' hitters rocked Jim Palmer for five circuit blasts, emphatically posting a new major league team record of 29 home runs in eight games.) The shutout evened Tiant's record through ten decisions. At that point, the Red Sox's record of 39–25 placed the team on top of the division, 4½ lengths ahead of New York and Baltimore.

But Boston proceeded to lose nine straight games, to drop a game behind the Yankees on the Fourth of July. From there forward, it was a three-team race in the American League East, between the Red Sox, Yankees and Orioles, all sporting very strong clubs.

Tiant pitched his best game on August 5, a walk-free, five-hit shutout of the A's in Oakland. The 1–0 win was Tiant's eighth, and the eighth win in a row for the Red Sox, who won three more times before losing. In mid–August, another victory stretch of five straight games lifted the Red Sox to a 3½-game, first-place advantage over the Orioles. But the streaky Sox lost eight of their next ten games and were overtaken—for good—by the Yankees. Boston finished two lengths in back of repeat-division-winning New York, in a second-place tie with the Orioles.

Though Tiant won his last four decisions on the season, he did not pitch consistently true to form. After the season, Tiant acknowledged the 4.53 ERA that accompanied his 12–8 record was not up to his standard. He encountered a persistent strain of criticism for the first time since arriving in Boston. While acknowledging that he did not pitch well, the pitcher also lashed out at local sportswriters whose criticisms, he said, affected him and his family.

In 1977, the veteran Tiant's skin was surprisingly not thick enough to weather the disapproving judgments of the same writers that had voted Tiant the Red Sox's most valuable pitcher for five straight seasons.

* * *

The following year, Boston won 99 games, two more than in 1977, but the season ended in folkloric heartbreak.

The prior season, Tiant had been three weeks late reporting to spring training because of contract issues. In 1978, Tiant signed for an undisclosed amount and came in on time, but dislocated a finger during camp and was not able to make his first start until April 23. The Red Sox had strengthened their pitching by signing free agent Mike Torrez and trading for Dennis Eckersley. These younger arms, and Bill Lee's 7–1 start, pushed Tiant to the back of the starting rotation. Bob Stanley brilliantly picked up the slack for relief specialist Bill Campbell, who, after pitching in nearly 150 games over the past two seasons, lost for good his station as a premier reliever with the team.

After closing April with four losses, the Red Sox seared through the American League with a 41–14 record over the next two months. Torrez had won 11 games, Eckersley and Lee eight each; Tiant ratcheted a fine 7–1 mark. (Tiant's sole loss came on June 30, in 11 innings, to Baltimore, 3–2.) On the morning of July 1, Boston stood eight games ahead of Milwaukee and nine in front of New York. And things got better. The Red Sox won ten out of their next 15 engagements, including their 62nd victory, in their 90th game, on July 19.

Immediately afterward, the Red Sox lost nine out of ten games. But the club collected itself and lost only five times in their next 16 outings. When Tiant, a loser of five of his last six decisions, beat the California Angels, 4–2, on August 16, the 75–44 Red Sox maintained a seven-game advantage over the second-place Yankees. The Red Sox scored twice in the ninth against Nolan Ryan, who committed one of three Angels errors in the inning, leading to the decisive scoring. For Tiant, the complete game win was extra special; it was the 200th of his stellar career.

Boston's lead in the division had been whittled to four games by the New York Yankees by September 5. The persistent Yankees had closed in on Boston's once seemingly unassailable 14-game lead on July 19. The New York team commenced a four-game series in Boston on September 7, wherein the Yankees kicked the Red Sox all the way up and down New England, from the lower half of Connecticut to the upper regions of Maine.

Inflicting pulverizing defeats on Boston in the first three games (15–3, 13–3, 7–0), the Yankees were on the brink of sealing the four-day humiliation with a Sunday win. Tiant, who was not scheduled to pitch in the series (having pitched a shutout over the Orioles the day before the Yankees came to town), sensed it was time for him to take the ball on three days' rest to try and stop the bloodbath. Tiant cried for the ball. But the plea fell mutely on the ears of the person in charge. Manager Don Zimmer opted not to pitch Tiant. With the Red Sox having had their brains beaten out for three days, Zimmer, inexplicably started Bobby Sprowl in the fourth game of the series, a pitcher with seven major league innings of experience under his belt. Sprowl did not make it out of the first inning; the Red Sox lost the September 10 finale, 7–4. The "Boston Massacre" henceforth conveyed a new meaning in New England's historic vernacular.

The Yankees eventually passed the Red Sox and took over first place. To the Red Sox's credit, the club finished the season with eight straight wins to tie the New Yorkers on the last day of the schedule. Tiant won three of the eight games—twice pitching on three days' rest. Tiant made three starts, hurling two complete games, including a 5–0 conquest of the Toronto Blue Jays in game 162, which, coupled with a Yankees' 9–2 loss to the Cleveland Indians, set up a one-game playoff for the American League East title.

In game 163, at Fenway Park on October 2, Ron Guidry decisioned the Red Sox, 5–4. Guidry, in 1978, recorded one of the greatest pitching seasons in baseball history. The left-hander won his 25th game; he received big assists from Bucky Dent and his infamous (from the Red Sox fans' point of view) three-run home run, and Goose Gossage, who registered the final eight outs of the game.

*   *   *

New Red Sox ownership, its principal leaders Buddy Le Roux and Haywood Sullivan, would not offer Tiant more than a one-year guaranteed contract for 1979. The principal owner of the New York Yankees seized an opportunity to get back at the Red Sox for signing away Mike Torrez the prior season and inked the free agent Tiant to a two-year guaranteed contract. George Steinbrenner also included a long-term scouting position with the Yankees as part of the contract.

"The loss of Tiant was a trauma for Boston fans," wrote New England sportswriter Jack Craig. "He was more than a superb pitcher. He was charismatic and a clutch performer."[48]

The Yankees team Tiant joined in 1979 were two-time world champions. Any dynastic aspirations, however, were ended the same season by the Baltimore Orioles. During the campaign, the Yankees suffered the tragic loss of their team captain. Thurman Munson was killed in a plane crash on August 2, an off day for the club. (The Yankees were 14 games behind Baltimore at the time.)

In the first game played by the Yankees following Munson's death, Tiant was the starting pitcher. The game was played at Yankee Stadium. In an emotionally charged game, the Yankees were defeated, 1–0, by the mound combination of Scott McGregor and Tippy Martínez of the Orioles. Tiant took the loss, allowing the run on two hits in eight innings.

Tiant made his pitching return to Boston on September 11. (He had split two starts against the Red Sox in New York.) Tiant left the game with one out in the sixth inning, after pulling his groin muscle. He was not involved in the decision, as the Yankees scored late and often to pull out an 8–3 win.

Even though he received only two starts in April, Tiant finished with 30 starts, tied with 1978 Cy Young Award winner Guidry for second-most on the team. Tiant pitched just under 200 innings and won 13 games. It was the final effective major league season for "El Tiante."

LEGACY

In 1980, New York left Tiant off its playoff roster for its American League Championship Series against the Kansas City Royals. The pitcher had posted an 8–9 record for the campaign with a 4.89 ERA, the highest of his career.

The Yankees did not try to re-sign the 40-year-old hurler after the season. Tiant hung on for two more seasons, but they were nothing more than brief hook-ups with clubs looking to supplement their pitching depth in the latter months of the season.

Tiant obtained his last major league win, 10–2, versus the Boston Red Sox on August 17, 1982, pitching for the California Angels. The West Coast club had recently purchased Tiant from the Tabasco franchise of the Mexican League. At Anaheim, the starter hurled eight innings and allowed one earned run, striking out eight. Less than three weeks later, Tiant was the losing pitcher in his last appearance on a major league mound. On September 4, Tiant, permitting seven of the runs, was defeated by the Milwaukee Brewers, 8–2. Robin Yount, who was eight years old when Tiant debuted in the big leagues, sent Tiant to the showers with a single in the sixth inning. The 27-year-old Yount was the last major league batter to whom Tiant pitched.

Luis Tiant, who may be the only pitcher in history to hurl shutouts the first time scaling the mounds of Yankee Stadium, Dodger Stadium and Fenway Park, as he did in his rookie season, felt he could still pitch, and did so in the winter of 1982 with the Santurce Crabbers. Tiant squeezed 112 more innings from his arm, pitching in Mexico in 1983, and then the 43-year-old stopped pitching competitively.

Apparently the scouting job with the Yankees did not pan out, and as often unjustly happens to former players who want to stay close to the game after they retire, there were no jobs in baseball available or offered to Tiant. He took a position with the Massachusetts Lottery to support the family that had grown to three children with the addition of a second boy, Daniel, in 1974.

It was not until 1992 that Tiant re-entered the game, at the calling of the Los Angeles Dodgers, who hired him as a minor league pitching coach. After six years as pitching coach, Tiant found a college managerial job in Georgia with the Savannah College of Art & Design. It was a brief tenure that Tiant enjoyed, especially in his second year when his eldest son joined him as an assistant at the NCAA Division III baseball program. Prior to the manager's stint, Tiant had been elected to the Red Sox Hall of Fame in 1997.

During the internet-enthusiastic period that followed, Tiant linked his named to a personalized website, where one could purchase a custom brand of cigars—not too unlike the victory cigars Tiant used to smoke in the showers and whirlpools to the gleeful amusement of clubhouse reporters.

Finally, in 2001, Red Sox general manager Dan Duquette brought Tiant back into the Red Sox family, giving him a dual field and executive level position as pitching coach for Boston's Class A Lowell Spinners, and as special assistant to the general manager.

"I've waited a long time—23 years," Tiant said at the press conference announcing his return to the organization for whom he had so measurably and memorably pitched. "I'm proud to work for the Red Sox…. I am grateful for the people here and the way they have treated my family."[49] Accompanying him was his wife Maria and two sons.

The 62-year-old was summoned off the field the very next year to take on the color-man role in the broadcast booth for the Spanish Radio network airing Red Sox games.

Prior to the Red Sox-Rays game on September 6, 2010, the former pitching great was paid homage by the Red Sox front office at Fenway Park. Marking 35 years since Tiant nearly pitched the Red Sox to the world championship, the tribute was accentuated by an on-field ceremony, which included Tiant's family. Tiant was presented with a luxury watch by Red Sox manager Terry Francona. Also on hand, lending their support, were former teammates Bill Lee and Dwight Evans, along with Red Sox legend Johnny Pesky. The almost–70-year-old Tiant capped the event by tossing out the ceremonial first pitch—his trademark "back turn" included—to David Ortiz, who was on the receiving end at home plate.

The Tiants have retired to Ft. Myers, Florida, where the former pitching great continues a relationship with the Red Sox as a spring training instructor.

Heart and Soul

Journalist and author Howard Bryant wrote in *Shut Out: A Story of Race and Baseball in Boston,* that Luis Tiant "was the first player in the city's history to be so totally embraced that he would enter a space usually reserved for white stars." In the same writing, Tiant defended Boston's reputation for racial intolerance. "Boston gets a bad rap," the former pitcher said. "I heard so many people say that Boston is racist. Everyplace is racist, even my own country of Cuba. Some people had problems there, and I do feel sorry for all of the Afro-Americans there and what they went through. But what happened to me, I can't say a bad word about Boston."[50]

When Tiant had returned to Boston for the first time, pitching for the Yankees in 1979, it was unintentionally upstaged by Carl Yastzremski, who was one hit away from 3,000. Tiant walked Yaz and popped him up, and after making two other outs in the 9/11/79 game, Number 8 had to wait another day to reach the hit milestone. Yastzremski—who battled behind Tiant for eight years and battled as hard as any pitcher could ask from a player for 23 major league seasons—also eloquently assessed the departure from the Red Sox of the Fu-Manchued hurler. "When they let Luis Tiant go to New York," Yastzremski said, "they tore out our heart and soul."[51]

The final vignette remaining to validate Luis Tiant's baseball life would be his induction into the National Hall of Fame. Tiant's allotted 15 years of post-retirement ballot placement have expired; his Hall of Fame fate lies with a revamped Veterans Committee. That committee (The Golden Era) did not offer a promising outlook for Tiant in 2011. A release of the tabulations reflected that Tiant had received three or fewer votes from the 16 member committee. Twelve votes (75) were required for induction, and were received by one player, Ron Santo, among a list of eight former players and two baseball executives on the ballot.

Tiant's numbers alone are worthy of induction: 229 wins, 49 shutouts, 3.30 ERA. Nearly 3,500 innings and over 2,400 strikeouts. Numbers as good as Hunter's and Bunning's and Drysdale's, all great and deserving Cooperstown co-habitants. Tiant recorded two score-less streaks of 40 innings. Walter Johnson is the only other major league pitcher with an equal accomplishment. Employing 21st century analytical data, Tiant's lifetime WAR (66.7) is higher than the great Bob Feller (63.6) and Juan Marichal (63.1). His career ERA+ of 114 is on par with Robin Roberts' 113 and his overall WHIP of 1.199 stands with Bert Blyleven's 1.198.

The Cooperstown admittance of Pee Wee Reese, a lifetime .269 hitter and the infield glue of the outstanding Brooklyn Dodgers teams from two generations ago, is credentialed on his Hall of Fame plaque for having "intangible qualities of subtle leadership on and off the field" and being "instrumental in easing acceptance of Jackie Robinson as baseball's first black performer." The following then could be vigorously offered for anyone who may find Tiant's baseball-only compendium insufficient for Hall of Fame entrance.

Should not the status of Luis Tiant as the "heart and soul" of the Red Sox and Boston's first "totally embraced," culturally diverse professional athlete, merit—as it did for Reese—favorable induction consideration from Cooperstown's Veterans Committee for *his* visceral leadership and social consequence in what was baseball's most reluctantly conformist city?

6

The 1970s—Mike Cuéllar, Dennis Martínez

Mike Cuéllar

Outstanding left-handed pitchers, more often than not, are as peculiar as they are rare. Mike Cuéllar was one of these peculiar and rare breeds of pitchers. Cuéllar possessed a parcel of superstitious practices that bemused teammates and fans. But idiosyncrasies aside, Mike Cuéllar was the top left-hander in the American League during most of the 1970s, and the winningest left-hander in baseball from 1966 to 1975. In that ten-year term, he won 175 games.

Cuéllar was, as are a majority of portsiders, a late bloomer. Arrival at stardom was a delayed one. As a 19-year-old in 1956, Cuéllar made his professional debut in the Cuban Winter League with Almendares, the team that had arranged his discharge from the army in order to enlist with its squad. The Cincinnati Reds, who had set their sights on Cuéllar during the conscripted time the teenager had spent hurling for the Cuban army's baseball team, signed Cuéllar in 1957. The major league prospect's life was not too dramatically altered after he signed with the Reds. The big league club placed Cuéllar on its affiliate Triple-A Sugar Kings team based in Havana.

Cuéllar's first game as a minor league professional was in a Sugar Kings uniform, in the opener of the International League's 1957 season. The nearly 20-year-old tossed four scoreless innings in relief versus Montreal. As a rookie, the 8–7 Cuéllar led the International League in ERA with a 2.55 mark.

After winning 13 games for the Sugar Kings in 1958, including five shutouts, the pitcher received an invitation to the Reds' Florida spring camp, in Tampa, in 1959.

In 20 Grapefruit League innings, Cuéllar allowed six earned runs, good enough to earn a trip north with the big club.

Cuéllar's major league debut came as a reliever in Cincinnati's sixth game of the 1959 campaign. Over two innings, the Philadelphia Phillies mistreated the young left-hander, scoring six runs, five earned, including a grand slam by Gene Freese. After another less than impressive two-inning relief stint, Cuéllar was returned to Havana, where, although not indicated by his 10–11 record, he pitched extremely well for the eventual International League champions.

He pitched well enough to justify a start in the second game of the so-called "Little World Series"—the championship challenge between the Triple-A titlists of the American Association and the International League. Cuéllar did not distinguish himself in the series, captured by the Sugar Kings with a thrilling seventh game victory, but he did manage a victory, in relief, in Game 4.

In April of 1960, Cuéllar was back trying to make the Reds, but as spring camp disbanded, Cuéllar and Rogelio Alvarez, another Sugar Kings player, were returned to Cuba. The two pitchers and the rest of their teammates were soon displaced by the politically forced relocation of the Sugar Kings' franchise that summer to the U.S. state of New Jersey. In one and a half seasons with Havana/Jersey City, Cuéllar logged an unimpressive 10–19 record. The pitcher was sent to Indianapolis midway through the 1961 season. From there, the Triple-A Indians traded him in July to Syracuse, where he finished the season.

Having pitched winter ball in Cuba every season since 1956, Mike Cuéllar, in the fall of 1961, simultaneously found himself as a player without a winter league team and a man without a country. Like most other Cuban professionals, Cuéllar turned to an alternate baseball nation to ply his trade. Cuéllar pitched for Valencia in Venezuela's winter circuit.

The Cincinnati Reds released the underperforming pitcher on April 26, 1962. Cuéllar spent the summer season in Mexico, pitching for the champion Monterrey Sultanes; he turned in an 11–6 record and led the league in strikeouts with 134. The Boer Indians selected Cuéllar from a list of eligible minor leaguer players and he spent the winter of 1962 pitching in Managua, Nicaragua.

The next spring, Monterrey sold Cuéllar back to the U.S. minor leagues, to the Jacksonville Suns, a St Louis Cardinals satellite. A Jacksonville teammate of Cuéllar was Rubén Gómez. The former major league pitcher, most prominently with the New York Giants during the preceding decade, talked Cuéllar into developing a new pitch—a screwball—and a strategy for using it. "Ruben inspired me to use the screwball," Cuellar stated. "He didn't have me throw it his way, but gave me advice on using the pitch."[1] The mastering and effective use of the pitch eventually helped elevate Cuéllar to a higher pitching plane.

Cuéllar began including the deviant pitch as a regular part of his pitching repertoire when he returned to the Suns the following season, 1964, after spending the winter pitching for Arecibo in Puerto Rico.

"This spring at Homestead, Fla., Jacksonville catchers saw little else from Mike besides the dipsy-do pitch," wrote sportswriter Bob Price. "Cuellar had kept his newly found screwball in the bullpen the latter part of 1963 while producing a 6–7 record for the cellar-dwelling Suns, but last winter in Nicaragua he began depending on it in the clutches. Confidence in the pitch came with practice. Mike hasn't hesitated to use it this year. His 5–1 record with a 1.81 earned-run average indicates his confidence is justified."[2]

Mike Cuéllar was signed by the Cincinnati Reds in the late 1950s. The Cuban later developed into the major leagues' greatest Latin American left-handed pitcher.

Price also identified, with the following comments, a Cuéllar personality trait, one that portrayed the pitcher as not one to wear his heart on his uniform sleeve, but that left no reservation about the pitcher's commitment: "Cuellar is a serious student of pitching, but he'll fool the average bystander because of his quiet nonchalant attitude. More than one fan has griped that Mike wasn't taking the game seriously enough. But it couldn't be further from the truth. He dies a little with every loss."[3]

Cuéllar's improved pitching at Jacksonville earned him a mid-season call-up to St Louis. On June 28, 1964, he made his initial major league start. His opponent was Chris Short, who was not short on anything that day. The Phillies left-hander blanked the Cardinals on five hits, 5–0. Cuéllar pitched seven innings and allowed three runs, and struck out rookie sensation Richie Allen four times. Cuéllar appeared in 32 games, starting seven, over the remainder of the season. His 5–5 rookie record with the Cardinals provided a mediocre snapshot of his up-to-then minor league career mark of 65–65.

St. Louis, in need of left-handed bullpen help, thought it was trading an average pitcher when it dealt Cuéllar, along with right-hander Ron Taylor, to the Houston Astros in June 1965, for pitchers Chuck Taylor and Hal Woodeshick, the desired left-handed reliever.

Cuéllar made four starts for Houston and did not win any of them, hurling for a team kept out of last place in the ten-team league only by the New York Mets.

* * *

In 1966 with the Astros, Cuéllar was given a chance to pitch regularly as a starter for the first time in the major leagues. He notched 12 wins and recorded the league's second-best ERA (2.22) in 28 starts and ten relief outings. Of his ten losses, two were by 1–0 scores (one in ten innings).

Cuéllar won his first six decisions in 1966. The sixth victory generated a career-high 15 strikeouts. It was a 3–2, nine-inning effort over the St. Louis Cardinals in the Astrodome on June 25. Trying for his seventh win on July 1, he battled three different Cincinnati Reds pitchers for 11 innings in a 1–1 tie game, before being removed for a pinch-hitter in the bottom of the 11th. The Astros gained a 2–1 win in the next inning. Cuéllar lost more games than he won over the next two months, but not necessarily because his pitching was off the mark. On September 10, he lost his second 1–0 game, hurling 9⅔ innings against the Los Angeles Dodgers and the combined pitching of Don Drysdale and Phil Regan. It was the second of four consecutive shutouts the Houston team suffered at Dodger Stadium, September 9–11.

In his last start of the season, on September 28, Cuéllar provided himself with an indispensable run in his 4–3 victory over the Cincinnati Reds at Crosley Field, socking the first of seven career home runs.

* * *

The Astros nudged into eighth place in the National League in 1966. In 1967, Cuéllar nudged himself to the front of the Astros' pitching corps and bettered by four his win total from the prior campaign.

Cuéllar was tabbed by second-year Astros manager Grady Hatton as the team's Opening Day starter against the Atlanta Braves on April 11. The left-hander tossed a five-hitter and downed the Braves, 6–1, in the Astrodome. Cuéllar was rocked in his next trip to the mound against the St. Louis Cardinals, but avoided a loss thanks to productive hitting from his teammates. Bob Gibson, allowing seven earned runs, was the 11–8 victor; Steve Carlton picked up a three-inning save. In start number three, April 21, Cuéllar threw nine innings, allowing one unearned run to Cincinnati. The visiting Reds scored two markers in the tenth to pull out a 3–1 win. Cuéllar was not involved in the decision. The pitcher then lost two out of three decisions, suffering losses to the Cardinals and Los Angeles Dodgers, while defeating the Philadelphia Phillies in between.

On May 21, Cuéllar spun his first shutout, an eight-hit, 2–0 indoor muffling of the San Francisco Giants. In his next start, on May 27, Cuéllar allowed the Cubs three singles at Wrigley Field, earning a 2–1 decision over Curt Simmons. A 4–1 victory over New York Mets rookie Tom Seaver followed on the first of June. Five days later, Cuéllar improved to 6–2 with a six-hit, 13-strikeout, no-walk performance against the Cardinals at Busch Stadium. Throwing his fourth complete game in a row, Mike allowed one earned run in the 3–2 triumph.

The streak came to an end in Cuéllar's next outing, but it did not prevent the pitcher from picking up a win. Allowing two earned runs at Crosley Field, Cuéllar defeated the Reds, 7–4, on June 11. He won again (6–2, at home, over the Giants) before the Cubs and Ferguson Jenkins defeated him, 3–2, on June 24. Both starters hurled the distance.

Cuéllar's 9–3 record on July 1 earned him a nomination for the All-Star Game in Anaheim. The pitcher's record especially stood out on the 28–47 Astros. In the longest Mid-Summer Classic on record—won by the Nationals, 2–1, in 15 innings—Cuéllar did his part and kept the American League stars off the board in two of the extra frames.

A dry spell of three weeks between victories ended for Cuellar on July 24. In the Astrodome, he downed the Philadelphia Phillies, 2–1, in 11 innings, a game in which Cuéllar scored the winning run. Cuéllar allowed only two hits and two walks, and the run he allowed was unearned. Houston was dead last in the league at the time, with only 39 wins. The Astros won just 30 more times on the season, and Cuéllar's 16 victories on the season accounted for nearly a quarter of his team's wins. The pitcher finished with a solid 3.03 ERA and struck out 200 batters for the first (and only) time in his career.

The Houston pitcher's last win, on September 28, came on another mighty, extra-inning effort against the Phillies. Again in the Astrodome, Cuéllar hurled 11 scoreless innings; his mound opponent, Jim Bunning, hurled nearly the same. In the bottom of the 11th inning, with two outs, Rusty Staub doubled and Chuck Harrison drove Staub home on a base hit for the game's only run.

*   *   *

After the 1967 season, the Astros thought it best if Cuéllar did not pitch over the winter. The habitual winter league pitcher reluctantly complied. (Cuéllar did manage to sneak in 12 scoreless innings with the Estrellas Orientales team in the Dominican Winter League championship series.) At the Astros' spring camp in 1968, Cuéllar developed a sore shoulder. The cause, the pitcher contended, was the months of prior inactivity.

Cuéllar was placed on the disabled list in April. Limited to 24 starts, he won but eight games. The left-hander lost 11 contests, but his ERA was a sharp 2.74. Skeptical of the pitcher's insistence that his arm was impaired from *lack* of use over the previous winter, the Houston Astros, heading toward the franchise's first last-place finish, grossly miscalculated and gave up on the burgeoning hurler.

Two springs earlier, the Astros had tried to trade the pitcher but found no takers. Trying again after the 1968 season, the franchise received interest from across the imaginary baseball boundary that separated the two major leagues. Baltimore Orioles general manager Harry Dalton pulled off what turned out to be one of the most lopsided trades in baseball history, wrangling Cuéllar from the Astros on December 4. The Orioles sent outfielder Curt Blefary and a minor league prospect to Houston for Cuéllar and shortstop Enzo Hernández, and a corresponding prospect that did not make the grade.

* * *

During a Florida interstate bus ride in 1959, a curled-up-in-his-seat, soundly sleeping Mike Cuéllar caught the attention of teammates, perhaps surprised at the pitcher's ability to find such complete repose in the less than comfortable environs. One of them said knavishly, "Probably dreaming of a 20-win season." Everyone in earshot laughed.

Ten years later, 32-year-old Mike Cuéllar, the "ten-year prospect" as he had been labeled in Houston, arrived in a new city and a new league with a sound arm, and proceeded, over the next seven seasons, to fulfill the highest aspirations the pitching profession can render.

Major League Baseball lowered the pitching mound from 15 inches to ten inches in 1969 to try and help its hitters, yet the season produced more than twice as many 20-game winners in both leagues than in 1968. The first time Cuéllar took the new, reduced mound as an Oriole, on April 10, 1969, he hurled ten innings and allowed one unearned run. Cuéllar was not around when the Orioles beat Boston, 2–1, in four more rounds for the team's initial win of the 1969 season.

Another ten-inning effort later in the month gave Cuéllar his inaugural American League victory; it came against the Detroit Tigers and Denny McLain on April 23. Orioles shortstop Mark Belanger singled in the winning run against McLain in the bottom of the tenth frame for the 3–2 victory. On April 27, Cuéllar tossed the first of his five shutouts on the campaign, a six-hit, 6–0 suppression of the New York Yankees, in the opener of a Cap Day doubleheader at Memorial Stadium.

His second shutout, a 2–0 win on May 18, against the expansion Royals of Kansas City, evened Cuéllar's record through eight decisions. After that, the left-hander's record soared to 19–7. The Orioles also engaged in an upward flight in the standings.

Cuéllar's first ten victories for the Orioles were complete game endeavors. The ninth, on July 8, was against the Yankees, on Babe Ruth Day, *in Baltimore,* the city of the legendary player's birth. Cuéllar defeated Ruth's former team for the third time on the season, 4–1, completing a doubleheader sweep for the Birds. Outfielder Ron Woods recorded all three of the Yankees' hits against Cuéllar, including a solo home run.

After the All-Star Game break, Cuéllar reeled off 12 victories in 13 starts. On August 10, the pitcher missed throwing a no-hitter by a few inches—the few inches a ball hit by the Twins' César Tovar sailed over the outstretched glove of shortstop Belanger and into the outfield. The lead-off, ninth-inning single broke up Cuéllar's no-hit bid. The pitcher retired the next three hitters and settled for a 2–0 win, his 15th against nine defeats. Cuéllar issued three free passes and fanned eight.

In his first September start, Cuéllar put the stratospheric Orioles team 50 games over .500, for the second time on the season; downing the Detroit Tigers, 8–4, the slender southpaw claimed his 20th victory. Less than two weeks later, on September 13, Baltimore, which had gone into first place on April 16 and had risen to double-digit leads over the rest of the new American League's East Division, clinched the first major league division title in history. A 10–5 win over the Cleveland Indians accomplished the deed.

Cuéllar's second-half pitching merited opening game assignments in the "Division Series," as the pennant playoffs were originally called, and then in the World Series. The left-hander received a no-decision in Game 1 of the best-of-five square-off between the Orioles and the Minnesota Twins. At Baltimore, he allowed three runs, two earned, in eight innings before he was lifted for a pinch-hitter. Boog Powell spoiled an equally fine effort by the Twins' Jim Perry with a ninth-inning solo home run to tie the game at three. Baltimore won, 4–3, in 12 innings. The Orioles took three straight from the West Division-winning Twins, including a second extra-inning, one-run affair in Baltimore. Game 2's victory was masterfully gained by Dave McNally, who tossed 11 scoreless innings for a 1–0 win. Game 3 was an 11–2 Orioles blowout in Bloomington.

The World Series commenced on the second Saturday of October in Baltimore. A most unexpected team represented the National League, the New York Mets. Twenty-five-game winner Tom Seaver faced Cuéllar and finished second-best. Cuéllar pitched a 4–1 triumph, a six-hitter in which the 23-game winner helped his own cause with a run-scoring single.

Flabbergasting the baseball world, the Mets came back to win four in a row, including the Cuéllar-Seaver rematch in Game 4 at Shea Stadium on October 15. The game was decided with a run crossing the plate on an error caused by a controversial base-running play in the tenth inning (2–1, the final score). Cuellar had been removed for a pinch-hitter in the top of the eighth inning with the score tied 1–1, a decision likely made by manager Earl Weaver, though he had been ejected from the game. The choice prompted Cuéllar, standing in the on-deck circle, to throw down his bat in disgust at the move which ended his day. There was one out and no one on base when the pitcher was yanked. Cuéllar had scattered seven hits, walked none and made only one bad pitch, which had been deposited out of the park by the Mets' Donn Clendenon.

Gil Hodges' Mets won it all the next day, and the post-season-inclusive 113-win Baltimore Orioles were left with a long winter to contemplate their astonishing World Series defeat. Cuéllar with a 23–11 record and 2.38 ERA, was named co-recipient of the American League Cy Yound Award, along with Denny McLain (24–9, 2.80).

*   *   *

The Orioles, in 1970, claimed what the Cinderella Mets had denied them the prior season.

Mike Cuéllar's year began on a personal high note as he was married four days into January. Three months later, beginning with his first start, Cuéllar struck elevated pitching chords all season long on the baseball diamond. Although his ERA rose to 3.48, more than a run higher than the exceptional 2.38 of 1969, Cuéllar received fertile run support when he was not at his most outstanding and won a career and league-best 24 games. The left-hander topped all American League pitchers in starts (40, tied) and complete games (21).

The Orioles took a bit longer in 1970 to establish a first-place stanchion than in 1969. The team encountered challenges from the Detroit Tigers and the New York Yankees during the first three months of the campaign. As June ended, the 47–28 Orioles were three games ahead of the second-place Yankees.

On July 3, Cuéllar tamed the Tigers, 4–0, at Memorial Stadium, stretching the club's division lead to five games. Four days later, New York arrived in Baltimore to open a three-game set. Brooks Robinson's tenth-inning grand slam gave Cuéllar a 6–2 victory in the first game of the series, and gained for the pitcher his tenth win. Baltimore took two out of three, and the Yankees left Maryland strapped with a deficit of 6½ games.

Earl Weaver's Orioles took command over the second half of the season and won 57 games after the All-Star Game. Cuéllar's record climbed by 14 wins over the same period. The savvy pitcher became a 20-game winner for the second year in a row on August 27. He downed the Oakland A's, 6–4, at Memorial Stadium. Cuéllar was insufficiently solved for ten hits and three earned runs by the Northern California team.

Cuéllar's two dozen wins tied him with Dave McNally at the head of an Orioles staff that sported three 20-game winners. The trio of exceptional hurlers, including Jim Palmer, did not miss a start all season, and won 68 games, the most by an American League starting triumvirate since 1944. Cuéllar and McNally started 40 games each, while Palmer started 39, accounting for 119 of the Orioles' 162 games. The New York Yankees won 93 games, yet finished a distant 15 games behind Baltimore in second place.

Though Cuéllar and McNally won the same number of games, Cuéllar's 10–1 record in his final 11 decisions influenced manager Weaver enough to give the Cuban left-hander the starting nod in the Division Series rematch opener against the Minnesota Twins on October 3. The game, played under blustery conditions in Bloomington, featured the league's third 24-game winner, Jim Perry. It was far from a classically pitched game as the starters gave up a combined 13 earned runs in less than five innings of work each.

A notoriously poor hitter (despite an occasional display of power), Cuéllar hit the first grand slam home run in league championship play, against Perry, in a seven-run fourth inning that knocked the 1970 Cy Young Award-winner out of the game. Cuéllar hit a high, lazy drive down the right field line that was blown fair by a stiff wind. The bases-loaded blow put the Orioles ahead, 7–2. The team marched on to a 10–6 win and added two more one-sided victories to attain a second straight sweep of the Twins in the post-season. The Orioles again advanced to the Fall Classic, this time to face the Cincinnati Reds.

The 1970 World Series was the first played on Astroturf, and the first in which a position player was named MVP as much for his work with the glove as his bat. Brooks Robinson's spectacular fielding helped the Orioles defeat the Reds in five games. Robinson was no slouch with the bat, slugging two homers and hitting .429. But it was his glove that the Hall of Fame called for after the World Series, which ended with Cuéllar's clinching win in the fifth contest on October 15. Cuéllar had gotten a no-decision in Game 2, allowing four runs, one earned, in less than three innings of work.

The Reds almost ended Cuéllar's day in Game 5's first inning, scoring three runs on four hits. Johnny Bench singled home Pete Rose with two outs to open the scoring. Lee May followed with a two-base hit to knock home Bench, and Hal McRae smacked the third double of the inning against Cuéllar for the third run. Weaver, up by two games in the Series, had some leeway to give his ambushed hurler. Though not much more. Had Tommy Helms, the next batter, reached, Weaver said later that he would have pulled his starter. Helms popped up, however, and Cuéllar settled down from there.

In fact, Cuéllar slammed the door shut on the Reds, allowing only two hits the remainder of the game. Baltimore scored six times in the first three innings and three more in later innings, and celebrated the capturing of baseball's ultimate championship on its home field with a 9–3 win. "Nothing can match winning the World Series and being called the best team in baseball," Cuéllar certified more than 25 years later in a *Baseball Digest* interview. "Whenever I think of my greatest day in baseball I will always remember my World Series victory over the Reds in 1970."[4]

* * *

A self-affirmed warm weather and second-half pitcher, Cuéllar's 13–1 start to the 1971 campaign was a most pleasant surprise to all in the Orioles camp.

The pitcher did have his usual slumberous April, winning only once: a 3–0 handcuffing of the Cleveland Indians on April 14. By the same token, Cuéllar did not suffer his first defeat until May 9. Following that initial 6–2 vanquishing at the hands of Catfish Hunter and the Oakland A's, Cuéllar won nine consecutive starts, all but one by complete game. He bounced right back from his first setback to record his second one-hitter, May 12. It was a 6–0 blanking of the Kansas City Royals at Memorial Stadium. The left-hander allowed only one other baserunner, via a walk. "The secret to Cuellar's success is his motion," imparted moundmate Dave McNally. "He throws all his pitches the same way. He changes his speeds as well as anybody I ever saw. He's come up with an excellent slow curve in the last two years and doesn't throw anything but strikes with it."[5]

On July 4, Cuellar topped the Detroit Tigers, 3–2, and improved to 12–1. The pitcher picked up his 13th win four days later, defeating the Washington Senators, 7–3. Cuéllar walked four in the complete game, and in spite of the ten runs scored, the time of game was two hours and eight minutes. Cuéllar was a fast worker on the mound once he dispensed with his inning-preparatory rituals.

Normally a 13–1 record at the season's midway point would guarantee a starting assignment from your league in the All-Star Game, but the American League was bedazzled that season by a left-handed sensation who fired blistering fastballs past the batters of both divisions with starlight success. Twenty-two-year-old Vida Blue was an unbelievable 17–3 when the Mid-Summer Classic's first pitch was thrown in Detroit on July 13. Blue, who had thrown 11 scoreless innings, with 17 strikeouts, in a no-decision start four days prior to the All-Star Game, was the overwhelming choice to start for the American League.

The National League stars were not impressed by the young Oakland A's pitcher, however, reaching him for two home runs in one of the most celebrated All-Star Games in history. Six home runs were hit by the super-talented teams during the Americans' 6–4 win at Tiger Stadium. Cuéllar flung a scoreless sixth and seventh inning in the winning cause.

The Orioles, with more players (five) participating in the game than any other team, continued their pursuit of a third division crown immediately afterward, holding a 5½-game lead over the second-place Boston Red Sox when the second half commenced.

Cuéllar slumped following the All-Star interlude and won only once over the next five weeks. That win came on August 10, against the Minnesota Twins. Cuéllar won it, 4–3, in ten innings. The game, at Metropolitan Stadium, featured Harmon Killebrew's 500th and 501st home runs. The historic shot was delivered in the first inning with no one on base against Cuéllar. The extremely personable Killebrew became only the tenth player to reach the monumental slugging plateau.

While Vida Blue took individual accolades from the mound in 1971, the Orioles' starting staff reaped collective honors. By the time Cuéllar won his 17th game on September 1, the Orioles had an 11½-game lead over second-place Detroit. The Orioles also had another pitcher with 17 wins and two others with 16 victories at the same time. On September 10, Frank Robinson hit home run number 498 of *his* illustrious career, against the Washington Senators, to help Cuéllar win his 18th decision, 7–1, at Memorial Stadium.

Two weeks and three starts later, on September 24, Cuéllar won his 20th game, largely offsetting nine setbacks. The 9–2, first-game-of-a-twi-night-doubleheader win, at Cleveland, also clinched Baltimore's third straight division title. Cuéllar joined Dave McNally as the staff's second 20-game winner. In the second game, Pat Dobson, who had been acquired in an off-season trade with San Diego, shut out the Indians, 7–0, and became the third Baltimore pitcher with 20 wins. When Jim Palmer entered the charmed circle two days after Cuéllar and Dobson, the Orioles had matched the 1920 Chicago White Sox as the only other team in baseball history with a quartet of 20-game winners. Inclement weather cheated each of

Cuéllar was a four-time 20-game winner for the tremendous Baltimore Orioles teams of the late 1960s and early 70s.

the starters out of an additional start as the Orioles were limited to only 158 games played in 1971. Nonetheless, the team won 101 times and captured the division by a dozen lengths.

The Orioles kept their perfect Championship Series record intact by sweeping the West Division's best team, Oakland, in three games. Blue was beaten by McNally, 5–3, in the first game, in Baltimore. Cuéllar followed McNally on October 4, and easily decisioned Catfish Hunter, 5–1, yielding six hits to the A's. The Birds flew across the country and ended things with Palmer on the mound, the very next day, 5–3. Earl Weaver used only four pitchers in the three games, with Eddie Watt spelling McNally for two innings in Game 1.

The World Series opened in Baltimore on Saturday, October 9. The Pittsburgh Pirates were the National League's representative, and the Orioles were prohibitive favorites to win it all again. In Game 1, McNally was on top of his game. Coming off his fourth consecutive 20-win campaign, the Orioles' studious left-hander allowed only three hits (two to Roberto Clemente) and no earned runs in a 5–3 complete game triumph. Rain prevented the second game from being played until Monday, the scheduled travel day. The Orioles came out hacking and took a 2–0 lead in games with an 11–3 win; Palmer, though battling control problems, was the winner.

Cuéllar made his fifth World Series start the following day, October 12, as the Series shifted to Pittsburgh. The left-hander was nicked for two runs through six innings, while the Pirates' Steve Blass befuddled the Orioles' hitters. In the seventh inning, after his own throwing error allowed Roberto Clemente to reach base, Cuéllar allowed a three-run home run to Pirates first baseman Bob Robertson, who missed a bunt sign on the pitch. The Pirates won, 5–1.

A first in World Series' play occurred on the *evening* of October 13, with the first night game played in the Fall Classic's history. The Pirates evened the Series with a 4–3 win under the lights. Making his first appearance of the post-season, Pat Dobson started, but was not involved in the decision. Pirates right-hander Nelson Briles then pitched the game of his career and beat McNally, 4–0, in Game 5.

At home, two days later on October 16, Palmer was up to the do-or-die task facing the Orioles. Setting up the extension of the Series to a full seven games, Palmer tossed nine innings of two-run baseball. Frank Robinson aggressively hustled home from third base on a fly ball with the winning run in the tenth inning for a 3–2 Orioles win.

The following day, Mike Cuéllar, in Game 7, took the same mound where he had hurled the Orioles to the World Series championship a year and two days earlier. Cuéllar pitched well, but not well enough. Roberto Clemente hit a solo home run in the fourth inning for Pittsburgh's initial hit. José Pagan doubled home Willie Stargell in the eighth inning. That was all Steve Blass, a 15-game winner on the season, needed. Cuéllar was lifted in the bottom of the eighth inning for a pinch-hitter, when the Orioles scored their only run of the game. Blass hurled the 2–1 win, the Pittsburgh right-hander's second complete game win of the Series. Although Clemente was named MVP in the Series, Earl Weaver reserved his biggest praise for Blass, in post-game comments.

*   *   *

Mike Cuéllar was more superstitious than most players, a condition that fed his dysfunctional nickname of "Crazy Horse." Cuellar's superstitions went beyond the common practice of wearing the same socks or undershirts during a lucky streak. His fortune-tapping whimsies were embroidered into his active daily routine.

Cuéllar had his warm-up cap and his game cap, and only Cuellar could tell them apart. The Mike Cuéllar "cap story" was well known around the Orioles' camp. The day before a start in Milwaukee, Cuéllar's game cap was nowhere to be found. The Orioles phoned Memorial Stadium to ask someone to search for the cap, which had mistakenly been left unpacked for the road trip. In less than 24 hours, Cuéllar's cap had to be trucked to Chicago, where it was placed on an air shuttle to Milwaukee, in order to arrive the next day. The cap reached the frenetic pitcher in time. Upon examining it prior to game time, Cuéllar let out a bilingual string of expletives before calming down with an explanation. "That's not my game cap. That's my warm-up cap!"[6] Cuellar did not make it past the third inning that night against the Brewers. Cuéllar and his game cap were presumably reunited shortly thereafter.

Apart from his caps, Cuéllar had his own personal pre-game warm-up catcher: coach Jim Frey. Teammate Elrod Hendricks—and only Elrod Hendricks—had to stand in like a batter during the warm-up session. Cuéllar's eccentric routine extended to the field as well. He began every inning by circling the mound and scaling it only from the front side. Cuéllar did not permit anyone but his game catcher to accept his warm-up tosses between innings. On the occasions his catcher made a half-inning's third out, Cuéllar waited patiently for his receiver to don his catching garb.

Cuéllar also abhorred anyone touching the baseball immediately before he did to start an inning. He did not want any of his teammates to retrieve or flip him the ball. These things did not escape the opposition. Detroit's Al Kaline, while playing first base, once recorded the last out of a half inning on a pop-up near home. Leaving the field, Kaline purposely overshot the usual target of the mound vicinity with his toss, and the ball rolled all the way down one of the base lines. Cuéllar, from the opposite dugout, calmly walked all the way over picked up the ball and calmly walked all the way back to the center of the diamond, then circled and paced up the front of the mound before finally beginning his warm-ups. The start of the inning took a full two minutes longer than usual.

In another gamesmanship instance, Yankees outfielder Bobby Murcer dallied coming in from the outfield after catching the third out, long enough to navigate a path intersecting with Cuéllar. Murcer wickedly flung the ball directly at the pitcher, whereby the pitcher had to catch the baseball or get hit by it.

That was one eccentric side of "Señor Caballo Loco," as his teammates fondly referred to their off-center lefty. But on the mound, Cuéllar did not resemble his translated nickname. He was difficult to rattle. The *Sporting News,* in a 1970 profile of Baltimore's "Big Three" of Cuéllar, Palmer and McNally, referred to them, respectively, as Mr. Calm, Mr. Cool & Mr. Collected.

In 1972, Mr. Calm won "only" 18 games, and the Orioles, after three straight division flags, slid to third place. Mike Cuéllar had won 67 games the past three years. Only six pitchers since the end of World War II had won more in a consecutive three-season span.

Cuéllar had averaged 39 starts over the prior three seasons. He received 35 starts in 1972, but the strike-curtailed schedule, along with two April starting assignment scratches because of a bad back, were inhibiting factors in Cuéllar reaching a fourth consecutive 20-win campaign. Cuéllar authored four shutouts on the season, and his 2.57 ERA was the second best he posted in Baltimore and third lowest of his 15-year career.

Cuéllar did not win his first game until April 29, a 6–1 triumph over the California Angels. Uncharacteristically, the pitcher had only ten wins through July, to go with eight losses. The tenth victory came on July 30, a 5–0, three-hit vanquishing of the Yankees. In August, Cuéllar won four games, and he added three more wins in September.

On October 1, the 35-year-old defeated Boston, 2–1, in a crunching setback for the Red Sox, who saw their first-place lead cut to one-half game with the loss and a same-day win by second-place Detroit. Had Cuéllar not beaten the Red Sox in that game, the Red Sox's last before heading to Detroit to play their final three contests of the season, the Tigers would have had to sweep Boston to win the division. Instead, the Tigers were able to capture the division flag in a less pressure-packed situation.

* * *

The Orioles bounced back in 1973, regaining the top spot in the division, and Cuéllar nearly duplicated his 18–12 record of 1972 with an 18–13 mark. The chronic slow starter had a worse than usual sluggish beginning. He was 1–4 through May 5, and by June 14 his record had sagged to 2–6. Cuéllar's poor opening led to some petulant behavior with manager Earl Weaver.

In a start May 31 against the Kansas City Royals, Cuéllar walked the bases loaded, then promptly surrendered a two-run hit to Amos Otis. The Orioles, at that point in the season were a .500-team, having split 40 games. Weaver could not have been faulted for having less patience than usual. The manager came out with the first-inning hook. Cuéllar turned his back on his manager before relinquishing the ball. Some of the pitcher's frustration may have stemmed from a small strike zone Cuéllar thought the home plate umpire had established with the first three Royals batters.

Weaver brushed off Cuéllar's impertinence as "a minor incident" and dismissed the possibility of a fine. "I never fine a player without talking it over and getting right to the problem for a solution." the cogent Weaver said. "You have to be careful when you speak to a bilingual person," he added, with commendable sensitivity, "so that all the facts are clearly known. I talked to Cuellar after the game in Kansas City and everything is fine and dandy."[7]

After two more ineffective outings, Cuéllar tossed a three-hit, 1–0, home shutout over the Texas Rangers on June 15. In his next start, the lefthander lost a 2–1 decision to the Yankees' Mel Stottlemyre, and then pitched 12 innings at County Stadium to defeat the Milwaukee Brewers, 4–3, on June 25. Cuéllar walked none and struck out nine, as the intuitive Weaver, possibly sensing a season-turning effort, let him hurl the distance. Cuéllar's record stood at 4–7. The Orioles had played 63 games and were three games over .500, in third place, but only three games out of first place.

Several more starts were required for Cuéllar to complete his turnaround. The pitcher took a few positive steps forward, winning three starts in succession in July, two over the California Angels (a team he had great success against) and Nolan Ryan. On July 11, at Memorial Stadium, Cuéllar defeated Ryan on an off-night for the California right-hander, 7–1. Two starts later, on July 19, the screwballer outdueled the Angels' fireballer in Anaheim, 3–1, in 11 innings.

A 4–2 Orioles victory pitched by Cuéllar over the Cleveland Indians on August 1 lifted the 56–45 Birds into a first place tie with New York; it was Cuéllar's eighth win against 11 losses. Cuéllar bettered his winning mark over the next few weeks, as did the Orioles their record, and Baltimore took over sole possession of the top spot in the AL East on August 15. A week later, Cuéllar defeated the Minnesota Twins, 4–3, for his 12th win. The Memorial

Stadium triumph evened Cuéllar record, as the Birds won their tenth game in a row. Stretching the team winning streak to 14, Cuéllar downed Texas, 6–1, five days later. With the win, Baltimore kept a five-game division lead on the second-place Red Sox.

On September 9, with an easy 13–4 triumph at Cleveland, Cuéllar gained his 15th victory and his 100th as an Oriole in just under five seasons. Baltimore won a robust 21 games in September and took the division by nine games. Cuéllar concluded the campaign with seven victories in eight decisions, a fine finish after his 2–6 start.

In his only start of the post-season, on October 9, Cuéllar lost a heartbreaker to the Orioles' league championship opponents. At Oakland, Bert Campaneris of the A's cracked a leadoff 11th-inning home run to hand Cuéllar a 2–1 defeat; Ken Holtzman three-hit the Orioles in the third game of the American League championship square-off. Oakland went on to win the series in five games, handing Baltimore its first playoff series loss in four appearances.

*   *   *

The same two teams played for the 1974 American League pennant the following season, with a similar outcome. The A's beat the Orioles in four games. Cuéllar, with a team-leading 22 wins, started the first and fourth games of the LCS. The left-hander defeated Catfish Hunter, 6–3, in the opener. Oakland won Games 2 and 3 on shutouts by Vida Blue and Holtzman. In Game 4, Cuéllar was overcome by a streak of wildness. He held Oakland hitless but walked nine batters in 4⅔ innings; Cuéllar allowed only one run before being relieved by Ross Grimsley. Reggie Jackson clocked Grimsley, in the seventh inning, with a game-deciding double. Hunter, who tossed the A's fifth-game pennant-winner last season against Baltimore, pitched seven scoreless innings. Reliever Rollie Fingers sufficiently closed the Orioles out over the final two frames, sending the A's, with a 2–1 victory, to the World Series for the third year in a row.

In order to reach the league championships, the Orioles had to overtake the New York Yankees to win the division, something the Maryland team achieved with a simply scorching stretch run. Baltimore posted a 28–6 record in its final 34 games. Over the final 11 days of the season, the Orioles won nine games in a row. The Yankees, in first place with less than two weeks to play, finished two games back. Cuéllar won his 20th game of the season in the middle game of a three-game sweep of the Yankees at Shea Stadium in mid–September. The series was part of a closing 2½–week stretch drive in which the Orioles rolled off a blistering 16–2 record.

Excluding the first month of the campaign, Cuéllar had been the Orioles' most dependable pitcher. The pitcher had lost his first three decisions, then won nine in a row. One of those wins took place on June 17. Renowned announcer Vin Scully once described the swift mound efficiency of Bob Gibson as someone "pitching like he was doubled-parked." A similar assessment could have been attached to Cuéllar's hill performance that evening. In one hour, 43 minutes, the disarming Orioles southpaw dispatched the Minnesota Twins, 1–0, on five hits, at Memorial Stadium. The win put the Birds one game over .500 at 31–30. The team shot upwards from there, with 60 wins in their final 101 games.

A no-decision followed Cuéllar's gem against the Twins, after which the Tigers and Mickey Lolich defeated the left-handed junkballer, 2–0, on June 25. Cuéllar came back to shackle the Yankees, 3–0, in his next start on June 30, for his tenth win. Cuéllar split his next four starts, the second loss absorbed at the hands of the A's and Vida Blue, 2–0, on July 17.

Cuéllar's next start was scheduled four days later, which fell on the Sunday before the All-Star Game (for which Cuéllar had been chosen). American League president Lee MacPhail, concerned about the losing trend incurred by his circuit, had worked out an agreement with clubs in his league to have more rested pitchers available for the contest. Cuéllar, rather than miss a start to conform with MacPhail's wishes, and then be idle for what amounted to more than a week of the regular season, convinced Weaver to start him on two days' rest on Saturday, when the Orioles had two games to play. On July 20, the diligent hurler tossed his second complete game in four days and defeated the California Angels, 5–2, in the second game of twi-night doubleheader at Memorial Stadium. As it turned out, Cuéllar was not used in the All-Star Game.

Afterward, it took the pitcher nearly four weeks to win again. Defeating the Chicago White Sox, 2–1, on August 15, Cuéllar improved his record to 14–9. He won eight of his final nine decisions as the ace of a staff that set a record with five consecutive shutouts in early September.

On September 6, Cuéllar recorded his second straight 1–0 shutout (and third of the season), this time victimizing the Cleveland Indians at Cleveland Stadium in the second game of a doubleheader. The blanking was the fifth shutout in a row hurled by Baltimore pitchers (Dave McNally was the first game's 2–0 winner). Four days earlier, Ross Grimsley and Cuellar had whitewashed the Red Sox in both games of a doubleheader by identical 1–0 scores. Jim Palmer chipped in with a third blanking of Boston (6–0) on September 4. Baltimore's bid for a major league record-tying sixth straight shutout the following day, September 7, was thwarted when the Indians' Charlie Spikes tagged Grimsley for a two-run home run—in the ninth inning. The Orioles and Grimsley (who also had three 1–0 victories on the season) settled for a 3–2 win. Baltimore's pitching staff still entered the American League record books with 54 consecutive scoreless innings over a seven-game span.

The double wins on September 6 tied the Orioles, a club in the midst of a ten-game winning streak, with the Red Sox for second place in the division, 1½ games behind New York. The team turned it on from there to nose out the Yankees at the end.

The 22–10 Cuéllar, as he was inclined to do, completed a majority of his starts on the season, a total of 20. The Sports Boosters of Maryland named Cuéllar and outfielder Paul Blair as co-MVPs of the team.

After six seasons in Baltimore, Mike Cuéllar counted some remarkable pitching statistics to his credit. The left-hander had averaged 38 starts, 278 innings, 19 complete games, and 20.8 wins per season with a 2.98 ERA. Moreover, Cuéllar had registered 125 victories in 228 starts, with 114 complete games.

* * *

At age 38 in 1975, Mike Cuéllar still had enough pitching guile to win 14 games, deliver 256 innings and match his high in shutouts in a season with five. In his initial start, Cuéllar blanked the Brewers, 2–0, on a cool, crisp April 16th evening, with temperatures in the 40s in Baltimore.

On May 31, the "cagey left-hander"—an oft-used description applied to Cuéllar over the years—one-hit the Angels, 1–0, at Anaheim. Only four hits were dispersed in the pitcher's duel. California's lone safety was delivered by Bruce Bochte in the third inning. Brooks Robinson blasted a solo home run against losing pitcher Bill Singer.

Cuéllar tossed his third shutout of the season on June 22, evening his record at 5–5. It came against the first-place Boston Red Sox, in the opening half of a Sunday doubleheader that also saw Luis Tiant pitch the nightcap. Cuellar defeated the Boston Red Sox, 3–0, throwing a six-hitter. Tiant earned a split for his team, downing the home club, 5–1, while striking out 12 Orioles. Thomas Boswell of *The Washington Post* sang the praises of the veteran pitchers' performances. About Cuéllar, the writer also focused on what had unavoidably become part of Cuéllar's superficial but amusing persona.

> He [Cuellar] had to arrive early to take batting practice. That's right. Even though pitchers don't bat in the American League. And after every out he had to be standing on the rubber before he would accept the ball from an infielder.
> Cuellar carries mystery with him. His teammates give him room and don't claim to have him figured out. Cuellar understands English perfectly and speaks it well—when he wants to, as he did after his shutout today. Those who have taken the time to look past the wall of superstitions find Cuellar shy, boyishly enthusiastic despite his 38 years, and totally dedicated to winning.[8]

Cuéllar's dedication took him to a seventh straight campaign with double figures in victories. On July 26, Cuéllar, who had won more games in the last six seasons than any other pitcher in baseball except Ferguson Jenkins, won his tenth of the season in grand fashion. The lefthander nearly silenced every Milwaukee Brewers' bat, while producing a 4–0 victory at County Stadium. Cuéllar yielded only a seventh-inning single to George Scott. In throwing his second one-hitter in two months, Cuéllar singled out ten of the "Brew Crew" as strikeout victims.

On August 11, as the second-place Orioles mounted another second-half charge, Cuéllar helped the team to its eighth win in nine tries and 22nd out of 29 since the All-Star break. The left-hander defeated the Kansas City Royals, 4–0, on two hits. It was Cuéllar's 35th career shutout. He managed only three more wins, however, to close out, at 14–12, his 13th big league campaign.

The Orioles, with a season-long exhibition of superior pitching from 23-game winner Jim Palmer, who hurled ten shutouts, and 20 victories from Mike Torrez, won 90 games. But the Boston Red Sox grabbed five more and the American League East Division with it.

* * *

Jim Palmer, Wayne Garland and Rudy May were the three reliably productive starters Earl Weaver governed in 1976. Cuéllar, Ross Grimsley, Ken Holtzman and Mike Flanagan all split time starting games. Cuéllar produced the least of the competing bunch. The decline was starkly evident throughout the season, as Cuéllar crashed to a 4–13 record in 19 starts.

After Cuéllar was knocked from the box in the first inning of a game against the Minnesota Twins on June 6, Weaver assigned the 2–6 pitcher to the bullpen to try and iron out his difficulties. Cuéllar made his first appearance out of the bullpen (in relief of Grimsley) the very next day. A scoreless three and two-thirds innings of work earned Cuéllar another start five days later, ahead of Grimsley. Cuéllar and the Orioles suffered a shutout at the hands of Kansas City's Doug Bird, 4–0. Nine days afterward, on June 20, Cuéllar pitched the last shutout of his career, corralling the Texas Rangers in Arlington, 2–0. It was also Cuéllar's fourth and final victory of the season.

By the All-Star break, Cuellar had been put back in the bullpen for a third time. Once, as Weaver was removing him from an unproductive showing, Cuéllar cursed at his manager. Outwardly, Weaver had shown Cuéllar continued support over the years. The incident appeared to have been a lamentable case of a once strong relationship deteriorated by one partner's denial of personal shortcomings and jarringly blaming the other. As such, Cuéllar felt short-changed by Weaver, believing the manager had not permitted him to pitch through his troubles. Weaver's not too lighthearted response became a famous baseball line. *I've given Mike Cuéllar more chances than I gave my first wife.*

The Orioles finished in second place, well behind the re-established New York Yankees in 1976. Following the forgettable campaign, Cuéllar headed to the place he had called his off-season home since his forced abandonment of Cuba. Tom Boswell caught up with the enigmatic pitcher in Puerto Rico, in January of 1977. It was a month after Cuéllar had been given his unconditional release by the Orioles and just after he had been signed by the California Angels on January 25. In his character examination, Boswell revealed some of the cultural impediments of North American baseball that sometimes forced Hispanic ballplayers to withdraw sullenly and therefore seem, on the exterior, detached or disinterested.

> So Cuellar has come home to pitch winter ball for the Caguas Criollos and try and turn back the clock. The Cuellar one meets here—calmly pitching his team into the island championship series with a 7–3 record and a 2.97 ERA—is an entirely different man from the reclusive left-hander that other ballplayers in the States call "Crazy Horse." Cuellar lives on the star washed beach here with his wife, Myriam, and his son, Mike, Jr.

"He has a phobia about sportswriters," says Cuéllar's best friend and catcher for eight years, Elrod Hendricks. "They either ignore him for months or quote him in pidgin English. It drives him crazy."

"Mike often goes into seclusion," says Hendricks, who is from the Virgin Islands. "He is a hard person to talk to about personal things. I know he hasn't seen his parents since he left Cuba, but we roomed together eight years and he has never mentioned Castro's name once."[9]

The aged hurler could not deliver for the Angels. On May 3, 1977, five days before his 40th birthday, Mike Cuéllar took the major league mound for the last time. At Yankee Stadium, Cuéllar was roughed up for seven hits and six earned runs in less than four innings of work. His mound opponent, Mike Torrez, who was making his first start in pinstripes after being traded by Oakland to New York for three players, earned the win, 8–1. The four-time 20-game winner's last major league pitch was whacked out of the park for a grand slam home run by the Yankees' Bucky Dent.

The Angels cut Cuéllar loose less than two weeks later.

LEGACY

Las Villas was one of the six provinces that jurisdictioned Cuba during its many decades as a republic. It was in that central province's largest city, Santa Clara, that Miguel Angel Cuéllar was born on May 8, 1937. According to Cuéllar's SABR Bioproject profile, written by Adam Ulrey, the future pitcher was one of four boys from a family who worked in the sugar mills.

Thirty-three years later and a long way from Santa Clara, Cuéllar, who made his first baseball glove out of burlap and played barefoot as a youngster, celebrated the final out of the 1970 World Series, on the infield of Memorial Stadium, as the first Hispanic pitcher to start and win a clinching World Series game. Cuéllar's victory that day required some rushed pre-game physical rehabilitation, as well as alternate in-game pitch selections. Cuéllar had to undergo heat treatments on his arm prior to warming up. He said his arm was stiff in the first inning but then he "got loose and had great stuff." He relied mostly on fastballs and sliders and very little on his screwball.

In the jubilant Orioles' clubhouse, big Boog Powell came over to Cuéllar with a keepsake—the ball he caught for the final out. Cuéllar took the baseball from the first baseman and kissed it, not once, but twice. "I love this game,"[10] Cuéllar said, with the ball close to his lips, in a future sports marketing catchphrase blinked over at the time.

At five feet, 11 inches and 165 pounds, Cuéllar was far from an intimidating presence on the mound. But from the same location, he brought to bear surpassing results. Cuéllar and his uniform number 35 was a despised sight to American League hitters, especially from 1969 to 1974. Those discouraged batters faced a pitcher who from the rubber stared in their direction, holding the ball out in front of him in his gloved hand, before initiating a fluid motion toward home. Cuéllar used a waist-high, bent-knee leg kick to propel his mostly over-the-top deliveries to the plate.

No other Latin American left-hander can match Mike Cuéllar's elevated level of major league excellence. (I make the distinction of Latin American because of Lefty Gómez.) Cuéllar collected 20 wins in four different seasons; he also won 18 games in two other seasons. Examining his lifetime ERA, Cuéllar's was a shimmery 3.14. Cuéllar's career ERA has been bettered by only two other Hispanic starting pitchers, minimum 2,000 innings. Miguel Angel tossed 36 shutouts, tied with Camilo Pascual and behind only Luis Tiant (49) and Juan Marichal (52) for most all-time by a Hispanic pitcher. The two-time major league All-Star completed a sensational 45 percent of the games he started (172 out of 379). From 1966 to 1975, the dependable pitcher averaged 256 innings a season, including a three-year stretch from 1969 to 1971 where he averaged 293 innings tossed per season.

In 1969, Cuéllar became the first Hispanic pitcher to win the Cy Young Award, tying for the prize with Denny McLain. Both outstanding pitchers received 10 of the 24 votes. (A points system was then established to try and avoid future ties.)

No Hispanic left-handed pitcher has been able to top Cuéllar's 20-win campaigns or 185 lifetime win total. His 2,808 big league innings are second only to Fernando Valenzuela's 2,930.

Cuéllar pitched seven winter seasons in Puerto Rico as a frontline pitcher, with seven other campaigns as a part-time contributor from the mound. He accumulated 59 wins and a 3.17 ERA in 873⅓ innings.

Over five seasons as a young hurler in Cuba's AAA-rated winter league, he managed 21 wins against 28 losses; his ERA was 3.09 over 455 innings. As a more seasoned pitcher with the International League Cuban Sugar Kings, Cuéllar won 37 and lost 39 in four campaigns. He holds the team record for best ERA (2.86) and most shutouts with ten (tied). His 32 complete games and 736 innings were the second-highest sums in franchise history. Cuéllar also pitched in Nicaragua and Mexico, pushing his career innings mark over 5,000.

In three World Series, Cuéllar started six games; he went 2–2, with a 2.61 earned run average. Both of his wins were by complete game. In the Caribbean Series, Cuéllar posted a 1–1 record, winning a game in relief for Almendares in the 1959 Caribbean Classic and losing a start, 3–1, for the Ponce Leones in 1970. In 1977, a few months away from his 40th birthday, Cuéllar earned a second CS opening assignment with the Caguas Criollos. He was spared a potential loss by the rallying bats of his teammates, who were eventual 9–8 winners over the Magallanes Navigators.

Uncharismatic and a "junkballer," Mike Cuéllar certainly did not get the media recognition he deserved as an outstanding pitcher. Cuéllar was sometimes overshadowed by other pitchers on his club, and he played on a team of stars, much like another equally productive left-handed Spanish predecessor of his. But unlike the incomparably gregarious Lefty Gómez, the language-inhibited Cuéllar had no regaling or ingratiating remarks to offer to the press, only pitching quirks that perhaps too often laughingly blinded the eyes of the media to the full grandeur of Cuéllar's accomplishments.

Cuéllar's teammate, Jim Palmer, echoed this sentiment following Mike Cuéllar's death on April 2, 2010, from stomach cancer. Cuellar was 72 and had retired to the Orlando, Florida area. "Mike was arguably the best left-hander in the game from 1969 to 1974," commented Palmer, "but never got his due."[11]

The lack of national recognition for Cuéllar has never been more evident since the millennium. Every "all-time Latino baseball list" that has been released or published, whether voted on by the fans or selected by higher-acumened Hispanic followers of the game, always reflects Fernando Valenzuela as the ethnic all-time best left-handed pitcher. With the utmost respect to the popular and charismatic Valenzuela, the placements have carried on a disservice to the game's legacy and an injustice to Cuéllar and his family.

As a 23-game winner in 1969, Cuéllar made $20,500, a paltry sum compared to the outrageous salaries of today. At the time of his sickness prior to his death, Cuéllar and his wife Myriam relied on a monthly pension as their sole means of support. As a result, Cuéllar was in store for a pauper's funeral, according to one newspaper story. But a charitable effort, led by a group of Central Florida Cuban American professionals, headed by former U.S. Senator Mel Martínez, helped raise more than $10,000 to cover funeral costs for Cuéllar's family in their grieving hour.

"Mike was a monstrous part of the great teams we had from 1969 to 1971," said Earl Weaver, shortly after learning of his former player's death. "He was an artist on the mound and a pitcher who put us over the top."[12]

Mike Cuéllar was also a mound artist and pitcher topped by few of his peers.

Dennis Martínez

In 1976, the Baltimore Orioles were grooming two players from Nicaragua for spots on their big league team. Both were Triple-A pitchers attached to the Orioles' Rochester, New York, affiliate. No player from Nicaragua had reached the major leagues. Initially, the Orioles had higher hopes pinned on Telica native Tony Chévez, who threw a knucklecurve and who was a year older than his Granada-born *conterráneo* named Dennis Martínez. As it came to pass, Silvio Antonio Chévez pitched in only four big league games, while José Dennis Martínez became one of the two dozen pitchers with the most career starts in modern baseball history.

Twenty-one-year-old Dennis Martínez made his major league debut on September, 14, 1976, at Memorial Stadium. The first Nicaraguan player in major league history struck out the first three batters he faced and picked up a 9–7 win in long relief. Less than two weeks later, on September 26, Martínez made his first start on the Memorial Stadium mound, that special plot of elevated topsoil which resonated with the grandiose pitching mantras of McNally, Cuéllar and Palmer. Martínez made a less than adequate showing. The starter was charged with five runs in less than eight innings of work and took an 8–3 loss against the Boston Red Sox. In his next start, on October 2, Martínez showed his potential. The game was the next to last one on the schedule; Martínez lost again, to the Red Sox, but the 1–0, complete came effort at Fenway Park left the Orioles and their fans something to pleasantly think about over the winter.

When the Orioles decided to bring Martínez up to the big club in September, he had developed a more impressive résumé than not only Chévez, but most Triple-A pitchers. Martínez had been named the minor leagues' top right-handed pitcher of 1976.

Baltimore had signed Martínez in 1973, after he came to the team's attention while pitching in the 1972 World Amateur Games held in Managua. Martínez came to the United States for the first time as a professional pitcher in 1974; as a 19-year-old, he was assigned by the parent club to the Miami Orioles. Young Dennis won 15 games for the Florida State League team. Martínez followed that with 12 more victories in 1975, when Baltimore moved him up a rung to Double-A Asheville, North Carolina. At the conclusion of the 1976 minor league campaign in Rochester, Martínez was summoned to his major league Eden in Maryland.

In 1977, Martínez's first full season, a three-team division race between the Orioles, Boston Red Sox and New York Yankees played out in the American League East. A fine rookie season also materialized for the right-hander; Martínez made valuable contributions to his team, which finished tied for second with the Red Sox. As a full-year freshman, Martínez pitched in 42 games, won eight of them in relief, and triumphed in six more as a spot starter. Martínez finished with twice as many wins as losses. The young hurler proved himself to be a hearty competitor and one savvy to the age-old doctrines of pitching, as displayed by an incident in June at Memorial Stadium. The Boston Red Sox were in town and mashing home runs at a near-record pace. Martínez faced the slugging squad in a start on June 21. The pitcher allowed two home runs that helped the visiting team tie a record for home runs hit in seven consecutive games (24). One of the long balls permitted was to George Scott, Boston's first baseman, in the fourth inning. In Scott's fourth at-bat of the game, in the ninth inning, Martínez drilled him with a pitch. Scott, a wide-load diesel, charged straight for Martínez, chasing the young and, fortunately for his sake, faster pitcher from the mound until other players intervened. Martínez, on the

Pitcher Dennis Martínez as a Baltimore Orioles rookie in 1977. Martínez toed the major league rubber for 23 years with five teams (photograph from Hall of Fame).

losing side of an eventual 7–0 defeat to Luis Tiant, was then withdrawn from the field of battle by his manager to pitch another day.

Martínez later scored two victories over the Red Sox, including his 14th, on September 17. The 11–2 victory was the first-year hurler's fifth complete game in his 13th and final start of the campaign.

*   *   *

Ross Grimsley's departure by way of free agency and Rudy May's trade to the Montreal Expos created two vacancies in the Orioles' rotation for 1978, and Martínez and Scott McGregor, a left-hander brought up to the big club at the same time of Martínez's promotion, were the appointed replacements. (A similar personnel shuffle had occurred on the staff at the end of the 1976 campaign with the release of veteran Mike Cuéllar and Wayne Garland's free agency auction, which opened the door partially for Martínez and fully for Mike Flanagan in 1977.)

Though Cuéllar and Martínez were pitchers in opposite transitional phases of their careers, Martínez always remembered advice he received from the veteran left-hander. "Cuellar helped me tremendously by teaching me to use patience and confidence to cope with pressure situations, " Martínez disclosed in a 1989 *Baseball Digest* interview. "And to set up different hitters with different pitches and speeds to outsmart them, the way he did. Cuellar taught me how to be a gracious winner and how to survive a losing streak."[13]

In Martínez's first start of 1978, in the second game of the season at Milwaukee, the pitcher failed to retire a batter during a Brewers eight-run first inning. The next day, Martínez returned with 4⅓ innings of sorely needed relief help, after starter Scott McGregor had given up ten runs in less than four innings. A 13–5 win that day closed out a humiliating, three-game, season-opening series sweep at the hands of the Milwaukee Brewers, in which the vaunted Orioles pitching staff allowed 40 runs.

The Orioles pitching straightened out though, as a team, it was no overall match for the New York Yankees and Boston Red Sox. Martínez, a full-time starter, split his first 14 decisions, but was not pitching that well. Pitching coach Ray Miller, who had helped Martínez as a raw Orioles recruit in the minors, stepped in again and remedied a detected "hitch" in the pitcher's motion to the plate whenever runners were on base. Correcting the flaw, Martínez won nine of his last 13 decisions and lowered his ERA, which had been above five, to 3.52. The second-year pitcher won 16 games and lost 11 on the campaign.

The Orioles, with Martínez among a starting staff of Jim Palmer, Flanagan and McGregor, finished in fourth place in the highly competitive American League East. The four pitchers totaled an impressive 71 of the Orioles' 90 wins on the season.

*   *   *

The following season, 1979, Dennis Martínez assumed the role of the Baltimore Orioles' top starter *and* the American League's most reliable pitcher, compiling the most starts (39), complete games (18) and innings (292⅓). The 24-year-old broke out to a 10–2 start (winning ten straight after losing his first two decisions), but then tailspinned to a 5–14 finish (though nine of the defeats came by one run). The Orioles coasted to the division title, completing a dominant 102–57 campaign.

Martínez' eighth win came via his second shutout on June 6. The 3–0, four-hitter at

Memorial Stadium, over the Kansas City Royals, put Baltimore into first place, one game ahead of the Boston Red Sox. The win was also the first of 22 victories in 25 games the Orioles would reel off. Baltimore closed out the month of June 4½ games ahead of a nearly-as-hot Red Sox team.

Ken Singleton was the biggest bat in Baltimore's lineup. The Orioles outfielder slugged home runs and drove in three runs in Martínez's 12th (6–1) and 13th wins, both versus the Seattle Mariners, on July 15 and 23 respectively. Baltimore moved 33 games above .500 with the latter 7–6 win.

Incidentally, according to Rory Costello in the Dennis Martínez SABR Bioproject entry, Singleton was responsible for giving Martínez his exalted nickname of "El Presidente." At a time Nicaragua was experiencing internal political upheaval from civil war, and the long-running dictatorial rule of the Somoza family had finally ended, Singleton quipped that Martínez—because of how well he was pitching—was going to become "El Presidente" of Nicaragua."

Martínez won only two more games from there, but one of them, his third shutout of the season in early September, put asunder for the rest of American League East Division teams any hopes of catching his high-flying Orioles club. With a home blanking the Toronto Blue Jays, 5–0, on September 6, Martínez increased the Birds' lead to 9½ games over the second-place Milwaukee Brewers. The final margin of victory was eight games.

The California Angels were the Orioles' American League playoff championship opponent that fall. Baltimore won the first two games. In Game 3 of the series, with Martínez the starter, the Orioles took a 3–2 lead into the bottom of the ninth inning. It appeared that the Angels were going to be dismissed in a sweep. But after a one-out double by Rod Carew, Martínez was replaced, and the Angels rallied for two runs for the win. There were no further comebacks for the Halos, however, as the Orioles wrapped up the series with a win in the following game.

The Orioles' third World Series appearance of the decade matched the club against the Pittsburgh Pirates—the team that had last opposed Baltimore in the Fall Classic of 1971. Martínez received a start in Game 4. The pitcher was bounced from the box in the second inning by five successive Pirates hits. The resulting four-run inning gave the Pirates an early lead, but good relief pitching and a six-run, eighth-inning outburst allowed the Orioles to win the game, 9–6, and take a 3–1 lead in the Series.

The "We Are Family" Pirates surprisingly came back to win three in a row, including the final two contests in Baltimore. In Game 7, Martínez was the last of five relief pitchers used by manager Earl Weaver in the ninth inning as Pittsburgh tallied two insurance runs for a 4–1 lead.

Kent Tekulve then closed the door on the last half-inning of the Orioles' unsatisfying season.

* * *

In the spring of 1980, the mustachioed Nicaraguan suffered a muscle tear in his right shoulder that cut down his starts by more than one-third from the prior season. The injury placed Martínez on the disabled list for the first time. The Orioles won 100 games, but were not good enough to overcome the 103-win New York Yankees. A healthier Martínez, who managed only six victories in 12 starts during the campaign, might have made a difference.

A fully healed Dennis Martínez came back strong and won 14 games to lead all American League pitchers in the 1981 strike-stunted season. Martínez also posted the best ERA of his career to date, 3.32. The shoulder injury from 1980 loomed as a big obstacle to overcome for Martínez in the face of the pitching-rich Orioles of 1981. Martínez was projected to be the fifth starter in a four-man rotation when the season began. But when Scott McGregor was not able to take his regular turn at the season's outset, Martinez stepped in. He also took advantage of an injury to 1980 Cy Young Award winner Steve Stone, and ended up with the most starts (24) on the staff.

The Orioles, while competitive, did not qualify for the disjointed arrangement that allowed additional teams into the post-season for the first time—from which emerged the Los Angeles Dodgers as champions.

The season included a detestable episode that involved Martínez and a fan in Chicago in July. From the stands at Comiskey Park, a hurled bottle struck Martínez, standing near the Orioles' dugout, flush on the head. The Baltimore pitcher was remanded to a local hospital where four stitches were needed to close the wound. The culprit was caught and battery charges were brought forth by Martínez, who fortunately was not seriously hurt.

The bottle that shattered over Martínez' skull was a beer bottle, and it was ironic that an alcoholic beverage container was used in the random incident. For Dennis Martínez, major league pitcher, pioneer and national celebrity of an entire Central American country, was a full-fledged, closet alcoholic.

* * *

He never drank the night before he was scheduled to pitch. "But I drank a lot on the other nights between starts,"[14] stated Martínez.

No one could have suspected that Dennis Martínez had a drinking problem in 1982, not by his won-loss record. Martínez led the Baltimore staff in wins, starts and innings.

The pitcher closed out June with four wins in a row and an 8–4 record, including a 14th consecutive Memorial Stadium win on June 26. Martínez defeated the Detroit Tigers, 4–1, on a seven-hitter. That personal home winning streak ended in his next start, July 1, against the Cleveland Indians. The 6–2 loss to the Indians left the Orioles in fourth place, five games in back of the first-place Boston Red Sox.

Baltimore made little headway in the standings over the next two months, and was staring at the same five-game deficit at the end of August. But using a 19-win month of September and gaining another three victories in the first days of October, the Birds managed a strong assault on first place. The American League East's penthouse had a new occupant, the Milwaukee Brewers, at the time the Orioles' rush upward began on August 28. Martínez delivered his 13th victory that day, 8–3, over the Texas Rangers, at Memorial Stadium, the first of ten consecutive wins for Earl Weaver's team. Previously, on August 24, Martínez had hurled a ten-inning home victory over the Toronto Blue Jays, 7–3 (finalized by a Joe Nolan grand slam). The right-hander picked up his third triumph in a row and 14th overall with a seven-hit, 5–2 road conquest of Toronto on September 1.

The Orioles battled for nine days in September without their top winner. Martínez was absent from the team due to the news of the accidental death of his father in Nicaragua. The elder Martínez was struck by a vehicle on a street and knocked into a moving bus, which took the 71-year-old's life. Upon his return from burying his father, the grief-stricken pitcher pledged to concentrate all the more on his profession. He refocused his attention on the Orioles' return to division contention.

Mike Flanagan won four times and Jim Palmer three in the final month as the Orioles drew to within three lengths of the Brewers, heading into the last weekend of the season ... and four games on tap between the Orioles and the Brew Crew at Memorial Stadium. Earl Weaver had announced his retirement after 15 years in the Orioles manager's chair, and there was a great deal of sentimentality surrounding the series, in which the Orioles had to win all four games to win the division.

Martínez's first start back from his absence came against the Brewers in the third game of a weekend set in Milwaukee, on the next-to-last Sunday of the season, September 26. Martínez pitched 7⅓ innings of two-run baseball and was credited with the 5–2 win that edged the Orioles to within two games of first place. Dropping two out of three games to the Detroit Tigers in their next series, the Orioles lost a game in the standings over the next four days. That brought the team to their hopeful series finale with the Brewers.

On October 1, Martínez won his 16th game in the Friday doubleheader opener of a memorable weekend of baseball at Memorial Stadium between the division's top two contenders. Martínez pitched well enough, holding the Brewers to three runs in 6⅓ innings, gaining an 8–3 victory. The Orioles trimmed the Brewers' lead to one scant game with a 7–1 win in the second game as Storm Davis tossed a six-hitter.

The Orioles came out swinging the next day and hacked out an 11–3 victory to tie Milwaukee for first place with identical 94–67 marks. The one-sided victory by Baltimore set up a nationally televised Sunday final to determine which team would play the California Angels for the American League pennant.

The three brink-of-elimination wins by the Orioles and the intrigue of extending Weaver's departure with a dramatic division title fanned the swirl of excitement leading into the last game of the season on October 3. But it was not to be for the Orioles or Weaver. Milwaukee pounced on the Orioles' best: Palmer, Martínez and Flanagan, the last two in relief, for nine of the ten runs the road team scored to secure the division. The 10–2 final was won for Milwaukee by future Hall of Famer Don Sutton, who hurled eight strong innings with two runs allowed.

* * *

The four-man starting rotation passed into history following the 1982 campaign. Only three managers were still subscribing to it up to that season. One of them, Weaver, retired, and his successor, Joe Altobelli, chose to fall in line with the rest of the pilots in the leagues who were rotating five top pitchers to open ball games. In 1983, Tommy Lasorda in Los Angeles and Pat Corrales in Philadelphia were the last field leaders to expand to five the decades-long scheme of utilizing a revolving quartet of frontline starters. (Corrales did not make a clean break, as he was not altogether averse to using Steve Carlton and the team leader in wins, John Denny, often on three days' rest that season.)

Altobelli picked Martínez as his Opening Day pitcher in 1983. The Orioles and Martínez were handed a 7–2 home loss by the Kansas City Royals. While not an auspicious beginning for the new Baltimore skipper, it was one of the few low points in a festive season that culminated with a world championship for the team from the "Old Line State" and that was festooned throughout by an MVP season from a home-grown, 23-year-old shortstop named Calvin Edwin Ripken, Jr.

Feeling the pressure of being tabbed as heir apparent to the aging Jim Palmer as new ace of the staff, Martínez said, in an evaluation to his ultimately poor season of 1983, that he felt an added burden when Palmer and Mike Flanagan went down during the season with injuries. Trying to do too much, the pitcher surmised, led to his downfall. The result was a 7–16 record for Martínez, one of the worst historically for a starting pitcher on a world championship club.[15]

It can be supposed that there were other factors involved for the sudden decline and that the "pressure aspect" was a well-suited excuse used by Martínez in denial of his behind-the-scene drinking addiction.

In December of 1983, the pitcher was forced to confront his problem. Martínez was arrested, for a second time, for driving under the influence of alcohol. "Finally I realized I had a problem when it became unmanageable. That's when I told myself ... I had to do something about it,"[16] Martínez stated, in one of his first interviews, after undergoing eight weeks of treatment for his drinking dependency, and three months following the second arrest.

"TO ME, HAPPINESS WAS DRINKING"

Within a span of just four days, the pitcher went from detox graduation to the Orioles' 1984 pitchers and catchers spring reunion. "My father was an alcoholic," Martínez divulged, in a sins-of-the-father insight, "and I believe that is what killed him. I think he was drunk when he was hit. I think that's the reason he is not here now. He didn't get any help. It was the alcohol."[17]

A two-year "drying out" period ensued for Martínez. Traveling city to city, as is the life of a ballplayer, Martínez used many a non-pitching day—the ones he used to spend drinking—attending various Alcoholics Anonymous regional chapter meetings throughout the United States. Martínez continued to speak with cleansing frankness about the disease he was defeating. "Before I use to be alone all the time," he said. "I wouldn't let anybody get close to me. To me, happiness was drinking. I found out what alcohol was doing to me—I was hurting myself, my family, my career, and my teammates."[18]

Martínez credited his agent at the time, Ron Shapiro, for forcibly redirecting him off the path to potential oblivion and toward personal salvation. But his agent could not help Martínez on the mound. The right-hander could not bring his ERA below 5.00 over three succeeding seasons in Baltimore. And while he showed an occasional flash of excellence (a 4–0, one-hitter against the California Angels, on June 5, 1985, for his 100th career win), Martínez was a very hittable pitcher from 1983–1985. He posted a winning record in 1985 (13–11), though his ERA remained over the five-run level.

By 1986, the pitcher's less than accomplished pitching of the past three seasons had soured him with the fans of Baltimore. Sportswriter Jim Heneman wrote about the pitcher's early season travails of 1986: "Martinez was booed during opening day ceremonies and before and after each of his two home appearances. In those two games, Martinez lasted only a total of two-thirds of an inning and gave up three runs."[19] In the pitcher's defense, his shoulder was not right. But when Martínez refused an assignment to the minors, the Orioles placed him on the disabled list after only four appearances, all in relief. (Martínez's shoulder was eventually diagnosed with tendinitis.) Martínez's name had been circulated in trade rumors for two years, and, after his shoulder strengthened well enough to make him somewhat salable, the Orioles made the talk a reality and sent the 31-year old right-hander to the Montreal Expos, in June, for a player to be determined at a future date.

* * *

After his trade to the National League, Martínez registered a 3–6 showing in 15 starts for the Expos. The seemingly "damaged goods" pitcher appeared not to figure strongly over the winter in the fourth-place Expos' plans for improvement. On top of that, Martinez's contract expired the end of the 1986 season and he became a free agent at the worst possible time. Martinez found himself firmly stationed at the proverbial crossroads that many athletes encounter at least once in their careers.

The unwanted pitcher, who had resisted an Orioles rehab assignment to Rochester the prior season, now, in 1987, in an ironic twist of baseball fate, was forced to accept a minor league contract in the Florida State League, pitching for his former Miami team, renamed the Marlins. "I had to be humble," Martínez stated the following spring. "I thank God he made me humble enough. I didn't quit."[20]

Baseball rules did not allow Montreal to re-sign Martínez until the first of May. The team did, and sent him to Triple-A. In June, the Expos recalled Martínez, and manager Buck Rodgers gave him a couple of starts. The arm problem of a year ago completely dissipated, Martínez turned in a superb performance in the second outing. The shaggy-haired hurler shut out the New York Mets, 4–0, on three hits. Following that June 15 start at home, Martínez became a regular part of the rotation for Montreal, an improved team that finished in third place in the National League East standings.

Martínez lost a 1–0 heartbreaker to rookie Joe Magrane of the division-capturing St. Louis Cardinals on September 29, in St. Louis. The loss was the first half of doubleheader shutout defeats suffered by the Expos to the Cardinals on the day and all but eliminated the third-place Expos' faint chances for a division crown.

The Expos finished four games behind St. Louis. Martínez's personal ledger showed that he had won half of his 22 starts, with only four losses. And his ERA, 3.30, was back to big league snuff.

* * *

Martínez found his fastball again in Montreal and mastered a forkball to complement his curve ball and change-up. A demonstrable pitching revival played out over the next six seasons for Martínez, with four campaigns with sparkling ERAs under 3.00 and a six-year win total of 86.

The Montreal Expos, following their 91-win season in 1987, backstepped a full ten games with their 1988 record. But the reversal could have been viewed less than harshly, as the New York Mets ran away with the division beginning in May. Martínez threw over 200 innings for the first time since 1982, and won 15 games, two more than he lost; he compiled an edgy 2.72 ERA.

In 1989, Martínez produced a 16–7 won-lost record, tying for the third of four times his career high for wins in a season. The Expos duplicated their .500 record of 1988, dropping a place in the standings to fourth.

In just a few seasons, Martinez had gained for himself the heady respect of National

League hitters. "Dennis Martinez has the best stuff of any right-hander I have ever faced,"[21] veteran slugger Mike Schmidt declared during that period.

*   *   *

The Expos of 1990 better resembled their 1987 improved selves, winning 85 games. The team placed third for the third time in four years in the National League East Division. Over most of the season, Martinez pitched better than his final sub-.500 record indicated. His ERA of 2.95 was nearly a quarter-run less than his 3.18 tabulation from 1989 when he won 16 games.

After 14 major league seasons, the first of four career All-Star selections arrived in 1990 for Martínez. At the time of the Nicaraguan's selection, his record was only 6–7, but with a 2.84 ERA. The appointment may have been a recompense for his omission from the National League squad in 1989, when he was 9–1 at the All-Star break. Martínez pitched a 1–2–3 fourth inning in the National League's 2–0 victory at Wrigley Field on July 10, and retired Cal Ripken, Jr., Ken Griffey, Jr. and Mark McGwire.

Martínez closed his 1990 All-Star season with a 10–11 record, the only time in seven full seasons with Montreal that he lost more games than he won.

"The whole country stood still"

Dennis Martínez was the Montreal Expos' Opening Day pitcher for six seasons, from 1988 through 1993. His best campaign in that half-dozen-year stretch was 1991. The 15-year veteran led the National League in complete games, shutouts, and ERA. Viewed against the landscape of Montreal's 90 loss-season and the team's placement squarely at the bottom of the East Division, the mound achievements become even more striking. Entering the 1991 campaign, the Expos rewarded their fine pitcher with a three-year, $9.5 million dollar contract, the largest of Martínez's career.

By the early 1990s, the frontiersman journey to the big leagues, and the longevity fastened to it, had made Dennis Martínez an immensely renowned person in his Nicaraguan homeland. Martínez was a source and symbol of great pride for a nation that had seen, up to then, only four more of their citizens follow Martínez into the major leagues. At that stage of his career, the only way Martínez could have improved his standing back home was to accomplish something as unprecedented as it was monumental ... win a World Series game or pitch a no-hitter. It was made evidently clear in the first few months of the 1991 season by the Expos' sinking record that playing in October did not have a legitimate place on Montreal's future agenda, so Martinez attained national demigod status the other available way.

On July 28, on a lazy, sunny afternoon like so many others in the City of Angels, Dennis Martinez took the Chávez Ravine mound and incandescently pitched himself and his country into the granite pantheon of baseball immortality, by throwing nine perfect innings in defeating the Los Angeles Dodgers, 2–0.

The Expos were retired in order by Dodgers starter Mike Morgan to open the game. (Earlier in the season, Morgan had lost a 1–0 game to Martínez in Montreal.) Martínez prodded the same course of inaction from the Dodgers in their half-inning. Leadoff hitter Brett Butler looked at a called third strike. Second baseman Juan Samuel grounded to short and Eddie Murray grounded to second baseman Delino DeShields, who was shading Murray up the middle.

Darryl Strawberry, the bottom of the second inning's first batter, bounced a pitch to almost the exact spot Murray had the previous inning, which DeShields fielded again and threw out the outfielder at first base. Left fielder Kal Daniels struck out swinging and Lenny Harris neglected to offer at a third strike called by home plate umpire Larry Poncino.

In the third inning, Mike Scioscia bounced a ball up the middle that was flagged down behind second by Deshields, who threw out the lead-footed Dodgers catcher. Eighth-place hitter Alfredo Griffin rolled to first baseman Larry Walker for an easy, unassisted putout, and pitcher Mike Morgan grounded out to DeShields, recording his fourth assist.

In his second time up, Butler slapped a 3-and-2 pitch (one of only three three-ball counts Martínez had in the game) to shortstop, where Spike Owen fielded and threw in time to nip the speedy center fielder. The next hitter, Samuel, kissed a hard bouncer to third baseman Tim Wallach, who, playing even with the bag, snagged it and tossed across the diamond to retire the opposing infielder. Pitching to Murray next, Martinez apparently felt a twinge in his back, causing the game to be momentarily delayed. The Expos trainer came out to check on the pitcher. The momentary discomfort was deemed not serious. Martínez re-engaged Murray, who pulled a bouncer down to first that Walker scooped and flipped to Martínez covering for the out.

Slugger Strawberry led off the fifth frame and grounded to Walker, who needed no help to record the out. The Expos defense had the next hitter, Daniels, played perfectly. The left-handed-hitting outfielder bounced a ball through the box which was handled by DeShields in good order and with time enough to throw out Daniels at first base. Third baseman Lenny Harris hit the first ball out of the infield against Martínez—a short foul fly to left field that outfielder Iván Calderón squeezed.

After five full innings, each pitcher had set down the opposition in unbroken order. The Expos mounted a mild threat in the sixth, on the heels of the team's first hit and a walk, but were retired without scoring by Morgan. In the bottom of the inning, Scioscia, as the first hitter, tested Deshields' fielding range again and was thrown out. Alfredo Griffin tried DeShields once more and was retired on a throw to first base by the busy second baseman. The throw was low and came close to pulling Walker off the bag, but the outfielder experimenting at first base that season kept his foot anchored long enough to record the out. Morgan batted and flied to Marquis Grissom in center field for the third out.

The Expos broke through against Morgan in the seventh inning, scoring two unearned runs on only one hit. Martínez took the scant lead into the lower half of the stanza with the Dodgers' top of the order due up. The pesky Butler fouled out to third baseman Wallach. Martínez fielded a bunt attempt by Juan Samuel and threw out the second sacker on an accurately needed and delivered throw to first. The prolific Murray then grounded out for a third time in the game, DeShields recording his eighth assist of the contest.

The Expos used back-to-back singles by Martínez and DeShields, with one out, to threaten in their turn to bat in the eighth. After throwing a wild pitch, Morgan coaxed two outs from the next two hitters, with runners on second and third, and prevented any scoring. In the bottom half of the eighth inning, the imposing Strawberry led off for the Dodgers, topped a Martínez offering to second and was routinely set down for the first out. Martínez then induced Kal Daniels to chase a third strike for his fourth strikeout of the game and his first since the second inning. Lenny Harris hit a tapper back to the mound that Martínez grabbed and relayed easily to first. Martínez had now gone through the order twice and two-thirds of another cycle without a batter reaching base.

The Expos went out quietly in the top of the ninth inning. Accompanied by the elusive specter of no-hit history and the more flighty penumbra of perfection, Martínez took the mound to meet the bottom of the Dodgers' order.

Mike Scioscia flied out to Calderón for the first out of the last inning. Dodgers broadcaster Vin Scully had called more than one perfect game in his grand career. He gave these impressions afterwards of the moment at hand: "This one was pretty quiet until Scioscia flied out to start the ninth. Then the entire ballpark seemed to get behind Martínez. It wasn't a World Series or a home team guy, but he was so-o-o perfect."[22] Stan Javier was sent in to pinch-hit for Alfredo Griffin. Javier could not put the ball in play and struck out swinging. Dodgers manager Tommy Lasorda requisitioned another hitter to take the place of his pitcher. Chris Gwynn was that batter, and he quickly fell behind in the count to Martínez, 1-and-2.

"I don't think anybody wanted the ball hit to them," center fielder Marquis Grissom said in post-game comments. "I was so over-excited out there. I was just thinking, 'Please no line drives, nothing hard. I don't want to be the one to ruin history.'"[23]

Grissom may not have been seeking the ball, but the ball found him. Gywnn swung and hit under the 1–2 offering, lifting the ball to center. Grissom nestled under the result of the 95th pitch of the game thrown by Martínez and only the third fair ball hit out of the infield by the Dodgers all day. Grissom embraced into his glove the descending sphere; Martínez raised his arms in triumph and was joyously mobbed by his teammates.

Within minutes of the 27th out, Martínez broke down and cried in front of reporters and cameras inside the Expos' dugout. The game was his 401st career start, and given the trials of his life dealing with alcoholism and the tribulations of re-establishing a seemingly dead-end career, it was easy to understand why Martínez was so wracked with emotion. Dennis Martínez had a met a destructive influence in his life head-on, and had overcome it, and professionally had persevered through unproductive seasons to continue pitching on the major league level, though few had given him a chance for success.

His personal demons vanquished, Martínez's tears of happiness also streamed, in part, for his distressed home country, brought upon by the emotion of knowing that what he had just accomplished would have a profoundly symbolic effect on his people. The Nicaraguan nation had suffered through, in recent times, a terrible natural disaster and violent internal discord, all of which had claimed many lives. "God gives us a gift for all to enjoy and share and be happy about, something my people needed after wars and earthquakes and tragedy,"[24] Martínez said retrospectively.

After his perfect performance, as he sipped Perrier, the 36-year-old pitcher accepted a congratulatory call from Nicaraguan President Violetta Chamorro. A few hours after the news reached Martínez's Granada birth community in Nicaragua, the town's main park filled with people reveling in their native son's grand achievement.

Alberto "Tito" Rondon, sports editor of Nicaraguan daily *La Prensa*, summarized the feeling of a country emerging from years of bloody civil strife with these comments: "Dennis Martinez is a great unifier in this country. He crosses party lines. Dennis Martinez was already the most popular person in the country before he pitched the perfect game. Now he's just more popular."[25]

"Only a Nobel Prize in literature could have more impact in this country,"[26] Justo Fernández, a teacher in Nicaragua, said.

René Cárdenas, Nicaraguan-born Spanish language broadcaster for the Dodgers, added, after the news of the game reached home: "The whole country stood still."[27]

Martínez was able to fly to Managua three weeks later, in between starts. The arrival date came two days after Martínez had gained his 12th win and fifth shutout (3–0) of the season, on August 17, against the St. Louis Cardinals. Martínez was greeted and treated in a manner befitting his national hero rank. He luncheoned with President Chamorro, then visited his hometown of Granada, where he disbursed gifts to needy children. A true glimpse into the Martínez character can be discerned through that generous act of kindness and goodwill, made in the midst of a national celebration in which *he* was the honoree. Martínez took the opportunity of an honorary return to his hometown to give back unpretentiously to the community of his youth.

The magnanimous sojourn was not an unknown trail traveled by Martínez. Twice in the past four years he had returned to Nicaragua, bringing with him humanitarian aid to a people beaten down by years of organized armed clashes. The Contras-Sandinistas conflict had reverberated back to Martínez in his adopted South Florida off-season home during the late 1980s. Tens of thousands of Nicaraguan immigrants fleeing the violence at home had come to the United States, the majority settling in the Miami area. One processing encampment, offering "temporary housing" for an overflowing number of refugees, had been Bobby Maduro Stadium in Miami, where Martínez had pitched during many spring trainings with the Orioles.

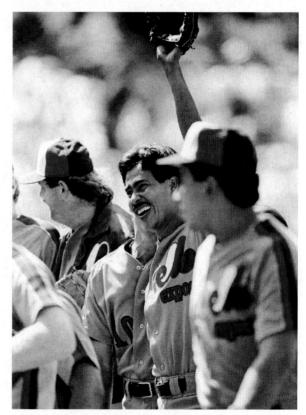

Following Martínez's return from Nicaragua, he won two more games for Montreal, a team that experienced its first losing season in the last five. His 14 victories for the 71-win Expos was testament to his outstanding pitching, as was his impressive, league-leading ERA of 2.39. The sour note to his fine campaign was as the National League's losing pitcher in the All-Star Game, permitting three runs, on four hits, to his circuit rivals, in the AL's 4–2 midsummer win at Skydome.

* * *

Buck Rodgers had lost his job less than one-third of the way through the 1991 season because of his team's poor performance. Rodgers' managerial replacement, Tom Runnells, was ousted due to a mediocre showing less than a quarter of the way through 1992. Runnells' substitute guided the Expos team

Moments after his perfect game, July 28, 1991, Dennis Martínez acknowledges the crowd applause at Dodger Stadium, surrounded by several of his Montreal Expos teammates.

to significant improvement. Felipe Alou took over a fourth-place team, three games under .500, through 37 games played in 1992; he steered the Expos to a second-place finish, with an upgraded record of 87–75. Alou's first game in charge, on May 22, was made easy by Martínez. The right-hander defeated the Atlanta Braves and Tom Glavine at Olympic Stadium on a two-hitter, 7–1.

Exemplified by that win, Martínez pitched exceptionally well in 1992, winning 16 times, tied with Ken Hill for most on the Expos' staff. Two of the first four losses Martínez (16–11) suffered on the season came by the score of 2–0, both to Doug Drabek and the eventual division-winning Pittsburgh Pirates. A third defeat was 2–1 to the San Francisco Giants.

The pitcher's 2.47 ERA was fourth-best among National League starters. Though Martínez did not record a shutout, in his final start of the season, on September 23, he threw nine innings without permitting a run. The effort was not squandered by Montreal; the club eventually won the game, 5–1, in 14 innings, on a grand slam by the manager's son, Moises.

*   *   *

The 1993 Montreal Expos won the second-most games in team history. The Quebec-based franchise had a newly naturalized citizen of the United States within its ranks. José Dennis Martínez Emilia became a United States citizen, along with his wife and two of his children, prior to the season.

On April 5, 1993, in the 123rd season of major league baseball, Dennis Martínez matched up against Dominican José Rijo of the Cincinnati Reds as the first Hispanic pitchers to oppose one another in a season-inaugurating game. Rijo came out on top, 2–1, with the save going to Rob Dibble. Following consecutive bad outings, Martínez won for the first time on April 23, beating the San Francisco Giants, 7–2.

Through 37 Expos games, Martínez had recorded seven decisions; his record stood at 2–5. The second-place Expos were trying to keep close to the 26–10 Philadelphia Phillies, 5½ games ahead of the Canadian club. Martínez then claimed eight straight 349 victorious decisions. One of the triumphs marked a milestone for the 38-year-old hurler. On June 18, against the Atlanta Braves, Martínez threw eight innings of one-run ball, and was picked up by John Wetteland for a 2–1 win, the 200th of his career. Martínez became the 92nd pitcher to reach this level, and the third Hispanic.

Martínez's winning streak came to a halt on July 15. The pitcher was defeated, 3–2, by a Los Angeles Dodgers pitching combination of Ramón Martínez, brother Pedro and Jim Gott. The Expos' Martínez tossed six innings, permitting all the runs, though one was unearned.

As the season progressed, the Expos lost ground in the standings to Philadelphia and slipped into third place. Martínez was prominently mentioned as the Expos player most likely to be moved prior to the trading deadline. The pitcher was in the last year of his contract and the Expos were not going to compete for him in the free agent arena. No such trade was consummated, however, and the pitcher remained in Montreal. (As a "10–5" man—a player with 10 years of major league service and at least five with one club—Martínez turned down a deal that would have sent him to the Braves.)

On the first of September, Martínez downed the Colorado Rockies, 11–3, for his 13th win. It was the Expos' seventh consecutive victory and its 11th in 12 games. The Expos stayed hot in September and regained second place. The club made a valiant showing. But Felipe Alou's squad could not come closer than three games to the Phillies, achieved on the last day of the season when they won their 94th and final game.

The Expos' 90th win, coming on September 28, registered as Martinez's 15th and last triumph for the campaign. The victory came against the Florida Marlins at Joe Robbie Stadium in Miami. Reporters from five Nicaraguan newspapers and 300 fans from Nicaragua flew into town to see their idol pitch. Martínez held the expansion Marlins hitless for the first six innings. In the seventh, the right-hander was reached for a couple of runs but held on, with help from reliever Wetteland, for a 3–2 win. Martínez had tried three times to secure his 15th victory, a cumulatively significant number in that it counted as the hurler's 100th National League win. The Central American pitcher was decorated as the sixth pitcher to collect 100 wins in both leagues, and the first Hispanic.

* * *

Three summers after his perfect game, Dennis Martínez was back in Nicaragua to accept honorary entrance into his country's Hall of Fame. The visit was a leisurely one, unlike the one in 1991, with no pressing requirement to rejoin his ballclub. Leisurely because, incredibly, there was no major league baseball being played that August in the United States. The players had recently initiated a work stoppage that would eradicate the last third of the 1994 season and eliminate the World Series.

Over the previous winter, Martínez had been signed to a two-year, $9 million contract by the Cleveland Indians, bringing to an end seven and a half predominantly successful years in Montreal. Leaving Montreal was not unexpected, as Martínez, who was known to speak his mind, had more than his share of clashes with the front office and teammates, and even pitching coaches during his tenure. Martínez's first choice had been to sign with the Florida Marlins, but the young team could not justify the pitcher's salary requirements against his age.

The Cleveland Indians had opened a new home park on April 4, 1994. Dennis Martínez was the first Indians pitcher to throw a pitch from the Jacobs Field mound. His opponent was Randy Johnson of the Seattle Mariners. Martínez parried with Johnson for seven innings, each pitcher allowing two runs. Neither hurler figured in the decision, which required 11 innings for Cleveland to win by a one-run margin, 4–3.

It took until May 6 for Martínez to win his first game back in the American League. The good result came against the Baltimore Orioles and was well earned. Eight days shy of his 39th birthday, Martínez pitched the Indians to a ten-inning, 4–2 win at Camden Yards. Martínez dropped his next start to fall to 1–4, but then won eight straight. His eighth win was a four-hit road shutout (2–0) over the Chicago White Sox on July 16.

Martinez's pitching coach at Montreal, Joe Kerrigan, had predicted the success the right-hander currently enjoyed, mentioning the new pitches developed by the competitor that unequivocally revived his career. "I think Dennis will have a significant advantage going back to the American League," commented Kerrigan, "because the last time he was there he didn't have a drop-down fastball and breaking pitch, and he certainly didn't have his split-finger changeup."[28]

The veteran had all of his pitches working for him on August 6, when he two-hit the Red Sox at Fenway Park, 2–0. Martínez's 11th win (against six losses) was his last start of the season for Cleveland, a team one-half game out of first place in its division. Five days afterward, with the conclusion of games played on August 11, the players' union acted on its threatened boycott and deserted the big league diamonds, not returning until the following April.

*   *   *

Upon cessation of hostilities between union and management in 1995, the 40-year-old pitcher picked up where he had left off the prior season. Martínez was pitching for a more powerful Cleveland club as well, one that made a shambles out of the American League Central Division on the way to a World Series appearance, the franchise's first in four decades.

A sampling of the run-scoring abilities of the Indians was provided on Opening Day, delayed until April 27 because of the labor impasse. Cleveland supplied Martínez with 11 runs, resulting in a five-run victory over the Texas Rangers in Arlington. The Indians, with a group of talented players blossoming into stars at the same time, and a balanced sprinkling of veterans, bored through any competition in their path. Martínez won his first nine decisions, and pitched for nearly three full months before losing his first game.

In the middle of August, with the Indians steaming toward a 20-game advantage in the standings, John Hart, Indians general manager, publicly cited Martínez as being the anchor of the Indians' staff and as good as any pitcher in the league since May of the prior season.

Martínez won 12 and lost 5 in 28 starts for Cleveland in 1995, and had the league's third-best ERA at 3.08. Against the Minnesota Twins on September 28, he made his last start of the season and won, 12–4. In the first inning, Martínez hit Twins All-Star Kirby Puckett with a pitched ball. The fast ball smacked the popular player on the side of the face and knocked him to the ground. Bleeding profusely from the mouth, Puckett's jaw was broken. Martínez was deeply affected by the results of the pitch he threw, saying the incident caused him to feel worse than at any other time on a baseball field.

Kirby Puckett never played another game. The following spring, he was diagnosed with glaucoma in his right eye and had to leave the sport permanently. At the news conference announcing his retirement, in July of 1996, a classy Puckett was unambiguous about exonerating Martínez and any connection from the beaning to his unfortunate affliction. Martínez himself was in the audience. "Dennis Martinez sitting back there has taken a lot of crap for an accident that happened last year," Puckett stated, dark sunglasses partially covering a large white bandage over his damaged eye. "I'm telling you now, I love Dennis Martinez, and he didn't do it on purpose. I was just leaning in there too far. I was what you call cheating, and I couldn't get out of the way in time."[29]

Hart's Indians ended the 1995 regular season the way they began it, in a powerhouse display of run production, plastering the Kansas City Royals, 17–7, on October 1. It was the team's 100th win on the season—in only 144 games played. The Royals finished in second place, *30* games behind the Tribe. Outfielder Albert Belle played in all but one of his team's games and accumulated an amazing 52 doubles and 50 home runs. Belle also topped the circuit in runs and RBI in one of the greatest slugging seasons in baseball history.

Prior to the 1994 players' strike, the biggest news for baseball off the field had come in the form of realignment. The 14 teams in each league were now sorted into three divisions, reflecting a more regionalized geographical format. The creation of a third division, the "Central" in each circuit, opened the way for two more teams in each league to make a bid for a World Series berth.

In the first American League Division Series, the Indians played the East Division-winning Boston Red Sox, a team with the second-best record in the league. The Indians dispatched the Red Sox in three straight games. Martínez was decision-less in Cleveland's Game 1 victory, decided in 13 innings, 5–4. The Seattle Mariners, who pulled off a stunning comeback against the "wild card" New York Yankees in its playoff round, including a spectacular extra-inning fifth-game win, stood as the Indians' remaining roadblock to the World Series.

Against the Mariners, Martínez was the starter and loser of Game 1, 3–2. A week later, Cleveland, holding a three-games-to-two lead in the American League Championship Series, was poised to move further into the autumn limelight. Trying to eclipse the Indians' shimmer was the elongated frame of Randy Johnson. The six-foot, ten-inch hurler opposed Martínez in Game 6 of the ALCS, at the Kingdome on October 17. Standing tallest at the end was Martínez, who hurled seven shutout innings and was the winning pitcher in the 4–0 clincher.

Making two starts in the 1995 Fall Classic, Martínez absorbed a loss in Game 2 and received a no-decision in the decisive Game 6 against the Atlanta Braves. The Indians' bats were mostly subdued by the superb pitching of the Braves, especially in the final game, when Tom Glavine and Mark Wohlers combined to shut out the hard-hitting Cleveland lineup on one hit, 1–0. Martínez was replaced in the fifth inning with two outs and two men aboard, and did not figure in the eventual outcome.

LEGACY

Fifteen seasons of double-figure win totals left Dennis Martinez, as he began his 21st big league campaign in 1996, within reach of Juan Marichal's Hispanic record of 243 victories. The three-decade pitcher entered the season 12 behind. Martínez could not gain on the total, losing 7–1 to the New York Yankees on April 2, while making his 11th Opening Day start, the most by a Hispanic pitcher.

The Indians were not as dominant a ballclub as in the prior season, but the team maintained a potent offense. By the arrival of summer, Martínez had won nine games, benefiting greatly from the high-powered Indians attack.

After a 14-pitch start on August 27 against the Detroit Tigers, Martínez was placed, for the third time on the season, on the disabled list. The causes were knee and elbow problems. The third DL trip, forced by a strained tendon in his pitching elbow, prevented Martínez from pitching any more that season. The late summer start against the Tigers, his 20th of 1996, also turned out to be his last appearance in the uniform of the Cleveland Indians.

Cleveland had reworked the option year of Martínez's contract in 1996, but was not interested in re-signing the pitcher. The club allowed its previously productive hurler to seek employment elsewhere for the 1997 campaign. The elder statesman pitcher found it, however short-lived, in Seattle. Making nine starts for the Mariners, and winning only once (against Cleveland), Seattle released Martinez on May 24, ten days after his 42nd birthday.

Idle the rest of the 1997 season, but not wanting to exit the game so abruptly, Martínez delightedly accepted an invitation to pitch for the Mayagüez Indios late in the winter season of 1997–1998. The junket to Puerto Rico was another fateful, full-circle experience in Martínez's long career, similar to his imposed return to the minor league Marlins in 1987.

As a young Orioles pitcher, Martínez had spent four winter seasons upgrading his trade, hurling for the Caguas Criollos, and a portion of another with Santurce. The return to Puerto Rico opened the doors to the major leagues again. A Braves minor league scout saw Martínez pitching for the Indios and gave a good review to his Atlanta superiors. The Braves had lost John Smoltz to elbow surgery. The team signed Martínez to a spring training tryout as potential insurance. Even minus Smoltz, Martínez faced the difficult task of making the pitching-strong Braves staff, and he did just that.

In 1998, with the Atlanta Braves, the durable hurler obtained the few wins required to supplant Marichal.

The Martínez major league mound ledger is a voluminous as well as luminous one. Only eight pitchers in history tendered longer service in the majors than Martínez's 23 years. The Nicaraguan finished one single out short of throwing 4,000 major league innings. Exactly 40 pitchers in MLB history have thrown as many.

From the mound, the right-hander delivered to the plate with a bent-knee leg kick elevating to his chest; he tucked his chin into his left shoulder, clasping the ball in his raised gloved hand, which he lifted above the bill of his cap. Martínez threw three-quarters overhand, and he pitched with a big chaw of tobacco bloating his right cheek. Martínez wore the uniform number 30 with the Orioles. He changed to 32 with the Expos, because the digits were owned, at the time, by Tim Raines. He kept the same alternate number with his last three major league teams.

Martínez came up as a six-foot, one-inch, 180-pound pitcher and retired within a few pounds of his original scorecard weight, a rare and noteworthy accomplishment for a ballplayer of any era.

As he seriously contemplated life without baseball in 1997, Martínez established a charitable foundation that bears his name, "with a main priority to help children in Nicaragua." Its services have branched out to include relief for hurricane and flood victims throughout Central America. The Miami-based non-profit organization is headed and primarily run by Martinez and his family of five, including wife Luz and sons Dennis Jr., Gilbert and Rick. Daughter Erika serves as chief administrator of the foundation.

In 2012, Martínez managed the Nicaraguan team that was bounced in a qualifying round for the 2013 World Baseball Classic. The former pitcher professed afterward a future desire to try again in the same capacity. It is unlikely he will be denied.

In Nicaragua, Dennis Martínez's relationship with the populace extends beyond idolatry. Martínez maintains a social station of iconic reverence not usually reserved for the living. Martínez has attained that which few athletes are capable of, or ever placed in a position to attain—complete and enduring capture of an entire country's imagination and affection through sport.

One day, another Hispanic pitcher may come along and exceed the ethnic mound marks of Dennis Martínez. And if that day comes, Martínez, or a descendent, might be present to applaud the achievement, fully knowing that the collective hearts of the Nicaraguan people will always remain, generation to generation, warmly affixed to the bosom of the Dennis Martínez baseball name.

The 1980s—Fernando Valenzuela

Fernando Valenzuela

There have been other rookie pitchers who have burst upon the baseball scene with awe-striking appeal—notably, overpowering ones like Herb Score and Dwight Gooden. But no first-year pitcher, with the possible exception of Mark "the Bird" Fidrych, captured and captivated the baseball public the way the seventh son of Avelino and Hermenegilda Valenzuela did in 1981.

Like Fidrych, Fernando Valenzuela possessed a combination of charisma and curiosity that excited and infatuated the public. But unlike Fidrych, who was exuberantly and giddily astonished by his own successes, Valenzuela's endearment lay in his nonplus demeanor and a unique pitching style that produced luxuriant results rarely seen from one so young.

Fascinating the fans and the North American baseball press was Valenzuela's "puzzled air" comportment, which was really nothing more than the affectation of a shy and overwhelmed foreigner. The basic character trait of youthful timidity plus an inability to speak English in his first season in the major leagues were responsible for the projected state of bewilderment. (Valenzuela was nicknamed "Señor Silent.") That he stayed so composed on the mound and displayed little emotion, unlike most Hispanic players, added anomalous intrigue to both Fernando the man and Fernando the pitcher. Early on, in front of a group of reporters, he was asked if he was intimidated by pitching in front of 50,000+ fans at Dodger Stadium. He replied, through an interpreter, that he was more intimidated by the 20 journalists he was now facing.

Valenzuela was remarkably comfortable on the mound for a rookie, and his command over an assortment of pitches, at just 20 years of age, added to everyone's amazement. Dodgers spring training pitching instructor Sandy Koufax commented how unusual it was for a pitcher as young as Valenzuela to have control over such a variety of pitches that he had.

A month into Valenzula first season, his catcher Joe Ferguson chimed to the press that he ran out of fingers when he gave Valenzuela the signs behind the plate. Ferguson was referring to two types of fastballs that Venezuela threw (straight and sinking), along with a changeup, slider, and sharp-breaking curve. There was also the "tornillera" or lanzamiento de tornillo. Valenzuela had already mastered a superb screwball.

Fernando Valenzuela was born in Navojoa, Mexico, November 1, 1960, and raised in Etchohuaquila, a dry farming village that had not many more residents than the town had letters. The extended Valenzuela clan, including Fernando, 11 siblings and assorted cousins, nieces and nephews, made up a good portion of the small community, approximately 20 miles north of Navojoa. Fernando described his early childhood as a poor one, but never lacking the basic necessities.

Fernando, the youngest of the 12 children, showed his baseball promise as a teenager. All of the Valenzuela boys played baseball in Etchohuaquila. It was his older brother, Rafael, who first saw something in the way Fernando threw the ball. Rafael, himself a pitcher, had played professionally. At the age of 15, Fernando was selected to play on an all-star team representing his home state of Sonora in a regional baseball tournament and did well enough to attract the calling of Guanajuato, a minor league team in the Mexican Central League. At that tender age, Fernando skipped his remaining high school years and opted for an $80-a-month, baseball-by-bus apprenticeship, traveling the dusty roads of the lower circuit's towns.

By 1979, Valenzuela had pitched his way to the Yucatan Leones in Mexico's most prominent league. "Birdog" scout Corito Verona first noticed Valenzuela, and then the Dodgers sent scout Mike Brito to investigate further. Brito assessed Valenzuela's potential and gave the Dodgers the "thumbs up" on the dumpy-bodied left-hander. Valenzuela's Mexican contract was owned by Puebla. Their owner negotiated a $120,000 purchase price for Valenzuela with the Dodgers. The New York Yankees were said to have made a bid for Valenzuela's rights in the neighborhood of $150,000, but it came too late.

In 1979, the Dodgers sent the 19-year-old to Class-A ball in Lodi, California, and then to Arizona for Instructional League training. There, Valenzuela developed the primary pitch that raised him to a higher pitching echelon and bewildered major leaguers for years to come.

Bobby Castillo, a third-year hurler with the Dodgers, showed Valenzuela how to throw a screwball. Valenzuela threw it so well that he drew unimpeachable praise from the master screwballer himself, Carl Hubbell. Hubbell stated after viewing Fernando's "fadeaway" that Valenzuela was the only pitcher he had seen in 40 years with as good a "screwball formula" as his own.

Valenzuela's big league ascension came after his first full year in the minors, at San Antonio. He was 6–9 at one point, pitching for the Dodgers' south Texas Double-A team, then won seven in row. The streak included a 35-scoreless-innings stretch. That earned him a call-up to Los Angeles in September 1980. In the heat of a nip-and-tuck pennant battle between the Dodgers and Houston Astros, Valenzuela made ten relief appearances and did not give up an earned run in 17⅔ innings.

El Coloso Mexicano

In 1981, Fernando Valenzuela's spring exhibition pitching earned him a starting slot in the Dodgers' rotation. As Opening Day approached, projected Opening Day starter Jerry Reuss pulled up lame and number two pitcher Burt Hooton had developed an ingrown toenail that needed more time healing. Manager Tommy Lasorda turned to the 20-year-old Valenzuela, who said, Why not? in a simple response to his manager's request to take the mound a few days earlier than scheduled. The rest was ... baseball history, combining elements of spontaneous enthrallment and snowballing brilliance.

Valenzuela stepped out to the mound on a sunny Chávez Ravine day in early April, in his first major league start, and five-hit the Houston Astros, 2–0. The Opening Day crowd of more than 50,000 and the Mexican and Mexican-descent majority of the roughly two million census-counted Hispanics of Los Angeles County fell immediately and proudly in love.

Five days later, on April 14, Valenzuela handcuffed the San Francisco Giants on four hits, 7–1, at Candlestick Park, striking out ten. The earned run was the first permitted by Valenzuela in 33⅔ major league innings, dating to last September. The televised game drew World Series–type TV ratings in the Los Angeles area and was the fifth-highest ranked show in the local Nielsen ratings that week. Beginning on April 18, Valenzuela threw three straight shutouts over a ten-day span. On the 18th, Valenzuela limited the San Diego Padres to five singles in his 2–0 triumph at Jack Murphy Stadium. After the game, Padres manager Frank Howard praised Valenzuela for having the "poise and command" of a man with at least five years of major league experience.

In the Astrodome on April 22, Valenzuela displayed the same poise and command, as he took matters completely into his own hands in defeating the Astros. Valenzuela knocked in the game's only run with a single. In gaining his fourth complete game victory, the left-hander walked three—one more than in his previous two starts—and impressed Astros manager Bill Virdon with the location of his pitches. Virdon stated that he could not remember anyone as young as Valenzuela with the type of control he showed, except for Juan Marichal.

Five days afterward, Valenzuela's appeal drew to Dodger Stadium over 49,000 fans on a Monday. Valenzuela humbled the Giants, 5–0, yielding seven hits. He started the scoring himself with a fourth-inning RBI single. He was not bothered all evening—until the ninth inning. A dark-haired female admirer, wearing jeans and a blue-sleeved baseball undershirt with VALENZUELA and "34" (his uniform number) imprinted on the back, scurried to the mound to plant a kiss on the cheek of her pudgy conquistador. She was whisked away by security, while the Giants were whisked away by Valenzuela, who closed out the month with a perfect 5–0 mark. Lasorda's team improved to 14–3 with Valenzuela's fifth win. When asked afterwards, Lasorda could not draw a comparison between Valenzuela and any other young pitcher he had seen, calling the pitcher's repertoire and initially sensational statistical accomplishments unique.

The Montreal Expos had drawn 30,003 fans as its Opening Day crowd. For Valenzuela's first start of May, 46,405 turned out at Stade Olympique. A 6–1, ten-inning win kept Valenzuela perfect on the season, but broke his complete game streak. The Dodgers scored five times in the top of the tenth inning, pinch-hitting for Valenzuela in the process. Steve Howe pitched the bottom of the tenth to lock up Valenzuela's sixth win.

Los Angeles, on its first Eastern road trip, headed south from Montreal and traveled to Philadelphia and then New York. Valenzuela's next turn came up in the opener of a three-game set against the New York Mets. (The Dodgers sent Valenzuela to New York ahead of the team to take on the one-per-city press conference to which the club was now confining him.) The fifth-place Mets had been averaging a little over 11,000 spectators per game. For Valenzuela's game, 39,848 fans were drawn in. Famed artist Leroy Neiman marked the occasion with sketched drawings of Valenzuela, and more than five times the usual number of radio stations that received Dodgers games in Mexico received broadcast beams from New York for the May 8 contest.

At the outset, Valenzuela was not sharp. He walked three and allowed three hits over the first two innings (the Mets were the first team to load the bases on the pitcher all season), but made clutch pitches to prevent the Mets from scoring in either inning. The Dodgers supported Valenzuela with one run in the entire game but the perplexing left-hander made it stand up. The 20-year-old registered his fifth shutout of the season—and the season was only 30 calendar days old! Valenzuela won with his "worst stuff" of the year, allowing seven hits and walking five.

The Dodgers finished their engagement in New York with two victories and a 6–4 road trip. The 20–9 team flew back across the country to entertain the same three Eastern city clubs in successive series. The first opponent for the first-place Dodgers was Montreal. The largest regular season crowd since 1974 (53,906) showed up at Dodger Stadium to witness Valenzuela's May 14 mound appointment. The Dodgers left-hander was involved in another tight contest. Valenzuela took a 2–1 lead into the ninth inning, having surrendered a home run earlier to Chris Speier, one of only two hits and three baserunners he had permitted. Valenzuela secured the first two outs of the ninth, but Andre Dawson deposited a Valenzuela pitch into the seats to tie the game. The pitcher retired the next batter. In the bottom of the inning, Pedro Guerrero slugged the third pitch he saw from reliever Steve Ratzer for a game-winning home run. If Dodger Stadium had a roof, it would have come off. Valenzuela won his eighth game, seven completed, and had an unbelievable ERA of 0.50.

The exciting win lifted to 10–0 overall—counting two wins in relief at the end of 1980—the record of El Coloso Mexicano, one of the nicknames the Mexican press had bestowed upon Valenzuela. His win completed a series sweep over the Expos and lengthened the team's division lead over the second-place Atlanta Braves to 5½ games. "In baseball, you win some, you lose some," Valenzuela said through a translator after the game. "I'm winning and I hope I can keep winning, but I'm prepared to take defeats. I don't have any idea how far I can go."[1]

Almost prophetically after his comments, Valenzuela was beaten by the Philadelphia Phillies four days later, May 18. The Dodgers were shut out by Marty Bystrom, 4–0, and all the runs in seven innings against Valenzuela were earned, including a home run by Mike Schmidt. Valenzuela's parents, watching him pitch in the major leagues for the first time, were among the 52,439 disappointed fans in attendance. Valenzuela, for his part, said he knew he had to lose eventually, and remained upbeat. The Cincinnati Reds and Atlanta Braves caught up with Valenzuela in his next two starts and hit the pitcher as he had yet to experience; Valenzuela endured a no-decision and suffered a second defeat. But the hindrances failed to diminish Valenzuela's appeal.

Much of the allure surrounding Fernando Valenzuela centered around his appearance and comportment on the mound. He did not talk to the ball, or himself, as had Fidrych, the last rookie pitcher to enchant baseball completely. He did not rush the ball to the plate with exceeding velocity. He had no outward showiness about him. He simply and calmly brought his 5'11," 210-pound, non athletic-looking body to the center of the baseball infield and delivered, pitch after pitch, to home plate in the same steady, unruffled manner. A puffy countenance made him look older than his young age, which was often questioned. A running gag was that an opponent's scout had seen numerous lines on the back of Fernando's neck and deduced that Valenzuela had to be older than listed.

"I've been doing Dodger games for 22 years," said Jaime Jarrín, who often translated for Valenzuela during media sessions, "and I've never seen anybody have an impact on the fans the way Fernando has. Not even Koufax or Drysdale or Maury Wills when they were at their peaks had this kind of wild devotion from the people. And I'm not just talking about Spanish-speaking people. I'm talking about everybody."[2]

Extenuating circumstances lamentably interrupted a most special first season for one most special left-handed pitcher in Southern California. An 18-month-long entrenchment between the players' union and management over free agent compensation reached unpardonable consequence in June of 1981 when the players went on strike. Valenzuela was 9–4 at the time with five shutouts.

Valenzuela spent the strike-induced layoff in the media's inescapable glare. He traveled and made acquaintances in high places. Valenzuela made a hero's tour through his former Mexican League pitching outposts. And he threw some exhibition innings in games in Tijuana and Mexicali (which was prohibited by the standard major league contract). Valenzuela also personally met the presidents of the Western Hemisphere's two most populous countries.

The labor impasse was eventually resolved and the season was restarted with the playing of the All-Star Game on August 9. Starting for the National League squad, Valenzuela tossed a scoreless inning and became the youngest Hispanic player to appear in the Mid-Summer Classic. The National League defeated the American League, 5–4, at Cleveland Stadium. The rest of the players returned to work the next day, after two months of inactivity.

It took Valenzuela three starts to pick up his tenth win after the restart of the campaign. He did so on August 22, with a 12-strikeout performance against the St. Louis Cardinals. Dave Stewart, in relief, obtained the last out of the 3–2 game. In front of another huge non-weekend crowd at Dodger Stadium on August 27, Valenzuela spun his sixth shutout, whizzing past the Chicago Cubs on four hits and ten strikeouts, 6–0.

The next time toeing the rubber, on September 1, Valenzuela attempted to become the major leagues' first 12-game winner. He pitched ten innings and allowed only one run, but got a no-decision against the Pittsburgh Pirates. The Dodgers came out on top, 3–2, with a Ron Cey RBI single providing the winning run. Dodger Stadium supporters, notorious for being "early exiters," that night were presented with more legitimate reasons for not sticking around to the end because of the game's eventual length of 14 innings. A sellout crowd of 50,134 attended; it marked the Dodgers' 19th sellout in 38 home dates and the seventh in eight home starts for Valenzuela. The only time Valenzuela had not drawn a capacity crowd at Dodger Stadium, occurred on August 11, the first game back after the two-month strike.

In his next outing on September 6, Valenzuela shut out the St. Louis Cardinals, 5–0, for his seventh whitewash, tying a National League rookie record. It was the second time in two weeks that Valenzuela had beaten Whitey Herzog's Cardinals. Herzog was asked if Valenzuela looked any different in this start compared to his last conquest of his Missouri team. "He's still as fat. He's still as ugly. He's still as good,"[3] said the St. Louis manager. (Perhaps unknown to Herzog, *Playgirl* magazine had named Valenzuela to its list of ten most desirable men. Also making the list from the sports world was Yankees owner George M. Steinbrenner.) Eleven days later, Valenzuela won his 13th game, three-hitting the Atlanta Braves at Dodger Stadium, 2–0. Twenty-six thousand-plus more fans were at the park than the prior evening's 19,905 attendees.

Valenzuela lost his final three starts of the season. Included was a 1–0 loss to the San

Diego Padres on October 1. In the game, Valenzuela struck out seven to nudge past Steve Carlton for the National League strikeout title with 180.

Valenzuela finished with a 13–7 record and a host of what-could-have-beens—if not for the strike. The left-hander had a 36-inning scoreless innings and tossed eight shutouts in a 110 game schedule.

The work stoppage uniquely affected the post-season as Major League Baseball crowned those teams in first place at the time of the walk-out "division winners," assuring them of a post-season playoff berth. All teams were given clean slates upon the resumption of the trun-cated schedule in August; those finishing first at the close of the campaign would also be deemed "division champions." (The set-up was similar to the "split-season" play favored in some Caribbean winter leagues.) The Los Angeles Dodgers unquestionably benefited from the plan. Lasorda's team held a tenuous one-half game lead over the Cincinnati Reds when the strike commenced and as such was one of four teams given a pass into the October play-offs. In the second half-season, the Dodgers placed fourth. In contrast, the Reds finished 1½ games behind the first-place Houston Astros in the second portion of the season, and, owning the best overall record in the National League, did *not* make the playoffs.

Houston won the first two games of the best-of-five inter-division series from the Dodgers. Valenzuela received a no-decision in his start in Game 1. Valenzuela locked up against the Astros' Nolan Ryan on October 6. Valenzuela allowed one run in eight innings. After he was lifted for a pinch-hitter, Alan Ashby reached reliever Dave Stewart for a two-run, ninth-inning home run. Ryan pitched a two-hitter for the 3–1 win. Three Houston pitchers combined to blank the Dodgers, 1–0, in 11 innings the following day. The series moved to Los Angeles for the next three games, if needed. The Dodgers won Game 3 behind Burt Hooton, and then called on Valenzuela, who evened the series with a sparkling four-hitter. Following those series-saving efforts, Jerry Reuss, who had pitched nine scoreless innings in Game 2, duplicated the effort in Game 5, and defeated the Astros and Nolan Ryan, 4–0, capping a fierce, three-game Dodgers comeback.

The Dodgers advanced to the National League LCS against the Montreal Expos and again fell to within one game of going home for the winter. The Dodgers opened at home with a win, 5–1. Valenzuela lost his Game 2 start to Ray Burris, 3–0. Then Reuss was defeated by Expos right-hander Steve Rogers, 4–1, when the series moved to Montreal. A Dodgers' 7–1 win in Game 4 by Hooton, his second win of the five game-series, set up the winner-take-all fifth contest, matching Valenzuela and Burris again.

Rick Monday's dramatic solo home run in the top of the ninth inning against Rogers, in relief, broke up a one-one tie and opened the way for the cardiac Dodgers into the Fall Classic. When Valenzuela walked two Expos batters in the ninth inning with two outs, Bob Welch was brought in, and he picked up the last out of the 2–1 victory.

Because of the extra round of playoffs, the World Series of 1981 had the latest starting date yet seen, October 20. As they had habitually done throughout their marvelous post-season run, the Dodgers dug themselves into a hole, losing the first two games on the road to the New York Yankees.

Everything changed abruptly for the Gene Michael-replaced-by-Bob-Lemon New York Yankees as the Series venue shifted across the country to Los Angeles. The team endured three losses to Lasorda's regrouped men at Dodger Stadium, then flew back to the Bronx where it was soundly defeated in Game 6. The World Series loss considerably rankled the

Yankees' demanding owner, as the Dodgers paid the New Yorkers back partially for two World Series conquests suffered a few years earlier.

The Series turned in Game 3—pitched by Valenzuela in front of a bursting-at-the-seams Dodger Stadium on October 23. Valenzuela vanquished the AL champions, 5–4, staunchly overcoming two home runs, nine total hits and seven walks issued. Although the Yankees were without the services of two of their star players, Reggie Jackson and Graig Nettles, the team had Valenzuela on the ropes early in the game but could not come up with the knockout blow. Valenzuela remained standing to the end, a proud victor.

Valenzuela, in all, won three games in the post-season for the world champion Dodgers, including the clinching game of the National League Championship Series versus Montreal.

Over the next six weeks, the Mexican marvel received Rookie of the Year and Cy Young Award trophies as the National League's most accomplished rookie and best pitcher. And still his year had one great accomplishment left in it.

Valenzuela married 21-year-old Linda Margarita Burgos, a comely girl from Merida he had met while in the Mexican League. Linda had been Valenzuela's girlfriend for two years, and on December 29, she became Valenzuela's girlfriend-for-life.

* * *

After the 1981 season, Valenzuela, humility intact, returned home to pitch for the Mayos de Navojoa in the Mexican Pacific League. As a league participant, Valenzuela qualified as a welcomed roster addition to the Hermosillo Orangegrowers, Mexico's Caribbean

Fernando Valenzuela is embraced by Mexican president José López Portillo, while U.S. president Ronald Reagan (partially eclipsed by Valenzuela) looks cheerily on. First Lady Nancy Reagan is at far left. The Mexican dignitaries were guests of honor at a 1981 White House luncheon.

Series team representative in February 1982. In a stroke of good fortune for Mexican fans, the Caribbean Series was scheduled to be played in their own backyard.

In Hermosillo, on the opening day of the tournament, February 4, Valenzuela and a reliever threw a combined two-hit shutout over the Ponce Leones. The 14–0 final score was undoubtedly the reason for not allowing Valenzuela to finish the game. At the time of Valenzuela's next start, five days later, 2–3 Hermosillo had been eliminated from championship consideration. In the closing game of tournament, Valenzuela received a no-decision as his team was defeated by the Escogido Lions, 7–2, on late-inning scoring. A third "Lions" team, from Caracas and managed by Chico Carrasquel, earned the big Caribbean prize, losing only once in the six-day competition.

The Dodgers did not approve of the off-season pitching, and the club also became more than miffed by Valenzuela's 22-day spring training holdout for more money.

The mid-season strike of 1981 had shocked every fan 30 and older into realizing that baseball had become Big Business and would never again be the game of their innocent youth. That became more apparent when the Dodgers' compensation offer of $350,000, a more than $300,000 increase over his rookie salary, was rejected by Valenzuela's people as not being equitable to the revenue stream Valenzuela had generated for the Dodgers. ("Fernandomania" had been a very pleasing boon to the deep coffers of the Dodgers.) "He is one-of-a-kind," Tony DeMarco, Valenzuela's lead agent, correctly pointed out. "I expected an offer that I would not find offensive," DeMarco said, upon receiving the Dodgers' tender for his client. "Their offer was not offensive; it wasn't what we want, but it should lead to serious negotiations."[4]

The salary haggle did not sit well with the working-stiff public, however, who were aware of the multiple endorsement deals Valenzuela had profited from in the past year. The Dodgers automatically imposed their offered salary, and when the contractually bound Valenzuela returned to the mound in the spring of 1982, there were boos and not cheers heard at Vero Beach. The boos carried over to Valenzuela's appearance in the annual "Freeway Series" between the Dodgers and Angels.

"Two years ago, his alarm clock was a rooster," Lasorda had said on more than one occasion, trying to put things in humorous perspective.

Lasorda gave Valenzuela his first start in the Dodgers' fourth game of the 1982 campaign. A capacity crowd showed up and as the April 11, 1982, *New York Times* reported "greeted the pitcher with a mixture of jeers and cheers." It rained in Southern California that afternoon and the weather delayed the game more than an hour. Valenzuela, having worked only five spring training innings, pitched six shutout innings against San Diego and picked up the win in the Dodgers' 6–0 triumph. The Dodger Stadium sellout, despite the weather, was the 16th in 17 games started there by Valenzuela.

April ended with the second-year pitcher owning a 2–3 record. Having played 21 games, the Dodgers were one game below .500 and did not resemble the team that gritted through the playoffs last season to seize the world championship.

Valenzuela then won six out of seven games, May 4 through June 5. Influenced by his pitching improvement, the segment of annoyed fans swayed back to him. The 21-year-old hurler tossed his first shutout (7–0) of the season on May 30, apportioning eight hits to the Chicago Cubs at Wrigley Field and earning his seventh victory.

Valenzuela had doubled his win total by the time of his next shutout, coming on July

31 over the Braves. Valenzuela improved his mounting record to 14–8 and topped his wins count from last season on the heels of the whitewash. The 3–0 triumph over the Atlanta Braves, at Fulton County Stadium, began a four-game series sweep by Los Angeles over the Braves. Heading into the series, the Dodgers were playing no better than mediocre ball for four months. The team trailed first-place Atlanta, a club that produced a scalding first half of the season pace, by 10½ games.

But the Dodgers re-entered the National League West Division picture with the sweep, and in less than a month's time were amazingly challenging the Braves for first place. On August 25, when Valenzuela topped the Cardinals in St. Louis, 11–3, the win moved the Dodgers—who had made up more than ten games in the standings in less than a month— into first place ahead of Atlanta. Winning for the 17th time, Valenzuela clubbed his first big league home run against the Cardinals' Steve Mura.

Valenzuela threw his second 1–0 shutout of the season on September 14, against San Diego at Dodger Stadium. The first had come three weeks earlier; Valenzuela two-hit the Pirates in Pittsburgh on August 20. Following Valenzuela's home blanking of the Padres, Tommy Lasorda's Dodgers held a 1½-game lead in the standings on the Joe Torre-led Braves. On September 19, Valenzuela hurled his 19th victory, 5–4, in ten innings over the Houston Astros. The Dodgers pulled out some of their late-season magic from a season ago, utilizing a two-out, two-run double by Pedro Guerrero in the bottom of the tenth inning to turn an impending defeat into victory. Los Angeles maintained a 2½-game lead on second-place Atlanta with 12 games to play. The Dodgers, in an unchampion-like manner, lost nine of those games, including eight in a row, and let the Braves retake the exalted territory from them. Valenzuela failed in three attempts at winning his 20th game.

The season entered its last weekend with Atlanta holding a one-game lead. The Dodgers traveled to San Francisco to play their final three games, while the Braves played the Padres farther down the California coast. The Dodgers answered each of the Braves' first two wins against San Diego with victories of their own. In game 162, the Dodgers needed to win and the Braves to lose in order to tie and force a one-game playoff to determine the NL West Division winner.

On October 3, Valenzuela started for the Dodgers against the Giants, who had entered the division-deciding weekend with an outside chance to claim the flag for themselves, but now were only playing for the relished desire of preventing their archrivals from broader success. With the score tied 2–2, the Dodgers loaded the bases with two outs in the seventh inning. Due up was Valenzuela; Lasorda pinch-hit for his pitcher. From the bench, Jorge Orta was called upon to try and put his team in the lead, but he grounded out. In the bottom of the inning, the Giants' Joe Morgan homered with two outs and two men on base against reliever Terry Forster. Two innings later, San Francisco completed a most satisfying 5–3 win.

*　*　*

Coming off his 19-win season, again, in 1983, Valenzuela held out for more money. But now he had labor leverage. As a third-year player, Valenzuela invoked his right to arbitration to settle the contract standoff. How far apart were the Dodgers and Valenzuela? Tommy Lasorda quipped the classic line, "He wants Texas back."

In February 1983, arbitrator Tom Roberts was more persuaded by Tony DeMarco's propping arguments than the Dodgers' council of denigrators. Roberts awarded Valenzuela a $1,000,000 salary and made the pitcher the highest-paid third-year player in baseball history—and the first Hispanic player to earn a seven-figure annual salary.

Valenzuela seemed inspired by the judgment and came into spring camp 15 pounds lighter than in previous years. The weight loss did not help in an Opening Day start against the Astros in the Astrodome. The pitcher was rocked for six earned runs in less than three innings. The Dodgers scored in bunches and he was spared a loss. Valenzuela bounced back with a home shutout over Montreal (3–0) five days later. The pitcher tossed a second whitewash, at St. Louis, defeating Joaquín Andujar, 8–0, on April 25. Both gems were seven-hitters. Valenzuela closed April with a 3–2 mark.

In May, Valenzuela obtained only three decisions, but they were all positive. Ten weeks into the season, Valenzuela appeared headed toward the 20-win campaign he had just missed last season and more validation for his sizable contract. Valenzuela garlanded his third shutout on May 28 at Dodger Stadium, against the San Francisco Giants. The left-hander allowed only four baserunners, walking two and permitting two hits, both harmlessly spaced doubles.

On June 13, when the pitcher defeated the Cincinnati Reds, 5–1, and bettered his won-lost ledger to 8–2, Valenzuela and the Dodgers appeared securely on the path to higher achievement. The win over the Reds boosted the first-place Dodgers to a 39–19 record. But Valenzuela tapered off from there, and so did the Dodgers—though each completed successful campaigns.

Valenzuela won 15 games and lost ten over the full schedule. Not throwing another shutout, his ERA swelled to 3.75, nearly a full run higher than in 1982. Valenzuela only completed nine games, but did pitch over 250 innings. As in last season, Valenzuela's value showed most in preventing extended losing spells. Twelve of Valenzuela's 15 victories followed Dodgers' losses, comparing favorably to Valenzuela's previous campaign of 11 wins that immediately nullified team setbacks.

Lasorda's team, riding the impetus of its fast start, won the division by three games over the Atlanta Braves. On September 28, despite losing a doubleheader to San Diego, through an attrition of games, the Dodgers clinched no worse than a tie for the division title. The next day, Valenzuela downed the Giants, 4–3, with relief help, and the Dodgers won their first "full season" division title in five years.

Los Angeles was one game better than the 90–72 Philadelphia Phillies, its East Division playoff opponent. Lasorda's men were defeated in four games by Philadelphia for the National League pennant. The only Dodgers victory in the championship series was registered by Valenzuela, a Game 2, 4–1 victory over the Phillies and John Denny in L.A, in front of just under 56,000 cheering fans.

*   *   *

In 1984, an upstart team in San Diego, piloted by Dick Williams, proved to be the class of the National League West.

Valenzuela did not show his good stuff in his early starts. It was not until April 20, against the San Diego Padres, that Valenzuela recorded his first win, 8–2, with a complete game effort. He was triumphant in his next two starts, giving him three wins in five decisions for the month of April. On the last day of the month, Valenzuela humbled the San Francisco Giants, 1–0, at Candlestick Park. It was "Kazoo Night," and the three singles and one double permitted by Valenzuela, mixed in with ten strikeouts, left little over which the 28,062 paid fans could toot their freebie toy trumpets.

Valenzuela lassoed another 1–0 shutout and the fifth of his young career on May 23 over the Philadelphia Phillies at Veterans Stadium. In a southpaw heavyweight pitching match-up, Valenzuela defeated Steve Carlton, while striking out a career-high 15 batters. Valenzuela drove in Mike Scioscia with the only run of the game with a ground out in the fifth inning. At the end of May, the Dodgers, only five games over .500, held a one-half-game lead on the second-place Padres.

Following that game, the Dodgers slid from five games over .500 to four under in a ten-week span. During the tailspin, Valenzuela's record slipped to 8–9, but his overall pitching was good enough to earn him a selection to the All-Star Game.

The game's best hitters added considerably to the stiff breezes of Candlestick Park when they fanned a record 21 times (for a nine-inning game) during the 55th Mid-Summer Classic on July 10. In the fourth inning, Valenzuela struck out the American League's Dave Winfield, Reggie Jackson and George Brett in succession. Three more American League batters went down swinging to Mets rookie sensation Dwight Gooden in the following frame, setting a record for consecutive strikeouts. The National League came out on top, 3–1, coincidentally on the 50th anniversary of Giants pitcher Carl Hubbell's legendary strikeout performance in the second All-Star Game, involving five fearsome American League batters in succession.

Both Valenzuela and the Dodgers went off course over the second half of the season. After a three-game sweep suffered against the Padres in San Diego on July 30–August 1, the floundering Dodgers found themselves staring at a 13-game deficit to the first-place club.

Valenzuela record of 12–17 at the final bell was not reflective of his overall pitching prowess. Valenzuela's ERA was nearly three-quarters of a run better than the prior season (3.03), and he lost several low-scoring contests. Valenzuela deserved better as the fourth-place Dodgers scored one run or none in nine of his defeats.

* * *

After losing more games than they won for the first time in five seasons, the Dodgers quickly returned to the division prominence it had known in recent years. But prior to that regained superiority, the club began the 1985 campaign with uninspired play, and dragged the superb pitching of Valenzuela down with it. Valenzuela started out pitching nearly as well as in his rookie season, but was particularly hampered by a feeble Dodgers offense.

The pitcher was defeated by the Astros and Nolan Ryan on Opening Day, 2–1; both runs against Valenzuela were unearned. Three starts later, Valenzuela lost a game to San Francisco by the same score and similarly bungled defense that permitted the Giants to score their two runs. In between, Valenzuela threw two shutouts. The first came in his first home start on April 13. The score was 1–0; Valenzuela allowed the San Francisco Giants five hits, while walking two and fanning five. The other came versus the San Diego Padres five days later. Valenzuela surrendered two hits and walked three in the 5–0, Jack Murphy Stadium victory.

At the time of his fifth start, Valenzuela's record was 2–2 with an ERA of 0.00. The left-hander then pitched eight shutout innings against the Padres on April 28, at Dodger Stadium, before allowing his first earned run of the campaign. In the ninth inning, with one out, Tony Gwynn drove a fastball into the seats for a home run. The Dodgers were shut out. Back in 1904, rookie pitcher Hooks Wiltse, as a reliever and starter, had opened the season with 40⅔ innings pitched without an earned run permitted, as a springboard to a career-starting 12 victories without a loss.[5] Valenzuela, who had sparred with Wiltse's ghost in 1981 for that very rookie victory record, had surpassed the mark of the New York Giants' pitcher of yore for most innings without an earned run to start a season by two outs when Gywnn connected (41⅓ innings). Valenzuela, for his part, was not discouraged despite the 2–3 start which, with some modest support, could have easily been 5–0 with four shutouts.

Valenzuela evened his record on May 4 with a gutsy effort at Pittsburgh in which he did not possess his best stuff. Hurling ten innings, Valenzuela defeated the Pirates, 6–5, allowing ten hits and four earned runs. Valenzuela could not consistently stay on the winning track immediately following, losing four of his next seven decisions. In the defeats, his pitching was not near the caliber of the opening month of play.

In late June, Valenzuela showily won for the seventh time, 6–3, over Houston's Astros. Following the 14-strikeout, complete game effort, Valenzuela made cross-over strides by engaging in English language interviews after the contest. Previously, any non–Spanish Q & A's had been extremely brief or conducted with a translator. For Valenzuela, the language barrier had provided a guarding presence, especially in his rookie year. Valenzuela elaborated on the point in another interview, recalling, "Not being able to speak English at that time was a big help. Not being able to talk to all members of the press individually, I didn't have to justify my work on the diamond to every single media member. In a way, that was my protection against an avalanche of people, and a blessing as far as my concentration on the game."[6]

Valenzuela steadily won ten more games over the next three months. His 17 wins were two behind starting mound cohort Orel Hershiser. The two pitchers headed a staff that led the National League in ERA and strikeouts. A defeat to the Cincinnati Reds and four no-decisions in his last five starts prevented Valenzuela from realizing a 20-win season.

The Dodgers, with a record of 57–33 from July 1 forward, won the division by 5½ games over Cincinnati and faced the St. Louis Cardinals in the first year of the seven-game League Championship Series.

Valenzuela, with relief help from Tom Niedenfuer, was a victor in the series opener against John Tudor, 4–1. The Dodgers also won Game 2 the next day, October 10, behind Hershiser, 8–2. The Cardinals rebounded to win their first two home games. In Game 5 at St. Louis, Valenzuela walked eight in eight innings of work, but yielded only two runs on four hits. Valenzuela left with the ball game tied 2–2. In the bottom of the ninth, with no scoring change, Cardinals shortstop Ozzie Smith yanked a Niedenfuer pitch down the line in right and over the outfield wall, and Cardinals fans went "crazy."

The Cardinals, after spotting the Left Coasters two games, won four straight, capped by Jack Clark's two-out, ninth-inning, three-run home run against reliever Niedenfuer in the sixth game at Dodger Stadium. The home team led by a run at the time.

*   *   *

Clark's crushing home run had a residual effect on Lasorda's team in 1986. The Dodgers plummeted to fifth place, 23 games in the rear of division-winning Houston. Also contributing to the decline was the loss, for most of the season, of the Dodgers' best run-producer,

Pedro Guerrero, to a knee injury in spring training. The only bright spot for the Los Angeles squad was their sixth-year Sonoran slinger.

Over the past five seasons, Valenzuela had compiled the best ERA (2.89) and second-most strikeouts (1,016) in the National League. Valenzuela had averaged 253 innings over the same span, including the strike-compressed year. The Dodgers rewarded their pitching ace in March with a three-year, $5.5 million contract.

The Dodgers began their forgettable season by losing 11 times in their first 15 games. In game 16, played on April 23, it was Valenzuela's turn to pitch ... and pitch. Valenzuela threw the most pitches he had ever thrown in a major league game. In what Dodgers beat writer Gordon Edes termed a "flawed masterpiece," Valenzuela defeated the San Francisco Giants, 6–4, requiring *163* pitches to do so. Valenzuela overcame three Dodgers errors and eight Giants hits in the laborious effort. He struck out two Giants in the bottom of the ninth inning to end the game.

Valenzuela closed the month of April by six-hitting the Pittsburgh Pirates, 2–1, for his third win. One start later, on May 3, Valenzuela tossed his initial shutout of the season and 24th in barely five full seasons. At Dodger Stadium, the 1985 National League champion Cardinals were the five-hit, 3–0 victims. With Valenzuela on the hill, the Dodgers won their seventh game in a row on May 20; the left-hander improved to 6–2 with the home stifling of the Montreal Expos, and the 4–0 two-hitter also produced Valenzuela's sixth complete game. Making a start on three days' rest on May 24, Valenzuela shut out the Philadelphia Phillies, 6–0, limiting them to two hits and striking out 11. A sellout Dodger Stadium crowd cheered perhaps their loudest as Valenzuela struck out Mike Schmidt and Glenn Wilson for the final outs of the game. In June, Valenzuela won three and lost two. The two defeats he was dealt were by scores of 3–2 and 2–1. The latter defeat's runs were both unearned. At the All-Star break, Valenzuela had recorded 11 of his team's 40 wins—a team eight games under .500. The Dodgers' staff leader received his sixth roster summons from the National League for the annual mid-season showcase game, played indoors in Houston that season. The 25-year-old Valenzuela followed 20-year-old Dwight Gooden to the mound for the National League and stole the limelight that had been placed on Gooden and his equally hard-throwing American League starting counterpart, Roger Clemens. Over two innings, Valenzuela consecutively struck out four of the American League's best hitters and its pitcher. The 11–6 Valenzuela won ten games following the All Star Game, seven by complete game. He finished with a 21–11 record, accompanied by a polished 3.14 ERA.

On September 17, with the elusive 20-win pendant dangling in front of him, he lost, 4–1, in Atlanta. In his next start, on September 22, he won number 20 in a breeze. In the Astrodome, site of several of his road pitching wizardries, Valenzuela two-hit the Astros, 9–2, permitting one earned run. Valenzuela became the first Mexican-born pitcher to win 20 games in a major league season. Valenzuela fell to 20–11, producing his worst campaign start on September 27 against the Giants in San Francisco.

In his final start, Valenzuela completely shook off that eight earned runs-allowed performance. In the next-to-last game of the season, on October 4, Valenzuela used his league-best 20th complete game to win his 21st game for a club that called only 73 victories its own. Not allowing an earned run, Valenzuela spun a 2–1, five-hit victory over the same Giants club that battered him less than a week earlier; the game took all of two hours and four minutes to conclude. A rather disappointing crowd of 24,466 were present at Chávez Ravine to see it.

Earlier that season, Tommy Lasorda had summed up his ace with these character-evaluating thoughts: "Fernando goes to the post, he never alibis, complains or blames anybody, he's one of the finest team players I've ever seen. From the day he arrived at the end of 1980, not one player has ever begrudged him that success. How many stars can you say that about?"[7]

*   *   *

The fifth-place Dodgers of 1986 had much room for improvement and took a small step in that direction in 1987. Valenzuela provided a fifth straight season of 250 or more innings and produced a 14–14 won-loss record with a circuit-best 12 complete games. He also posted the highest ERA of his career to date, 3.98.

In his second start of the season, on April 12, Valenzuela gained his 100th career win. He defeated the San Francisco Giants, 7–5, giving up only two of the opposition runs in seven innings of work. Don Drysdale, three months younger than the 26-year-old Valenzuela at the time, was the only Dodgers pitcher to win 100 games at a younger age.

A promising 4–1 start for the left-hander regressed to 5–5 during a four-week stretch from May 22 through June 11. The fifth loss, June 11, was particularly difficult to take—1–0 to the Houston Astros at Dodger Stadium.

Valenzuela's pitching remained inconsistent from that point on through the rest of the season. He tossed his lone shutout, a seven-hit, 7–0, home conquest of the Pittsburgh Pirates, on July 16.

*   *   *

In 1988, things took a downward turn for Valenzuela, but the Dodgers made a tremendous turnaround from the previous season's 73–89 record. Led by Orel Hershiser's late-season historic pitching, and the no-nonsense leadership of Kirk Gibson, the Dodgers won their division and upset the New York Mets and powerful Oakland A's to capture their second world championship of the decade.

Valenzuela lost five of his first eight decisions, then struggled for months while his team flourished. Sporting a record of 5–8, Valenzuela made a start against the Houston Astros on July 30 and stretched the anterior capsule tissue in his shoulder. The next day, after 255 consecutive starting assignments, Valenzuela was placed on the disabled list for the first time in his eight-year career. "I always felt that something was wrong," said Lasorda. "But he would never tell you because he is such a tremendous competitor. He feels like he is letting the team down. I told him that even the best car, when it's eight years old, gets a flat tire."[8]

Lasorda obviously felt Valenzuela had not been pitching at full strength due to a physical impairment. It was written that his fastball's velocity had lost several miles an hour; his screwball was also hanging more and more. An ERA of 4.39, more hits than innings pitched, and fewer strikeouts than walks all reinforced the manager's supposition.

The injury sidelined Valenzuela longer than expected. He did not return until late in the season. He made one start and one relief appearance, earning his first save since 1980 in a season-ending series against the San Francisco Giants. The Dodgers did not place Valenzuela on the team's post-season roster, and the hurler missed out on a second trip to the World Series.

*   *   *

Valenzuela acknowledges one of the countless ovations he received over the years at Dodger Stadium. Manager Tommy Lasorda characteristically leads the applause from inside the dugout.

Valenzuela came back in 1989, but he was not the pitcher he had been. There was a new staff ace in Hershiser and several other pitchers had moved ahead of Fernando in the starting rotation. Valenzuela did not win his first game until June 7, ending a winless span of 19 starts, including the prior season (the longest such streak for any former Cy Young Award-winning pitcher). From that date, the 0–5 Valenzuela's pitching improved. Though more wins than setbacks accumulated after that, Valenzuela's final ledger was 10–13, with a more than respectable 3.43 ERA.

After the season, one in which the Dodgers failed in all respects as a defending world champion, Tony DeMarco, Valenzuela's agent and confidant, was quoted as saying that his free agent client felt "morally obligated" to re-sign with the Dodgers, and that Valenzuela's desire "stemmed from the club's help and patience during his recovery and his love for the city of Los Angeles."[9] But when DeMarco did not accept the initial front office offers, the sides appeared headed toward arbitration. The Dodgers sharpened their pencil and offered a one-year, $2 million contract, with another $500,000 in incentives, which was then accepted by arguably the National League's pitcher of the decade.

* * *

The next season, 1990, a 22-year-old fireballer named Ramón Martínez dominated the pitching scene in Los Angeles. The Dodgers challenged the wire-to-wire, division-winning Cincinnati Reds into late September. But never coming closer than 3½ games, the Dodgers finished five back, in second place. Valenzuela allowed the most earned runs in the league. The left-hander was an average pitcher at best, reflected by a 13–13 record and bloated 4.59 ERA.

But with one of the 13 wins, on the last Friday of June 1990, Valenzuela found enough of his old self to throw a no-hitter against the St. Louis Cardinals at Dodger Stadium. Valenzuela, who had not won in six prior starts, pitched the second of two no-hitters that occurred on the 29th of June. The other was tossed earlier by Dave Stewart of the Oakland Athletics in Toronto, as the major leagues set a record for most no-hitters in a month with four.

No-hitters are seldom thrown without one or two good defensive plays in support. Valenzuela's was no exception. Shortstop Alfredo Griffin made two stellar plays to throw out Cardinals roadrunners Vince Coleman and Willie McGee in the first and seventh innings, respectively, and center fielder Stan Javier hauled down a deep drive against the outfield wall to end the eighth inning. McGee's out was important because Valenzuela walked the next two hitters before retiring two Redbirds.

In the eighth inning, facing the lower third of the order, Valenzuela retired Rex Hudler on a grounder to shortstop. The next batter, Ozzie Smith, flailed at a third strike. Then Cardinals utility man Craig Wilson made the bid for extra bases that Javier snuffed at the wall. Los Angeles added the last of its six runs in their half-inning at bat.

The bespectacled Valenzuela (he had taken to wearing glasses in 1986) took the mound for the ninth inning and faced the top of the Cardinals order. The pitcher's own reflexes played a part in securing the no-hitter. Valenzuela struck out Coleman looking, the call protested loudly by Coleman. Valenzuela then walked McGee. Former teammate Pedro Guerrero hit a hard grounder through the box that deflected off Valenzuela's glove to second baseman Juan Samuel, who stepped on second and threw to first to double up Guerrero. It appeared that the ball would have headed into center field had Valenzuela not redirected it with the late movement of his glove. The pitcher-assisted double play was turned, and announcer Vin Scully urged all Dodgers fans to throw their sombreros into the air after the final out in celebration.

"The only thing that has escaped Fernando over the years has been a no-hitter, and tonight he accomplished that," said Lasorda. "It couldn't have happened to a greater guy. He pitches his heart out every time he goes out. He is without a doubt one of the greatest competitors in the game."[10]

"Really, I'm happy to have this game," said Valenzuela, who issued three walks in the game. "Every pitcher is looking for this game in his career."[11]

* * *

There were only three players remaining on the 1991 Dodgers' spring roster that had been with the team since 1987. The number dwindled to two when the Dodgers, in late March, released their six-time All-Star and 141-game winner, shortly before the club would have been contractually obligated to pay him a full year's salary ($2 million).

Before his release, Valenzuela had the opportunity to pitch an exhibition game with the Dodgers in Monterrey, against the Milwaukee Brewers and Mexican compadre Teddy Higuera. Dodgers owner Peter O'Malley made the trip to Monterrey with his team and marveled at the reception Valenzuela received from the sellout crowd. " We all knew of Fernando's popularity in his country," said O'Malley, "but to come down here and see it, hear it, feel it … it is one of the most extraordinary moments in my time with the Dodgers."[12]

The same O'Malley was not as nostalgic with his comments after cutting loose Valenzuela. "All great careers must come to an end," he said, less than a week later. "I think the fans will understand. This is something we had to do."[13]

Valenzuela was extremely hurt. But as a merit to his character, he did not snipe at the team with the antagonistic parting shots that many athletes, in similar circumstances, fire off; Valenzuela never publicly bad-mouthed the Dodgers organization. He did, however, file a salary grievance with the Players Union, contesting the Dodgers' decision as purely a monetary one.

At 30 years of age, Valenzuela had no thoughts of retiring. The American League Angels signed the pitcher less than two months after his Dodgers dismissal.

In early June, Valenzuela made his first start for his new club. It was a box office success, drawing nearly 50,000 fans to Anaheim Stadium to see Valenzuela pitch against the Detroit Tigers. But that was all it was as far as the home team was concerned. Valenzuela gave up nine hits and five runs, four earned, in five innings of work. After another poor start, a one-sided defeat to the Milwaukee Brewers and Teddy Higuera, the Angels snipped Valenzuela aside, then re-signed him to a minor league contract from which he was released two months later.

The following year, 1992, with no major league suitors apparent, "El Toro" went back to Mexico and its summer league, where the Dodgers had originally discovered him. Valenzuela pitched and won ten games for the Jalisco Charros.

Then the Baltimore Orioles gave Valenzuela another shot at the Big Time in 1993. Valenzuela responded with 31 starts for the second-division Orioles. The pitcher gained but eight wins, outweighed by ten losses. Valenzuela threw the second-most innings (178⅔) on the staff, with an ERA a shade under 5.00. He displayed flashes of his former brilliance when he allowed just three runs in 41⅔ innings during a five game, mid-season stretch.

The Philadelphia Phillies brought the unsigned free agent pitcher back to the National League in June of 1994, for what turned out to be a short, seven-start stint because of the extended players' strike.

The San Diego Padres next signed the 34-year-old hurler in April 1995. Valenzuela found a second home with Padres and stood out with 21 wins and only 11 losses in two seasons with San Diego. Thirteen of the triumphs came in his second season with the club.

The Padres rewarded Valenzuela with a $1.65 million dollar contract for 1997. It was not money well spent. The team spared Valenzuela another release by including the 2–8 pitcher in a six-player trade with the St. Louis Cardinals in June.

Fernando Valenzuela's 17-year major league pitching career was brought to a close with his release from the Cardinals on July 15, after five starts without a win.

LEGACY

Fernando Valenzuela exploded on the baseball scene the way few players ever have, and the way no Hispanic player ever has. Valenzuela galvanized a legion of Hispanic fans, none more so than the Mexican-predominant population in Southern California. The broad-faced left-hander earned Rookie of the Year and Cy Young Awards in 1981; the first rookie Cy Young Award winner in baseball history propelled the Dodgers to the franchise's first world championship since 1965.

Major league stadiums were filled with spellbound spectators ogling the pouch-prominent hurler and his pernicious screwball. So much in demand was Valenzuela in his rookie season that the Dodgers implemented congregational-style press conferences to accommodate the large number of local and national media that engulfed the team. The appointed groupings also shielded Valenzuela from the distractions of constant requests for his time. The Dodgers may have been the first sports team to channel media access to a player in this type of multi-gathering scenario, eventually widely adopted by all sports teams.

The media attention Valenzuela garnered by dominating National League batters as a rookie was embellished by his unique pitching style. During his wind-up, Valenzuela routinely rolled his eyes to the heavens and gave batters the "cold shoulder." Valenzuela delivered the ball from the mound from a one o'clock overhand motion, winching up from a high, bent-knee leg kick that reached the armpit level of his raised arms. On his follow-through, Valenzuela flashed the red number 34 on the front of his ample Dodgers jersey to hitters and fans. (To this day, his number has been unofficially off-limits to any Dodgers player.)

Valenzuela had a confidence and fearlessness that all great pitchers own. Particularly remarkable was the inborn possession of these normally acquired attributes displayed by Valenzuela from the outset of his career. Valenzuela, who ranks in 20th century, big league, left-handed Hispanic stature behind only Mike Cuéllar and Lefty Gómez, was unafraid of throwing any of his pitches in crucial situations, or when he was behind in the count.

In nine post-season games, eight as a starter, he posted a 5–1 mark, with a brilliant 1.98 ERA in 63⅔ innings. He won his only World Series start.

From the time of his marriage to sweetheart Linda, the Valenzuelas had become "Angelinos." The couple's four children attended Los Angeles schools, and the Valenzuela home was located a relatively short distance from Dodger Stadium. But Valenzuela resisted all

Fernando Valenzuela's unique pitching delivery involved rolling his eyes to the sky prior to every pitch.

overtures from the team to return for tributes to him and other Dodgers players after his retirement in 1997. It was written that Valenzuela was still bitter over the way in which Los Angeles had released him in 1991. The Tony DeMarco people offered that Valenzuela was just a private person. No jobs interested Fernando, though many were proffered by the organization. Over the years, the former pitcher passed up Jaime Jarrín Hall of Fame Night and an invitation to Fernando Valenzuela Bobble Head Doll Night.

Finally, in the summer of 2003, Fernando Valenzuela returned to the franchise that made him rich, the franchise he helped enrich, the franchise that made him a star, the so-called "franchise of the stars."

"I was on vacation," came Valenzuela's answer to the prevailing question of his whereabouts for the past 12 years, as he was re-introduced to the media as the Dodgers' new Spanish broadcast radio color man. Looking svelte in a suit and tie, Valenzuela further explained his absence by saying, "I didn't want to do anything or have any celebration until I had completely stopped playing."[14]

With the "vacation comment," the former pitcher unveiled a "lighter" personality side about which the general public knew little. Vin Scully affirmed as much in his comments on Valenzuela joining the broadcasting ranks. "When he was in uniform, he was Fernando the pitcher," said Scully. "When he was in the clubhouse, he was Freddy, full of humor. He may start as a broadcaster as Fernando, but when he's at ease, he'll be Freddy again."[15]

Valenzuela threw out the ceremonial first pitch, opening the Caribbean Series, on February 1, 2013. It coincided with the inauguration of Estadio Sonora, a gleaming, state of the art baseball park that was built for the Hermosillo Naranjeros of the Mexican Pacific League. The park may have inspired Mexican representative Obregón Yaquis, which won the 2013 Caribbean Series by defeating the Dominican Republic's Escogido team in a marathon championship game, 4–3.

The same month of the Caribbean Series, Valenzuela was honored with entrance into the Caribbean Hall of Fame. The most popular Mexican player to play in the major leagues had delayed his own induction by refusing to hang up his spikes. A winner of 173 big league games and 50 more in the minor leagues (including 30 in the Mexican League), Valenzuela pitched well into his forties, toiling in the Mexican Pacific League. He finally called it quits in 2006.

Two decades earlier, Valenzuela had more easily surrendered another piece of his equipment to benefit the Los Angeles Chamber of Commerce. In 1985, "Freddy" contributed one of his pitching gloves as a cultural keepsake to a time capsule Los Angeles city fathers interred to publicize a gentrification project in the city's downtown.

When the preserved glove inside the capsule, scheduled to be re-opened in 2085, is removed, it will reawaken archival memories of the man who, by then, will have passed into history, comfortably sealed in his own vestibule of baseball immortality.

8

The 1990s—Pedro Martínez

Pedro Martínez

A great deal of expectation, Pedro Martínez has stated, was placed upon him during his early years as a pitcher in the minor and then major leagues, well before his own unique talent elevated him into one of the game's greatest pitchers.

Pedro Martínez was the three-year-younger brother of Ramón Martínez, a young pitching prodigy who at the age of 16 was chosen to the Dominican national team for participation in the 1984 Olympics. Ramón, a tall, lanky right-hander, was signed the same Olympics year by the Los Angeles Dodgers and, at the age of 22, was a 20-game winner in the major leagues. An illusory Olympics experience—consisting of hanging around his big brother with the Dominican team as it trained—convinced 13-year-old Pedro Martínez, who could throw hard for his age, to pursue a baseball career in earnest.

In the 1980s, the Dodgers were one of several major league teams to have established vocational camps in the Dominican Republic as wholesale scouting and development vehicles for the island's burgeoning baseball talent. Pedro often accompanied Ramón on the two-hour bus rides from where the boys lived in Manoguayabo, which was outside of Santo Domingo, to "Dodgertown-Dominicano" in Guerra, an interior town to the northeast. Pedro was a raw talent "discovered" by the Dodgers through Ramón's signing. Pedro was nurtured by the Dodgers from age 16, after they signed him to his first professional contract in June of 1988.

The Martínez boys—four of them: Nelson, the eldest, followed by Ramón, Pedro and Jesús—grew up playing baseball in Manoguayabo. The three youngest Martínez siblings were signed to professional baseball contracts. A competitive bond between the middle brothers developed from a young age. Among other things, they competed at throwing pebbles the farthest distance. Anything resembling a ball was usurped by the Martínez brothers in order to play baseball or test their arm strength, including the plucked-off heads of dolls that they pillaged from their sister Anadelia's meager collection.

In all, Paolino Jaime and Leopoldina Martínez had six children. (Paolino Jaime had himself been a pitcher in his athletic youth, a ball-playing contemporary of the Alou brothers.) The common practice in parts of the Dominican for sons and daughters to take their mother's maiden name as surnames was perhaps more easily adopted for the Jaime children following the break-up of their parents. Pedro was nine years old at the time, and while staying under his mother's care through the difficult period, he leaned on his brother Ramón, who became a guiding influence during Pedro's formative years.

Pedro, in young manhood, grew to be five inches shorter than his six-foot, four-inch older brother and 25 pounds lighter at a wispy 145 pounds. The difference in physical stature was a cause for consternation for Pedro as he followed Ramón's path through the Dodgers' minor league system. Playing on the same teams Ramón had a few years earlier, Pedro often was overlooked because of his size and tagged by prejudgments that he would never measure up to his brother on the hill.

As an 18-year-old in 1990, after two years of summer league pitching at home, the Dodgers sent forth their teenage ward to Rookie League ball in Great Falls, Montana. The northwestern U.S. state could not have removed him much farther, both geographically and culturally, from his Dominican Republic birth-place. Pedro Martínez had an adequate command of English. He had been introduced to the language through courses in upper-grade schooling in the Dominican and at the Dodgers' Dominican baseball camp, which like other similar major league sponsored-academies throughout Latin America were now preparing Hispanic big league prospects for cultural acclimation abroad.

Martínez was struck down by stomach infirmities related to the unaccustomed diet of foods he encountered in his first year in "Big Sky" country. Unlike his Hispanic predecessors, however, he had no trouble ordering foods of his choice in restaurants, though he had difficulty finding or arranging food prepared to his flavorful liking. Martínez made it through the rookie ball short-season and won eight games, losing three.

The following year, 1991, Martínez made an eye-catching, class-level ascension through three Dodgers minor league teams. The third promotion was to Triple-A Albuquerque, where Ramón had won ten out of 12 decisions three years earlier. After an 8–0 start at Single-A Bakersfield, Pedro was bumped up to San Antonio in the Double-A Texas League. A 1.76 ERA, three shutouts and seven wins in 12 decisions spurred the promotion to Alberquerque, where he posted a 3–3 mark.

In 1992, Martínez's first full year at Albuquerque was less than spectacular. He made 20 starts and won only seven games. The showing contrasted poorly to the prior season when he was named *Sporting News* "Minor League Player of the Year" and rated the best right-handed minor league pitcher by *Baseball America*. The residual honors were derived from the 18–8 combined three-team record in 1991. It was a sore left shoulder that halted Martínez's progress in 1992 (injured swinging a bat during practice) and that twice placed him on the disabled list.

That same fall, Martínez was fit enough to be called to Los Angeles by the big club. On September 24, a month and a day before his 21st birthday, Martínez made his first major league appearance as the fifth Dodgers relief pitcher in a game against the Cincinnati Reds. Less than a week later, on September 30, Martínez made his initial big league start and took a 3–1 loss at Cincinnati, allowing two runs in six innings before being lifted for a pinch-hitter.

In October, Martínez had reconstructive surgery on the ailing shoulder. In 1993, fully recovered from the previous year's shoulder mishap, Martínez had a great spring training with the parent Dodgers. The right-hander expected to make the big league team, but was demoted as camp was disbanding. The last-minute cut left Martínez disheartened and disenchanted, until he was reminded by his brother Ramón that *he* had been called up by the Dodgers in 1989, pitched a shutout, and then was immediately returned to the minors.

Martínez did not stay long in the minors. On May 5, in his ninth relief appearance, the youngster gained his first major-league win. It came as a middle reliever. Martínez kept the

New York Mets scoreless for two innings, while his teammates scored twice to gain a 6–5 win. Ramón Martínez had opened the game; Pedro was the third of four pitchers used by manager Tommy Lasorda. Earlier in the season, Pedro had relieved his sibling in the seventh inning of a one-run game. The Dodgers announced it was the first time two brothers had pitched in the same game for their franchise.

Los Angeles improved from a last-place finish in 1992 to fourth position in the National League West in Pedro Martínez's first extended major league season of 1993. Martínez factored into the improvement, compiling a 10–3 record in 63 appearances out of the bullpen, including eight wins in a row. Martínez received two September starts, both of which he lost. Martínez's ERA for the campaign was a crisp 2.61. It was a gratifying season for Martínez. He had reached the major leagues at a young age and he was playing on the same team as his brother, whom Pedro would publicly call "his hero" and, in later years, "the reason I am what I am."

At the close of 1993, Los Angeles could not come to terms with second baseman Jody Reed and was unsuccessful in luring free agent Robby Thompson from the San Francisco Giants. The team was facing the prospect of gathering for spring training, three months away, without a major league-experienced second baseman. So the club pulled the trigger on what turned out as probably the worst trade in franchise history. The Dodgers dealt Pedro Martínez to the Montreal Expos for Delino DeShields. At the time, the Dodgers were exchanging a young relief pitcher for a young, quicksilver second sacker who had racked up nearly 200 steals in four big league seasons.

Neither of the Martínez brothers was expecting the news. Pedro did not want to leave the Dodgers because it meant separation from Ramón. It was Ramón who wisely put a positive spin on the deal for Pedro to accept more easily. The trade gave Pedro a chance at becoming a starting pitcher right away, Ramón explained, and an opportunity to get out from the shadow of Ramón Martínez.

* * *

In his first season in Montreal, Pedro Martínez became the fourth starter for Felipe Alou's Expos. The Canadian club accumulated the best record in baseball before the players' strike of 1994 trainwrecked the baseball season. Martínez made 23 starts, won 11 and lost five, with a 3.42 ERA. He also led the league in hit batsmen, with a number equal to his win total.

Winding up on the mound, Martínez looked almost marionette-like because of his pencil-thin build and the way his elbows jutted out from his pinned-back-shoulders delivery to the plate. But, belying his lightweight looks, Martínez was a bona-fide dart-thrower, and like most young speedballers, he was not immune to having some pitches get away from him.

One incident to exemplify this was in the 23-year-old's second start for Montreal. Martinez had a perfect game on the board through 7⅓ innings when, with a 2–0 lead, he unintentionally hit Cincinnati's Reggie Sanders with an 0–2 pitch. The Reds outfielder, who had struck out his previous two times at bat after being pitched too inside to his liking, overreacted and charged the mound. Sanders was ejected, and after both squads returned to their vacated dugouts, Martínez collected himself and kept the no-hitter intact for the next two outs. Martínez lost the no-hit bid in the ninth and was removed from the game, only to be failed by his relievers. Martínez went unrewarded for the outstanding effort after the Reds tied the score in their last at-bat. The Expos, though, were victors in the game, 3–2, scoring the winning run in the ninth inning.

It took three more starts for Martínez—0–5 as a starter so far in his career—to record his first major-league win in the starter's role. It came as a 5–3 home decision on April 30 against the San Diego Padres. Martínez received impeccable help from four relievers to secure the victory.

Martínez was involved in two other highly charged incidents in 1994, in which resentful batters rushed him after being struck by pitched balls. He developed a reputation as a reckless thrower, if not a "head-hunter." A Montreal newspaper referred to him as "Señor Plunk." The pitcher had hit a league-leading ten batters in three months, but it was not as bad as indicated by the number. "Half of my ten hit batters were on breaking balls. Why doesn't the media say anything when I hit someone with a breaking ball?" Martínez questioned. "I'm a power pitcher. I'm supposed to go in and get people out. I'm just in my second year in the league, and I'm learning."[1] The secondary comments implied that the young hurler had already attained a firm grasp of what it took to be a successful pitcher in the major leagues. His manager defended his pitcher, lobbying the press to change their focus.

On June 9, Pedro threw his first major league shutout, a three-hitter against the New York Mets at Shea Stadium, 9–0. Martinez then won six of his final eight decisions, including his last five in a row.

On August 10, Martínez pitched the 74th and last win of the season for Montreal, a team stationed in first place, seven games over the Atlanta Braves in the National League East. One out shy of his second shutout, Martínez gave way to John Wetteland, who obtained the 27th out in the 4–0 road victory over the Pittsburgh Pirates.

Two days later, the players walked.

* * *

"When I'm fine, I can do a lot of stuff"

When the union and management finally resolved their differences and the 1995 season began in late April, the Montreal Expos were a team changed for the worse. Key players that the Expos could not afford to re-sign had been traded. Starter Ken Hill, who led the National League in wins with 16, was packaged off to the Atlanta Braves, and closer John Wetteland was sent to the New York Yankees. Felipe Alou lost two-thirds of his outfield when Larry Walker left via the free agent route and when Marquis Grissom, looking down the same path, was traded as well. The Expos also lost promising player Cliff Floyd for most of the season to a severely broken wrist and ligament tear.

Martínez moved up to the number two man in the rotation behind Jeff Fassero. Martínez won three more games (14) in 1995 than he had in 1994, against ten losses. The pitcher led the Expos in victories, innings pitched and strikeouts. In a side note, Martínez also hit the first batter he faced on the season. The Expos tanked into last place, playing a 144-game schedule.

One of Martínez's 14 victories came on the first Saturday of June in Southern California. That June 3 evening, Pedro Martínez walked to and from the mound at Jack Murphy Stadium ten times. After completing every one of the first nine round trips, Martínez had retired the opposing side in unbroken succession: nine three-up, three-down, 1-2-3, good-morning, good-afternoon and good-night innings. Twenty-three-year-old Pedro Martinez set down 27 San Diego Padres batters in a row! But his teammates, faring only slightly better with their bats against Padres starter Joey Hamilton, did not score throughout the pitching gem by Martínez, witnessed by fewer than 10,000 fans. The lack of scoring necessitated an extension of the game.

The Expos scored a run in the first extra inning, and Martínez walked to the hill for a tenth time, beseeched to expand his flawless masterpiece. He could not. The damaging stroke came off the bat of the 28th hitter, Bip Roberts. It was a clean hit, pulled inside the right field line, that went for a double. Perfection was lost, but not the game as Martínez, with relief help, became the victorious pitcher, 1–0.

Martínez used the grand game to speak up for himself and try to shed some of the negative press that had attached to his aggressive pitching style. "This shouldn't be my first reputation as a pitcher," Martinez offered in post-game debriefings, "because I have been here not very long, but long enough to show what I can do. When I'm fine, I can do a lot of stuff. I don't want to fight anybody."[2]

Sometimes, though, it seemed people were picking a fight with Martínez. In his third start after the "near-perfect" game, Martínez was warned by the plate umpire after hitting the game's third batter. Earlier in the season, an umpire had issued a similar warning to Martínez—following his *third* pitch of the game. Felipe Alou petitioned Expos management to file a grievance with the National League. Expos general manager Kevin Malone issued this statement: "It seems to me that he's being singled out for some reason and we want to know what it is. It doesn't seem fair to us."[3]

Martínez matter-of-factly confirmed what his bosses had intimated as a situation shaded with racial undertones. "I'm a young black kid from the Dominican Republic,"[4] commented Martínez.

The young black kid from the Dominican Republic pitched in turn for nearly one month between wins; on July 4, facing the St. Louis Cardinals and former moundmate Ken Hill, Martínez threw a four-hit shutout (5–0), striking out seven and issuing one free pass. The win gave the Expos a 32–32 record.

The team struggled for the next two months to stay at the break-even level, but lost its fight. When Martínez tossed his second shutout of the season on September 11, against the New York Mets, the Expos claimed their 60th win, with only six more to be netted along the darkened horizon of a disconsolate 66–78 season.

* * *

In 1996, Montreal regained its competitive edge, and Pedro Martínez topped 200 innings and strikeouts for the first time in his career.

Hitters may have been more on their toes, or he may have developed a bit more control or restraint, for the pitcher who had hit 11 batters in each of the prior two campaigns, smacked only three. Martínez won 13 games, accompanied by ten losses.

Martinez threw his only shutout of the campaign on May 1, a two-hitter on the road. The New York Mets, as victims, now accounted for three of his four career blankings. The Mets also had provided Martinez with eight of his 38 lifetime wins (without a loss). Two weeks later, the two most diverse pitching staffs in baseball met at Dodger Stadium when the Expos paid the first of their bi-annual visits to Los Angeles.

Prior to the Montreal series, manager Tommy Lasorda had substituted Korean-born Chan Ho Park for an injured Ramón Martínez in the Dodgers' rotation. Park joined Japanese import Hideo Nomo, Mexican Ismael Valdéz, Dominican Pedro Astacio and Californian Tom Candiotti in a starting staff representing five countries. Felipe Alou, when he briefly

Pedro Martínez won the first of his three Cy Young Awards as a Montreal Expo in 1997.

used Mexican-born Tavo Alvarez along with Caracas native Ugueth Urbina, Canadian Rheal Cormier, North American Jeff Fassero and Martínez as his starting five, matched the multi-national mound contingent of the Dodgers. The Dodgers bested the Expos in the series, with Candiotti and Ramón Martínez winning two of the three games. The Dodgers took nine of the 12 meetings on the season between the two clubs.

It was Montreal's poor season record versus the Dodgers and another team—the Atlanta Braves—that kept the Expos from seriously contending. (Montreal also dropped nine of their dozen games against the Braves.) Montreal, 88–74, finished in second place, a full eight games behind the East Division-winning Bravos.

* * *

After three seasons with earned run averages ranging between 3.42 and 3.70, Pedro Martínez matured and became the pitcher of the highest order that had been suggested at San Diego two years earlier.

In 1997, Martínez became the National League's most dominant pitcher, winning his first eight starts and nine more over the remainder of the season. With a sensationally sliced ERA of 1.90 in 31 starts, Martínez allowed the fewest hits per nine innings (5.89) in the league and led the circuit in complete games (13), in what can be called a personal coming-out party that left National League hitters perpetually hung over.

Martínez's first win was delayed until April 15, because of having to sit out the initial seven days of the season due to a suspension from a helmet-throwing incident in his final start of 1996 (thrown at the opposing pitcher). Martínez defeated the Houston Astros, 7–5, allowing only one run in six innings. The scoring level in the game was not duplicated often by the Expos throughout the season when Martínez pitched. The pitcher lost eight times on the season, and five of the defeats came by scores of 2–1 (twice), 2–0, 1–0, and 3–1.

Martínez's success during the season was attributed to mastering an off-speed pitch—the circle change. Martínez was originally taught how to throw the pitch by Guy Conti, his Rookie League pitching coach in Great Falls, Montana.

Ironically, it was the New York Mets, whom Martínez had beaten ten consecutive times (eight with the Expos) who handed the pitcher his first loss of 1997. On May 28, New York mistreated the rising star, reaching him for seven hits and seven runs, though only two earned, in five innings of work. The Mets' Bobby Jones shut out the Expos, 7–0.

Jones, with help from John Franco, defeated Martínez again six days later, 2–1; Martínez struck out a dozen in the complete game setback. Martínez was brilliant two starts afterwards, on June 14 against the Detroit Tigers. The right-hander struck out 14 Tiger batters in a 1–0, three-hit, two-walk home win.

A 10–4 record during the first week of July earned Martínez a second consecutive trip to the All-Star Game, where he pitched an inning of hitless ball for the National League in its 3–1 loss at Jacobs Field. Also in July, Martínez threw his third and fourth shutouts of the campaign, his final total that would leave him one behind teammate Carlos Pérez for the league lead. On July 13, an extremely hot Sunday afternoon in Cincinnati, Martínez allowed only one hit and one walk to the Reds, while defeating them, 2–0. Three starts later, on July 29, Martínez plowed through a hard-hitting Colorado Rockies, yielding only five hits, with 13 strikeouts, in a rare 3–0 Coors Field shutout.

The Expos peaked at 11 games over .500 in June. But Alou's team was never able to climb higher than third place. The club dropped to fourth place when it lost six more games than it won in the month of July. The sag seemed to coincide with a cost-conscious management announcement that it would not pursue any trades to bolster the team for a wild-card run.

As the Expos fell completely out of the race in August, Martínez set his sights on a personal goal for impersonal reasons. "Pedro Martinez is taking dead aim on the N. L. Cy Young Award," reported the *Sporting News*, "and if he wins it, he plans to dedicate the award to Juan Marichal. 'It would be a pleasure to let Juan Marichal carry the award back to the Dominican Republic, because he deserved to win one in his career,' says Martinez."[5] Showing he had as much grit as he did class, with the announcement, the young hurler pitched the last month of the season with a sore right thumb. Martínez won only once but still struck out 50 batters in his five final starts to finish with 305.

No pitcher who had struck out 300 batters with an ERA under 2.00 in a season had failed to win the Cy Young Award. Martínez was not the exception. He easily beat out Greg Maddux for the prize, and with it, Martínez received a $100,000 bonus perk to his $3.5 million salary.

*   *   *

The previous gun-for-hire trading tactics, where a team sent a player, usually a veteran, to a contending team for a prospect or two or three, had been transformed through an increased attention to baseball team economics. Now, budget-constrained teams, like the Expos, traded a quality player on the eve of free agency for as much in return as possible.

Two weeks following the announcement of a $13 million operating loss, the Expos, knowing they would not be able to offer Pedro Martínez anywhere near his increased market value, traded him. Montreal received pitcher Carl Pavano and a player at a later date (Tony Armas, Jr.) from the Boston Red Sox for Martínez, and Martínez received $75 million to pitch for the next six years in Boston.

It was love at first pitch in Beantown. On the second Saturday of April 1998, a day after the Red Sox scored seven runs in the bottom of the ninth inning for the most dramatic home Opening Day win in Red Sox team history, Pedro Martínez took the Fenway Park mound for the first time. In attendance was Juan Marichal, in a contemporary North American scenario akin to Kerry Wood pitching with Nolan Ryan in observance.

"Marichal ... sat for the first five innings or so with the fans behind home plate with an entourage from the Dominican Republic," wrote Michael Vega of *The Boston Globe*. "Marichal, who is Dominican Minister of Sport, said he 'had my breath taken away' when Martinez presented him with his 1997 Cy Young Award."[6] (Martínez, over the winter at the Boston Baseball Writers annual fete, had made good on his dedication and presented his Cy Young Award to Marichal, in a gallant gesture of magnanimity and historic cognizance that too often is lacking among modern day ballplayers.)

Also present at Martínez's first Fenway game, along with many pockets of Dominican fans in the stands, was home city favorite Luis Tiant. The two stately monarchs of the mound were among 32,403 who beheld Martínez dazzle, with 12 strikeouts, the Seattle Mariners. Martínez held the visiting team to two hits, in a performance of less than two and one-half hours, reminiscent of Marichal's and Tiant's era of under-150-minute ballgames. A more filled-out pitcher now at 170 pounds, Martínez thrilled the Boston crowd with each blazing fastball and awed them with each mystifying change-up. Oversized Dominican flags waved in the spectator sections of Fenway Park, a cultural celebration circulating in the stands to a degree sportswriter Bill Koening compared with the atmosphere of a World Cup soccer match.

The festive Fenway gathering was Martínez's third start of the season and second win. The new Red Sox ace had opened the season on April 1, on the road, against the Oakland A's. Martínez, in a seven-inning scoreless debut, earned his first Red Sox win (2–0), striking out 11. He followed that with a one-run, seven-inning, no-decision against the Angels in Anaheim on April 6. The Angels won the game, 2–1, in 11 innings. Boston was victorious 18 times in its first month of games, aided more by pitcher Bret Saberhagen's four wins without a defeat, than by Martinez's 2–0 record.

In May, Martínez turned in four victories in five decisions. The Red Sox were in second place, and destined to remain there all season, ahead of the rest of the division, but forlorned like distant flotsam in the wake of the juggernaut New York Yankees, managed by Joe Torre. Though the Yankees flattened all competition in 1998, not even their record-breaking season could dampen the enthusiasm of Fenway fans for their new Caribbean prince.

The Boston Globe began running, in Spanish, next-day accounts of home games in which Martínez pitched. The day after Memorial Day, the Spanish headline in *The Globe* told of the pitcher's first loss, after five wins: "Martinez Cae Ante Los Azulejos." "Martinez Falls Against the Blue Jays." Doing in the pitcher in the 7–5 loss were home run pitches thrown to José Cruz, José Canseco and Shawn Green.

Martínez received considerable offensive support to win two of his next three starts. The only loss, on June 5, came against Al Leiter and the New York Mets, in which Martínez was tattooed for four home runs and six runs in four innings, in the 9–2 home setback. The effort, Martínez's third rough outing in row, displeased many fans. After he was showered with boos for the first time at home, it was written in the next day's newspapers that Martínez, with his forced exit from the mound, received as warm a reception as Mets coach Mookie Wilson.

Martínez bounced back strongly and boasted an 11–2 record when the leagues met for the annual All-Star extravaganza. The Red Sox hurler last pitched the Thursday before the All-Star Game and, though fully rested, was passed over for the starting assignment by American League manager Mike Hargrove. Left-hander David Wells, with the same record as Martínez, had pitched a perfect game earlier in the season, and received the start. Martínez was not used at all in the American League's 13–8 win at Coors Field.

In his second start following the Mid-Summer Classic, on July 15, Martinez threw his second-best game of the season. Improving to 12–3, the Red Sox hurler flung a 1–0, four-hit victory over Hargrove's Indians, in a fastball-roaring night at Fenway Park, against opposing pitcher Bartolo Colón.

Boston climbed 20 games over .500 with its 64th win on August 1, versus the Anaheim Angels; Martínez claimed his 15th win in the game at Anaheim, an 11–3 decision that was cracked open by Boston with five runs in the ninth inning. The right-hander lost for only the fourth time in his next time out, a 4–3 reversal to the Texas Rangers, in spite of 13 strikeouts recorded in only 6⅔ innings. Two outings later, Martínez was back on the winning track and stayed there through three starts.

In September, Martínez hit a bit of a rough patch. On the eighth day of the month, at Fenway Park, an 18–4 Martínez matched-up against an 18–5 David Cone of the New York Yankees. Cone edged Martínez, 3–2, when Martínez gave up two runs in the eighth inning. Six days later, Martínez was defeated again by the Yankees and Orlando Hernández, 3–0. Martínez lost his third game in a row, 5–2, to the Chicago White Sox on September 19, allowing only two earned runs in seven innings.

He won his last start of the season (and 19th game) on September 24, versus the Baltimore Orioles, allowing five earned runs in 6⅓ innings. The Tom "Flash" Gordon-saved win, 9–6, was the Red Sox's 90th and earned the team a wild card playoff invitation. The save was also the 42nd in a row for Gordon, a new record for relief pitchers.

The Red Sox won two more games to complete a 92–70 season, finishing the same heavy number of games behind the 114-win Yankees as the team finished above .500.

Boston had everything working for it in Game 1 of the Division Series against the Cleveland Indians. Martínez threw seven innings and allowed three runs as the team cruised to an 11–3 road win. Cleveland jumped on Boston starter Tim Wakefield the next day, September 30, and won handily, 9–5, to send the 1–1 series to Boston.

Four solo homers by Cleveland, including a pair by RBI-machine Manny Ramírez, were enough to edge Boston, 4–3, in Game 3.

Facing elimination on the morning of October 3, Red Sox manager Jimy Williams stuck to his plan to use Martínez as his fifth game starter and slotted, instead, Pete Schourek. The left-hander pitched teeteringly well, yielding no runs in 5⅓ innings, with two hits and four walks allowed. Boston held a 1–0 lead going into the eighth inning, and brought in their record-setting reliever to pitch. But Gordon, who had not blown a save in five and a half months, permitted two runs in the top of the eighth inning to the defending American League champions. The Red Sox failed to answer in their remaining at-bats and saw their season end by losing, 2–1.

Following the final out, extended rounds of applause emanated from the Fenway faithful, who clapped with collective appreciation for their conquered heroes as the Indians celebrated in the visitors' clubhouse.

"This is as good as it gets"

The Red Sox lost a pillar of their team, Mo Vaughn, to free agency in December 1998, but had signed second baseman José Offerman to a surprisingly lucrative multi-year deal prior to losing Vaughn. Martínez echoed the sentiments of most, saying the Red Sox were going to miss their 40-HR slugger. Moving forward, Jason Varitek became the regular catcher, and the team inked pitchers Mark Portugal and Pat Rapp to bolster a supporting cast of starters around Martínez. General manager Dan Duquette also made an all-out but unfruitful effort to sign Yankees star Bernie Williams prior to the new season.

It was Martínez's pitching in 1999 that did more to make Vaughn a memory in Boston that anything else during what turned out to be a more successful Red Sox campaign than the prior season.

Offerman collected four hits in Martínez's 5–3 Opening Day win over the Royals, at Kansas City on April 5. Martínez downed the Tampa Bay Devil Rays by the same score five days afterward, but lost his next start when the Red Sox were shut out by three Chicago

White Sox pitchers, 4–0. Martínez then defeated the Detroit Tigers, 1–0, pitching 7⅔ innings of scoreless baseball. Five days later, on April 25, Martínez pitched his first complete game win, 3–2, at home over Cleveland's Indians.

The Red Sox had split 22 games when Martínez took the mound on the first of May and struck out 13 Oakland A's in a 7–2 home win. With a record of 5–1, Pedro Martínez began setting himself apart from his peers—far apart. Beginning on May 7, with eight shutout innings and 15 strikeouts, Martínez subdued the Anaheim Angels at Fenway Park, 6–0. In his next turn on the hill, in which he recorded double-digit strikeouts for the sixth time in a row, Martínez matched the career high in strikeouts he had set in his previous outing. Putting the clamps on a strong lineup of Seattle Mariners hitters for eight innings, Martínez raised his record to 7–1 with the 9–2 home triumph.

From May 1 to June 4, the Red Sox won 22 of 31 games. Their ace won every time out during the stretch, racking up seven of the wins. The winning ways propelled the Red Sox into first place. On May 29, on the strength of Nomar Garciaparra's three-run home run, Martínez won his tenth game. The Cleveland Indians were the 4–2 victims, in front of their own fans.

Martínez's eighth game on the season with ten or more strikeouts came as an interleague doozy against the Atlanta Braves on June 4. In throwing his second complete game of the season, the 27-year-old hurler subjugated Atlanta's batters on three hits, while striking out 16 and walking two. One of the hits was a chintzy home run by Ryan Klesko inside Pesky's Pole in right, the only run for Atlanta in the 5–1 final. After Martínez made Brett Boone his 14th strikeout victim to close the eighth inning, the capacity Fenway crowd rose with applause and chants of "Pe-dro, Pe-dro, Pe-dro," entreating from their masterful pitcher the increasingly popular "curtain call" most commonly reserved for home run hitters. With an inning to go, Martínez wisely resisted, and came out to pitch the ninth to wild cheering. The delirium progressed throughout the stands when Martínez struck out the first two batters of the inning and then deflated some when Braves catcher Javy Lopez put a two-strike pitch into play for the 27th out of the game.

The following week, Martínez suffered only his second defeat, to his former team, Montreal, allowing four runs in six innings. The resulting 13–1, lopsided loss dropped the Red Sox out of first place, a position the team would not regain again for the rest of the season. Following the loss, Martínez won his next four outings, completing the month of June with a domineering 14–2 pitching record. Martínez had started off with four victories in April, six more in May, and pulled in another four over the season's third month. Martínez was named "Pitcher of the Month" three straight times, a feat never accomplished since the league began the recognition.

At the All-Star break, with a 15–3 record, Martínez was named the starting American League pitcher. The game was played at Fenway Park. It was an electric night in Boston, and all of baseball glowed from the charge that radiated from the last, memorable public appearance by Ted Williams, who, unsteadily but determinedly, threw out the honorary first pitch. Williams, sitting in a golf cart, was surrounded by a fawning group of the game's greatest past and present players.

Pitching the first two innings for the American League, Martínez struck out five of the six batters he faced (one reached on an error and was erased trying to steal). Included were home run impressarios Sammy Sosa and Mark McGwire. The American League captured the game, 4–1, with Martínez gaining the win.

Martínez's first start after the mid-season break was his worst of the campaign. The pitcher was bruised for seven earned runs by the last-place Florida Marlins. The day after the July 18 start, which Martínez escaped without losing thanks to a Red Sox rally, Boston placed its number one hurler on the disabled list with an inflamed right shoulder. The team brought him back slowly, limiting him to five innings in each of his first two post-DL starts. The second one, on August 8, was a 9–3 road decision over the Anaheim Angels; it was Martínez's 100th career victory.

The next turn for Martínez was scheduled for August 14. But Martinez arrived late for the Saturday afternoon game and was disciplined by manager Jimy Williams. The pitcher (who apparently carried a streak of tardiness about him) did not make it to the ballpark within the team's hourly requirements, imposed on all players, and he lost his starting slot in the game. (Two hours before game time was the arrival standard.) The veteran was not pleased with his manager's actions and let it be known. Martínez did apologize to his teammates, citing an extended session at his home with his personal physical therapist as the reason for his late arrival. Yet Williams all but handed his discontented pitcher an easy win later. He called Martínez into the game, in relief, to start the sixth inning with the Red Sox holding a 7–1 lead. As the third Red Sox hurler of the game, Martínez became the discretionary pitcher of record from the official scorer; he received his league-leading 17th victory by throwing a one-run, four-inning close-out of a 13–2 Red Sox win over the Seattle Mariners.

In an example of how injured pride can quickly contrive with petulant behavior, prior to Martínez's next outing, five days later, *The Boston Globe* reported that Martínez arrived at "the players' parking lot at 3:50 p.m." and "stayed in his vehicle for 10–12 minutes" before entering the clubhouse "exactly two hours before the 6:05 game time." Moments later, irked by the horde of reporters he encountered waiting to chronicle his punctuality, Martínez lashed out with some unkind remarks directed at the press, his manager (again), and his general manager. The verbal vitriol prompted the Red Sox's media director to clear the clubhouse of reporters. A few hours later, in the early evening game, Martínez was bested by Oakland A's rookie pitcher Tim Hudson. Martínez registered his 50th career game with ten or more strikeouts in the 6–2 loss.

Martínez soon returned to the level of pitching superiority that he had shown throughout the season's first 100 days. Two subsequent victories, in which Martínez struck out 26 batters in only 14 innings, brought his victory total to 19 as September rolled around. Four days into the new month, Martínez reached the pitcher's vanguard for the first time; his 20th win was a scoreless eight-inning, 15 strike-out performance at Seattle. Following the 4–0 victory, the 76–60 Red Sox held a one-game wild card lead over the Oakland A's.

That lead had increased to three as the team opened a three-game set at New York on September 10, against the first-place (+ 6½ games) Yankees. The Sox starter in the opening game, Martínez, imposed his will on all but one of the Yankees' hitters on the night, striking out 17 batters in the most dominating performance by an opposing pitcher ever witnessed at Yankee Stadium. Martínez allowed one hit—a home run to Chili Davis with two outs in the second inning—and faced only 28 batters. He was a human dynamo on the mound, seemingly growing stronger with each out he recorded. He set down the last 22 hitters in the game, fanning seven of the last eight. Martínez struck out the side in the ninth.

Martínez was master and commander of each of his devastating pitches—fastball, curve and changeup. "I felt great," he said. "I felt in control of every pitch. This is as good as it gets. I won't lie."[7] After Martínez struck out Chuck Knoblauch to end the game, he pointed to the heavens, a mannerism started by reliever Tom Gordon and one that was adopted by Martínez, along with many, many other ballplayers in the coming years, following an exhibition of on-field prowess.

The Red Sox won the next two games. Their road sweep cut the Yankees' division lead to 3½ games. The deficit was trimmed to three when Martínez blanked the Blue Jays, 3–0, on September 21, in his only shutout of the season.

But by the time of Martínez's next start, Boston's hope of catching the Yankees was reduced to a highly unlikely mathematical one. But with the wild card all but clinched, Martínez started the Red Sox's final home game on September 27, and coasted to his 23rd victory. In the 5–3 win against the Baltimore Orioles, he allowed one earned run in eight innings and struck out 12. It was Martínez's final start of the regular season. In his final seven starts, Martínez compiled a 6–0 mark with an ERA under 1.00. Six times in 1999, Martínez (23–4) struck out 15 or more in one game, and he rang up 14 in two others. Martínez struck out 300+ (313) batters for the second time in his career. He became the second pitcher, after Randy Johnson (this same season), to strike out 300 men in a season in both leagues.

The Red Sox concluded the campaign with six road games, and a well-rested Martínez toed the rubber for the 94–68 Red Sox in the Division Series' opening game against the Cleveland Indians on October 6. But Martínez had to retire after throwing four scoreless innings. A muscle strain in his back prevented him from continuing. The repeat Central Division champions, trailing by two runs when Martínez left, came back to win, 3–2. The Red Sox lost the next game, and a duplicate outcome of the prior season's opening playoff round results seemed likely. However, following the venue shift to Boston, the Red Sox won twice—one game 9–3, and the other by a football-like 23–7 score—to force a fifth and deciding game back in Cleveland. (Prior to the Fenway Park victories, the Red Sox had lost 18 out of their last 19 postseason games.)

His back having responded to treatment, Martínez was not ruled out for the fifth game. But the questionable factor of how long he could pitch persuaded the Red Sox to choose Bret Saberhagen as their starter for the decisive game. The Indians scored five runs against Saberhagen and knocked him from the box without having retired a batter in the second inning. Saberhagen's replacement, Derek Lowe, fared moderately better but, in the third inning, surrendered the two-run lead his teammates had secured, following a five-run uprising in top of the inning and two runs scored in the first frame.

The resilient Red Sox tied the slugfest at 8–8 with a run in the fourth inning. Seizing on the opportune moment of a clean slate, Jimy Williams brought in Pedro Martínez. It was planned that he would pitch a middle inning or two. Martínez, also seizing the moment, pitched longer. Martínez pitched as long as he physically could, as long as the Red Sox needed him. The right-hander retired all three Indians he faced in the fourth inning and then set down the heart of the order in the fifth, with only an interrupting walk to Manny Ramírez. Another base on balls to Sandy Alomar in the sixth inning broke up an otherwise 1–2–3 inning for Martínez.

Red Sox outfielder Troy O'Leary hit a three-run homer in the top of seventh, to nicely complement the grand slam he had hit earlier; Boston took an 11–8 lead, one that Martínez was not going to relinquish. Of the three sequential outs Martínez recorded in the seventh, two were by strikeouts, giving him six over three innings. In the Indians' eighth, DH Harold

Baines coaxed a one-out walk. Baines was forced at second by the next batter, before the fourth hitter of the inning popped up. The Red Sox added another run in the ninth. In the Indians' turn at bat, Martínez recorded his third perfect inning of the night, capping an inspiring three-game series comeback for the franchise most often conditioned to the role of the beguiled rather than the beguiler.

Martínez's performance was remarkable. Unable to summon his best fastball, he still kept one of baseball's most potent offenses at bay, not allowing a solitary hit and only one fair ball out of the infield. Seconds after whiffing Omar Vizquel for the game's final out, an ecstatic Pedro Martínez was lifted up on his engulfing teammates' shoulders, in the center of the infield, reveling in his team's success, which only a few days earlier had seemed so improbable.

The Jacobs Field celebration was the last for Boston, however. After an off-day, the New England club dropped four out of five games to the New York Yankees in the ALCS. Martínez won the only game, a ballyhooed but one-sided match-up versus Yankees pitcher Roger Clemens.

* * *

The final game of the ALDS against the Indians was a defining moment for the pitcher, who had long since stopped being known as the brother of Ramón. The six-inning, hitless endeavor, the century's second longest by a pitcher in post-season play, sanctified the Martínez name and presence on a baseball diamond. If performance was the sole measure, in all but a few ways the idol of Manoguayabo was even better in 2000 than in 1999.

Not as good in 2000 was the Red Sox team, which gave the Yankees a half-hearted run for the division. The Boston linchpins in its underachieving 85–77 campaign were Martínez, reliever Derek Lowe, whom the Sox had stolen, along with Jason Varitek, from the Seattle Mariners in a 1997 trade, and Nomar Garciaparra, who won his second consecutive batting title.

Martínez won his first five starts; Lowe saved three of them. The first loss of the season for Martinez came in a 17-strikeout, 1–0 heart-breaker to the Tampa Bay Devil Rays on May 6. Steve Trachsel out-pitched Martínez with three hits allowed to Martínez's six. The flame-throwing right-hander followed that start with a 9–0, 15-strikeout, no-walk shutout on May 12 over the Baltimore Orioles. Martínez improved to 7–1, with a 0.90 ERA, five days later with seven scoreless innings in an 8–0 win over the Blue Jays at Skydome. Six days afterward, Toronto came back to defeat the dynamic pitcher, 3–2, in Boston.

Martínez shut out New York at Yankee Stadium in a nationally televised Sunday night game on May 28 that pitted him against Roger Clemens. Both pitchers were on the beam and held their opponents scoreless through eight innings. In the ninth, with Clemens having struck out 13, Trot Nixon popped a two-run homer. The Yankees attempted to rally in their final at-bat and loaded the bases with two outs. But Tino Martínez grounded out to end the game. Boston sportswriter Dan Shaughnessy likened this masterful 2–0, nine-strikeout exercise from Martínez to the 17-strikeout game on the same Yankee Stadium mound eight months earlier as "a little like the Beatles' second appearance on the *Ed Sullivan Show*," in the *Boston Globe*, May 29, 2000. The shutout win put the Red Sox, at 28–18, into first place, one game above the Yankees in the American League East.

Soreness in a side muscle, following the apparently strenuous four-hit effort against the Yankees, forced the 8–2 Martínez to be scratched from his next scheduled start and placed the pitcher on a precautionary pitch count the night of June 8, versus Cleveland. In the game, a makeup contest from an April rain-out, Martínez retired 14 of the first 15 Indians hitters (an error allowing the only baserunner). With two outs in the fifth inning, Martínez permitted his only hit, a double to Russell Branyan. He retired the next ten batters, completing eight innings of one-hit, one walk-yielded work. Closer Derek Lowe pitched the final frame of the 3–0 victory. The Red Sox were in the middle of a travel-tough interleague stretch of games and needed to spare an over-worked bullpen. The performance by Martínez against the Indians highlighted his value to the team.

The next two outings for baseball's best pitcher came against New York. Martínez received a no-decision in a "semi"-rematch against Clemens on June 14—the Rocket exiting after an inning with a strained groin. Martínez pitched six stanzas with one run allowed, but Boston dropped the 2–1 road decision. On June 20, a day after suffering the franchise's worst home loss ever, 22–1, to the hated Yankees, the Sox were shut out, 3–0, by Andy Pettitte and Mariano Rivera. Martínez, bopped for three home runs, was the loser. Martínez also surrendered three homers five days later to the Toronto Blue Jays, but was not involved in the Jays' 6–5, extra-inning home win. The loss dropped the Red Sox into third place, behind the Yankees and first-place Toronto.

Six long balls in two starts against Martínez was too suspicious-looking for the Red Sox front office. They suspected the oblique muscle in his side was bothering him more than he let on. Against Martínez's protestations, the team placed their star on the disabled list with a strained oblique muscle. The move made Martínez ineligible for the All-Star Game; he next pitched a week following the game, on July 18. More than three weeks since his last start in Toronto, the pitcher's return, against the Montreal Expos, at once refocused playoff hopes for the Red Sox.

The start following his July 18 3–1 win versus the Expos left no doubt that Martínez was back to full, fluid strength. The Chicago White Sox, through nearly 100 games played, had the best record in baseball when they visited Fenway Park for a weekend set in late July. The teams split two games and in the rubber game, the heavy-hitting White Sox's bats were "turned into matchsticks" (*The Boston Globe*, July 24, 2000) by Martínez, who struck out 15 and walked no one in a six-hit, 1–0 scintillator. In the three-team AL East race, the Red Sox moved into second place, now behind the Yankees and in front of Toronto.

Martínez won his third and fourth successive starts, then dropped a tough 2–1 road decision to Ramón Ortiz of the Anaheim Angels on August 8. The following week, stiffness in his shoulder (in between starts, the pitcher had slept awkwardly on it) became the root cause for Martínez's shortest junket of the season, with a pitching line of six hits and three runs permitted in four innings against the Tampa Bay Devil Rays. Martínez was uninvolved in the final outcome, one that ended grandly for the Sox on Rico Brogna's bottom-of-the-ninth, two-out, bases-loaded home run. Martínez showed all was well with seven shutout innings on August 19 against the Texas Rangers, collecting his 14th win. Five days later, Jimy Williams' squad overcame Martínez's worst start of the season—six runs allowed in eight innings—and defeated the Kansas City Royals in extra innings, 9–7. The win was the 67th for Boston and put the team ten games over .500, a threshold it could not exceed through the remainder of the season.

The worst was followed by the best. On August 29, at Tampa, Martínez plunked Devil

Rays leadoff batter Gerald Williams on the left wrist. Williams rushed the mound and flailed at Martínez as the benches emptied. Both combative players were knocked to the ground by the first arrival of opposite charging troops. Williams was ejected, one of eight Devil Rays to be thumbed out by two umpires during the course of the game, including manager Larry Rothschild. When order was restored, Martínez was collected enough to retire the next three batters, with pinch-runner Jason Tyner advancing only as far as second. Martínez set the side down in order in the second, registering two strikeouts. He induced three consecutive ground outs in the third. A fly out and two strikeouts took care of the home team's three challengers in the fourth. In the fifth, holding a 3–0 lead, Martínez struck out the side. He whiffed his sixth straight hitter to start the sixth, then retired the next two batters on harmless lofts into the airspace of enclosed Tropicana Field, making for 18 Devil Rays set down in a row since the first hit-by-pitch batter. Martínez faced three hitters in the seventh inning and struck out two of them, giving him 12 in the game; he popped up the other. In the eighth, Martínez recorded his 22nd, 23rd, and 24th straight outs on a ground out, fly out and whiff.

The Devil Rays' eighth-place hitter, John Flaherty, had grounded to short and struck out swinging in his previous trips, but his third time up, leading off the ninth inning, the catcher lined a clean single to right-center, breaking up the no-hit bid. Martínez resignedly dispatched the next three men and settled for a 13-strikeout, one-hit win. The final was 8–0. According to catcher Jason Varitek, his pitcher "had the best fastball he's had all year" in the game.

In his next outing, at Fenway Park, Martínez won his 16th game with eight innings of six-hit pitching against the Seattle Mariners. A home run served up to Mike Cameron accounted for the only blemish in the 5–1, 11-strikeout victory.

Boston headed into a three-game home series with the Yankees on September 8, trailing the top-seated New Yorkers by six games. The Yankees swept the set, with Martínez the pitcher of record in a 5–3 loss to Andy Pettitte in the middle game. The three losses crumpled Boston's wild card chances, as two 90-win teams jockeyed in the AL West for half of the apportioned four league playoff spots. For the first time since Martínez had arrived in New England, the Red Sox did not reach the post-season.

But Martínez could not be blamed. The pitcher's final and spectacular ERA of 1.74 (lowest in the DH era) was an incredible 3.17 lower than the 4.91 American League average! An opponents' batting average of .167 and pinpoint control resulted in 6.64 baserunners allowed per nine innings, the best ratio ever recorded by a starting pitcher. Martínez, who struck out a stagger-

Martínez reached remarkable pitching levels with the Boston Red Sox at the turn of the 21st century (photograph from Hall of Fame).

ing 284 batters in 217 innings (with only 32 walks), dominated the Designated Hitter league in 2000 even more so than in the prior season, though he did not win 20 games (18–6). Perhaps because of this and without any post-season pitching heroics, his 2000 year—with more complete games (seven) and shutouts (four) and an ERA better than a quarter of a run lower than in 1999—drifted a bit, at least in the national spotlight, behind the splashier performance wake left by his 1999 season.[8]

Securely in tow for Martínez was his third Cy Young Award, as the peerless pitcher's 11.7 WAR ranking surpassed Adolfo Luque's 10.8 rating from 1923 as the highest all-time by a Hispanic hurler.

* * *

Early in the 2000 off-season, after failing to hook free agent pitcher Mike Mussina, the Red Sox more than made up for it by snaring run-producer extraordinaire Manny Ramírez. It took the second largest contract in baseball history (eight years, $160 million) to land the outfield hitting star.

Boston was dealt a severe blow when it lost two-time batting champ Nomar Garciaparra to wrist surgery performed on the same day of the team's 2001 inaugural. In Baltimore, on April 2, as the Red Sox shortstop's season was all but wiped out by the intricate operation, Pedro Martínez stepped onto the hill at Camden Yards and did what he did best. He threw seven innings against the Orioles, was nicked for one run, and departed with the game in a 1–1 tie. The Red Sox lost, 2–1, in 11 innings.

There were better results for Martínez and the Red Sox in his second start. The Devil Rays of Tampa continued their trend of hitting ineptitude against the Boston right-hander, going down swinging 16 times to Martínez in his first home appearance on April 8. On a very chilly day, Martínez left after eight innings, and Derek Lowe closed out the ninth and the 3–0 final. Two starts later, Martínez speared 13 more Devil Rays with his strikeout harpoon, and won his second game, 8–3, with a six-inning effort.

On the first of May, Martínez raised his record to 3–0, beating the 20–5 Seattle Mariners, 2–0, the first right-hander all season to do so. An umpiring decision incited the verbal wrath of Martínez following his eight shutout innings. The Mariners' Edgar Martínez was bonked on the helmet by a Martínez curve ball. The home plate umpire issued a warning to a perplexed pitcher. A misinterpretation of the updated "no-tolerance" rule by the umpire caused the unjustified warning, but vindication for Martínez was still forthcoming when he lashed out in post-game remarks.

> It's just unbelievable. [Pitching inside] It's been here forever. Now they want to change it. Why? It must be because of me, because they're not picking on Roger [Clemens] or anyone else. If I wanted to hit Edgar, I would not use a breaking ball.
> They've done so many things to me. One thing they've never done is appreciate what I do for baseball, what I do off the field. They don't recognize the things I've had to overcome, to come from the Dominican to become a star in the game. They don't recognize any of that, but now the bad things they want to point out.[9]

The day before the game against Seattle, Ramón Martínez announced his retirement at age 33. Two comeback attempts, one with the Red Sox, following rotator cuff surgery in 1998, had failed to pan out for the former 20-game winner.

The season's first defeat for Martínez came on May 24, a 2–1 setback against the Yankees in New York. Mike Mussina's pitching line matched that of Martínez, inning for inning (8/8), hit for hit (6/6) and strikeout for strikeout (12/12), but had bettered Martínez by one in the runs-allowed department. Mussina yielded to Mariano Rivera, who threw a scoreless ninth.

Martinez had absorbed a no-decision earlier against New York and had now gone five starts (0–3) without a win versus the Yankees. Insinuations abounded that Martínez had been gripped by the strain of bad karma that for generations had supposedly pervaded the Red Sox franchise. A New York newspaper circuitously picked up on it and proclaimed, "New York Has Martinez's Number," prior to the defending champions' second visit to Boston at the end of May.

The pot is always boiling, the furnace always stoking when the Red Sox and Yankees play. The newspaper headline was an incendiary remark that the teams did not need to gear up for head-to-head competition, but one that Martínez may have drawn from to make a more pronounced effort in his May 30 start against New York. With eight shutout innings, the pitcher made his statement on the field, and then made a few after the game. "I'm starting to hate talking about the Yankees," said Martínez after his four-hit, 13-strikeout performance that led the Red Sox to a 3–0 win. "It's getting kind of old.... I don't believe in damn curses. Wake up the damn Bambino and have me face him. Maybe I'll drill him in the ass."[10] The closing comment, unabashedly Pedro, was one of two popular quotes attributed to him in his Bostonian-era confrontations versus the Yankees.

The media scrutiny major sports cities place upon their teams and star players can be suffocating at times, and Martínez, it seemed during the first part of June, was seeking more breathing space from the press. The pitcher, who, according to the *Boston Globe*, was regarded as "a most accommodating celebrity athlete," left the park for a second consecutive start without uttering a word to the news media. The second cold shoulder followed a loss suffered at home to the Philadelphia Phillies, in which Martínez gave up five earned runs in seven innings. Five days earlier, on June 4, Martínez ignored reporters in the clubhouse following a no-decision against the Yankees at Yankee Stadium. The Yankees rallied to win that game, 7–6.

Martínez, it turned out, was physically ailing. He had developed a sore shoulder; he was scratched from his next start to give the shoulder a respite. When he gave up four runs in less than five innings to Tampa Bay on June 26, it was clear there had to be something physically wrong. The next day, the Red Sox placed Martínez on the DL with an inflamed rotator cuff. Rest was prescribed and it was anticipated Martínez would miss a month. He was gone twice as long, and the Red Sox floundered without him.

On the day Martinez was disabled, Boston held a three-game lead over the second-place Yankees in the American League East. When Martínez returned to the mound on August 26, the Red Sox had flipped positions with New York and were four games behind. The team had also lost its manager. Jimy Williams became a casualty of a 14–17 record following the All-Star Game and was replaced with pitching coach Joe Kerrigan.

Martínez did not return at full strength and made only two more starts, both against the Yankees. He accepted a loss and a no-decision; Martinez finished the season with a 7–3 record. The Red Sox continued their poor performance under Kerrigan and quickly dropped out of the race.

Contention arose between Martínez and front office leader Dan Duquette as to the hurler's physical wellness and the severity of the shoulder injury. Upon further examination of the prized shoulder by another medical source, a small rip in the area of the rotator cuff was diagnosed. Duquette maintained the severity level was not incapacitating. Martínez did not appreciate, in his mind, Duquette's over-extended opinion and the pressure that it implied to continue to pitch.

As the points of view of the two men unplacatingly played out in the press, Martínez made his last start on September 7. Martínez pitched his last three innings of the season, with three runs allowed, and was removed. He was branded with his third defeat, 3–2, to the Yankees and Orlando Hernández. Soon afterward the Red Sox, out of playoff contention, decided to shut down their star pitcher.

With 17 games left in the season and no prospect of pitching again, Martínez was allowed to leave the team to return home to the Dominican and begin the healing process that all of New England hoped would be swift and complete.

* * *

A concerted rehabilitation effort over the winter brought Martínez back to the upper level of the American League pitching ranks.

At the 2002 spring camp, new manager Grady Little greeted a physically changed and, hopefully healthy, Pedro Martinez. Three-quarters of the way through the exhibition schedule, reporter Bob Hohler glimpsed, in the following newspaper account, the corporal conversion the 30-year-old pitcher had undergone: "As his recent outings have underscored, Pedro Martinez is in the midst of a crucial passage in his career. He is learning to pitch with a new body, laden with more than 15 pounds of muscle he amassed to try and bolster his ailing shoulder."[11]

Ken Rosenthal in the *Sporting News* detailed more fully the muscular enhancements of the high-performance pitcher in this report: "Martinez lifted weights this winter (a first) and undertook an exhaustive training regimen. He reported to camp two inches thicker in the chest, one inch thicker in the neck. Rather than a string bean, he now looks more like a healthy stick of broccoli, and the additional muscle in his upper body and legs has increased his weight to 191 pounds."[12]

The healthy stick of broccoli stunk up the joint on Opening Day, April 1. Martínez was pounded by the Toronto Blue Jays for seven earned runs and nine hits in three innings. A strong counter-offensive by the Red Sox spared Martínez a loss.

The Red Sox took full advantage of an early season "soft" schedule and raced off to a fast start. The club blazed to 40 wins in its first 57 games. The biggest mound contribution came from Derek Lowe, who, converted into a starter, won nine games, two more than an undefeated Martínez.

As Memorial Day neared, the Red Sox were monitoring and managing the 7–0 Pedro closely. He had an unofficial pitch count range of 110–115 throws per start. Little juggled the rotation and threw Martínez every sixth day, as often as possible, in order to give the pitcher an extra day's rest (even passing over a Martínez scheduled start on one occasion when merely the threat of inclement weather was in the forecast). Strong run support from his teammates had helped Martínez dodge the defeat demon a few times so far. Martínez was involved in 12 starts without a loss before eventually suffering his initial setback, on

June 8, to the world champion Arizona Diamondbacks and Curt Schilling. Martínez allowed three runs in six innings, all that the Diamondbacks would score in the game, and came up on the short end of a 3–2 decision.

Despite his impressive record, Martínez was categorized as a pitcher unsure of whether he could ever recapture his former dominance over American League hitters. The right-hander finished June with a 9–2 record, an ERA of 3.09, and 119 strikeouts in 102⅔ innings. Martínez lost back-to-back starts that month for the first time since September of 1998. However, any self-doubt the pitcher, or his followers, may have still had quickly dissipated over future outings, as Martínez was victorious in all five of his decisions in July.

A scoreless eight-inning, seven-hit, 14-strikeout performance against Toronto on July 1 cemented Martínez's selection to his sixth All-Star team, but the pitcher, on the advice of his Red Sox pitching counsel, elected to rest rather than participate in the game. On July 19, the Red Sox and Yankees waited through a game-delaying rain of more than two hours in the Bronx in order to stage a Martínez versus Mussina match-up. Martínez emerged the 3–2 victor, pitching into the eighth inning, yielding both Yankees runs, and striking out nine. It was the 100th decision for Martínez in a Red Sox uniform, and he had won an incredible *78* of those 100—an all-time record for any pitcher with any team.

While Martínez was obviously back, the Red Sox had squandered much of their sensational 40–17 start with a cumulative 23–26 record in their next 49 games. At the end of July, the team was lodged in second place, trailing the surging Yankees by four games.

In August, Martínez beat the Minnesota Twins, 2–0, in a non-route-going, four-hit effort, for his 16th win. But in a rematch six days later, on August 16, the Twins scuffed Martínez for three earned runs, handing him a 5–0 defeat. It was the first loss by Martínez to an American League team other than the Yankees in nearly two full years. The same Yankees beat Martínez on August 28, 7–0 at Fenway Park, as Mussina exacted revenge for his earlier Yankee Stadium loss. Martínez allowed four runs, three earned, in a game that was broken open in the seventh inning. So close was the game until the seventh (1–0) that Martínez was permitted to exceed by ten his previous season high of 117 pitches. The loss pushed the 74–57 Red Sox nine games away from first place and left alive only wild card aspirations for the post-season.

Over the next two weeks, it became more and more apparent that the American League's fourth playoff team was not going to come out of the AL East. Oakland and Anaheim battled for the West Division crown, and concurrently fought the Yankees for the best record in the league. During that period of "playoff-sorting," Martínez was sidelined with a strained hip. Two weeks after his loss to the Yankees and after recovery from the hip strain, he defeated the Devil Rays, 6–3, on September 11, for his 18th victory and 150th career win.

Martínez won his next two times out and earned a second 20-win campaign. He joined 21-game winner Derek Lowe as the first pair of Red Sox starters to win 20 in a season since Mel Parnell and Ellis Kinder more than half a century earlier. Martínez accrued 30 starts (for the first time since 1998) and won 20 games with only four losses. He missed 200 innings pitched by two outs and became only the third pitcher (Bob Grim, 1954 Yankees and Clayton Kershaw, 2014 Dodgers) to garnish 20 wins in a season without 200 innings of work.

Martínez placed second behind Oakland's Barry Zito for the Cy Young Award.

* * *

In their second year under new ownership led by John W. Henry, the previous owner of the Florida Marlins, the Boston Red Sox, with a core of heavy-hitting players in their line-up, slugged their way back to the post-season. The DH-advantaged team did enough long hitting in 2003 to top the 75-year record-holding 1927 Yankees in all-time team slugging percentage, .491 to .488.

Boston's augmented offense—resembling some of its powerful hitting teams of past eras—was evidenced in the season's first week. The Red Sox twice tallied double-figure run counts and fell one and two runs shy of ten runs on two other occasions. The scoring abundance delivered a 5–2 start, with Martínez involved in, but not held responsible for, the losses.

Pleased with the results of his rehab training from the prior winter, Martínez repeated the off-season conditioning that entailed swimming and working with dead weights to strengthen shoulder tissue sheathing. But pleased Martínez could not have been with his performance in the Red Sox home opener at "new-and-improved Fenway Park." Baseball's oldest ballpark had undergone a painting facelift and refit. Included in the upgrades were the addition of MLB-trendy and high-priced, fan-intimate field level seating. Also coming soon to Fenway Park were "Green Monster seats," above the park's famed left field wall. After a ten-game road trip and a rained-out first try at the home opener, the worst start of Pedro Martínez's career occurred on April 12, in the Red Sox's 103rd home inaugural. Contrasting two previous road starts, in which Martínez permitted one earned run in 15 innings, Martínez was raked across the coals for ten runs and nine hits in 4⅓ innings by the Baltimore Orioles. Rebounding from the aberrant outing, he won four of his next five decisions. Included was his initial victory of the campaign, on April 17, versus the Tampa Bay Devil Rays, a 6–0 combined shutout with reliever Mike Timlin.

Martínez marched out to a 4–2 record before a trip to the disabled list halted him in mid–May. A strained back muscle kept Martínez out of action for a month. The Red Sox missed him, playing under .500 baseball during his absence. The Red Sox were 26–14 at the time of Martínez's fourth victory, and thanks to the good start, the team still found itself neck and neck with the New York Yankees for the division lead upon his return.

The right latissimus dorsi muscle that Martínez had strained was tested on June 11, and it held up during a three-inning starting stint against the St. Louis Cardinals. The premium arm responded well during a longer five-inning trial five days later. One start afterward, Martínez was back pitching deeper into games. He won two starts leading up to the All-Star Game.

Martínez traveled to the Dominican Republic following his start on the Saturday before the All-Star break, and then eased back into the rotation, rather leisurely, in the team's fourth game of the second-half schedule. The Red Sox again excused their star pitcher from the team at the beginning of August, so Martínez could participate in the opening ceremonies of the XIV Pan American Games, which were held in Santo Domingo. Kevin Baxter in *The Miami Herald* described him as one of "more than a half-dozen of the Dominican's most distinguished athletes" to participate in a torch-carrying relay that included Juan Marichal's ceremonial cauldron-lighting as the official start to the Games.

The Dominican pitcher returned to the Red Sox and seemed to be still brimming with pride from the experience, translating into his second complete game of the season, and eighth win, on August 6. At Fenway Park, Martínez downed the Anaheim Angels, 4–2, striking out 11 in the nine-inning endeavor.

Martínez split his next two starts and then was sidelined for eight days with a severe throat inflammation that required a hospital stayover. He came back with a six-inning, six-hit effort against Seattle for his tenth win (8–1), on August 25. The Red Sox were battling with the Mariners for wild card supremacy. The Washington state club was also engaged with the Oakland A's for the top spot in its own division.

Martínez split decisions against the New York Yankees in consecutive starts. The pitcher followed those stalemated showings with three straight wins, including his last winning start of the season on September 21. At Jacobs Field, Martínez hurled seven scoreless innings of four-hit ball against the Cleveland Indians, before handing off the 2–0 contest to his inconsistent bullpen. Boston's relief corps had been shaky all season long, especially where Martínez had been concerned. But in this game, the tandem of Mike Timlin and Byung-Hyung Kim did not disappoint any Red Sox rooter, as they evenly and efficiently split the victory-preserving chore.

The Red Sox were six games behind the Yankees at that point with seven games to play. Gearing up for an anticipated first-round playoff meeting with pending West Division champion Oakland, Boston elected to give its ace only a "tune-up" appearance on September 26. Martínez tossed three scoreless innings against Tampa Bay.

On the season, Martínez won 14 games, along with an estimable *fifth* ERA title. His bullpen betrayed him more times than a starting pitcher deserved, costing him a handful of victories in games with leads it failed to protect.

The West Division champions hosted and won the first two games of the ALDS. A well-rested Martínez was not involved in the final outcome of the October 1 opener. The right-hander allowed three runs in seven innings, but a bullpen-blown ninth-inning lead cost him a victory; the A's pulled out a 5–4 win in 12 innings. Boston dropped the next game, 5–1, and then rallied to win three do-or-die games. Martínez, with the help of four relievers, was the winning pitcher in the 4–3 Game 5 clincher.

The exciting, come-from-behind series win was the precursor to a seven-game, toe-to-toe League Championship Series fight with the despised New York Yankees.

Martínez had pitched two effective but unspectacular games in the first round of the playoffs. He repeated the competent pattern in his initial appearance of the American League Championship Series, a 4–3 loss to Roger Clemens in a brawl-marred third game of the series at Fenway Park on October 11. The Yankees' win nudged the team to a 2–1 advantage in games in the ALCS. Trailing in the series, the Red Sox displayed the tough determination reflective of their belt-strapping "Cowboy Up" team slogan, battled back and won two out of the next three games, avoiding elimination in the sixth game at Yankee Stadium.

The seventh game, played on October 16, was a promoter's dream. Martínez versus Clemens. But the Rocket fizzled early, allowing four runs in three-plus innings. Martínez responded with seven innings of two-runs work. Yankees relievers, including Mike Mussina, provided stellar relief, and through seven innings, Martínez held a 4–2 lead. The Red Sox scored once more in the eighth inning to give Martínez a three-run advantage. As close to the World Series as any Red Sox team had been in 17 years, a nightmarish meltdown for the Red Sox squad ensued in the home half of the eighth. Martínez recorded the inning's first out on a pop-up, then rapidly gave up the lead on four consecutive hits: three doubles, with a single in between. The Yankees scored three times before Martínez was relieved. The game extended into extra innings.

Leading off the 11th inning, Yankees third baseman Aaron Boone smashed a pitch into the left field seats against Tim Wakefield, a winner of two games in the series as a starter. The Yankees, with the 6–5 victory, advanced to play in the 99th World Series against the Florida Marlins.

After the game, Martínez assumed the largest responsibility for the team's defeat, deflecting what turned into a New England firestorm of criticism directed against manager Grady Little for leaving Martínez in the game too long. (Some follow-up comments by Martínez at a later time reflected a less gracious view of the matter.) Little was fired after the season, publicly for "other reasons" and not for his decision to stick with his number one pitcher while the Yankees mounted their three-run, game-tying comeback.

The fateful eighth inning of the ALCS seventh game in New York branded itself beside other infamous moments of torturous, championship-denying defeat in Red Sox history, perpetuating all the more the media-exalted supernatural malediction that had supposedly possessed the franchise for more than 80 years.

LEGACY

Boston's 13th straight post-season game loss in 1995 had prompted the following season-ending, melancholy prose from Dan Shaughnessy: "They are the Red Sox. Good turns into bad. Victory dissolves into defeat. Joy gives way to sadness. We go to the theatre and enjoy the performances, but the script never changes.

"In the end, the Titanic sinks, Hamlet dies and the Red Sox lose the last game that matters."[13]

That staining string of post-season defeats was ended by Martínez in the 1998 AL Division Series opener against the Cleveland Indians. But with the three straight defeats that followed, the eighth championship-absent decade in Boston quickly inscribed its discredited place in New England baseball lore.

The personage of Pedro Martínez, with heralded excitement, first arrived upon the scene in 1998. Almost instantly, Martínez was anointed by the Boston commonwealth of fans as the messianic knight of the Yawkey Way pitching circle. Martínez's mound exploits repeatedly delighted and infrequently slighted the Red Sox gentry. His terribly swift arm loosed fateful lightning on opponents from coast to coast, as he carried the Red Sox into a new century of hope, and heartache, and finally ultimate triumph. In doing so, Martínez represented the same self-resonating cult of celebrity as The Kid and Tony C and Yaz and Looie.

It is ironic, then, that Pedro Martínez's statistically weakest season with Boston (excluding his mostly injured 2001 year) was the Red Sox's most gloriously successful.

Boston, in 2003, had tried to extend his contract, but unable to reach an agreement, instead only picked up the option year for 2004. In the winter of 2004, Martínez signed with the New York Mets as a free agent and pitched four seasons for that team, winning 32 games. (He became the first Hispanic pitcher to strike out 3,000 big league batters on September 3, 2007.) Martínez's final major league campaign arrived in 2009 with the Philadelphia Phillies, a club that signed the pitcher to bolster an unsuccessful run at a second consecutive world championship.

Pedro Martínez pitched in 18 seasons and won 219 games, with only 100 losses. The winning percentage of .687 is the third-best all-time for modern era starters with at least 1,000 innings pitched (Spud Chandler, .717, and Whitey Ford .690). Martínez's lifetime ERA of 2.93 is truly amazing considering the offense-laden era in which he pitched. Just as amazing were his *five* ERA titles. From 1997 through 2003, Martínez compiled an ERA (2.21) less than one-half of his league's average (4.58) for the period. Factoring statistical peer comparisons and governance over hitters, Martínez recorded perhaps the most dominating back-to-back seasons in 1999 and 2000 in baseball history. A winner of three Cy Young Awards in four seasons, Martínez irrefutably engraved his name into baseball's 20th century pantheon of greatest pitchers.

It cannot be overlooked, however, that Martínez was not overly taxed with regard to his expected pitching commitments. Even before clubs lowered the starting pitching bar, Martínez, in his career, never threw more than 241 innings in a season. His 11 percent ratio of complete games to starts was reflective of the game's specialized age, but, nonetheless, appears as a shortcoming for any premier pitcher, as do his 17 career shutouts.

In the post-season, Martínez was not a dominant pitcher. (His most extraordinary pitching exercise came as reliever in 1999.) Martínez won six and lost four in 14 post-season starts; his ERA checked in at 3.46 over 96⅓ innings. He permitted 74 hits and walked only 30 batters, while striking out one batter per inning.

Pedro Martínez was no longer a premier pitcher when Theo Epstein, Dan Duquette's 29-year-old replacement in 2003, snapped the Red Sox Nation out of its oppressive gloom, six weeks after Aaron Boone's crushing home run, by trading for and signing thoroughbred pitcher Curt Schilling. But Martínez was still great enough to make Boston, following the trade, possessors of the most formidable 1–2 starting pitching combination in either league.

One of the youngest general managers in baseball history, Epstein also addressed a weak spot in the bullpen, signing 2003 American League saves leader Keith Foulke in January of 2004. A month later, Epstein and the Red Sox fell just short of executing what would have been the biggest trade in franchise history. But a three-team transaction that would have landed arguably the game's best player, Alex Rodríguez, in Boston, did not happen, and then seemingly blew up in the Red Sox's face when their arch nemesis, the New York Yankees, hooked Rodríguez in their place. The Red Sox gathered at Ft. Myers, Florida, for spring camp, a stronger team than last season, but knowing that they had been, once again, upstaged by the "evil empire" of George Steinbrenner.

On April 4, 2004, Pedro Martínez lost his first Opening Day start in a Red Sox uniform, to the Baltimore Orioles at Camden Yards. Nicked for three runs, two earned, in six innings, the output was enough to pin him with the defeat in the Orioles' 7–2 win. Martínez won his next three decisions, then alternated winning and losing over four starts. It took two months for the 32-year-old pitcher to deliver a vintage performance.

On June 8, Martínez grabbed a 1–0 victory with eight innings of two-hit pitching over the San Diego Padres, at Fenway Park. Martínez improved his record to 6–3.

The prize-winning pitcher won four more games in six attempts. By the time of his tenth win (4–2) on July 16, against the Anaheim Angels, the first-place New York Yankees had opened a seven-game lead over the Red Sox in the American League East. The lead puffed out to 8½ games after play on July 31. The same day, Epstein pulled the trigger on a quaking trade that sent packing the extremely talented and popular Nomar Garciaparra and reaped a reliable replacement, Orlando Cabrera, plus first baseman Doug Mientkiewicz, as part of a four-team, eight-player exchange.

On the day the trade was completed, the Red Sox's record stood at 56–46. The club modestly bettered the mark over the next two weeks. When Martínez downed the Tampa Bay Devil Rays at Fenway Park, 6–0, on August 12, the team moved to a season-best 13 games over .500. The six-hit blanking, with no walks and ten strikeouts, was the first shutout for Martínez in four years and also acquired for the Red Sox a solitary grip on the wild card station over three other contending teams. The double-digit strikeout total against the Devil Rays eased the special pitcher into 21st place on the all-time strikeout list, ahead of towering greats Bob Feller and Warren Spahn.

Martínez next win, on August 28, came in the middle of a ten-game Red Sox winning streak. Pedro followed the inspired stretch with two more triumphs, including his 16th on September 8. That 8–3 victory over the Oakland A's was the 20th in 22 games for scalding Boston; the win lifted the club 30 games over .500, at 84–54, and to within two games of first-place New York.

Boston had six games remaining with the Yankees, and split them. Martínez started in two of them and lost both. He was hit hard in one loss. In the other, Martínez, in a nearly identical repeat of last season's seventh-game playoff in New York, failed to hold a late-inning lead. This time it was Terry Francona, new Red Sox manager hired away from the bench coach position with the Oakland A's, who was put through the wringer by the Boston press for not removing Martínez in due course. When the dust settled from the divided square-off with New York, the Yankees held a 3½-game advantage. Boston had seven games left to play.

The losses to New York played a part in a dubious novelty for Martinez. On September 29, for the first time in his career, Pedro Martínez lost a fourth consecutive start, and to the bottom-scraping Tampa Bay Devil Rays. Punched out after five innings, with ten hits and five earned runs surrendered, Martínez, who had averaged less than five losses a season with the Red Sox, lost his ninth game. The runs allowed in the defeat raised Martínez's ERA to 3.90, creditable for many pitchers, but the highest of his stupendous career to date.

Martínez did not make another regular season start, but with his 16 wins, he exceeded 200 innings for the first time since 2000. He also made the most starts (33) since his 33 in 1998. The Red Sox couldn't overtake the Yankees, but the team easily won the wild card with a very lofty 98 wins.

It was 21-game winner Curt Schilling who received the starting nod in the first game of the ALDS against the Anaheim Angels, to be followed by Martínez. Both pitchers took advantage of strong run support and benefited from impeccable relief pitching to win their respective starts, 9–3 and 8–3. In Game 3, David Ortiz, who had come into his own as a power-hitting DH, hit a two-run home run in the bottom of the tenth inning to provide the Red Sox, the league's top offensive team, with an 8–6 win and a series sweep. Up next were the New York Yankees, and a series without equal.

In the first two games, the Red Sox tried the same opening combination they had used against the Angels, but without the same positive results. In the Bronx, Schilling was peppered for six runs in three innings in a 10–7 Game 1 loss. Martínez also saw defeat, albeit by the much more respectable count of 3–1.

On October 14, a travel day, the Red Sox revealed that Schilling had pitched the opener with a dislocated tendon in his right ankle and faced corrective surgery. Two days later, the Red Sox played their first home game of the ALCS and received a resounding paddling from the Yankees, 19–8.

Going into the series, the Red Sox, with Schilling and Martínez available for two starts each in an extended series, seemed to have an edge over a Yankees squad that could not boast a pitcher with more than 14 victories. But after three games, the Yankees had out-pitched and out-hit their fall-guy rivals and owned a historically insurmountable advantage.

In Game 4, on October 17, Orlando Hernández faced Derek Lowe. Both pitchers were long gone when Mariano Rivera, casting the dark silhouette of the Grim Reaper in most New Englanders' eyes, stepped onto the mound in the ninth, for his second inning of work, with a 4–3 lead. But the intrepid Red Sox kicked loose the scythe of cut-fastball death Rivera brandished and used a walk, a critical stolen base and a single by Bill Mueller to tie the score and send the game into extra innings. Red Sox relievers Alan Embree and Curt Leskanic combined to keep the Yankees off the board in the 10th, 11th and 12th innings. Leskanic was the fifth pitcher that Terry Francona had used to keep Joe Torre's team from scoring since the sixth inning. Former Red Sox closer and now set-up man for the Yankees, Tom Gordon, held Boston at bay in its first two extra-inning at-bats, following Rivera's rare blown save. In the lower half of the 12th inning, Ortiz hit his second walk-off home run of the post-season, against Paul Quantrill, New York's fifth pitcher of the game. A man was on base, and the 6–4 win reprieved the potential humiliating sweep.

Martínez matched up against Mike Mussina the next day, October 18. No American League Championship game had lasted longer than the five-hour and two-minute experience of Game 4—until Game 5. Martínez was less than mediocre, allowing four runs on seven hits and five walks in just six innings. Trailing 4–2 in the eighth, Ortiz set off a game-tying rally with a leadoff home run. The Red Sox manufactured the tying run on a walk, single and sac fly (against Rivera, though the run was not charged to him). Three scoreless innings later, both teams' middle and short relievers had been spent, and two pitchers who were normally starters were called upon by their respective clubs to plot through the extra-inning tenseness.

Beginning in the top of the 12th, Tim Wakefield, who had been rocked for five runs in Game 3, knuckled his way through three scoreless innings. The Yankees' Esteban Loaiza had induced an inning-ending double play coming out of the bullpen in the 11th, and had faced only six men in the 12th and 13th innings, neatly retiring the side in order twice. In the bottom of the 14th inning, the Tijuana-born right-hander allowed a one-out walk, then walked another man with two outs. With runners on first and second, David Ortiz came up and delivered a run-scoring single, his third game-winning hit of the post-season. The Red Sox had suspensefully staved off a series defeat again and pushed the championship clash back to New York for a sixth game.

In the Red Sox's third elimination game, Schilling, the hurler slated for surgery a few days earlier, but who instead underwent a radical and literal patchwork procedure to staple his dislodged tendon to healthy ankle tissue, pitched again—and inspirationally well. Adding a new definition to the term "gamer," Schilling, with the white sanitary sock of his tacked-together right ankle noticeably splotched with blood, limited the Yankees to one run and four hits in seven innings. Schilling and two relievers used the game's biggest offensive blow, a three-run home run by second baseman Mark Bellhorn in the fourth inning, to win, 4–2. The Red Sox forced a seventh game for the first time in baseball history after a team had lost the first three games of a championship series.

Before the seventh game, the Yankees brought out Bucky Dent to throw out the ceremonial first pitch. Neither Dent nor the legend of his New England-infamous home run, had any negative effect on the self-asserting Red Sox. In the first inning, David Ortiz a/k/a "Big Papi" (and the series MVP) blasted a home run with a man aboard to give Boston two quick runs. In the second frame, team catalyst Johnny Damon banged a bases-loaded home run to put the Red Sox up 6–0 before the Yankees' cleanup hitter had come to the plate. From there, Derek Lowe and three Red Sox pitchers, including Martínez, kept the bewildered Yankees effectually contained in their Bronx home. Boston won decidedly, 10–3. The Red Sox had finally laid the hammer down on the New York Yankees and in the most franchise-crushing manner imaginable.

In an almost impossibly imagined scenario from a week earlier, the World Series opened, at Fenway Park, on October 23. In Game 1 of the Fall Classic, the Red Sox wielded a collectively stronger, run-producing mallet against a formidable St. Louis Cardinals squad and out-bludgeoned the National League team, 11–9. Each team's starter, Tim Wakefield and Woody Williams, was hit hard.

In the second game, Schilling, and his stitched and pain-numbed ankle, threw six effective innings, holding the Redbirds to four hits and no earned runs. In the same number of innings, Schilling's teammates ground down Cardinals starter Mike Morris and two relievers for eight hits and six runs. Three Red Sox bullpen men closed out a decisive 6–2 win.

Busch Stadium was where Pedro Martínez threw his first World Series pitch, on October 26, in Game 3. Johnny Damon staked the pitcher to a 1–0 lead with a leadoff homer. The Cardinals threatened in the first inning but Martínez escaped a one-out, bases-loaded jam, when left-fielder Manny Ramírez threw out Larry Walker at home plate trying to score on a potential sacrifice fly. In the third inning, the Cardinals failed to score a "gimme" run following two consecutive hits. Cardinals pitcher Jeff Suppan singled and raced to third base on an Edgar Renteria double, with no outs. Still early in the game, the Red Sox elected not to try and cut off the run at third and defensed accordingly. Larry Walker, the next batter, grounded out to Red Sox second baseman Mark Bellhorn. Suppan hesitated advancing down the line—twice—in what appeared to be an easy progression from third base to home on the ground ball hit to the right side of a normal depth infield. Caught in "no man's land" by the indecision, Suppan was thrown out trying to get back to the base he had been so uncertain about vacating. Following the 4–3–5 double play, Martínez retired the next hitter, Albert Pujols, stranding Renteria at second.

The starting pitcher who would retire with the best ERA+ (154) in history then set down 12 more hitters in a row over the next four innings, en route to a seven-inning, three-hit, six-strikeout, two-walk golden effort. The Red Sox scored three more runs during Martínez's middle-inning dominance. St. Louis avoided the shutout in its last at-bat on a Walker home run, as reliever Keith Foulke wrapped up the 4–1 win.

The next evening, October 27, Derek Lowe, a much-maligned pitcher on the season because of poor performance numbers, duplicated Martínez's seven-inning scoreless achievement of Game 3, then turned things over to the Red Sox bullpen with a 3–0 lead. Bronson Arroyo and Alan Embree combined to retire the home team in the eighth inning, stranding a walked baserunner. In the ninth, Foulke found himself on the mound again in his closer's role. Trying to preserve a shutout win, Fouke allowed a single to the first hitter, then retired the following two hitters. The next batter, Edgar Renteria, whose dramatic, extra-inning single had won the 1997 World Series for the Florida Marlins, tapped back to Foulke, who lurched toward first base before tossing the ball to first baseman Doug Mientkiewicz.

The Titanic sailed into New York harbor, Hamlet lived and the Red Sox won every last game that mattered.

The 2000s and 2010s—Mariano Rivera, Johan Santana, Félix Hernández

Mariano Rivera

One inning. One pitch. One arm angle. That was the implausible formula for unprecedented success for one Mariano Rivera.

A soccer aficionado as a young man who idolized Pele, Rivera hailed from humble origins, far from the big city limelight under which he would eventually thrive and become revered. Born November 29, 1969, in Puerto Caimito, Panama, a fishing village on the Isthmus country's south central coast, Rivera was unearthed by the New York Yankees' head of International Scouting, Herb Raybourn. A year after first seeing Rivera pitch in Panama's national baseball tournament in 1989, Raybourn, a dual citizen of the U.S. and Panama, signed Rivera. It cost the Yankees a mere $2,000 to sign the future peerless reliever.

Leaving Panama for the first time at the age of 20, Rivera spent five years and part of a sixth in the Yankees' farm system, before he was given an opportunity with the varsity team. The 25-year-old was promoted to the Yankees early in 1995, in the role in which he had been exclusively pitching for the past three seasons—starter. The Yankees were strapped for a starter in late May and they chose Rivera from Triple-A Columbus.

Rivera opened for the Yankees, on the road, on May 23, 1995, against the California Angels. The right-hander, who owned a 95 mph fastball, struck out the first batter he faced, Tony Phillips. Rivera pitched two scoreless innings but the second time through the order, in the third, the Angels reached him for two runs. The home team knocked the inexperienced pitcher out of the box in the fourth inning. The Angels won, 10–0, behind Chuck Finley; Rivera was charged with half of the runs.

Undaunted, Rivera bounced back five days later and recorded his first big league win. He defeated the Oakland Athletics in their home ballpark, 4–1. He obtained one out in the sixth inning prior to his removal. Bob Wickman and John Wetteland held the A's scoreless over the remaining 3⅔ innings.

After two poor starts, Rivera was sent back to Columbus on June 11 and then recalled for a Fourth of July start in which he hurled eight spotless innings against the Chicago White Sox at Comiskey Park. Rivera allowed two hits and struck out 11. John Wetteland was scuffed for a run in the ninth inning as the Yankees prevailed, 4–1. Rivera remained with the Yankees from that date forward.

His first major league relief appearance came on August 1. Pitching in middle relief, he failed to protect a lead, but was credited with a win (his fourth) after a Yankees' three-run, seventh-inning rally defeated the Milwaukee Brewers, 7–5, at Yankee Stadium.

The rookie pitcher (5–3, 5.51 ERA) received his first taste of the post-season as the Yankees eked out a wild card berth over the California Angels. New York's first-round opponent was the Seattle Mariners. In one of the most memorable ALDS, the Yankees won the first two games in New York and then swallowed three straight defeats at the Kingdome, including a crushing fifth-game, 6–5 loss in 11 innings. Edgar Martínez drove home the tying and winning runs with a double off Jack McDowell, pitching in relief. Rivera appeared in three games in the series. He secured his first post-season win in Game 2, tossing 3⅓ scoreless innings in the Yankees' 15-inning, 7–5 victory in the Bronx.

Rivera was converted to a full-time reliever for the 1996 season. The sophomore pitcher excelled in his assigned setup role to Yankees closer John Wetteland, who led the league in saves with 43. Rivera won eight games in relief, the fifth-highest win total on the club. Division winners, the 92-win Yankees gelled as a team in the playoffs and pulled off one of the most stirring and surprising World Series comebacks to capture their first world championship since 1978.

Rivera posted a 2.09 ERA in 61 appearances. In 107⅔ innings, he struck out 130 batters, the most by a Yankees reliever since Goose Gossage (122, in 1978). He accumulated a stretch of 26 scoreless innings during the campaign, including 14 straight without allowing a hit. Twice during the season (4/26 and 4/28), he bridged the middle inning divide to John Wetteland's final-inning save territory by hurling three hitless frames. Both times, Rivera received the win. The right-hander chipped in with five saves of his own.

The Yankees defeated the West Division champion Texas Rangers in four games in the ALDS. Managed by first-year skipper Joe Torre, they dispatched the wild card Baltimore Orioles in the ALCS. Rivera gained his second post-season win in Game 1. The game was tied by the Yankees in the eighth inning, on a disputed Derek Jeter home run, involving fan interference. With no further scoring in regulation, Rivera was brought in to keep the Orioles off the board. He did, for two extra innings. The Yankees scored in the bottom of the 11th inning to win the game, 6–5. The Yankees stumbled in Game 2, but won three in a row in Baltimore to advance to the World Series.

The American League champions were embarrassed in the first game of the World Series, 12–1, by the Atlanta Braves. Nineteen-year-old, Curacao-born Andruw Jones became the youngest player to hit a World Series home run when he smashed a second-inning offering off Yankees left-hander Andy Pettitte to open the Braves' scoring. The Braves won again the following evening, October 22, behind Greg Maddux and Mark Wohlers, 4–0. Torre's team then roared back with four straight victories. Rivera surrendered the first post-season run of his young career in Game 2, after 16 unscored-upon post-season innings.

After the season, Rivera received the 1996 Buck Canel Award from the BBWAA as the majors' best Latin American player.

* * *

In 1996, John Wetteland had won the American League "Rolaids Relief Man of the Year" Award and, with four recorded saves, the World Series MVP. The Yankees, in a calculated move, allowed Wetteland, having completed the final year of his contract, to pursue free agency, with the intent of making Mariano Rivera their closer. The decision vaulted the

New York Yankees franchise to dynastic heights over the next few seasons and transformed Mariano Rivera into the most proficient pitcher in baseball history.

A strong Baltimore Orioles team turned the tables on New York and forced a 96-win Yankees squad to settle for a wild card draw to reach the 1997 post-season. In his first year as Yankees closer, Rivera converted 43 saves with an ERA of 1.88, both marks second-best among AL relief specialists. He missed converting on saves nine different times, and garnered a 6–4 record. His innings pitched total was 71⅔.

Rivera blew three of his first six save attempts as the new Yankees closer in 1997. But he righted himself enough to earn an All-Star Game invitation in July. Rivera punctuated his first All-Star selection with a 1–2–3 ninth-inning save against the National League in the junior circuit's 3–1 win at Jacobs Field on July 8. The game-winning blow, a two-run home run, was delivered in the seventh inning by Cleveland's Sandy Alomar.

The Indians catcher would later be responsible for Rivera's first post-season blown save. It came on October 5, at the same Jacobs Field, in Game 4 of the ALDS. The Central Division-winning Indians, trailing two games to one in the series, were inching closer to the brink of elimination as Rivera was called into the game with one out in the eighth inning and the Yankees holding a 2–1 lead. Alomar smacked an opposite-field home run against Rivera to tie the game, and the Indians won, 3–2, in the next inning, scoring a run against Ramiro Mendoza. The dramatic win inspired another tight Indians victory (4–3) the following night.

The comeback series win against the Yankees propelled the Cleveland club to reach the most extended post-season point a sports team can travel without achieving championship glory. On October 26, Edgar Renteria's bounding single off Charles Nagy painfully ended for the Indians an extra-inning, seventh-game World Series engagement against the Florida Marlins, in the Marlins' favor.

Rivera shook off the series-altering home run to Sandy Alomar and went on to set an unapproachable standard for October relievers over the next four post-seasons.

The Yankees entered the 1998 playoff joust as a record-setting club that tore through all regular season competition, setting a new American League standard for wins with 114. Rivera saved 36 of the victories, including 22 saves in a row, with five opportunities missed. He won three games (without a defeat) and posted an ERA of 1.91 in 61⅓ innings.

Against the Texas Rangers in the ALDS, Rivera appeared in all three games and saved two of them. Rivera added a five-out save in Game 5 of the Yankees' six-game ALCS triumph over the Cleveland Indians. The Panamanian then preserved three games in the Yankees' World Series sweep over the San Diego Padres, including the championship-crowning 125th victory of the season for the redoubtable New York club. Rivera accumulated his six post-season saves in 13⅓ scoreless innings.

In 1999, the Yankees, with a regular season record of 98–64, were actually more dominant in the post-season than in their record-shattering season of 1998. Joe Torre's team lost only one playoff game en route to the 17th World Series sweep in history and the team's second in row.

Rivera was intrinsically involved in the team's success, all season long, out of the bullpen. He accounted for 49 of New York's wins, saving 45 games out of 49 attempts, and coming up with four other wins against three defeats. Rivera's ERA of 1.83, in 69 innings, reflected his ascendant pitching.

Mariano Rivera's consistent pitching delivery and nearly unhittable cutter made him baseball's greatest closer.

In a repeat of 1998, the Yankees swept the Texas Rangers in the ALDS. Rivera saved two games, one of a two-inning duration, and he retired eight of the nine men he faced in the series. Rivera saved two of the Yankees' four wins over their ALCS opponent, the Boston Red Sox, and reckoned in three of the four consecutive World Series triumphs the Yankees inflicted over the National League champion Atlanta Braves.

After saving Game 1 for Orlando Hernández, Rivera gained his first World Series victory in the third game, pitching two shutout innings. Outfielder Chad Curtis capped off the 6–5 win with a tenth-inning solo home run against Braves reliever Mike Remlinger. Rivera secured the final four outs of Roger Clemens' clinching 4–1 win the following night, October 27. For his 4⅔ innings of precision work, Rivera was named the World Series MVP. He became the third relief specialist and third Hispanic pitcher to win the award.

Rivera finished the season as an untoppable reliever. Including his impenetrable post-season run of 12⅓ innings, the exceptional bullpen man did not allow an earned run over his final 43 innings pitched, a total of 36 appearances.

Shortly after the World Series, Rivera traveled back to his home country to proudly receive the Manuel Amador Guerrero Order as part of Panamanian Independence Day celebrations in Panama City.

*   *   *

In 2000, "Mo," as he was being affectionately referred to, tallied 36 saves, with five other lost opportunities on his record. The pitcher's ERA scaled up to 2.85 in 75⅔ innings.

Rivera posted his first Opening Day save, on April 3, despite being nicked for a run by the Anaheim Angels in the bottom of the ninth inning. The visiting Yankees won, 3–2. Rivera won the first of his seven campaign victories (against four defeats) on April 17. He pitched two innings, allowing one run, in the Yankees' 11-inning, 5–4 win over the Texas Rangers at Arlington. The run was scored in the bottom of the tenth inning; the blown save was Rivera's first since July of 1999, and the trip-up broke a string of 27 successive saves over that time.

Rivera recorded two saves on July 8, in a unique day-night, home-and-home double-header between the Yankees and New York Mets. In the afternoon affair at Shea Stadium, Rivera notched his 20th save of the season with a perfect ninth inning of work, sealing the home team's fate, 4–2. In the nightcap at Yankee Stadium, which featured a nasty beaning of Mets All-Star catcher Mike Piazza by Roger Clemens, Rivera once more closed the door on the Mets, assuring a 4–2 Yankees win.

In October, the New York Mets were the Yankees' World Series adversaries in the first Subway Series since 1956. The Yankees dispatched the Mets in five games. Rivera recorded the final out of the World Series for the third consecutive year.

Entering the 2000 post-season, the Yankees closer had not permitted a run since Sandy Alomar's 1997 home run, a span of 27 innings. Rivera added 7⅓ innings to the streak during the first two rounds of the playoffs. In the process, the Panamanian pitcher established a new record for consecutive scoreless innings in the post-season, 34⅓. "I'm just happy to break the record as a Yankee because it was a Yankee who held it,"[1] said Rivera, referencing previous record holder Whitey Ford's 33 straight unscored-upon innings (all in the World Series as a starter).

The streak ended on October 17, against the Seattle Mariners in the sixth game of the

ALCS, when Rivera gave up a two-run double to Mark McLemore, one of the runs belonging to him. The Yankees were victorious in the game, 9–7, which clinched their World Series berth.

In the Fall Classic, with the Yankees having captured three games, Joe Torre summoned Rivera in Game 5, on October 26, to ensure a new Yankees dynasty and Rivera did not let his manager down. Holding a two-run lead, Rivera retired Mike Piazza, the tying run, on a deep fly to center fielder Bernie Williams and set off intimately familiar celebrations for the closer on the mound.

In preserving the 4–2 win, Rivera set a new record for World Series saves with seven.

* * *

In 2001, Mariano reached the relief pitchers' rarely attained 50-saves mark. Establishing a new Yankees team saves record, Rivera secured 50 out of 57 rescue attempts. He won four and lost six, throwing 80⅔ innings, with his ERA at 2.34.

On May 13, in a 10–5 home loss he suffered to the Baltimore Orioles, Rivera allowed five runs in one game for the first time in his seven-year career.

On the first of August, the steady reliever pulled in his 35th save of the season and 200th as a fireman. He did it with a two-inning, no-hit, two-strikeout showing against the Texas Rangers at Yankee Stadium; the final score was 9–7.

In a runaway, the Yankees won their fourth successive AL East title. For the second season in a row, the Yankees were maximally tested by the Oakland A's in the first round of the playoffs. The Yankees won a deciding fifth game, 5–3, with Rivera earning a six-out save. The New Yorkers had an easier time against the Seattle Mariners in the ALCS, losing only one game to the AL West champions, who had won a record 116 regular season games.

In the World Series, the Yankees ran into an inspired duo of Arizona Diamondbacks starters named Randy Johnson and Curt Schilling. The Series took seven games to decide, with the Diamondbacks winning the first two contests, played in Arizona, and the Yankees coming back to register victories in all three games played in New York.

In actuality, with more effective relief pitching, Arizona could have won the Series in five games. As it was, the Series played out as one of the best on record, with memorable highs and lows experienced by both clubs. When the last pitch was thrown—by Mariano Rivera—the emotional tide ebbed lowest for the Yankees.

Rivera appeared in all three Yankees wins in New York, saving one, winning one and holding the lead in the other. After a Game 6 blowout won by Johnson, Rivera was on the mound in the bottom of the ninth inning the next evening, November 4, needing three outs to bestow upon the Yankees its fourth consecutive world championship. Protecting a slim 2–1 advantage, Rivera had converted 23 consecutive post-season save opportunities. In the eighth inning, he struck out the side around a two-out single, giving all indication that October save number 24 was a foregone conclusion. (This was the first World Series to spill over into November, due to the September 11 terrorist attacks that interrupted the regular season schedule late in the season. Incidentally, Rivera would donate his 2001 Rolaids Relief Award to the New York City Fire Department.)

The Diamondbacks tied the game on a hit, a sacrifice bunt botched by Rivera, and a double. With the loaded the bases and one out, Arizona outfielder Luis González muscled a pitch over a drawn-in infield for a base hit and a stunning, 3–2, walk-off triumph. Entering Game 7, Rivera had not given up a run in 45 of 51 career post-season appearances.

* * *

Injuries limited Rivera to only 28 saves in 2002. Three separate DL stints trimmed his appearances to 45 on the season. In 46 innings, he managed a 1–4 record and a 2.74 ERA. But the physical setbacks did not deter Rivera from becoming the Yankees' all-time saves leader. The franchise-best 225th successful rescue came on May 9 versus the Tampa Bay Devil Rays. At Tropicana Field, Rivera recorded four outs to close out a 3–1 Yankees victory.

Rivera was chosen for his fifth All-Star Game in 2002. He pitched one scoreless inning at Miller Park, in the only All-Star Game to end in a tie not caused by the weather. (Both managers ran out of pitchers.) Five days after the All-Star Game, on July 14 in Cleveland, Rivera permitted a walk-off grand slam to the Indians' Bill Selby. Rivera allowed six earned runs—the most in one inning in his career—in blowing the save and being pinned with the 10–7 loss.

The Yankees, as a team, did just fine with and without the injury-plagued star reliever. The club won 103 games, but were upset in the first round of the playoffs by the Anaheim Angels. Although reaching the post-season as the wild card team, the Angels had won 99 games. The team won three more against New York. Rivera saved the first game of the ALDS for the Yankees, and then was not seen again as the Angels won the next three straight from the Bronx Bombers.

* * *

Rivera trimmed his ERA by more than a run in 2003, to 1.66, while saving 40 games for the division-topping Yankees, who tied with the Atlanta Braves for most wins in baseball with 101. Also derived from the reliever's 70⅔-inning workload was a 5–2 record. The right-hander missed the first 25 games of the season after suffering a groin injury during the last week of spring training.

On June 13, Rivera buttoned down Roger Clemens' 300th career win. It was an efficient three-out, three batters-faced, ninth-inning save by the extraordinary fireman, in the Yankees' 5–2 interleague win over the St. Louis Cardinals at Yankee Stadium.

Rivera concluded the season with 15 consecutive saves, after earlier in the summer registering 14 straight saves.

The "lights out" closer saved two games in the ALDS, as the Yankees surged to three successive victories over the Minnesota Twins after losing the opening playoff game. In an unforgettable championship series match-up with their hated division rivals, the Boston Red Sox, Rivera turned in an MVP performance. He allowed one run in eight innings pitched, with six strikeouts and no walks. He saved two games. Additionally, he was the winning pitcher in the seventh-game ALCS thriller that featured a late-inning comeback by New York and an extra-inning, game-winning home run by third baseman Aaron Boone. Rivera hurled the last three scoreless innings of the 11-inning, 6–5 victory.

In the World Series, the heroics were monopolized by the Florida Marlins. The North Miami team defeated the favored Yankees, four games to two. The clinching sixth game victory for the Marlins was tossed by young right-hander Josh Beckett. In a game reminiscent of Brooklyn's Johnny Podres' Game 7 World Series win over the Yankees at Yankee Stadium in 1955, the 23-year-old Beckett hurled his own 2–0 shutout in the Yankees' famed ballpark.

All Rivera could do was hurl the final two innings, keeping the Marlins from further scoring.

* * *

In 2004, Rivera led the major leagues with 53 saves, and became only the second fireman to record two 50-save seasons. He missed converting on only four save opportunities during the campaign. His record was 4–2 with an ERA of 1.94, tabulated from 78⅔ innings of bullpen assistance.

Career save number 300 came against the Tampa Bay Devil Rays on May 28. New York defeated the Devil Rays at Tropicana Field, 7–5. Notching his 17th save of the season, Rivera pitched a scoreless ninth frame.

Six weeks later, on July 10, against the same Devil Rays team at Yankee Stadium, Rivera extended a perfect save conversion record he held against the western Florida club. The save was a vintage "nothing across" final inning of work in a Yankees' 6–3 win. It was Rivera's 32nd of the season and gave him a 28 for 28 saves record versus Tampa in his career. Rivera's 32 saves at the All-Star break were the second-most attained by a reliever, behind John Smoltz's 2003 record of 34.

On July 24, Rivera allowed his fifth game-deciding home run, and second walk-off blast, to the Red Sox's Bill Mueller. Rivera could not protect a two-run lead, surrendering three ninth-inning runs, two on Mueller's home run, as the Red Sox pulled out an arresting 11–10 victory at Fenway Park. (Rivera had strung together 23 consecutive saves prior to this.)

A month later, on August 28, Rivera was credited with his most unusual final-score save in an 18–6 Yankees win over the Toronto Blue Jays at Skydome. Rivera entered the game in the lower half of the eighth inning to quell a Blue Jays rally, and then the Yankees scored nine runs in their final turn at bat. The four-out save was Rivera's 45th.

Winning 101 games for the second year in a row, the Yankees hung on to win their division by three games over the wild card Boston Red Sox.

In early October, the Yankees eased past the Minnesota Twins in their American League divisional faceoff, three games to one. Joe Torre's team won three in a row after being shutout by Johan Santana and two relievers in the first game, 2–0. Rivera was the winner in the decisive game for the Yankees; he pitched two scoreless innings in the 6–5, 11-inning win at the Metrodome on October 9.

The Yankees won the first three games against the Boston Red Sox in the ALCS, and then suffered the most historic meltdown in baseball post-season history. The Red Sox won four straight games and eliminated their arch-enemies of the diamond to advance to the World Series. Rivera, after notching saves in the first two games, blew the save in the potential Game 4 clincher for the Yankees—a 6–4 Red Sox win in 12 innings. The reliever also missed out on a save opportunity in the fifth game by allowing an inherited runner (from third base) to score, in the eighth inning of another eventual marathon win by Boston, this one 5–4 in 14 innings. The back-to-back blown saves were a first in the post-season for Rivera.

* * *

At age 35, Mariano Rivera recorded the best ERA of his career in 2005—1.38. He achieved it by pitching 78⅓ innings and finishing 67 games, the most by an American League reliever. He racked up 43 saves, plus two more in a brief post-season. His 7–4 record and miserly ERA were good enough to win Rivera his fourth "Rolaids Relief Man of the Year" Award, and second in a row.

For the second time in four years, the Yankees were ousted in the first round of the playoffs by the Anaheim Angels. The ALDS extended to its full complement of five games. Rivera saved both Yankees wins.

In 2006, Rivera scored 34 saves to climb into fourth place on the all-time saves list with 413. Rivera pitched 75 innings on the season; his ERA was a shining 1.80.

On June 6, the reliever topped Dennis Eckersley for fourth place on the all-time saves list with his 391st career save. It came against the Boston Red Sox at Yankee Stadium. Rivera did away with the fifth-, sixth-and seventh-place hitters in the Boston lineup to preserve a Yankees 2–1 win.

Six weeks later, on July 16, Mariano gained his 400th save. The victory-protecting effort was of the two-inning variety against the Chicago White Sox. At Yankee Stadium, the bullpen magistrate registered his 11th career regular season save of a two-inning duration in the Yankees' 6–4 win. Four days hence, the late-inning specialist was touched for an 11th-inning walk-off home run by Toronto's Vernon Wells. It was the first dinger allowed by Rivera since August 16, 2005 (Eduardo Pérez), a span of 74 innings. It was the third career walk-off home run surrendered by Rivera and only the 12th walk-off loss for the pitcher.

In his 700th appearance, on July 22, Rivera pitched a perfect ninth inning to tally his 23rd save of the season. The Yankees won, 5–4, over the Toronto Blue Jays at the Rogers Centre.

Prior to gearing up for another post-season run, Rivera missed 22 games in September with a strained right forearm. In his first appearance back from the injury, on September 22, he struck out the side to record his 34th save (allowing one hit).

In the quest for October glory, the Yankees were once more ousted in the earliest session of the playoffs. The Detroit Tigers consigned to the Yankees a longer winter than the team would have desired, by defeating the perennial American League East champions in four ALDS games. Rivera saw action in the only Yankees win, in a non-save situation.

* * *

After nine straight division titles, the New York Yankees settled for a wild card ticket in 2007 to enter the World Series sweepstakes draw.

For the first time as a reliever, Rivera posted an ERA over 3.00 that season. Rivera's 3.15 earned runs mark was calculated over 71⅓ innings of work in 67 appearances. Given 34 opportunities, he saved 30 games; his record was 3–4.

Early in the campaign, on April 15, he allowed a walk-off home run to the Oakland Athletics' Marco Scutaro. The home run was blasted on an 0–2 pitch—the fourth walk-off home run allowed by Rivera in his career and first home run surrendered by him when the batter was that far down in the count since 1997. Scutaro's three-run home run provided the Athletics with an exciting 5–4 win, witnessed by a Sunday crowd of 35,077 at McAfee Coliseum.

That same month, on April 28, Rivera began a streak of 19 straight save conversions that lasted until August 12. From June 12 to August 15, Rivera pitched 27 innings in a row without walking a batter (23 appearances). And during a five-save stretch from August 24 to September 9, Rivera set down 21 straight batters.

In the ALDS, the Yankees were beaten by a hungrier Cleveland Indians team. Rivera appeared in three games, tossing 4⅔ scoreless innings without a save opportunity.

The elimination game for the Yankees occurred on October 8 at Yankee Stadium. The Indians' 6–4 playoff-advancing win was the last game managed by Joe Torre in Yankees pinstripes.

*   *   *

In 2008, Rivera bounced back from his "off year" to pile up 39 saves in 40 chances, the second-best conversion rate since Flash Gordon's 46-for-47 in 1998. Rivera's won-lost mark was 6–5, with a 1.40 ERA in 70⅔ innings. He finished fifth in American League Cy Young Award balloting, and his opponents' batting average of .165 was second-stingiest in all of baseball behind only Carlos Marmol of the Chicago Cubs (.135). Rivera, on the season, did not blow a save at Yankees Stadium—20 for 20. The right-hander finished the season with 230 saves at Yankee Stadium—the most by any one pitcher in one ballpark.

Rivera commenced the campaign by converting 28 consecutive saves, before being charged with a failed attempt. He would allow runs in just two of his 39 saves on the season. The first run to be charged to his pitching ledger did not come until May 13 (his 15th appearance). He allowed a game-winning single in the bottom of the 11th inning at Tampa. Rivera had entered a 1–1 tie game in the prior inning; he did not retire a batter in the 11th frame and suffered a 2–1 defeat.

Rivera collected 22 saves through June. The 38-year-old reliever was virtually an automatic selection for his seventh All-Star Game, in which he chipped in with 1⅔ innings of scoreless work for the American League. Pitching in his home ballpark, Rivera was one of a full complement of 12 pitchers used by AL manager Terry Francona in his league's 4–3, 15-inning victory on July 15. The game tied the longest All-Star Game on record in innings, and, at four hours and 50 minutes, became the longest Mid-Summer Classic, by time.

For the sixth time in his magnificent career, from August 22–24, Rivera saved all the games of a three-game series for the Yankees. The saves came against the Baltimore Orioles at Camden Yards. Ten days prior to the Baltimore series, Rivera experienced his only blown save of the campaign. At the Metrodome, he surrendered a one-out, three-run gopher ball to the Twins' Delmon Young in the bottom of the eighth inning, which tied the score. Two inherited runners and Young's tying run denied Rivera's save chance. The Yankees scored three runs in the top of the 12th inning to win, 9–6.

On September 15, the right-hander moved past Lee Smith into second place on the all-time saves list. At Yankee Stadium, Rivera induced three groundouts from the three Chicago White Sox batters he faced in the top of the ninth inning, tying up his 36th save of the season and 479th of his career. The Yankees doubled up the White Sox, 4–2.

Awarding the 2008 All-Star Game to Yankee Stadium was baseball hierarchy's fitting salute to the great cathedral of the game. The famed "House That Ruth Built" was scheduled to be demolished at the end of the season to make room for parking and other public amenities for a new, ultra modern Yankee Stadium being constructed right beside the original. In the final game played at Yankee Stadium, on September 21, Rivera threw the final pitch (a groundout to first base by the Orioles' Brian Roberts). He had come on to symbolically finish a Yankees' 7–3 victory.

Though Rivera methodically chalked up saves as usual, this season's affluent Yankees team had trouble stockpiling the necessary win total to qualify for the post-season. The 89–73 squad was excluded from October baseball for the first time since 1993.

* * *

Right shoulder surgery on his acromioclavicular joint in October 2008 did nothing to slow Rivera down in 2009. Over 66⅓ innings, he hoarded 44 saves, while missing on only two other opportunities. A 3–3 record and 1.76 ERA summarized his continuing brilliance.

Again, Rivera put together an extended streak of faultless save chances, stringing up 36 in a row (a career best) from April 30 to September 14. On May 29, Rivera saved an Andy Pettitte victory for the 59th time, the most by one reliever for one starter. Rivera's tenth save on the campaign guaranteed Pettitte's fifth win (3–1), and broke the previous reliever-starter duo high mark of 58 by Dennis Eckersley and Bob Welch.

On June 24, Rivera struck out all four batters to come to the plate against him. In doing so, the reliever secured his 16th save and an 8–4 interleague win over the Atlanta Braves at Turner Field. Four days later, he reached a significant milestone, recording his 500th career save. At Shea Stadium, Rivera retired all three bottom-of-the-ninth-inning batters he encountered, as the Yankees completed a sweep of their three-game interleague match-up with the Mets, 3–2. "I don't look for records or things like that," said Rivera afterwards. "I'm not here for that. I'm here to play baseball and win the World Series. If it happens, it happens. But I don't come here to chase records."[2]

The following month, Rivera's tenth All-Star Game selection resulted in his eighth appearance and fourth career save, topping the previous All-Star high held by Dennis Eckersley. Rivera retired three straight elite National League batters to wrap up the American League's 4–3 win at Busch Stadium on July 14.

Exactly a month later, Rivera appeared in his 900th game; he garnered his 34th save on groundouts induced from three Seattle Mariners batters and preserved a 4–2 Yankees win at Safeco Field.

Rivera's perfect save conversion string ended on September 18. Back in Seattle, facing the Mariners, the reliever showed he was human by surrendering a two-out, two-run home run to outfielder Ichiro Suzuki. The blow joyously lifted the home team to a 3–2 victory and hung Rivera with his third loss of the campaign. (It was only the fifth walk-off home run allowed by Rivera in his long career.) Ironically, two batters earlier, Rivera had recorded his 1,000th strikeout, victimizing Mariners pinch-hitter Mike Carp. (Rivera allowed seven home runs on the campaign, the most since he permitted 11 in 1995.)

Rivera's Yankees lost their first two games of the season, then won 103 of their next 160 contests to qualify their bullpen star easily for his 12th post-season appearance. Rivera was never better during the Yankees' determined run through the playoffs. The already legendary relief artist was five-for-five in save chances, while allowing a scant run in 16 innings of stellar relief. He was on the mound in the clinching games of all three rounds of the post-season, as the Yankees resoundingly recovered from their post-season shortfall of 2008 to win their 27th World Series title.

Rivera saved the third game of the ALDS, a 4–1 eliminating win over the Minnesota

Twins at the Metrodome. Against the Anaheim Angels, he saved game one (4–1) and the final Game 6 of the ALCS, 5–2. In the World Series—for which his All-Star Game save helped secure the home field advantage for the Yankees—he saw action in four of the six games played. He collected saves in two contests and packaged up a 7–3 World Series win at Yankee Stadium, as Joe Girardi's Yankees dethroned the defending champions of baseball, the Philadelphia Phillies.

*   *   *

With five World Series rings to his name, Mariano Rivera, in 2010, recorded 33 saves. He won three games lost three, and posted another sub-2.00 ERA (1.80). He tossed 60 innings, the fewest since his injury-plagued 2003 season. Only one of his 33 saves extended beyond one inning. Rivera also had five blown saves, his highest total since 2003. In the playoffs, however, Rivera let no one down; he was three-for-three in save chances.

The Yankees, in their familiar autumnal role, advanced from a wild card seed to the American League Championship Series. But an emerging team from the American League West, the Texas Rangers, made its presence known to all by eliminating Girardi's Yankees in six games.

In 2011, Mariano Rivera cemented his place in history as baseball's greatest closer. Rivera hauled in 44 saves, while failing at five other opportunities. At age 41, he became the oldest pitcher to record 40 saves in a season.

On May 25, Rivera appeared in his 1,000th game, the most by any player with one team. Rivera pitched the last inning of a 7–3 home win over the Toronto Blue Jays, in a non-save situation.

Rivera finished the season with 15 straight saves and became only the second pitcher to record 600 saves. On September 13, facing the Seattle Mariners, Yankees catcher Russell Martin threw out Ichiro Suzuki trying to steal second base for the last out of the game, to hand Rivera his 600th save. Rivera had allowed a single to Suzuki and retired two batters, when Martin made the Japanese star pay for his gamble to get into scoring position. The Yankees won, 3–2, at Safeco Field. At Rogres Centre, four days later, Rivera tied Trevor Hoffman's record for career saves with 601. The relief master set down the Blue Jays without a peep in the home half of the ninth inning, securing a 7–6 Yankees triumph.

History was made by Rivera on September 19. The 16-year veteran prompted a ground out, a line out, and a called strike three against Chris Parmelee of the Minnesota Twins, to close out a 6–4 Yankees win at Yankee Stadium. Rivera claimed his 43rd save on the season and number 602 lifetime. Rivera was able to attain his sizable piece of baseball history with his entire family in attendance. His father, Mariano, Sr., and mother, Delia, along with the pitcher's wife, Clara, and their three sons, Mariano III, 17, Jafet, 14 and Jaziel, 8, all bore witness to the remarkable achievement. "It's a blessing," Rivera said in the clubhouse. "I never thought that I'd be doing this for so many years and be able to accomplish this record."[3]

Rivera made two cameo appearances in the ALDS for his division-winning team, throwing 1⅓ innings. In neither of the brief outings were the Yankees protecting a lead. Rivera and the Yankees were forced to swallow a premature ending to their season, bowing to the Detroit Tigers in five first-round games.

*   *   *

On Opening Day 2012, Rivera suffered a blown save to the Tampa Bay Rays. Rivera was rattled by three Rays hits, one a triple, and allowed two runs. Tampa Bay carried away a 7–6 win. Coming into the game, Rivera had been 60 of 61 in save opportunities against the Sunshine State team.

Rivera saved his next five games after that, the last of which came on April 30, when he battened down a 2–1 Yankees victory over the Baltimore Orioles at Yankee Stadium . He threw a double play ball to Nick Markakis to end the game. It was the last pitch Rivera threw on the season.

At Kauffman Stadium on May 3, while shagging flies during batting practice—a regular routine of the relief hurler—Rivera injured his knee. A closer examination revealed a torn ACL. Surgery five weeks later wiped out the remainder of Rivera's season.

The Yankees, as repeat Eastern Division champions, admirably reached the ALCS without their irreplaceable closer. But the team was dismissed from there in four straight games by the Detroit Tigers.

Rivera, who was under contract for only the 2012 season, announced during his recovery period that he would not end his career on such a disappointing note and that he would return for the 2013 season.

The Yankees, of course, accommodated Rivera and signed him for 2013, and the reliever without equal came back to slam the door on opponents 18 times in a row before a misstep.

Three days into the season, on April 4, Rivera was presented with his first save opportunity since his injury. Facing the Boston Red Sox, the closer was nicked for a run on a ninth-inning walk and hit, but otherwise seemed his old self in bundling three outs and fastening a 4–2 home win. The winning Yankees pitcher was veteran Andy Pettitte, who benefitted for the 69th time from Rivera personally locking up a victory.

It was vintage Rivera for the first two months of the season. The 43-year-old pitcher, who had announced that the 2013 campaign would be his last, did not slip up until May 28. After 18 straight saves to open the season, Rivera let one get away, allowing three last-at-bat hits to the New York Mets at Citi Field. A broken-bat hit by the Mets' Lucas Duda scored the game-winner for the home team in their 2–1 win over their crosstown rivals.[4] (It was the first blown save of Rivera's career in which he did not record an out.)

On Father's Day, June 16, Rivera converted his seventh straight save since shrugging off the misfortune against the Mets. Opposing the Anaheim Angels in their home ballpark, Rivera came in to quell a valiant attempt by the home club to tie and possibly win a game that seemed out of reach when the last inning started. Trailing 6–0, the Angels struck for five hits, including three base knocks against Rivera, to plate five runs. With the bases loaded, the unflappable closer struck out Albert Pujols on three pitches to put out the fire and record his 25th save.

Rivera's 28th save provided C.C. Sabathia with his 200th career win on July 3. At Target Field, Rivera pitched the ninth inning, allowing one hit and nothing else, in sowing up a 3–2 victory over the Minnesota Twins. Four days afterward, Rivera blew his first save at Yankee Stadium in 41 chances, and only his second missed save opportunity in 31 chances on the season. In a 1–0 game in the ninth inning, Orioles center fielder Adam Jones tagged Rivera with a two-run home run. It was the second big fly Rivera allowed on the season. The Yankees went down without a fight in their last at-bat and Baltimore prevailed, 2–1.

The amazing Rivera obtained his 30th save on July 12, and achieved that many saves by the All-Star break for the second time in his career. At Yankee Stadium, the bullpen specialist pitched a flawless ninth inning to preserve New York's 2–0 win over the Minnesota Twins.

His ninth and final All-Star Game appearance delivered for the hurler his first MVP trophy, the third Yankee to win the prize. At Citi Field on July 16, Rivera pitched the eighth inning, keeping the National League off the board in the American League's 3–0 win. (The scoreless inning increased Rivera's All-Star Game mark to nine innings pitched without allowing an earned run.) At the start of the inning, Rivera warmed up on the mound, to a standing ovation from fans, teammates and opponents. Except for catcher Salvador Pérez, his AL teammates refrained from taking their defensive positions on the field to allow Rivera the individual spotlight prior to his farewell All-Star Game appearance. Rivera retired three batters in a row and was named the game's top player in a selection that was unofficially dedicated as a lifetime achievement award. Rivera became the first relief pitcher and first Panamanian player to be bestowed with an All-Star Game MVP trophy.

On August 6, Alex Rodríguez returned to the Yankees lineup for the first time in 2013, following hip surgery. Coincidingly bearing the weight of a 211-game suspension handed down by MLB for PED abuse, the suspension-appealing infielder was one of numerous key injuries that had decimated the Yankees squad from the beginning of the season. The next evening, Rivera, who was 35 out of 37 in save conversions with a 1.56 ERA, failed in his attempt at number 36. Facing the Chicago White Sox, he allowed a two-out hit to Adam Dunn in the bottom of the ninth inning that tied the game at 5–5. The White Sox won the game in the 12th inning, 6–5, and dropped the injury-riddled New Yorkers to a non-contending 57–56 record.

Two nights later, the game's greatest hitter spoiled another save attempt by the game's greatest closer. The Detroit Tigers' Miguel Cabrera hit a two-out, two-strike, two-run home run to erase a 3–1 Yankees lead in the top of the ninth inning, at Yankee Stadium. The Yankees salvaged the game by scoring a run in the tenth frame to win, 4–3. It was the first time since 2007 that Rivera had failed to nail down back-to-back save attempts. In the finale of the three-game series, Rivera squandered another save opportunity when the reigning Triple Crown winner and Victor Martínez blasted ninth-inning solo home runs against the usually automatic closer. Cabrera became the first batter to hit home runs in consecutive at-bats off Rivera as the Panamanian blew three straight saves for the first time in his renowned career. Rivera earned a 5–4 victory in the two home run-allowed game, following a Brett Gardner walk-off home run in the Yankees' immediate turn at the dish.

A week later, on August 18, Rivera made the least stressful of save chances a bit dicey before nailing down a Yankees' 9–6 win at Fenway Park. Entering the game with a three-run lead in the bottom of the ninth inning, the career saves leader broke his mini-string of lack of successes by securing the game's final three outs, the last coming as the tying run at the plate. It was the previously elusive 36th save for Mariano.

The 13-time All-Star clicked off four more saves, attaining his 40th save at home on September 3. Facing the Chicago White Sox, Rivera tossed a scoreless ninth inning with two strikeouts. He reached the 40 saves mark for the ninth season, equaling Trevor Hoffman for most all-time. (Rivera finished with 44 saves and a 2.11 ERA in 2013.)

To their credit, the Yankees battled back to challenge for a wild card berth in the American League at the start of September. The wild card hopes were staggered with three losses

One of the more innovative farewell gifts received by Rivera in 2013 was this rocking chair made from the broken bats of Minnesota Twins hitters. Twins manager Ron Gardenhire (jacket) and Justin Morneau make the presentation.

in four games to the division-pacing Boston Red Sox, from September 5–8. Rivera failed on two save attempts in the series, nudging up to seven his blown saves count, which matched a career high.

The last major league baseball player to wear the number 42 regularly had his uniform number retired by his team in Yankee Stadium's Monument Park on September 22. The elaborate, pre-game ceremony included the presence of Mrs. Rachel Robinson and a live performance by Metallica. The heavy metal group, whose "Enter Sandman" refrains, since the early 2000s, had accompanied Rivera's entrance into a game as a portent to its imminent conclusion, played their hit song live for the humbled 19-year veteran.

In the end, the 85–77 Yankees faded in their wild card quest. The playoff-less campaign, however, did provide for Rivera his 15th season with 30 or more saves, breaking a tie with Trevor Hoffman and Lee Smith for most all-time.

Legacy

Baseball writer Tom Verducci wrote in *Sports Illustrated* after the Yankees won their 27th World Series in 2009 that "God touched Mariano Rivera one June afternoon in 1997."[5] That blessed afternoon Rivera discovered, during a routine throwing session with pitcher Ramiro Mendoza, that his ball was moving in a way neither he nor Mendoza had ever seen. Rivera assured Mendoza that he was not trying to make the ball change direction just prior to smacking into Mendoza's glove—the ball dipped and darted on its own. Mariano Rivera's amazing cutter was born, and a hard-throwing pitcher would go on to become baseball's most successful relief pitcher for baseball's most successful franchise.

At 6'4" and 185 pounds, Rivera was a model of consistency from the mound for 19 years. He maintained his slim build throughout his career as rigidly as his singular, smooth-striding overhand delivery to the plate. Batters never saw Rivera deviate from his pitching motion. Remarkably, it was always the same. The same arm movement forward, from the same arm angle—with mostly the same deviant pitch. Batters knew the manner in which the ball was coming, from where it was coming, and what was coming—and they still could not hit the pitch squarely. The pitch, of course, was the cutter, a pitch that would run in or out on a hitter, with such late movement, that the most skilled batsmen could not anticipate its speeding, skittish course.

For all of Rivera's immense success—he was a seven-time recipient of the *Sporting News* "Fireman of the Year" Award and a five-time winner of the Rolaids "Relief Man of the Year"— he never acted anything but professionally from the hill. He never pointed his fingers in a threatening or dismissive fashion at batters he had finished retiring; he never engaged in any antics or theatrics after a save; he never showed up an opponent. The humility Rivera displayed on the mound came from his upbringing as the son of a struggling fisherman, growing up far from the stages of glory he could never have imagined conquering in his youth.

A boating accident, in which the fishing boat he was in capsized, dissuaded a young Mariano from wanting to become a fisherman like his father. Rivera, a deeply religious man, has said he would have probably pursued some call to religious ministry had his baseball career not panned out. Like many star players, Rivera, who earned over $150 million in his career, has established a charitable foundation, in his name, to help disadvantaged youth.

The Mariano Rivera Foundation has helped build an elementary school and church in Rivera's seaside hometown of Puerto Caimito in Panama. The foundation's dollars have also been put to work more recently for the construction of a new church in New Rochelle, New York.

The only man to record the last out of the World Series four times fittingly established a World Series record for saves that will be difficult to surpass: 11. So will his post-season records for consecutive scoreless innings, 34⅓, and for saves, 42, including 23 in a row. His 0.74 ERA in 141 October innings will be nearly impossible to better.

Eleven times in his career, Rivera posted an ERA under 2.00, and during four separate seasons he did not miss converting a save opportunity in his home ballpark. (In 2011, he was 23-for-23 at home; 24-for-24 in 2009; 17-for-17 in 2008, and 20-for-20 in 2006.)

It was at his home ballpark that Rivera made his final major league mound appearance, the 1,115th of his career—a record for a Latin American pitcher. (Santa Barbara, California-born Jesse Orosco appeared in 1,252 games.) On September 26, Rivera entered the Yankees' final home game of the season in the eighth inning and retired four successive batters. With two outs in the ninth, Andy Pettitte and Derek Jeter came out to the mound to remove their "Core Four" colleague.

The ceremonial removal caused a rush of emotion from Rivera. Watery-eyed, he hugged both of his longtime teammates, and exited to a standing ovation from the sellout Yankee Stadium crowd.[6]

Mariano Rivera's Career Statistics

G	GS	GF	CG	SHO	SV	SVO	INN	HR	BB	SO	W	L	ERA	PCT	ERA+	WHIP
1,115	10	952*	0	0	652*	732	1,283.2	71	286	1,173	82	60	2.21	.577	205*	1.00

*major league record

Johan Santana

It is not often that a Rule 5 draft choice comes back to haunt a team. It is even rarer for one to traumatize two teams, as Johan Alexander Santana has done. Two teams let the young left-handed pitcher slip through their organizational fingers. The Houston Astros signed Santana as a 16-year-old prospect from Tovar, Merida, Venezuela, in July of 1995. Four and one-half years later, the Florida Marlins plucked Santana from Houston's roster as a Rule 5 unprotected player. On the same day of what could have been a marvelous find, December 13, the Marlins (by prior arrangement) traded Santana to the Minnesota Twins for career minor leaguer Jared Camp.

As a youngster in Venezuela, Santana wanted to be like Omar Vizquel, with runner-up choices of Ken Griffey, Jr. and Rickey Henderson. But his live arm changed any position player aspirations he may have had in following in the steps of his idols.

Santana's conversion to his pitching calling occurred during his stay at a baseball academy near Valencia. The academy was co-founded by Andrés Reiner, a Hungarian-born and Venezuelan-raised Houston Astros scout who first discovered Santana. The 15-year-old Santana was playing the outfield in an amateur national championship tournament held in Carabobo (the same Venzuelan state in which the academy was located) when Reiner first spotted him.

Just prior to Santana turning 16, Reiner convinced Santana's parents, Jesús and Hilda, to virtually hand over their son to him to take to his baseball academy. Reiner had to make the half-day's journey by car to reach the Santana home in Tovar, which lay along mountainous countryside.

When he was of age, Santana was sent to the Astros' Rookie League team in the Gulf Coast League. He lost all four of his decisions. The next year, at age 19, in Single-A Ball, Santana logged a 7–6 record in 16 starts. The following year, 1999, also in Single-A Ball, the young left-hander received 26 starts with the Michigan Battle Cats; he split his 16 decisions. Having not shown much to date, it was understandable why the Houston organization left him unprotected over the winter.

In 2000, Santana made his new Minnesota Twins team as a bullpen arm reinforcement; he was assigned uniform number 57, a number he would wear throughout his career. Three weeks after turning 21, Santana saw action in his initial major league game. On April 3, at the Metrodome, Santana was called upon to pitch the ninth inning of a disappointing Twins home opener. The club was losing 7–0 to the Tampa Bay Devil Rays, and Santana pitched a scoreless final frame. He allowed one hit and struck out the second big league batter he faced—DH José Canseco.

Santana received his first major league start four days later in Kansas City. At Kauffman Stadium, in the Royals' season inaugural, Santana pitched five innings, allowing one run. He was denied a chance for his first victory, as the Royals scored late and often for a 10–6 win.

The keepsake win for Santana did not come until June 3. Ironically, it was achieved against his original team, the Houston Astros. Santana relieved Twins starter Eric Milton, who had to retire after only two innings. Santana pitched five middle innings and gave up one run. The Twins scored three runs in the eighth inning, and two relievers preserved the team's 3–1 victory and Santana's first.

Appearing in 30 games overall for the last-place Twins, Santana was 2–3, with an ugly ERA of 6.49, in 86 innings.

Arm trouble in 2001 forced Santana to spend more than three months on the disabled list. The pitcher was limited to 15 appearances with the Twins, a team that improved considerably in the standings from the prior dismal season. Four of the appearances were starts, in one of which he picked up his only decision of the season, an 8–3 victory over the Detroit Tigers. Santana pitched five innings and surrendered two runs in the home triumph.

Santana opened the 2002 season at Triple-A. It turned into a short, but career-altering tenure. Edmonton Trappers pitching coach Bobby Cúellar worked with Santana on how to perfect his change-up, to throw it the same way, with the same release point, as his two-seam fastball. The change-up would develop into Santana's strikeout pitch. Over 60 percent of Santana's strikeouts have come via the change.

After posting a 5–2 record with the Trappers, Santana was recalled by the Twins. With the big club, he started 14 games and relieved on 13 other occasions. He notched an 8–6 record, throwing 100 innings (108⅓) for the first time. He maintained his ERA below 3.00 (barely—2.99). The left-hander recorded the only save of his career, through 2013, on July 19, 2002. Tossing three scoreless innings in relief of starter Kyle Lohse, Santana was credited with the save in a 5–1 Twins win over the Detroit Tigers at Comerica Park.

The vast majority of the saves registered by the Twins' bullpen that season belonged to

Eddie Guardado, who led the league with 45. Another reliever, J. C. Romero, won nine games out of the pen. Along with Santana's effectiveness, the trio was dubbed "The Three Amigos," a reference to a popular, comedic motion picture of years past.

After moving all the way up to second place in the American League Central Division in 2001, the Twins, in 2002, won their division. The club made it past the Oakland A's in the first round of the playoffs but were eliminated by the Anaheim Angels in the LCS, in five games. Santana absorbed the loss, in relief, in the clinching game for the Angels on October 13.

In 2003, Minnesota repeated as champions of the Central Division. The team was ousted, however, by the New York Yankees in the ALDS. Santana, once more, suffered the defeat in the opponent's playoff clinching victory. This time as a starter, Santana was tagged for six runs over 3⅔ ineffective innings. The Twins, down two games to one, fell to the Yankees, 8–1, and were sent home searching for their golf clubs.

Santana had helped his team make the playoffs, with exceptional work as a reliever and starter. In 45 appearances, including 18 starts, Santana tallied a 12–3 record, the best winning percentage in the league.

*   *   *

A trade which brought veteran pitcher Kenny Rogers to the Twins prior to the 2003 campaign had derailed Santana's chance at becoming a full-time starter. But in 2004, the hard-throwing lefty could be held back no longer. The 25-year-old assumed an exclusive role as a frontline Twins starter. Though he started off slowly in his new role, Santana came on like gangbusters over the second half of the season. His record was only 2–4 after 12 starts. In the off-season, Santana had submitted to surgery on his throwing elbow to remove bone chips. He said later he did not feel fully recovered until early June.

His 6–2 record from June 3 to July 22, with an ERA of 1.74, resoundingly reflected his improved physical health. During that stretch of fabulous pitching, he allowed more than two runs only two times in 22 starts. Santana also tossed the first shutout (and first complete game) of his career. It came on July 6 against the Kansas City Royals. Thrilling a Metrodome crowd of 18,083, Santana struck out 13 and pitched a three-hitter. He walked two. His two defeats suffered in the same span were by the scores of 2–1 and 2–0. In a ten-start span, between June 15 and August 1, Johan pitched at least six innings without giving up more than four hits in a game. He allowed only 27 hits in 77 total innings. From June 20 to July 11, Santana recorded five consecutive games with ten or more strikeouts.

Santana was named American League Pitcher of the Month for July, August and September. He became the first pitcher since Pedro Martínez (1999) to be three times honored with the award in the same season. His record in six July starts was 3–2, with a 1.17 ERA and an opponents batting average of .095 (14–147). In August, he went 6–0 with a 2.08 ERA, 7 walks and 52 strikeouts. In September, the lefthander posted a 5–0 mark, with a minute 0.45 ERA (two earned runs in 40 innings).

Over his last 15 starts of the season, Santana was absolutely stupendous. He had mastered his change-up, and in tandem with his 94-mph fastball, he used it with devastating effect. A third pitch, a slider, also caused great consternation among American League batters. Santana went 13–0, with two no-decisions and a 1.21 ERA. He recorded a 33-inning stretch in which he did not permit a run. He struck out a career-high 14 Baltimore Oriole on September 19, pitching the Twins to a 5–1 win; Santana threw eight scoreless innings in recording his 19th victory of the season.

Santana became a 20-game winner in his next start, five days later. With six innings of work, he defeated the Cleveland Indians, 8–2, at Jacobs Field. He was reached for one run. Santana was named AL pitcher of the Month for July, August and September.

The strongest numerical proof that Santana had mastered with precision his three main pitches was his strikeout/walk totals of 265/54. Santana headed the league in strikeouts and ERA at 2.61. With a 20–6 record, Santana led the Twins to a runaway division title; the team bested the second-place Chicago White Sox by nine games.

Santana pitched the Twins to an opening-game Division Series victory over the New York Yankees on October 5. The Twins ace threw seven scoreless innings at Yankee Stadium and won, 2–0. Four days later, with the Twins facing elimination, Santana came back on three days' rest and pitched only five innings. He was removed from the game, perhaps over-cautiously by Twins manager Ron Gardenhire, holding a 5–1 advantage. The Twins' bullpen blew the lead and the Yankees won in 11 innings, 6–5.

In November, Santana was unanimously named the American League's Cy Young Award winner, the first pitcher from his country to be so honored. Santana's native land exploded with excitement and pride over the news.

> "I knew it would be a big deal in Venezuela, but not to this extent," Santana stated the following spring. "It was much more than I ever imagined. The reactions of all the people, seeing their faces, was amazing. People were crying.... What I was most proud of was that everybody forgot about all the political unrest in my country. For two months, they forget about everything and talked nothing but baseball. That was the best feeling."[7]

Andrés Reiner, Santana's discoverer, called the selection the biggest sports day in Venezuela since the day in 1984 when Luis Aparicio was elected into the National Baseball Hall of Fame.

Venezuelan president Hugo Chávez arranged for Santana to visit him at Miraflores, the presidential palace in Caracas. In a nationally televised event, Chavez bestowed upon Santana el Orden del Libertador, the Order of the Liberator, a prestigious designation to citizenry for outstanding national achievement.

Among the more highly publicized rash of social problems plaguing Venezuela, under Chávez, was the tendency for successful, returning major league players and their family members to become targets for kidnappers. To assure the safety of the pride of their country, the Venezuelan president assigned armed guards to protect Santana and his family (wife Yasmile and young daughter Jasmily) throughout the winter.

* * *

Prior to the 2005 season, Venezuela's most celebrated athlete signed a four-year, $40 million deal, the most lucrative contract at the time in Twins franchise history.

Manager Gardenhire opted for veteran Brad Radke over his Cy Young Award winner for his team's Opening Day assignment. It worked in Santana's favor, as the Twins were held to just one run on the day by four Seattle Mariners pitchers and suffered a 5–1 setback. The next day, April 4, Santana benefited from eight runs scored by his club at Safeco Field. The left-hander pitched only five innings and exited with a 7–4 lead. The Mariners would score no more the rest of the game, while the Twins added one insurance run.

On April 20, Santana celebrated the birth of his second child, named Jasmine. She was born minutes prior to a home start Santana was scheduled to make against the Kansas City Royals. Informed that his wife and child were fine, Santana went out and made his appointed start, receiving a no-decision. Although he struck out ten, he allowed four runs in seven innings, in an excusably distracted outing.

Winning his first four decisions of the 2005 season, Santana had a 17-game victory streak end on May 1. He was beaten, 2–1, by the visiting Anaheim Angels. Santana allowed two hits in the game in eight innings of work, but both were solo home runs. The 17 wins in a row were the most recorded by a Hispanic major league pitcher (tied by José Contreras in 2006).

In July, Santana was named to the All-Star squad for the first time. With a 7–5 record at the time, it was a selection perhaps tied to his Cy Young Award season. At the All-Star break, the Twins were a struggling club, nine games behind the eventual division-capturing Chicago White Sox.

Santana came on strong in the second half; he won nine games and was defeated but twice. On August 12, in Oakland, the pitcher tossed his second shutout of the season. He outdueled the A's Dan Haren, 1–0. Both hurlers threw three-hitters. Two starts later, inside the Metrodome on August 23, Santana outpitched White Sox pitcher and compatriot Freddy García, 1–0. Santana threw eight innings, with Joe Nathan picking up the save with one inning of faultless relief. A masterful García surrendered one hit in eight innings—a home run to Twins outfielder Jacque Jones.

Santana's eye-catching, year-end numbers were: 16–7, a 2.87 ERA, and a 0.97 WHIP. He walked only 45 batters in 231⅔ innings and led the majors in strikeouts with 238. Santana, however, could not inspire successful results from his club. The Twins lagged farther back over the final months and settled in third place, 16 games out of contention.

* * *

In 2006, Santana received his first career Opening Day start. He lost to Roy Halladay and the Toronto Blue Jays, 6–3. Santana was tagged for ten hits and four runs in less than six innings. Over his next three starts, Santana lost twice and obtained a no-decision. On April 27, Santana picked up his first win, downing Kansas City, 7–3. He permitted all of the Royals' runs over eight innings and struck out ten. The game was played at the Metrodome, where Santana did not lose a game all season.

Santana won his next three starts before he was defeated in a pitchers' duel on May 17 by Justin Verlander. The Detroit Tigers rookie hurled eight scoreless innings and closer Todd Jones kept the Twins off the board in the ninth to preserve a 2–0 Tigers win. Santana struck out a dozen in an eight-inning complete game.

On June 13, at the Metrodome, Santana registered a season-high 13 strikeouts against the Boston Red Sox, including the 1,000th of his career; Red Sox DH David Ortiz was the milestone casualty. The 13 whiffs were recorded in eight innings, over which Santana surrendered one lone run. The Twins won the game in exciting fashion, 5–2, on an 11th-inning grand slam by Jason Kubel. That no-decision notwithstanding, Santana was in the middle of a five-game winning streak, all brought to fruition by the Twins bullpen.

Santana's 9–4 record by month's end was good enough to merit an invitation to the All-Star Game. He pitched one scoreless inning, with one walk and one strikeout, as the American League scored twice in the top of the ninth inning to pull out a 3–2 victory, at PNC Park.

Santana had lost his final start right before the Mid-Summer Classic, but was defeated only once more over the remainder of the season. He posted a 10–1 mark over the second half of the campaign.

Santana's Twins ballclub surged right with him. The team overcame the early torrid pace of the Detroit Tigers to win the Central Division for the third time in four years. Santana paced the American League in pitching's glamour categories to win the Triple Crown. He logged 19 wins, 245 strikeouts and a 2.77 ERA. He also led the circuit in starts, 34, and innings pitched, 233⅔.

The Twins were unbeatable at the Metrodome in all of Santana's starts, extending the team's consecutive victory total to 23 in home games started by Santana, a modern era record for one pitcher. (The streak was begun in 2005.) However, the lucky streak came to an end in the first game of the ALDS. The Oakland A's, behind Barry Zito, defeated Santana, 3–2. The uncommon home loss with Santana on the hill may have psychologically affected the Minnesota club, as it lost the next two games to bow out of the playoffs quickly.

Santana had his own bows to take after being unanimously selected for a second Cy Young Award. Receiving all 28 first-place votes, Santana became the fifth hurler to win the league's best pitcher award twice unanimously (joining Koufax, Clemens, Maddux, and Martínez). "This was not such as a big surprise as 2004," the six foot, 195-pound pitcher commented. "[But] Today we made a lot of people happy. This is a matter of pride for me, my country, my family and the Minnesota Twins. The only downside is that I couldn't take our team to the World Series."[8]

* * *

The Minnesota sportswriters' "Pitcher of the Year" for three years running opened the 2007 season for the Twins with a 7–4 Metrodome win over the Baltimore Orioles. Santana hurled six innings and surrendered all of the Orioles' runs in the April 2 opener. Two starts later, on April 13, Santana suffered his first regular season home loss since August 1, 2005. He was defeated by Scott Kazmir and the Tampa Bay Devil Rays, 4–2, with Santana charged with all of the visitors' runs.

Santana won three games in April and three more in May. After 52 games, the Twins were in third place in their division, a couple of games above .500.

In June, Twins broadcaster Bert Blyleven challenged Santana to extend himself on the mound. The future Hall of Fame inductee, who tossed 242 complete games and 60 shutouts in his illustrious career, announced on air that he would shave his head if Santana would throw a shutout. Santana had only five complete games and three shutouts in 142 starts entering the 2007 season. On June 19, Santana whitewashed the New York Mets on four hits, 9–0, at Shea Stadium. Blyleven, the next day, sat down to have his hair lopped off to a buzz-cut by the Twins' winning, and slightly gloating, pitcher himself.

The shutout win was the left-hander's seventh; he won four more starts to improve to 11–6, before suffering his next setback. Prior to that loss—3–2 to the Detroit Tigers on July 18—Santana had been picked to his third All-Star team. He pitched a scoreless inning in the showcase game, won by his American League mates, 5–4, at AT&T Park.

The second-half surge that Santana seemed to summon regularly over the past few years, did not materialize this season. Santana won only four games after the All-Star Game. One of those victories was a dominant 17-strikeout performance (his career high) against

As a Minnesota Twin in 2004, Johan Santana became the first Venezuelan pitcher to win the Cy Young Award. Here he holds the second of such awards he won with Minnesota.

the Texas Rangers, at the Metrodome, on August 19. Santana allowed only two hits in eight innings and walked no one in the tight 1–0 victory saved by Joe Nathan.

Santana may not have been long on shutouts or complete games, but he had been a consistently reliable starter to a significantly valuable extent. His streak of 123 starts in a row with five or more innings pitched ended due to a rain delay on September 26 (the third-longest such streak of the past 50 years, behind Curt Schilling, 147, and David Cone, 145). Santana was not allowed to continue in the restarted game at Comerica Park after throwing the first three innings.

Santana finished the campaign with a 15–13 record and 3.33 ERA. In 33 starts, he maintained his strikeout wizardry, fanning 235 in 219 innings. Santana continued to flabbergast hitters, inducing swings and misses on 27.6 percent of pitches thrown, the highest ratio in the American League. Santana also led the league in most home runs allowed with 33, and he won his first Gold Glove Award.

The Twins, with only one other pitcher with a double-figure win total, expectedly floundered. The team placed in their division's third position, 17 games behind a new Central Division champion, the Cleveland Indians.

* * *

On January 30, 2008, the Minnesota Twins traded Johan Santana to the New York Mets for four players.[9] The Twins had committed to long-term deals with Justin Morneau ($80M over six years) and Michael Cuddyer ($24M for three years) days before the trade. The newest New York Met, with a year remaining on his lucrative contract, signed a jaw-dropping six-year extension for $137.5 million, turning him into baseball's highest paid pitcher.

After barely missing out on the post-season in 2007, the Mets were looking for that star player to lead them to October splendor. The high-priced pitcher did not disappoint expectations on Opening Day, March 31. He hurled seven innings, allowing three stingy hits and two runs, in the Mets' 7–2 win over the Florida Marlins, at Dolphin Stadium. Santana was tagged with his first loss as a Met in his next trip to the mound, as his hitters deserted him in a 3–1 loss to the Atlanta Braves. He was nicked for only one of the victors' runs in seven innings.

Santana's much-awaited initial home start came on April 12. In front of 54,701 embracing fans, Santana was not sharp. He was beaten by the Milwaukee Brewers, 5–3, allowing four earned runs in 6⅔ innings. Santana closed the month with a 3–2 record, all the wins coming on the road. The Mets said goodbye to April two games over .500 (14–12), but only one-half game out of first place.

Santana earned his first home win on May 10. He was stung for ten hits and three runs in six innings, but the Mets broke out the heavy lumber and paddled the Cincinnati Reds, 12–6. Over 55,000 fans were on hand at Shea Stadium to applaud what was hoped to be the first of many more home victories to come for Santana wearing the Mets' orange and blue. The game was the first of a day-night doubleheader; the Reds won the evening contest, 7–1, with 47,673 of the Mets' faithful in attendance. Santana won twice more in May to improve his record to 6–3.

On June 1, Santana won his seventh game, allowing one run to the Los Angeles Dodgers in 7⅔ innings. The six-hit, 6–1 victory occurred in front of another Shea Stadium crowd of over 50,000. It was Santana's 100th career victory, but turned out to be his only win of the month.[10]

As July began, luckily for the Mets, no team had established a vast superiority over the National League East Division. The 40–42 Mets were in third place, 3½ games behind the front-running Philadelphia Phillies. Santana managed just two wins in July, but as he had shown in the past, he turned it on over the season's latter months.[11]

In mid–August, the Mets won ten out of 11 games, with Santana victorious in three of them. Santana hurled a shutout on August 17 at PNC Park for his 12th win. Santana was reached for only three Pirates hits; he struck out seven and did not walk a batter in the 4–0 conquest. During the hot streak, the Mets took over first place.

The Mets opened September in first place, one game ahead of the Phillies. Santana did his best to keep the team from relinquishing the slim lead; he was unbeaten in September with a 4–0 record. (In his last nine Shea Stadium starts, Santana posted a 6–0 mark.) But the Phillies edged past the Mets and took over first place by one-half game following a Mets three-game winless streak in mid–September.

Pitching eight innings, Santana won his 15th game on September 23. The 6–2 home win over the Chicago Cubs moved the Mets to within a game and a half of first place. With one series remaining on the schedule, Santana came back on three days' rest and hurled his second shutout of the campaign, beating the third-place Florida Marlins, 2–0. The three-hit shutout was only the fifth of his career and came before a crowd of more than 54,000 Shea Stadium hopefuls. Alas for Mets fans, the Phillies, with a home triumph over Washington, clinched the Division title the same day.

Santana had done his best to pitch the Mets back into the playoffs, but in the end the club fell just short again, missing out on a wild card berth by one game to the Milwaukee Brewers. Santana could not be faulted. He led the National League in innings and ERA. It was the Santana's third ERA title. The 29-year-old tied his career high in starts with 34, and finished tied for second in strikeouts. His season totals included a 16–7 record, 234⅓ innings, 206 strikeouts, and a 2.53 ERA.

Santana finished third in the NL Cy Young Award balloting.

* * *

Unusually for Santana, the pitcher came out of the blocks quite quickly to open the 2009 season. Through four starts, his record was 3–1 with an minuscule ERA of 0.70. His only defeat had been to the Florida Marlins, 2–1, on April 12. Both runs charged to Santana were unearned, and Santana struck out 13 Marlins in seven innings.

The Mets inaugurated their new ballpark the next day. Santana's first start at home came five days afterward, on April 18. Santana was on top of his game in his Citi Field debut. Facing the Milwaukee Brewers, he tossed seven scoreless innings, yielding five hits and striking out seven. J. J. Putz and Francisco Rodríguez protected Santana's 1–0 lead to the end.

On May 6, the NL Pitcher of the Month for April defeated the Philadelphia Phillies, 1–0, at Citi Field. Santana (4–1) handcuffed the Phillies for seven innings, permitting two hits and striking out ten, before handing it off to a pair of win-preserving relievers.

Santana won four out of his next six starts. He was 8–3 heading into an opening assignment against the New York Yankees on June 14, but suffered the worst drubbing of his career to date. He was knocked around for nine hits and nine runs in three innings, in the rubber game of an interleague weekend series between the Yankees and Mets. With the 15–0 home win, the Bronx Bombers took the series, two games to one. Santana was not affected by the smarting; he returned with an superior outing six days later. As luck would have it, his mound opponent, James Shields of the Tampa Bay Rays, was slightly better. Shields and two relievers outpitched Santana and three of his bullpen men, 3–1. Santana was responsible for two runs.

After recording his ninth win, Santana suffered a pair of setbacks, one in tough luck fashion. On July 5, Joe Blanton and Phillies bettered the Mets ace, 2–0. Blanton, pitching into the eighth inning, required three pitchers to help conserve his victory. Santana left after seven, with both runs (solo homers) charged to his pitching ledger. The Mets fell three games below .500 (39–42) but only four games behind the first-place and defending World Champion Phillies.

Though selected for the fourth time, Santana did not appear in the 2009 All-Star Game.

Santana improved his record to 12–8 on July 30. At Citi Field, in the first game of a day-night doubleheader, Santana muffled the offense of the Colorado Rockies over seven innings. Holding a comfortable lead, Santana handed off things to the bullpen. Two innings later, Santana had a 7–0 victory. For Santana, it was the seventh time that season in which he had pitched six innings and allowed no earned runs (second most to Félix Hernández, who did it nine times in 2009). The Rockies rebounded to win the evening game, 4–2. The loss dropped the fourth-place New Yorkers 9½ games off the picked-up pace of the Phillies.

Unlike past seasons, Santana put together an erratic August. He was 1–1 with two ineffective no decisions. On August 25, the up-to-now very durable pitcher was placed on the disabled list with bone chips in his pitching elbow. With the Mets completely out of playoff contention, it was decided the 13–9 Santana would not throw another pitch for the rest of the season.

During the season, no base runner attempted to steal against Santana on a delivered pitch to the plate during any of his 25 starts.

* * *

Santana made his fifth Opening Day start and third with the Mets on April 5, 2010. He threw six innings, allowed one run, and took away a 7–1 win over Josh Johnson and the Florida Marlins. In his second Citi Field start six days later, he was not as proficient. A first-inning grand slam by Josh Willingham of the Washington Nationals doomed the pitcher to a 5–2 defeat. Santana was pulled after five innings, all of Washington's runs charged to his record.

On April 17, Santana tossed seven scoreless innings against the St. Louis Cardinals at Busch Stadium. Incredibly, the game would progress another 12 innings before the initial run of the clash was tallied and another inning after that for the game to be decided. In a nearly seven-hour-long contest, the Mets outlasted the Cardinals 2–1, in 20 innings. The Cardinals used two position players on the mound, including outfielder Joe Mather, who surrendered both Mets runs and suffered the loss.

Santana won two more Citi Field starts before the conclusion of the month. On April 22, he defeated the Chicago Cubs, 5–2 and permitted one run in six and one-third innings. It was one of 16 starts on the season in which Santana limited the opposition to one run or less (tied for most in the major leagues). Another came five days later. Santana was unscored upon for six innings, prior to retreating from an eventual 4–0 victory over the Los Angeles Dodgers.

On May 2, the Philadelphia Phillies pounded Santana for ten runs in under four innings. Six days later, Santana could not hold an eighth-inning, 4–2, home lead over the San Francisco Giants. The Mets bullpen could not rescue Santana, and the Giants scored twice to tie the game. But the Mets prevailed in 11 innings, 5–4. After 30 games, the 17-13 Mets trailed first-place Philadelphia by one game.

Following two no-decisions in which he gave up a combined two earned runs, Santana gained his fourth win on May 23 against the cross-town rival New York Yankees. The pitcher was touched for only one run and worked into the eighth inning of a 6–4 win. Two more starts and 15 consecutive scoreless innings yielded two more no-decisions for Santana and, worse for the Mets, two losses. Milwaukee's Yovani Gallardo shut out the Mets, 2–0, the winning runs scoring on a walk-off home run by outfielder Corey Hart. Santana threw eight innings of three-hit ball. Five days later, on June 2 at San Diego, the Padres' Adrián González clubbed a bottom-of-the–11th-inning grand slam to lift the Padres to a 5–1 victory.

Despite these tough losses, the Mets were centrally involved in the NL East race, trailing by only two games to the new first-place club in the division, the Atlanta Braves. Santana dropped his next decision to the same Padres, 4–2, at Citi Field. Thanks to solid offensive support, he bounced back to defeat the Cleveland Indians, 7–6, on June 15. However, on June 20, C. C. Sabathia enacted a measure of revenge for his earlier defeat to Santana on May 23. The Yankees left-hander downed Santana, 4–0, at Yankee Stadium. Santana dropped to 5–5 with another shutout defeat on June 26, this time to Carl Pavano and the Minnesota Twins. Santana allowed five of the Twins' six runs in the home loss.

At Citi Field on July 6, Santana recorded a memorable game not only on the mound, but with the bat as well. The grand left-hander blanked the Cincinnati Reds, 3–0, on three hits and five strikeouts. He also slugged his first major league home run, for the Mets' first run of the game. The blast came against Reds pitcher Matt Maloney. The win moved the Mets ten games over .500 (47–37), two games behind the front-running Braves.

Santana turned in a handful of superior pitching performances following the All-Star break. Very little about the Mets' play over the second half could be categorized as high quality, however. Santana tossed three complete games and another shutout. He blanked the Colorado Rockies, 4–0, on August 12, for his tenth win. In spite of this good stretch by their number one pitcher, the Mets steadily dropped off the pace set by the contending NL East teams. The team finished the season four games below .500, 18 games out of the running.

Following a start on September 2, Santana felt discomfort in his pitching arm. (He had undergone off-season surgery to remove bone fragments from his pitching elbow.) Less than two weeks later, Santana went under the knife to repair the anterior capsule of his left shoulder. The pitcher with the best ERA in the major leagues (2.89) and second-most strikeouts (1,479) since 2004 was devastatingly lost to the Mets and their fans for not only the rest of 2010, but for all of 2011.

* * *

Santana made a most encouraging return to the mound on April 5, 2012. In the Mets' home opener, and 19 months since his last mound appearance, the 33-year-old pitcher threw five scoreless innings against the Atlanta Braves. Scoring the only run of the inaugural match in the sixth inning, the Mets sent a crowd of 42,080 home contented.

Six days afterward, Santana paired up against the Washington Nationals' young strikeout sensation, Stephen Strasburg. Santana allowed one run in five innings and was charged with the loss in the 4–0 Nationals victory at Citi Field. In a rematch against the Braves at Turner Field on April 17, Santana was knocked out of the box in the second inning. Six runs, four earned, were scored by the Braves off Santana, en route to a 9–3 win. A week later, on April 24, Santana displayed a classic routine from his not too distant past, striking out 11 in 6⅔ innings of mound labor against the Miami Marlins. The left-hander allowed one run on three hits, and received a no-decision in the Mets' eventual 2–1 victory.

On May 5, Santana picked up his first win of the campaign and first since September 2, 2010, 20 months ago. The Arizona Diamondbacks fell 4–3 victims to Santana and two other Mets pitchers at Citi Field. Santana won only once more in the month, and it was a stifling effort over the San Diego Padres. Santana shut out the West Coast club, 9–0; he allowed four singles, struck out seven and did not walk a batter.

As exceptional as that endeavor was, it paled in comparison to the results of Santana's subsequent start, five days later, on June 1. At Citi Field, Santana completely suppressed all offense capabilities of the St Louis Cardinals, throwing a no-hit, no-run game and the first no-hitter in New York Mets franchise history. Santana walked five and struck out eight. The walks and strikeouts racked up the pitch count for Santana on the evening. He threw a career-high 134 pitches. The Venezuelan also became the first pitcher since Dave Righetti in 1983 to throw a shutout and a no-hitter in consecutive starts. The feel-good game for Santana and his teammates was assisted by an apparent missed umpire's call on a ball ruled foul, instead of fair, down the third base line, struck by the Cardinals' Carlos Beltrán.

As often happens, the outing following his masterpiece was not a good one. Santana was smacked around by the New York Yankees a week hence. Two starts later, on June 19, Santana seemed to be back in the groove, tossing six scoreless innings against the Baltimore Orioles. The bullpen wrapped up a 5–0 victory over the visiting American League squad. Santana closed his eventful month with a victory over the Los Angeles Dodgers on June 30. At Dodger Stadium, Santana threw eight scoreless frames while permitting three hits and two bases on balls; he improved his record to 6–4 as the Mets won, 5–0. The Mets, after three months of play, were in second place, 2½ games in back of the surprising first-place Washington Nationals.

Santana, a traditionally great pitcher over the season's second half, followed with multiple poor starts through the month of July. A sprained ankle landed him on the disabled list for 15 days during the underachieving month.

Things did not improve for him upon his return. He remained a hittable pitcher in August. Lower back problems placed him back on the disabled list a handful of days after another poor start on August 17. Inflammation in his lower back shelved the pitcher for the remainder of the season.

The Mets' fortunes turned with Santana's string of bad outings. Santana stumbled to a 6–9 record, his first losing mark since his 2–3 rookie season. At season's end, the Mets had sunk into fourth place, 24 games behind the upstart and division-conquering Washington Nationals.

In April 2013, Johan Santana underwent surgery on the same anterior capsule of his left shoulder that had been repaired in 2010. Santana had re-torn the shoulder tendons. Twelve strikeouts away from the grand total of 2,000, Santana saw his 2013 season wiped out and his career left in serious doubt.

Félix Hernández

Unlike many anointed phenoms, Félix Hernández has more than lived up to the buzz and hype surrounding him when he broke into the major leagues in 2005 at age 19. Over multiple seasons since his big league arrival with the Seattle Mariners, Hernández has continued to reap his share of deserved accolades, as he established himself as one of the American League's best pitchers.

His debut on August 4, 2005, against the Detroit Tigers, stamped Félix Abraham Hernández as the youngest pitcher to start his first major league game since 1978 (Britt Burns). In the five-inning, big league testing on the road, Hernández allowed three hits, two runs (one earned), struck out four, walked two, and was hung with a 3–1 loss. Five days later

Santana pitched the first no-hitter in New York Mets franchise history. His injury-plagued tenure with the team caused him to greatly underperform the contract of abundant riches the club laid at his feet.

at Safeco Field, *Baseball America's* top-rated major league pitching prospect tossed eight scoreless innings, striking out six and walking none. He defeated the Minnesota Twins, 1–0. Hernández started ten more games the rest of the season. He concluded his eight-week, top-level indoctrination with a 4–4 record and eye-catching 2.67 ERA. He held major league hitters to a .203 batting average in 84⅓ innings.

After Hernández proved he could hold his own against major league hitters, Seattle obligingly gave him the opportunity to make the big club in 2006. The youngster earned a spot with the team, overcoming shin splints that put him out of commission for a couple of weeks toward the end of spring training. As the team's fifth starter, Hernández posted a 12–14 record in 31 starts, missing by nine the 200 innings pitched plateau. His ERA was 4.52, the highest of his nine-year career through 2013.

The 20-year-old Hernández tossed his first major league shutout on August 28 against the Anaheim Angels. He permitted five hits and struck out four. The 2–0 Safeco Field win was conducted in one hour and 51 minutes.

The following season, 2007, after two last-place finishes in the American League West, the Seattle Mariners improved to second place. Hernández, with a 14–7 record, stood out along with fellow starter and 16-game winner, Miguel Batista. The 88–74 Mariners placed six games behind the division-capturing Angels of Anaheim.

Hernández started the season opener for the Mariners on April 2 at Safeco Field. In front of a crowd of 46,003, he pitched eight shutout innings and struck out 12 in the 4–0 Mariners win. On April 11, three days after his 21st birthday, Hernández pitched a marvelous, one-hit shutout over a strong Boston Red Sox club at Fenway Park. The only hit in the 3–0 victory was a leadoff, eighth-inning single by Red Sox outfielder J. D. Drew.

Those two starts notwithstanding, Hernández struggled during the first half of the 2007 season. He was placed on the disabled list with a strained elbow early in the season. On July 22, after an 8–0 defeat at Toronto, his record stood at 6–6. Hernández recorded an 8–1 record over his final 13 outings. In 30 total starts, he maintained his ERA below 4.00 (3.92) in 190⅓ innings.

Although certainly monitoring their pitching prodigy's progress, the Seattle Mariners never tried to curtail or cap Hernández's innings per season or pitches per game during his initial campaigns. Apart from his extraordinary right arm, Hernández was blessed with a 6′3″ 230-pound physique that projected an outward capability to meet the challenges of his new, increased major league workload.

Hernández had vaulted through the Mariners' minor league system starting in 2003, a year after the Mariners signed the 16-year-old to a contract featuring a $710,000 signing bonus. Born in Valencia, Venezuela, Hernández was discovered by Venezuelan-based, Mariners scout, Pedro Ávila.

As a 17-year-old in Class A, Hernández posted a 7–2 record and followed that up with 14 wins and only 4 defeats in Double-A in 2004. His record was 9–4 at Triple-A Tacoma, with 100 strikeouts in 88 innings, when the Mariners decided to bring him up to the Show in August of 2005.

The teenage Hernández was an extremely confident young pitcher, with a 97 mile per hour fastball that helped back up any of the traceable swagger. During his call-up trial, Hernández was given the uniform number 59. In 2006, he switched to 34, a number he has worn since and the number worn by his favorite pitcher as a Seattle Mariner—Freddy García.

(One of the reasons Hernández signed with Seattle was because it was the team of Garcia, his Venezuelan schoolboy idol.)

* * *

In 2008, the Mariners regressed, and that regression affected Hernández. The power pitcher reached the 200-inning mark for the first time, nudging past it by ⅔ of an inning. He produced a 9–11 record and 3.45 ERA in 31 starts. The Mariners, who entered the season with high expectations following a big off-season trade to land pitcher Erik Bedard, lost 101 games. The team dropped like a rock in the standings from an early 11–11 record to a final 61–101 mark.

Against the Florida Marlins on June 17 at Safeco Field, Hernández struck out the side on nine pitches. The three-pitch Marlins victims were Jeremy Heredia, Jorge Cantú and Mike Jacobs. Hernández won his sixth game of the season, 5–4, with relief help.

Six days later, during interleague play, the infrequent hitter recorded his second major league hit and first home run. At Shea Stadium, Hernández, a right-handed batter, smashed an opposite field home run against the Mets' Johan Santana. Adding to the thrill, the bases were loaded. The Mariners won, 5–2, but Hernández did not figure in the decision. He injured his foot and had to leave the game before completing five innings.

Hernández won only three more games, while losing six, the rest of the season.

* * *

Passed over in favor of Bedard by manager John McLaren to open the 2008 season, Hernández was reinstated to the number one slot on the staff by new manager Don Wakamatsu in 2009. The pitcher responded and started the Mariners off on the right foot with a 6–1, Opening Day win over the Minnesota Twins at the Metrodome.

Hernández led a marvelous 24-win improvement from 2008 for third-place Seattle with an outstanding 19-win season. Hernández was defeated only five times in 34 starts. He pitched 238⅔ innings, recorded two complete games and one shutout, and had a distinguished 2.49 ERA. Hernández reached the 200-strikeout plateau for the first time, ending up with 217.

The lone shutout came at San Diego, a 5–0 two-hitter on June 16. The young pitcher struck out six Padres and walked four.

Hernández was 9–3 at the mid-season break and earned his first All-Star Game selection. He pitched one inning in the Mid-Summer Classic and retired all three batters he was pitted against, doing his part in the American League's 4–3 win at Busch Stadium.

Two more wins immediately following the All-Star Game raised his record to 11–3. He won his 12th game on August 1, a 7–2 decision over the Texas Rangers; Hernández pitched seven innings and allowed two runs. From that point, Hernández endured several weeks without claiming a win. He dropped to 12–5, following a 6–1 defeat to the Cleveland Indians on August 23. Half the runs Hernández coughed up were unearned.

He rebounded and won his final seven decisions, including his campaign's other complete game. It came against the New York Yankees on September 18 at Safeco Field. The Mariners' Ichiro Suzuki smacked a two-out, two-run, bottom-of-the-ninth-inning home run off Mariano Rivera to turn Hernández from an apparent 2–1, dejected loser into a 3–2, elated victor. Rivera had compiled a stretch of 36 consecutive saves before the Ichiro blast.

Validating all the early appraisals from the so-called "experts," Hernández continued his strong pitching over the second half. Team saves leader Dave Aardsma preserved four of eight combined August and September wins. The last came on the final day of the season, October 4. Hernández won his 19th game, defeating the Texas Rangers, 4–3. He allowed three hits and two earned runs in 6⅔ innings. Aardsma pocketed his 38th save with a perfect ninth inning.

In nine of his starts, Hernández pitched a major league-topping six innings or more with no earned runs permitted.

* * *

In 2010, Hernández, who was being referred to as "King Félix" in the press, reigned majestically from the hill. Opening the campaign for the Mariners on April 5, Hernández did not have his best stuff; he walked six and allowed three runs in 6⅔ innings to the home team Oakland Athletics. He left a tied game that the Mariners won two innings later, 5–3. Hernández also received a no-decision in his next start. The winning Mariners (4–3) scored too late to benefit their starter, who departed after seven innings after allowing two earned runs.

In his first home start, on April 16, Hernández gained his first win, with 6⅔ innings of work against the Detroit Tigers. The Mariners were victorious, 11–3. The runs output by the Mariners was not reflective of the support the club provided for Hernández during the campaign. Nor was the win indicative of any sustained victory trends the last-place Mariners were destined to establish that season.

The inferior team scored three runs or fewer in 18 of Hernández's career-high matching 34 starts. He threw eight innings or more, allowing one or no runs, in 13 starts. Over a span of seven successive starts by Hernández in mid-summer, the Mariners' bats steered home a grand total of eight runs for their beleaguered pitcher. Hernández compiled a 2–5 record despite a 1.93 ERA in those seven starts. Hernández's best game of the season came prior to that difficult stretch, on June 30. He authored his sole shutout, blanking the New York Yankees, 7–0, at new Yankee Stadium. Hernández allowed two hits, struck out 11 and walked three. It was the pending hard-luck pitcher's sixth win to go along with five setbacks.

At Fenway Park on August 25, Hernández became the fourth youngest pitcher to reach 1,000 career strikeouts. In the sixth inning of the second game of a day-night doubleheader, Hernández victimized Red Sox DH David Ortiz for the milestone whiff. Following the 4–2 Mariners triumph, Hernández, who required 1⅔ innings of relief help from Brandon League to nail down the win, identified his original strikeout victim while talking about the game conditions and how he struggled, at times, throughout the effort. "I remember my first strikeout, Ivan Rodríguez," Hernández said. "Tonight, the mound was wet and slippery. I couldn't push off like I usually do. I fell behind in the count. I had to work really hard."[12]

The 61–101 Mariners scored 104 runs for their ace pitcher all season, explaining to a great extent his 13–12 record. Hernández led the American League in starts (tied with two others) and innings with 249⅔. He topped the circuit with a stupendous 2.27 ERA. He threw six complete games, one fewer than his lifetime total entering the season. He produced the best pitching WAR in the league (7.1) and allowed the fewest hits per inning (6.993). Hernández did not place in the top ten in wins, but the baseball writers, recognizing his plight and offering the most validation to date of newer, 21st-century statistical player evaluations, voted the 24-year-old pitcher the American League Cy Young Award.

* * *

Hernández began the 2011 campaign as if he were planning to take all pitching matters into his own hands. He tossed a five-hit, walk-free, 6–2, complete game victory over the Oakland A's, at the Oakland-Alameda County Coliseum. However, Hernández infrequently captured that type of top-notch performance over the remainder of the long season.

Although still the Mariners' best pitcher, Hernández was not the dominant entity on the rubber as he was the prior season. He won 14 games and lost as many, with a 3.47 ERA. Thirty-three starts delivered 233⅔ innings and helped him accumulate 222 strikeouts, his third straight season of 200 or more whiffs. Hernández was selected to his second All-Star team (but did not pitch), as the Mariners remained mired in last place in their division for a second consecutive campaign.

In 2012, nothing changed for the Mariners as far as their positioning in the American League West. Hernández, though, was consistently brilliant throughout the year: 33 starts, 232 innings, 223 strikeouts and a 3.06 ERA. He became the first Mariners pitcher to string together four seasons of 200 innings and 200 strikeouts. In 17 of his starts, he allowed one run or none. In four of them, he threw eight or more innings and received a no-decision, tying a major league record dating back to 1918.

The first of those eight-inning frustrations came on Opening Day, 4,770 miles from Hernández's home base of Seattle. The Mariners and Oakland Athletics faced one another to open the season again, this time in Tokyo, Japan, on March 28. The early-season opener parceled itself into Major League Baseball's adopted strategy of "internationalizing" the game in the 21st century. In the first of a two-game series at Tokyo Dome, Hernández produced a stalwart effort for the 44,227 enthusiastic Japanese fans on hand. He was reached for only one run on five hits. He struck out six and displayed impeccable control by not walking a single batter. The A's were victorious in 11 innings, 3–1.

On the season, the 2010 Cy Young Award winner diversified his talents, showcasing a league-leading five shutouts, one whitewash more than he owned coming into the season. He joined only three other American League starters in tossing as many as five shutouts in one season since 1989.

The Seattle pitcher was virtually unhittable during a 14 start-stretch from June 17 to August 27, in which he posted a 9–0 record and 1.40 ERA. He was the runaway pitcher of the month in August with a 4–0 mark, 1.08 ERA and three shutouts—all by a *1–0* count.

His first shutout did not occur until June 28, and it was a hard-fought effort. Facing the Boston Red Sox, Hernández was involved in a scoreless contest until the Mariners finally scored the lone run of the game in the bottom of the ninth inning, rewarding their pitcher and a crowd of 20,692. Hernández was touched for five hits; he struck out 13 and walked only one, to bump his record over .500 at 6–5.

After two no-decisions, in his first start after the All-Star Game, Hernández tossed his second shutout on July 14. The Mariners backed their prized hurler with four runs in the first inning. Hernández cruised to a 7–0 win over the Texas Rangers and their golden talent from the Orient, Yu Darvish. Facing the two-time-defending American League champions, Hernández allowed three hits and no walks, and fanned 13.

In his second 1–0 shutout, he vanquished the Yankees at Yankee Stadium on August 4. Hernández permitted two hits and two bases on balls, and struck out six. The two-hitter was the first 1–0 victory by a visiting pitcher over the Yankees in their home ballpark since 1988. The marvelous effort improved Hernández's record to 4–1 with a 1.13 ERA in five career starts at the Yankees' new $1.5 billion home.

Two starts later, on August 15, Hernández was totally infallible while registering 27 outs against the visiting Tampa Bay Rays. Hernández threw the 23rd perfect game in major league history, the seventh by a 1–0 score and the *third* perfect game pitched in 2012!

A section of Safeco Field had been appropriated by ardent Hernández followers, wearing easily identifiable yellow "King Felix" T-shirts, for some time. The fans in that area would hold up "K cards" in unison every time the Venezuelan struck out an opposing batter. On this historic Wednesday afternoon, the "King's Court" was especially engaged, acknowledging 12 outs recorded by their ruler via the punch-out. Gaining strength as the game progressed, Hernández fanned eight batters after the fifth inning. He struck out the side in the sixth and eighth frames. (The monumental game was his third shutout with 12 or more strikeouts, the first pitcher to accomplish this feat in one season since Pedro Martínez in 2000.)

The only ball hit into play that resembled a safe hit came during the very first at-bat of the contest. Rays leadoff hitter Sam Fuld smoked a ball into the gap that Mariners rightfielder Eric Thames ran down in right-center, his momentum carrying him into the outfield wall. Following that, Hernández exhibited an overwhelming dominance over the next 26 hitters he faced. He displayed faultless command of the wide assortment of pitches he had developed since coming into the league. His "12-to-6" curveballs, filthy sliders, nasty change-ups, fastballs and split finger fastballs were swung at and missed a combined 26 times, an extremely high number of missed pitches in any game. Of the 113 pitches he delivered, 77 were strikes—the final three of which were to the last batter of the game. Hernández fell behind, 2–0, to ninth-place hitter Sean Rodríguez, then wheedled from him a swinging strike before freezing him on two consecutive change-ups.

In an on-field interview shortly after the final out, Hernández recognized the 21, 889 fans in attendance. "I don't have any words to explain this," he said. "I've been working so hard to throw one and today is for you guys."[13] Impressively, Hernández became the fifth Venezuelan pitcher to throw a major league no-hitter.[14]

At Target Field on August 27, Hernández tossed his fourth 1–0 shutout of the season. He improved to 13–5 with the five-hit suppression of the hometown Minnesota Twins. He struck out five in copping his final win of the campaign.

The pitcher struggled in four of his six remaining starts to the close the season at 13–9. But saddled with the second-poorest run support in the league (3.65), resulting in 11 no-decisions, the record could easily have been much better.

*   *   *

Opening the season against Oakland for the fourth consecutive year, Hernández made his sixth career Opening Day start in 2013. He pitched into the eighth inning without allowing a run and giving up only three hits. The April 1, 2–0 road triumph was already his fourth season-initiating victory and 99th of his career.

Four more attempts were required before Hernández gained his 100th career victory.

The youthful Houston Astros were the historic casualties on April 22. At Minute Maid Park, Hernández tossed six shutout innings and was backed by three home runs, in coming away with the 7–1 win. Hernández surrender five hits and one walk, struck out nine and trimmed his early-season ERA to 2.08. As a precaution, he was removed after six innings with tightness in his back.

Hernández became the third Mariners pitcher (after Randy Johnson and Jamie Moyer) with as many franchise victories. The hefty run support broke an early trend of sparse scoring by the Mariners behind the 27-year-old hurler (seven runs in the three previous starts). "Finally. Finally," Hernández expressed to reporters after the game. "It took too long. But it felt great. One hundred wins in the big leagues, Hopefully I can get more and more."[15]

Hernández then defeated the Angels, the Blue Jays and the Pirates, pitching eight innings against each and not allowing more than one earned run per start.

At Yankee Stadium on May 14, Hernández pitched six innings and left the game as the pitcher of record on the winning side. But the Mariners bullpen could not hold the 3–1 lead Hernández had provided. Hernández had been involved in a collision with a baserunner earlier and, as a safeguard with 97 pitches thrown, manager Eric Wedge pulled his star pitcher. The Yankees rallied with a three-run seventh and won, 4–3.

Hernández dropped to 5–3 and Seattle fell to 20–24 with a road loss to Cleveland on May 19. All of the Indians' runs were charged to Hernández (five earned) in five innings, as three Indians pitchers held the Mariners offense to four singles. Six days later, on May 25, Hernández had his strikeout pitch working but not much else, as the last-place Mariners tumbled to their eight consecutive defeat, 5–2, in front of their largest crowd since their home opener (35,024). The Texas Rangers spoiled "Félix Hernández Bobble Head Night" at Safeco Field, pelting Hernández for 11 hits and all the runs in less than six innings. Hernández struck out nine, as his ERA jumped from a league-best 1.53 to 2.51 in the span of two starts.

Hernández sailed to 7–1 triumph over the San Diego Padres on May 30. The pitcher hurled eight innings; only six Padres batters reached base against the pitcher, three on hits and the same number on walks. The Mariners slugged five home runs at usually hitter-unfriendly Petco Park.

Backed by early run support in his next start, Hernández defeated the Chicago White Sox, 7–4, at Safeco Field. All the White Sox runs were charged to Hernández, who was removed from the game with one out in the eighth inning.

On June 9, at Safeco Field, Hernández battled against the New York Yankees and poor run support again. Hernández was clipped for one run over seven innings before departing with the score tied at 1–1. The Yankees scored a run in the ninth and Mariano Rivera recorded a shaky save, his 23rd, for the 2–1 New York victory. The low-scoring game marked the 91st time in 252 career starts that Hernández has received one or fewer runs of support.

Six days later, Hernández threw seven shutout innings in defeating Oakland, 4–0, on the road. Hernández was solved for only five hits; he struck out eight and lowered his ERA to 2.32. The key hit was a grand slam by newly signed veteran catcher Henry Blanco.

Facing one of the few teams against whom he has not had good success, Hernández took the mound against the Angels of Anaheim on June 20. But on a night when Hernández was given a fine opportunity to improve his lifetime 7–12 record against the Halos, the right-hander delivered a subpar pitching effort. For the first time in his career, the Seattle pitcher surrendered more than six hits in one inning. He was reached for 12 hits in five innings, while allowing seven runs (six earned). The Mariners' offense responded with a run total sufficiently high enough to spare their ace a loss, but not enough to prevent their squad from falling to the home team, 10–9.

Hernández was back in form six days later, allowing two runs in seven innings while striking out 11. His mates could not provide more than two runs of offensive support so he had to settle for a no decision. The Mariners, who left ten men on base, lost to the red-hot Pittsburgh Pirates, 4–2. Hernández nearly mirrored the performance on July 3, versus the Texas Rangers. He threw seven innings of two-run baseball, struck out seven, but had no record improvement as the Mariners scored twice in the ninth to pull out a 4–2 road win.

The Mariners provided Hernández with the team's second highest runs output on the season on July 8. At Safeco Field, the Mariners defeated the Boston Red Sox, 11–4. Hernández retired after seven innings with a 10–2 lead. Taking the hill again, prior to the All-Star break, on July 13, Hernández tossed eight scoreless innings against the Anaheim Angels at Safeco Field. In obtaining the 6–0 win—his tenth—Hernández lowered his league-leading ERA to 2.53.

On July 16, the 10–4 Hernández was one of ten American League pitchers manager Jim Leyland used to combine to shut out the National League, 3–0, at Citi Field.

Over the second half of the season, however, Hernández disappointingly managed only two more wins. He logged a 2–6 record over the final ten weeks of the campaign.

The Mariners' hitters disappointed Hernández with their scoring output on July 26 against the Minnesota Twins. One start after the Mariners had backed their ace with an unusual 12-run scoring spree versus the Houston Astros (July 21), to deliver Hernández's 11th win, the team's bats regressed to one run of support over nine innings for their star pitcher. At Safeco Field, Hernández allowed one run in nine innings but did not figure in the final outcome of the game, a 3–2 Minnesota victory in 13 innings.

On August 1, the Mariners' bullpen let Hernández down in a big way when they could not hold on to a 7–1 lead over the final two innings at Boston. The Red Sox rallied with six ninth-inning runs to pull out an electrifying 8–7 victory.

Hernández suffered through a rough August. He won only one game and was knocked around in several starts, including one on August 28, in which he yielded a career-worse eight runs to the Texas Rangers in three innings of work. In the home loss, Hernández dropped to 12–20, with a 4.20 ERA, in 39 lifetime starts versus Texas.

Feeling tightness in his lower back, Hernández was removed in the seventh inning of his next outing against the Kansas City Royals on September 2. Trailing 3–1, he was pinned with the road loss. In a throwing session between starts, Hernández was diagnosed with a strained oblique muscle and was sidelined until September 22. He returned from the nearly three-week layoff with his strikeout pitches working to their fullest. In a curtailed outing against the Anaheim Angels, the right-hander whiffed ten Angels batters. He also walked four and was pulled after only four innings (allowing one run) with 92 pitches thrown.

Following that no-decision, Hernández made his final start of the season on September 27. Early ineffectiveness led to a first-inning, three-run home run by the Oakland A's Brandon Moss and the pitcher's downfall. Pitching at Safeco Field, Hernández settled down to pitch six innings without allowing any more runs, but the Mariners were not able to produce more than two runs during the span; the game concluded 8–2, in Oakland's favor.

A reaction shot of the Mariners' Félix Hernández, following the last out of his perfect game, is superimposed on the section of Safeco Field where fans cheer his strikeout efforts by displaying yellow and black "K" placards. The photograph was distributed on the press conference date when Hernández signed his extraordinary $175 million contract.

The off-kilter second half performances cost Hernández not only chance at capturing his second American League ERA title, but also snapped a string of six seasons in a row as Mariners' ERA leader. That honor went Hisashi Iwakuma (14–6, 2.66 ERA), who also displaced Hernández as the team's best pitcher.

Hernández's final numbers were 12–10, a 3.04 ERA and 216 strikeouts. Hernández became the third pitcher in history to record eight seasons of 150 or more strikeouts by his age 27 season. He joined the illustrious company of Bert Blyleven and Walter Johnson. The pitcher succeeded in pitching 200 innings for the sixth straight year. He matched Detroit's Justin Verlander as the only active pitchers with five consecutive seasons of 200 or more innings and 200 or more strikeouts.

Prior to the 2013 season, the husband to Sandra, and father of two young children (daughter Mia and son Jeremy) had signed a seven-year contract for $175 million dollars that made him, for a short time, the highest paid pitcher in baseball history.

The contract signaled an obvious commitment on the part of the Seattle Mariners franchise to try and improve their ball club, with their most talented and popular player as a centerpiece to their strategy. The 71–91 team finished in fourth place in the AL West Division in 2013.

THE BEST HISPANIC MAJOR LEAGUE PITCHERS

In this personal all-time ranking list, based solely on major league performance, I have included three "non-native" pitchers. Though he was not fundamentally tied to any Latin American culture through language or custom, I felt I should list Lefty Gómez. The Yankees great may not have openly embraced his heritage, but he did not shun it, either. In the 1940s, Gómez managed in the winter leagues of Venezuela and Cuba. With a last name like Gómez, and his descendancy from the mother country of all Spanish-speaking lands, how could he not warrant inclusion?

Also listed is Mike García. As a Mexican descendant raised in California, García spoke Spanish and seamlessly bridged the Anglo-American world as so many U.S.-residing Hispanics do today. (Bobby Ávila credited García with helping him overcome the daunting language barrier and easing his overall transition into the big leagues with the Cleveland Indians.) Mike García was a nose-to-the-grindstone pitcher for the Cleveland Indians during the 1950s. Over a seven-year stretch, he appeared in 287 games as a starter and reliever, an average of 41 appearances per season. García's career was delayed by the Second World War and cut short by a back injury. His major league numbers speak for themselves.

Brooklyn-born John Candelaria was a 20-game winner in 1977 with the Pittsburgh Pirates and led the league with a 2.34 ERA that same year. The Puerto Rican descendant posted especially fine career victory, ERA+ and WHIP totals.

I could not comparatively rank reliever Mariano Rivera. I have listed Rubén Gómez non-numerically simply to provide his major league statistics.

About the evaluation process. I weighed individually all of the accompanying established pitching categories, including a pair of new age ones. Wins mattered to me—a lot. So did ERA, complete games, shutouts and innings pitched, which I view as staple measures encompassing the true art of starting pitching. Younger fans may find this to be outdated thinking or reasoning, and in today's baseball, it may very well be. But I will not apologize for being a product of my generation, for lauding men who finished what they started, on a regular or semi-regular basis. Who accepted, without complaint, much heavier workloads, at pennies on the dollar, in comparison to today's coddled and highly compensated hurlers. Men who took the mound with the mindset that abundant reliance on other pitchers would be the exception and not the rule. Men who were prepared to battle with the opposing starter deep into a close game, and sometimes even extra innings.

In the days before the extinction of the term: "pitchers' duel."

Appendix

Rankings for the All-Time Great Hispanic Pitchers

Rankings Based on Major League Records

	G	GS	CG	SHO	SV	INN	HR	BB	SO	W	L	ERA	PCT	ERA+	WHIP	20*
1. Juan Marichal (HOF) *Dominican Republic*	471	457	**244**	**52**	2	3,507	320	709	2,303	243	142	**2.89**	.631	123	1.101	**6**
2. Pedro Martínez *Dominican Republic*	476	409	46	17	3	2,827.1	239	760	**3,154**	219	100	2.93	**.687**	**154**	**1.054**	2
3. Luis Tiant *Cuba*	573	484	187	49	15	3,486.1	346	1,104	2,416	229	172	3.30	.571	114	1.199	4
4. Lefty Gómez (HOF) *United States*	368	320	173	28	9	2,503	138	1,095	1,468	189	102	3.34	.649	125	1.352	4
5. Mike Cuéllar *Cuba*	453	379	172	36	11	2,808	222	822	1,632	185	130	3.14	.587	109	1.197	4
6. Adolfo Luque *Cuba*	550	366**	206	26	28	3,220.1	113	918	1,130	194	179	3.24	.520	118	1.288	1
7. Dennis Martínez *Nicaragua*	**692**	**562**	122	30	8	**3,999.2**	**372**	**1,165**	2,149	**245**	**193**	3.70	.559	106	1.266	0
8. Johan Santana + *Venezuela*	360	284	15	10	1	2,025.2	220	567	1,988	139	78	3.20	.641	136	1.132	1
9. Félix Hernández + *Venezuela*	303	303	23	9	0	2060.2	161	572	1,951	125	92	3.07	.576	130	1.170	0
10. Mike García *United States*	428	281	111	27	23	2,174.2	122	719	1,117	142	97	3.27	.594	117	1.318	2
11. Camilo Pascual *Cuba*	529	404	132	36	10	2,930.2	256	1,069	2,167	174	170	3.63	.506	103	1.287	2
12. Fernando Valenzuela *México*	453	424	113	31	2	2,930	226	1,151	2,074	173	153	3.54	.531	104	1.320	1
13. Bartolo Colón + *Dominican Republic*	442	436	35	12	0	2,786	330	832	2,101	204	141	395	.591	111	1.308	2

#	Player / Country																
14.	John Candelaria *United States*	600	356	54	13	**29**	2,525.2	245	592	1,673	177	122	3.33	.592	114	1.184	1
15.	Joaquín Andújar *Dominican Republic*	405	305	68	19	9	2,153	155	731	1,032	127	118	3.58	.518	99	1.276	2
16.	Ramón Martínez *Dominican Republic*	301	297	37	20	0	1,895.2	170	795	1,427	135	88	3.67	.605	105	1.311	1
17.	Juan Pizarro *Puerto Rico*	488	245	79	17	28	2,034.1	201	888	1,522	131	105	3.43	.555	104	1.325	0
18.	José Rijo *Dominican Republic*	376	269	22	4	3	1,880	147	663	1,606	116	91	3.24	.560	121	1.262	0
19.	Javier Vázquez *Puerto Rico*	450	443	28	8	0	2,840	373	763	2,536	165	160	4.22	.508	105	1.249	0
20.	Mario Soto *Dominican Republic*	297	224	72	13	4	1,730.1	172	657	1,449	100	92	3.47	.521	108	1.186	0
21.	Ed Figueroa *Puerto Rico*	200	179	63	12	1	1,309.2	90	443	571	80	67	3.51	.544	105	1.330	1
22.	Orlando Hernández *Cuba*	219	211	9	2	2	1,314.2	177	479	1,086	90	65	4.13	.581	110	1.263	0
23.	Liván Hernández *Cuba*	519	474	50	9	1	3,189	362	1,066	1,976	178	177	4.44	.501	95	1.440	0

*20-win seasons

**Author's discrepancy with official records, which lists 367.

+ Active player

HOF= Hall of Fame members.

Category leaders in bold.

Lifetime player statistics from retrosheet.org and baseball-reference.com.

WHIP and ERA+ are from baseball-reference.com.

The Top Hispanic Major, Minor, Negro and International League Hurlers

This classification is augmented by three Hispanic pitchers not shown on the preceding list and one that was shown but not ranked, Rubén Gómez. Two never received an opportunity to pitch in the major leagues: Ramón Bragaña and Martín Dihigo. Their combined International and Negro league win totals, as delineated in this writing, rightfully earned their placements here. The other two, Ramón Arano and Rubén Gómez, racked up such indelible pitching marks from the mounds of their home countries' baseball leagues, as to catapult them to the ranks of all-time ethnic greats.

Unlike the prior list, because some Minor, International and Negro league records remain incomplete, attempting to incorporate any such available data with Major League statistics, for player comparative purposes, would not have been viable.

Rankings Based on Major, Minor, International and Negro League Records

1. Juan Marichal (HOF)
   Dominican Republic
2. Pedro Martínez
   Dominican Republic
3. Adolfo Luque
   Cuba
4. Luis Tiant
   Cuba
5. Mike Cuéllar
   Cuba
6. Dennis Martínez
   Nicaragua
7. Juan Pizarro
   Puerto Rico
8. Camilo Pascual
   Cuba
9. Lefty Gómez (HOF)
   United States
10. Johan Santana +
    Venezuela
11. Félix Hernández +
    Venezuela
12. Fernando Valenzuela
    México
13. Mike García
    United States
14. Bartolo Colón +
    Dominican Republic
15. John Candelaria
    United States
16. Rubén Gómez
    Puerto Rico
17. Ramón Arano
    México
18. Orlando Hernández
    Cuba
19. Martín Dihigo (HOF)
    Cuba
20. Joaquín Andújar
    Dominican Republic
21. Ramón Martínez
    Dominican Republic
22. Ramón Bragaña
    Cuba
23. José Rijo
    Dominican Republic
24. Ed Figueroa
    Puerto Rico
25. Javier Vázquez
    Puerto Rico
26. Mario Soto
    Dominican Republic
27. Liván Hernández
    Cuba

Honorable mention to Negro League Hall of Famer José Méndez
+ Still Active
HOF= Hall of Fame members.

Chapter Notes

Chapter 1

1. Roberto González Echevarria, *The Pride of Havana A History of Cuban Baseball* (New York: Oxford Press, 1999), 258.

2. Alfredo L. Santana Alonso, *El Inmortal del Béisbol Martín Dihigo.* (Editorial Científico-Técnica, Ciudad de la Habana, Cuba, 2006), 20. Dihigo is quoted as using the word "gringos." Although not specified, it is assumed he meant white gringos or North Americans. It should also be noted the book's biographer is a Havana-based historian. A later passage in his book depicts Dihigo as having openly spoken out against dictators of the period, such as "Trujillo, Batista, Pérez Jiménez and company." The author conveniently makes only one mention of Fidel Castro in his work and refers to him as Commander-in-Chief of the Cuban Revolution.

3. Larry Lester, *Black Baseball's National Showcase: The East-West All-Star Game 1933–1953* (Lincoln: University of Nebraska, 2001), 72.

4. Monte Irvin, with James A. Riley. *Nice Guys Finish First* (New York: Carroll & Graf, 1996), 93.

5. Gerald F. Vaughn, "George Hausmann Recalls The Mexican League of 1946," The Baseball Research Journal 19, 1990, 59–63.

6. Santana Alonso, 24.

7. Roberto González Echevarria, *The Pride of Havana A History of Cuban Baseball* (New York: Oxford Press, 1999), 181.

8. Bob Broeg, "Lloyd, Dihigo Had Talent to Burn." *The Sporting News*, March 19, 1977.

9. Tracey Eaton, "Cuban Baseball Great Pushed for Blacks' Rights." *The Dallas Morning News*, September 4, 1999.

10. Santana Alonso, Alfredo L., *El Inmortal del Béisbol Martín Dihigo. Editorial Científico-Técnica, Ciudad de la Habana*, Cuba. 2006. First Edition, 1996, 109.

11. Gilberto Dihigo's blog is called *Palenque de Dihigo*. It is written is Spanish and can be found at dihigo. blogspot.com. He mentions the year of his father's birth as 1906, not 1905, as several other sources state.

Chapter 2

1. Russell Schneider, "Tribe Given Red Rug Welcome in Mexico." *The Sporting News*, March 25, 1967.

Cleveland made the trip minus pitchers Sam McDowell and Gary Bell, and Rocky Colavito, who was in a contract dispute with Gabe Paul. The Cleveland GM wanted to cut Colavito's salary by 25 percent following an off year by the popular outfielder. McDowell and Bell were said to have remained at the Indians' Tuscon, Arizona, training camp to get into better shape. Vic Davalillo, nursing a sore knee, and Joe Azcue were the other frontliners who did not make the trip. (The Cuban Azcue could not obtain the necessary papers to enter Mexico.)

2. Television interview with Megadeportes, Veracruz. Youtube.com. April, 2010

3. "Puerto Rican Fans Acclaim Ruben Gomez on His Return." *The Sporting News*, October 20, 1954.

4. Phone interview with José Santiago, May 21, 2013.

5. Thomas Boswell, "A Baseball Paradise Flourishes in San Juan." *The Washington Post,* January 20, 1977.

6. Phone interview with José Santiago, May 21, 2013.

7. Steve Fainaru and Ray Sanchez, *The Duke of Havana: Baseball, Cuba and the Search for the American Dream* (New York: Villard Books 2001). This was Hernández's reply to the official, as relayed in the book: "I told him, 'I'm going to play baseball again before I die, even if I have to play in Haiti.' "His response was the same response they always gave you: an ironic little laugh and the face of victory. The look of having defeated the enemy. But you cannot claim victory while the enemy is still standing."

8. During a 1996 trip to Cuba, Hernández Nodar unfortunately was swept up during the Cuban government's harshest crackdown period on ballplayers' defections and was arrested for encouraging "illegal departure." He was unjustly convicted and sentenced to 15 years of incarceration. He spent nearly 13 years in a Cuban prison before he gained his release in 2009.

9. The three U.S. Senators were Florida's Bob Graham and Connie Mack, grandson of the Philadelphia A's Hall of Fame owner and manager, and New Jersey's Robert Torricelli. On the state congressional side from Florida were Ileana Ros-Lehtinen and Lincoln Diaz-Balart, and also from New Jersey, Bob Menendez.

10. El Duque's loyalty to his friends was well rewarded. Had he accepted the original U.S. entry, he

would have had to wait a full year to obtain permanent residency status before he could have begun the process of trying out and then signing with a prospective major league club. (It was this lengthy procedure that delayed Rene Arocha's arrival in the major league by two years from his original defection date in 1991.) Once El Duque had established residency in a third country, as he did in Costa Rica, the pitcher was viewed as a free agent under Major League Baseball's eyes, and was free to sign with any big league club.

    11. Steve Fainaru and Ray Sanchez, *The Duke of Havana: Baseball, Cuba and the Search for the American Dream* (New York: Villard Books, 2001).

    12. The Cuban Sports Hall of Fame (*Salón de la Fama del Deporte Cubano*) has incorporated the Cuban Hall of Fame members and also names amateur players for enshrinement. Heading the election committee is sportswriter and founder Marino Martínez. Hernández and Luis Giraldo Casanova's lifetime Cuban League statistics were taken from *The Duke of Havana*.

    13. Jerome Holtzman, "Jet Start Pushing Pizarro on Path Toward 20 Wins," *The Sporting News*, June 6, 1964.

    14. Phone interview with José Santiago, May 21, 2013. During a trip I made to Puerto Rico in 2011, to research a previous book, Pizarro was described to me by several people as being a notorious no-show to commemorative Winter League events and as one who rarely did interviews. Pizarro, late in life, can be best described, it seems, as a private person. A striking example of this characterization was delivered to me by Pantalones Santiago, who told me he considered Pizarro to be a good friend. I asked him about Pizarro's family and he could not confirm whether his "good friend" was currently married or had any children.

Chapter 3

    1. *Secrets of Baseball Told by Big League Players*, D Appleton & Company, 1927. Reprint Applewood Books, Bedford, Massachusetts.

    2. Long Branch, a team composed of nearly all Cuban players, was the runaway pennant winner of the league in 1913. Adolfo Luque emerged as its star pitcher with a 22–5 record. A few members of the team played in the major leagues, including Mike González and Angel Aragón.

    3. The other two players were outfielders Angel Aragón and Luis Padrón. Padrón was listed in *Who's Who in Cuban Baseball* by Jorge S. Figueredo as being the "first Cuban invited to a major league spring training in 1908 with the White Sox, but was not signed due to a racial accusation." Unlike Aragón, Padrón never played in the major leagues.

    4. Harry Bloom, "Couldn't Revive it if they Wanted To," *The Sporting News*, August 1, 1918.

    5. Luque has been given credit for ten starts in 1918 when he only had nine. Pitching in both ends of the doubleheader this day may have been a root cause to the confusion.

    6. This was *Cincinnati Enquirer* reporter Jack Ryder's

June 27 summary of the causes for the Luque-Klem battle (Unlike ungracious journalism graduates who followed, Ryder used proper grammar and spelling when conveying Luque's comment in newsprint. Judging by similar quotes attributed to Luque in another Cincinnati daily, it also seemed Ohio newspapermen, at least with this Hispanic player, interpreted comments in their own writing style, possibly for the sake of clarity and/or better copy. Many of the words said to have been spoken by Luque do not have a verbatim ring.):

"Luque's explanation of the assault was that umpire Klem called him a vile name which he would not stand for and also alluded to him as belonging to the negro race. Luque bitterly resented both of these remarks and said he would never stand for either of them being uttered about him. Umpire Klem admitted that he had used a bad term in speaking to Luque, but denied flatly that he had added anything about his nationality or had repeated the epithet a second time, as was claimed by Luque.

"Stock had opened the eighth with a single. Hornsby bunted to the box and Luque threw Stock out at second. Luque made a snap throw to first and caught Hornsby off the bag. This made two out with no one on, and it looked to be the last moment in the world for any trouble with the umpire.

"Luque explains his actions as follows: 'After throwing Hornsby out at first, I was getting ready to pitch to Fournier, when Klem said to me, "Go ahead and pitch out there." I made a motion with my hands which evidently he didn't like, for he said again, "Go ahead and pitch," adding an epithet which any man would resent. I said to him, "What's that you said, Bill?" and he repeated it, adding the term "nigger," and at the same time walking onto the diamond toward me. That's all there is to it and I would do it again any number of times under the same provocation.'"

"He was corroborated in his statement by catcher Nick Allen, who had taken Wingo's place and was in a position to hear all that was said. Jack Fournier, the Cardinals' batter, was a dissenting voice, saying he had not heard Klem utter anything offensive." [Fournier was also the runner who was called safe on the close play at the plate by Klem in the sixth.]

"Umpire Klem, who had a rough afternoon, was seen shortly after he returned from filing charges in Police Court against one of the pop bottle throwers of the sixth inning. His statement: 'It is true that I applied a wrong epithet to Luque. After the pitcher had thrown Fournier [sic Hornsby] out at first, I told him to go ahead and pitch to the next batter. He responded by making a motion with his arms and hands, which I took to be an expression of contempt and designed to incite the crowd to get after me. It was at this time that I used the term to which Luque objected so vigorously. It is not true that I repeated it or called him a nigger. As a matter of fact, I have always stood up for the Cubans, and when players on opposing teams have tried to annoy them by the use of that term I have always prevented them from doing so. I have never lied in my life or sent in an unfair report on any ball player, and so I will admit that I used a bad term to Luque, for which I am sincerely sorry. As for repeating this term or calling him by another name I can only enter a firm denial'"

7. Peter T. Toot, in a footnote in "Armando Marsans, A Cuban Pioneer in the Major Leagues," said that a $100 fine was handed down to Luque because of the incident with Klem.

8. F. C. Lane, "The Strange Case of Adolfo Luque." *Baseball Magazine*, May 1923.

9. Ibid.

10. "Luque's Pitching Blanks Giants, 7–0," *The New York Times*, May 19, 1923.

11. W. A. Phelon, "Phelon Sings Song of Joy in His Work." *The Sporting News*, July 26, 1923.

12. Peter T. Toot, *Armando Marsans, A Cuban Pioneer in the Major Leagues* (Jefferson, NC: McFarland, 2004), 156.

13. W. A. Phelon, "Great is the Fall of One Bill Phelon." *The Sporting News*, August 23, 1923.

14. Toot, 153. Over time, Luque's version has been completely discarded in most readdressing accounts, with writers preferring the sarcastic irony associated with McGraw's defense.

15. "Giants Are Beaten Twice by The Reds." *The New York Times*, August 16, 1923.

16. "Luque Given Big Welcome in Cuba." *The Atlanta Constitution*, October 4, 1923.

17. Luque's great 1923 major league campaign may have swayed the owners of Habana into letting Luque manage their marquee club in place of Mike González, who had been the team's manager for the past five seasons. Beginning again in 1924–1925, González once again became the Habana team's skipper—and for the next 29 years after that.

18. Untitled. *The Sporting News*, July 17, 1924.

19. Prior to the Thursday afternoon game, the Giants welcomed their greatest, earliest stars to mark fifty anniversary years of Senior Circuit baseball. The invited players were from the formative years of the franchise, some of whom played in the *original* Polo Grounds, which dated back to the National League's rudimentary seasons. On hand to help commemorate the National League's Golden Jubilee, complete with bunting-adorned grandstands and a Conway jazz band, was Commissioner Kenesaw Mountain Landis. Among the invited baseball luminaries: Jim Murtrie, the first manager of the Giants, and future Hall of Famers Amos Rusie, Roger Connor, Mickey Welch and Dan Brouthers.

20. Tom Swope, "Hendricks Status to be Known Soon." *The Sporting News*, September 24, 1925.

21. Swope, "Discarded Yankees Welcome in Cincy," *The Sporting News*, January 21, 1926.

22. Swope, "Reds Match Mound Let-up With Punch," *The Sporting News*, July 1, 1926.

23. Untitled. *The Sporting News*, July 1, 1926.

24. Swope, Tom. "Cincinnati Hears More Than Earful," *The Sporting News*, January 27, 1927.

25. Swope, Tom. "Cincy Reds Have No Kick on Condition," *The Sporting News*, April 27, 1927.

26. Swope, Tom. "Reds Dip Into Red at Columbus Farm," *The Sporting News*, October 27, 1927.

27. Tommy Holmes, "Robins in Tailspin As Machine Cracks," *The Sporting News*, August 21, 1930.

28. Holmes, "Many Dodgers Fail to Sign Contracts," *The Sporting News*, February 18, 1932.

29. Official records list 367, but I am respectfully removing one of ten credited starts from 1918. See footnote 5.

30. Three days earlier, on April 23, the National League's largest Opening Day crowd packed the Polo Grounds to herald Babe Ruth's return to New York. The Babe, in the uniform of the Boston Braves, went hitless in three at-bats, with a walk. According to a game report, the Babe made a spectacular one-handed catch against the right field wall. Ruth was removed after the visitor's half of the eighth inning, doing little more to excite the crowd of 47,009. Ruth's exit was saluted with applause and a "shower of torn papers" as he climbed up the clubhouse steps. The Braves, trailing 5–3, rallied for two runs in the ninth, with the 44-year-old Luque coming in to choke off further scoring. The game entered extra innings, tied 5–5. Mel Ott singled home the winning run in the 11th for the Giants (Luque starting the decisive inning with a single). Pitching the game's final two and two-thirds innings, Adolfo Luque gained his 194th and last big league victory. Three weeks later, facing a roster decision, the Giants removed Luque's standing as a player and appointed him as their pitching coach, ending the 20-year major league career of the pitching pride of Cuba.

31. Jorge S. Figueredo indexed the game in *Cuban Baseball: A Statistical History, 1878–1961* as follows: "When his staff was depleted due to injuries, Adolfo Luque took the mound on February 1, 1945 for the last time in his career. Luque allowed two runs and four hits and struck out four certainly chagrined batters." During the same stage of his life, Luque had packed on the pounds. A newsreel shot of Luque hitting ground balls at the Giants' spring encampment in Lakewood, New Jersey, in 1945 showed an overweight man with a wide backside, his piped stirrups riding high up his calves giving his legs a spindly look. His appearance was almost Babe Ruth-ish, except more heavily compact. For anyone seeing Luque's "heavyweight" disposition at that time, it would be almost impossible to believe that a month or so earlier he had hurled three innings of competitive professional baseball against men his junior by multiple decades and multiple pounds.

32. Roberto González Echeverria, *The Pride of Havana. A History of Cuban Baseball* (New York: Oxford University Press, 1999), 145–147.

33. Ibid.

34. Untitled, *The Sporting News*, May 21, 1947.

35. In presence and action, the big Californian was as intimidating a force as any pitcher to stride up the major league hill. Drysdale was strictly possessive of the inside part of the plate. Possessive compulsive, if judged by the number of hit batsmen he racked up. Five times Drysdale led the league in plunking batters.

36. Author's correspondence with Carlos Pascual, April 13, 2004.

37. Ibid.

38. Author's correspondence with Jorge S. Figueredo, May 5, 2004. Some of the negative stories associated with Luque, involving Ted "Double Duty" Radcliffe, Terris McDuffie and Babe Pinelli, are, to me, the reactive responses of a snorting bull met by the unfurled red cape of a witless matador. Though there can be no excuse for brandishing a firearm as a tactic of intimidation as Luque apparently did on at least one occasion, it is clear certain indolent conduct, or excuses, from ballplayers, simply were not tolerated by Adolfo Luque and incited volatile behavior from the man.

39. "Adolfo Luque, 66, Baseball Pitcher," *The New York Times*, July 4, 1957.

40. Gerald F. Vaughn, "George Hausemann Recalls the Mexican League of 1946–1947," *Baseball Research Journal* 19, 1990, 59–63.

41. Arturo Flores, "Luque Warms Up Old Giant Gems at 'El Pitcher,'" *The Sporting News*, October 23, 1946.

42. Jorge S. Figueredo, *Beisbol Cubano: A un Paso de las Grades Ligas 1878–1961* (Jefferson, NC: McFarland, 2005), 334.

Chapter 4

1. Author's correspondence with Carlos Pascual, December 20, 2003. Carlos Pascual was signed by Joe Cambria in 1949 and preceded his brother to the minor, then major leagues. The brothers played together for the Class B Havana Cubans in the early fifties. (Carlos once pitched a 14-inning game against the Miami Beach Flamingos that was ended by curfew tied at 1–1.) *The Sporting News* of August 5, 1953, reported on an incident wherein the two were ejected during a Florida International League game: "Policemen were summoned to escort the Pascual brothers, third baseman Carlos and pitcher Camilo of Havana, from the opening game at Tampa, July 28. The brothers were banished for tossing gloves, bats, and jackets in protest to a fourth inning balk decision on Camilo." Carlos Pascual pitched for the Washington Senators in 1950, and had a curt two-game major-league career, resulting in one victory and one loss. On September 24, Pascual defeated Philadelphia, 3–1. Four days later, he lost to the Red Sox, 4–3. Both were complete games. In 1962, Carlos Pascual retired as an active player and became a scout for the Minnesota Twins, the year his brother became a 20-game winner for the same team. Carlos Pascual passed away May 12, 2011.

2. Arno Goethal, "Pascual Traveling Glory Road after Start as Bus-Weary Boy," *The Sporting News*, October 5, 1963.

3. Pascual had spent the spring and summer of 1952 and 1953 playing for the Havana Cubans. The pitcher was traded in the middle of 1952 to the Tampa Smokers for outfielder Claro Duany, then was returned in 1953 to the Havana team, which happened to be bought by Bobby Maduro from Clark Griffith earlier in the year. The young Pascual was exposed to another historic Hispanic baseball figure at that time. Armando Marsans, early major-league Hispanic standout, was Pascual's manager with the Cubans in 1953. (The sharp-eyed Maduro that winter traded for the 19-year-old Pascual in the Cuban Winter League's most one-sided trade ever recorded.)

4. "Pascual Credits Ex-Twirler for Help with Curve," *The Sporting News*, April 18, 1962.

5. Shirley Povich, "Hat's Off, Camilo Pascual," *The Sporting News*, May 21, 1958.

6. Ruben Rodriguez, "Old Favorite Nelson Aims at HR Mark," *The Sporting News*, November 20, 1957. This, more than likely, was a "medical deferment" diagnosed in order to permit Pascual to draw some type of salary.

7. Shirley Povich, "This Morning," *The Washington Post*, September 22, 1959.

8. In the sabermetric world of Bill James, the hailed baseball analyst has Pascual earning the Cy Young Award not only in 1959, but again in 1963. The novel James' pitching point system ranks Pascual as the best pitcher in baseball both years, as the award did not dually recognize one pitcher from each league until 1967. Among other things James takes under calculative consideration, are strength of opponents faced and a ballpark's pitching friendliness.

9. Shirley Povich, "Reds' Million Offer for Pair Nixed by Nats," *The Sporting News*, December 23, 1959. In a ten-month period, from mid–April, 1959, culminating with the Caribbean Series in February, 1960, Pascual, threw a stupendous 410 innings and recorded 383 strikeouts. He compiled a cumulative 34–15 record between the major and Cuban Winter leagues.

10. Bob Addie, "Cuban Fans 15, Aided by 4 Homers," *The Washington Post*, April 19, 1960.

11. A final retrospective note on the 1961 season, generated from Billy Crystal's marvelous baseball feature "61*." Pascual is misidentified as the Opening Day pitcher who shuts out the Yankees at the Stadium (it was teammate Pedro Ramos). In the film, glimpsed delivering a pitch in that game, wearing number 14, is a black actor purported, by voice-over, to be Pascual. Camilo's uniform number has already been referenced as number 17, and Pascual is Caucasian. (In his playing days, Pascual had the dashing good looks of a cinematic leading man. A look at his 1960 Topps baseball card reveals Pascual to be the spitting image of actor Robert DiNero, with corresponding facial birth mark and all.) Baseball-Almanac.com lists uniform numbers 14 and 28 for Pedro Ramos for the 1961 season. Therefore, it may have been number 14 pitching for the Twins on April 11, 1961, at Yankee Stadium. But Ramos is also Caucasian.

12. The winning run in the heartbreaking loss was set up by a rare error by sensational fielding first baseman Vic Power. The same day, Pascual's second child was born, a daughter named Maria Isabel.

13. "A Righty Would Make Things Right," *Sports Illustrated*, April 8, 1963.

14. Max Nichols, "Camilo's Mom, Dad Permitted to Leave Cuba," *The Sporting News*, September 5, 1964.

15. Ibid.

16. Nichols, "Camilo's Curve Sharper Than Ever," *The Sporting News*, April 2, 1966.

17. *The Sporting News*, October 23, 1965.

18. Max Nichols, "10 Degrees Below Outside as Camilo Smiles Warmly at 46-Gee Pact," *The Sporting News*, February 12, 1966.

19. Having high hopes for Sturdivant, the Yankees held on to him, but never let the trade completely fizzle. Over the winter of 1958–1959, the Yankees' patience with Sturdivant had run out and they reopened negotiations for the Cuban pitcher. But the Senators, by then, with Pascual's stock having risen, wanted young infielder Bobby Richardson to be included with Sturdivant. The Yankees would not agree.

20. Max Nichols, "Camilo's Fast Ball Crackles—Back Surgery a Huge Success," *The Sporting News*, October 2, 1965.

21. Nichols, "Pascual After 11 Long Years Pass .500," *The Sporting News*, June 5, 1965.

22. Shirley Povich, "This Morning," *The Washington Post*, July 8, 1969.

Chapter 5

1. As related by Marichal in his 1967 autobiography, the death was brought about by too much drink, or *romo*, a Dominican slang equivalent of "booze."

2. Juan Marichal, with Charles Einstein. *A Pitcher's Story*. (Garden City, New York: Doubleday, 1967).

3. Ibid.

4. Bob Stevens, "Why Does He Run? He Remembers $1 Fines," *The Sporting News*, July 20, 1968.

5. "When It Was A Game III," Home Box Office, Inc. 2000.

6. Jack McDonald, "Hats Off! Juan Marichal," *The Sporting News*, August 3, 1960.

7. Harry Jupiter, "The Dominican Dandy," *Baseball Digest*, Oct–Nov, 1962. Marichal's bride, Alma Rosa Carvajal, was a girl from Santo Domingo who lived near countryman and fellow ballplayer Felipe Alou. Alma Rosa was a close friend of Alou's sister. Through the Alou family connection, the two young people had met. Marichal had proposed marriage to Alma Rosa, only 16 at the time, after the 1961 season.

Alma Rosa's father had served in the armed forces under Trujillo and the Dominican Republic was in political turmoil following the dictator's assassination in 1961. Trujillo oppositionists, gathering strength and becoming bolder, were now eyeing former "loyalists." Alma Rosa's father was branded because of his military background, even though he maintained no political ties to Trujillo. Marichal wanted to take Alma Rosa away from the volatility and, with Dark's permission, flew home and married his sweetheart in her hometown

church of San Juan Bosco. The dainty ingénue would flower into a radiant woman who would bear Marichal four daughters over the next 11 years. According to SABR bioproject author Jan Finkel, the Marichals have six children and celebrated 50 years of marriage in 2012.

8. Bob Stevens, "Juan Issues Only Two Walks in Holding Houston Hitless," *The Sporting News*, June 29, 1963.

9. Stevens, "Torture to Watch Declares Hub, Giants Last No-Hit Hurler in '29," *The Sporting News*, June 29, 1963.

10. "Juan Rates No-hitter as Number 2 Thrill," *The Chicago Tribune*, June 16, 1963.

11. Curly Grieve, "Willie Knew His Blast Was Homer," *The San Francisco Examiner*, July 3, 1963.

12. Ibid.

13. Orlando Cepeda and Herb Fagen, *Baby Bull. From Hardball to Hard Time and Back* (Taylor Publishing Company, 1998), 93

14. Curly Grieve, "Willie Knew His Blast Was Homer," *The San Francisco Examiner*, July 3, 1963.

15. Ibid.

16. On September 1, 1967, Marichal's moundmate Gaylord Perry started and pitched 16 scoreless innings at Crosley Field—the last time a pitcher has thrown as many innings in one baseball game. Goose eggs galore reigned in that game, which lasted 20 scoreless innings before the Giants pushed across a run in the top of the 21st to take a 1–0 victory. Perry, a right-hander and future Hall of Famer, the next day said he had to comb his hair with his left hand because he could not lift his other arm. Five days later, though, Perry had no problem with his arm. He pitched a shutout in his regularly scheduled start against the Houston Astros.

17. After the July 2 game, Spahn's teammates greeted the warrior pitcher—the last player to enter their clubhouse because of an interview session—with their own tribute. Quoting Braves teammate Bob Sadowski, writer Jim Kaplan described it as follows, in a *National Pastime* article from 2007: "When Spahn arrived, everyone stood, applauded, and lined up to shake his hand. 'If you didn't have tears in your eyes, you weren't nothing,' Sadowski says."

18. "Scorecard Too Much Heat," *Sports Illustrated*, March 16, 1964.

19. Further friction between player and manager developed when Dark decided to call the pitches in an outing Marichal made against the Mets, reasoning that the New York team—which had never beaten Marichal—was due to solve the right-hander and a change in pitching tactics was needed. On another occasion Dark had, in the dugout, openly criticized his pitcher for using his screwball too much, even though it was striking out batters during the game. Dark sarcastically rebutted the success of the pitch by saying it would have a disabling affect on Marichal's arm within a few years. The latter comments, in dugout context, can be attributed less harshly than the off-the-cuff remarks by the manager.

20. Juan Marichal with Charles Einstein. *A Pitcher's Story* (Garden City, NY: Doubleday, 1967).

21. Ibid.

22. Ibid. (quoted from *Sport Magazine*).

23. The first Hispanic "sportsman" to grace the cover of *Time* was José Raúl Capablanaca. The Cuban chessmaster was featured on the December 7, 1925 cover.

24. Richard Dozer, "Santo Spiked in Left Knee by Marichal's Slide at 3rd ," *The Chicago Tribune*, June 23, 1966.

25. Leonard Koppett, "Mets Defeat Marichal First Time," *The New York Times*, July 5, 1967.

26. John Wiebusch, "Marichal Unseats Reds With One-Hit Gem, 1–0," *The Los Angeles Times*, September 6, 1969.

27. Ibid.

28. Pat Frizzell, "Juan Reels in And Starts Over After Seeing Old Movie," *The Sporting News*, August 15, 1970.

29. Frizzell, "Juan Feeling Wonderful—And Giants Look Healthy," *The Sporting News*, April 17, 1971.

30. Jan Finkel, "Juan Marichal" at Bioproject. Sabr.org

31. Bob Stevens, "Juan Gets a Kick Out of Pitching," San Francisco Giants Yearbook 1973.

32. Jack Lang, "Brooks Robinson, Marichal to Enter Hall of Fame," *The Sporting News*, January 24, 1983.

33. Ibid.

34. "Marichal Salutes Roseboro," *The Miami Herald*, August 25, 2002.

35. Luis Tiant and Joe Fitzgerald, *El Tiante: The Luis Tiant Story* (Garden City, NY: 1976).

36. The strikeout of Ruth by Tiant, it should be mentioned, occurred during a barnstorming game in New York in 1935, and Ruth was 40 years old.

37. Luis Tiant and Joe Fitzgerald, *El Tiante: The Luis Tiant Story* (Garden City, NY: Doubleday, 1976). Staying in Mexico, Tiant hurled for the Reynosa Oilers in the winter of 1961. In the season opener, he tossed a no-hitter, defeating the Montemorelos Eagles, 2–1.

38. Ibid.

39. Russell Schneider, "Lucky Luis? Modest Hurler Tiant Thinks So," *The Sporting News*, August 3, 1968.

40. Ibid.

41. Russell Schneider, "Sweet Lou Weary, But He's Delighted to Join the Indians," *The Sporting News*, July 13, 1968. Tiant was the starter and loser for the American League. The score, emulating a couple of hard-luck losses Tiant incurred throughout the season, was 1–0. The only run was set up by a bad pick-off throw to first by Tiant himself.

42. Luis Tiant and Joe Fitzgerald, *El Tiante: The Luis Tiant Story* (Garden City, NY: Doubleday,1976).

43. Ibid.

44. Ibid.

45. Larry Claflin, "Red Sox Fans Cheer Tiant as Comeback Hero," *The Sporting News*, October 7, 1972.

46. Luis Tiant and Joe Fitzgerald, *El Tiante: The Luis Tiant Story* (Garden City, NY: Doubleday, 1976).

47. Ibid.

48. Jack Craig, "Do Bosox Owners Want Profits or Pennants?" *The Sporting News*, February 3, 1979.

49. "El Tiante Rejoins Red Sox Family." www.ourredsox.com

50. Howard Bryant, *Shut Out: A Story of Race and Baseball in Boston* (New York: Rutledge, 2001).

51. Ibid.

Chapter 6

1. Thomas E. Van Hyning, *Puerto Rico's Winter League: A History of Major League Baseball's Launching Pad* (Jefferson, NC: McFarland, 1995).

2. Bob Price, "Cuellar Masters Screwjie; Calls Tune for Int Batters," *The Sporting News*, June 20, 1964.

3. Ibid.

4. Mike Cuellar, as told to Tom Capezzuto, "The Game I'll Never Forget," *Baseball Digest*, July 1977.

5. "Cuellar Wins 10th, Has a Chance at 30," *New York Times*, June 13, 1971.

6. Don Zminda, *From Abba Dabba to Zorro: The World of Baseball Nicknames*" (Norton Grove, IL, Stats Publishing, 1999).

7. 1981 Orioles Yearbook.

8. Thomas Boswell, "Tiant, Cuellar Last of a Breed," *The Washington Post*, June 23, 1975.

9. Boswell, "Cuellar Treats His Age to Puerto Rico Cure," *The Washington Post*, January 21, 1970.

10. "Cuellar Wins Without His Screwball," *The Washington Post*, October 16, 1971."

11. Matt Schudel, "Mike Cuellar, Ex–Baltimore Orioles pitcher, Dead from Cancer," *The Washington Post*. April 4, 2010.

12. Mike Klingman, "Prioles Pitching Great Mike Cuellar dies at 72," *The Baltimore Sun*. April 2, 2012

13. Tom Capezutto, "Dennis Martinez Finds Success on Comeback Road," *Baseball Digest*, October 1989.

14. Ibid.

15. Martínez was left off the Orioles' post-season rosters, and his record was the worst ever for a starting pitcher on a World Series-winning team until David Cone posted a 4–14 mark for the Yankees in 2000.

16. Jim Henneman, "Martinez Blames Woes on Alcohol," *The Sporting News*, March 5, 1984.

17. Ibid.

18. Henneman, "Orioles Glad they Held On to Martinez," *The Sporting News*, March 11, 1985.

19. Henneman, "O's "Martinez Nixes Rochester Rehab," *The Sporting News*, May 19, 1986.

20. Ian MacDonald, "Alcohol, Minors Humbled Martinez," *The Sporting News*, April 11, 1988.

21. MacDonald, "Martinez Gains N.L. Respect," *The Sporting News*, August 8, 1988.

22. Alan Malamud, "Capturing the Perfect Fantasy," *The Los Angeles Times*, July 29, 1991.

23. Bill Plaschke, "Expos' Martinez Pitches 15th Perfect Game Ever," *The Los Angeles Times*, July 29, 1991.

24. Ken Gurnick, "Next? Is Perfect Query for Martinez," *The Sporting News*, August 12, 1991.

25. James Buckley, Jr., *Perfect* (Chicago: Triumph Books, 2002).

26. "Nicaraguans Celebrate After Perfect Game," *The New York Times*, July 30, 1991.

27. Rob Rains, "Martinez Made it a Perfect Day—National Celebration Followed Achievement," USA Today *Baseball Weekly,* August 2, 1991.

28. Sheldon Ocker, "Cleveland Indians AL Report," *The Sporting News*, January 24, 1994.

29. Michael Kinsley, "Farewell, Old Friend," *The Sporting News*, July 22, 1996.

Chapter 7

1. "Valenzuela Wins on Homer in 9th," *The Chicago Tribune*, May 15, 1981.

2. Ronald Yates, "Rookie Pitcher ValenzuelaIs Numero Uno with the Dodgers," *The Chicago Tribune,* May 3, 1981.

3. Mark Heisler, "Can a Guy Win Rookie of the Year Twice?" *The Los Angeles Times*, September 7, 1981.

4. "Valenzuela Set for Record Pact," *The Sporting News*, January 30, 1982.

5. Along with Wiltse, Butch Metzger is the only other big league pitcher to start a career 12–0. Metzger's wins were strictly in relief and accrued over three seasons. Rookie Atley Donald of the Yankees won 12 games in a row to open 1939, but he had been spotted with a loss in an earlier 1938 trial.

6. Fernando Paramo, "Fernando Valenzuela," *Sport*, July 1986.

7. Ken Gurnick, "Valenzuela Masterly Amid Dodger Mishaps," *New York Times*, August 10, 1986.

8. Sam McManis, "Dodgers Win One, But Lose Valenzuela," *The Los Angeles Times*, August 1, 1988.

9. Untitled. *The Sporting News*, October 23, 1989.

10. Untitled. *The Sporting News*, July 9, 1990.

11. Ibid.

12. "Out of the Blue," *Sports Illustrated*, April 8, 1991.

13. "Valenzuela's Release 'Tough to Swallow,'" *The Sporting News*, April 8, 1991.

14. Paul C. Gutierrez, "Fernando Is Back Home After His 'Vacation,'" *The Los Angeles Times*, June 6, 2003.

15. *The Miami Herald*, June 7, 2003.

Chapter 8

1. Steve Marantz, "Pedro Martinez Says He Has to Pitch High and Tight to Be Effective," *The Sporting News*, July 18, 1994.

2. "Paradise Lost: Martinez Loses Perfect Game in the 10th," *The New York Times*, June 5, 1995.

3. "NL East Notes," *USA Today Baseball Weekly*, June 28–July 4, 1995.

4. Ibid.

5. "Bullinger's Woes Won't Cost him as Turn," *The Sporting News*, August 18, 1997.

6. Michael Vega, "New Ace Had Support of Many Nations," *The Boston Globe*, April 12, 1998.

7. Buster Olney, "1 Hit, 17 Strikeouts, No Way for the Yankees," *New York Times*, September 11, 1999.

8. Also, according to 38pitches.com, ranking as all-time best marks by a pitcher for any one season were the .213 On-Base and .259 Slugging Percentages permitted by Martínez in 2000. Many sabermetricians (along with the MLB Network) have ranked Martínez's 2000 season as the greatest by any pitcher of the modern era. Cited are the incredible statistical differentials compiled by Martínez against American League hitters in comparison to his peers. The caveat of only 29 starts and 7 complete games can be presented to temper the claim. Nonetheless, Martínez, in 1999 and 2000, posted a combined 41–10 mark with 597 strikeouts!

9. Bob Hohler, "Day After, Warning Hits Nerve with Ace," *The Boston Globe*, May 3, 2001.

10. Dan Shaughnessy, "Sox Spares No Yankees, Puts an End to Streak, Talk," *The Boston Globe*, May 31, 2001.

11. Bob Hohler, "Weighty Issue: Martinez Adjusting," *The Boston Globe*, March 23, 2002.

12. Ken Rosenthal, "Ace in a Hole," *The Sporting News*, March 4, 2002.

13. "Same Old Story," *The Miami Herald*, October 8, 1995.

Chapter 9

1. "Super Mariano," cnnsi.com, October 14, 2000.

2. Bryan Hoch, "Rivera Takes Place in History with Save No 500," mlb.com, June 29, 2009.

3. Ian Begley, "Marinao Rivera Sets New Saves Record," ESPN/New York.com, September 20, 2011.

4. Rivera had long since made a habit of breaking opposing hitters' bats. In early July, the Minnesota Twins, during the Yankees' last trip into Minnesota, bestowed upon Rivera a unique gift. The pitcher's announced plan to retire at the end of the season prompted some type of ceremonial recognition from the front offices of every road city he visited. The Twins presented Rivera with a rocking chair made of Twins' bats splintered by the closer over the years. Rivera celebrated receipt of the gift by recording a two-pitch save, his 27th, in the game that July 2 night at Target Field.

5. Tom Verducci, "The Sure Thing," *Sports Illustrated,* November 11, 2009.

6. Ronald Blum, "Iconic Reliever Closes out Hall of Fame Career," *The Miami Herald,* September 29, 2013.

7. Bob Nightengale, "Venezuela's Favorite Son Returns Favor," *USA Today Baseball Weekly*, February 23–March 1, 2005.

8. "Santana Unanimous Choice for AL Cy Young Award," November 18, 2006, espn.com.

9. The four players were: Carlos Gómez, Phillip Humber, Kevin Mulvey and Deolis Guerra (non-major leaguer).

10. Santana maintained a sparkling winning percentage as he reached the triple-digit win total. With only 47 defeats, he became baseball's fifth left-hander to achieve 100 wins with fewer than 50 losses. The others: Lefty Gómez, Whitey Ford, Don Gullett, Ron Guidry.

11. In one of those July starts—July 22—in which he pitched very well and received a no-decision, Santana

recorded his 1,500th strikeout. The Phillies' Chris Coste was Santana's fateful victim. The strikeout total was reached in 1,425 innings, the fifth fewest number of innings pitched to attain this strikeout level. Santana ranked behind only the following great strikeout artists: Pedro Martínez (1,325⅔), Randy Johnson (1,361), Nolan Ryan (1,366⅔), and Sam McDowell (1,417).

12. Larry Larue, "Milestone for Felix. Split for M's," The newstribune.com. August 26, 2010.

13. "Felix Hernandez Perfect Game. Mariners Ace Records 27 Straight Outs in 1–0 Win Over Rays," Huffingtonpost.com. August 15, 2012.

14. The other Andean no-hit pitchers are: Wilson Alvarez, Anibel Sánchez, Johan Santana, and Carlos Zambrano.

15. Greg Johns, "Felix Dominates in 100th Win as Seattle Bats Come Alive," Mlb.com. April 23, 2013.

Bibliography

Bryant, Howard. *Shut Out: A Story of Race and Baseball in Boston*. New York: Rutledge, 2001.

Buckley, Jr. James. *Perfect*. Chicago: Triumph Books, 2002.

Dickson, Paul. *Baseball's Greatest Quotations*. New York: Harper Collins, 1991.

Fainaru, Steve, and Ray Sanchez. *The Duke of Havana: Baseball, Cuba and the Search for the American Dream*. New York: Villard Books, 2001.

Figueredo, Jorge S. *Beisbol Cubano A un Paso de las Grades Ligas 1878–1961*. Jefferson, NC: McFarland, 2005.

Figueredo, Jorge S. *Cuban Baseball: A Statistical History 1878–1961*. Jefferson, NC: McFarland, 2003.

Figueredo, Jorge S. *Who's Who in Cuban Baseball 1878–1961*. Jefferson, NC: McFarland, 2003.

Gonzalez Echevarria, Roberto. *The Pride of Havana: A History of Cuban Baseball*. New York: Oxford University Press, 1999.

Kerr, Don. *Opening Day: All Major League Baseball Season Opening Games, By Teams, 1976–1998.* Jefferson, NC: McFarland, 1999.

Klein, Alan M. *Baseball on the Border: A Tale of Two Laredos*. Princeton, NJ: Princeton University, 1999.

Lester, Larry. *Black Baseball's National Showcase: The East-West Baseball Game, 1933–1953, with a Foreword by Joe Black*. Lincoln, NE: University of Nebraska Press, 2001.

Marichal, Juan, with Charles Einstein. *A Pitcher's Story*, Garden City, NY: Doubleday, 1967.

Nathan, David H. *The McFarland Baseball Quotations Dictionary*. Jefferson, NC: McFarland, 2000.

Regalado, Samuel O. *Viva Baseball! The Latin Major Leaguers and Their Special Hunger*. Champaign, IL: University of Illinois, 1998.

Rhodes, Greg, and John Snyder. *Redleg Journal*. Cincinnati, OH: Road West, 2000.

Secrets of Baseball Told by Big League Players. D Appleton & Company, 1927. Reprint Applewood Books, Bedford, Massachusetts.

Thorn, John, and Pete Palmer, Michael Gershman, David Pietrusza with Matthew Silverman and Sean Lahman. *Total Baseball*, Sixth Edition. Champaign, IL: Total Sports, 1998.

Tiant, Luis, and Joe Fitzgerald. *El Tiante: The Luis Tiant Story*. Garden City, NY: Doubleday, 1976.

Toot, Peter. T. *Armando Marsans: A Cuban Pioneer in the Major Leagues*. Jefferson, NC: McFarland, 2004.

Van Hyning Thomas E.. *Puerto Rico's Winter League: A History of Major League Baseball's Launching Pad*. Jefferson, NC: McFarland, 1995.

Vincent, David, Lyle Spatz, David W. Smith. *The Midsummer Classi:c The Complete History of Baseball's All-Star Game*. Lincoln, NE: University of Nebraska, 2001.

Zminda, Don. *From Abba to Zorro: The World of Baseball Nicknames*. Morton Grove, IL: STATS Publishing, 1999.

Articles

Anderson, Kelli. "2 Seattle Mariners." *Sports Illustrated*. March 31, 2008

Blum, Ronald. "Iconic Reliever Closes Out Hall of Fame Career." *The Miami Herald*, September 29, 2013

Boswell, Thomas. "A Baseball Paradise Flourishes in San Juan." *The Washington Post*, January 20, 1977.

Capezutto, Tom. "Dennis Martinez Finds Success on Comeback Road." *Baseball Digest*, October 1989.

Chen, Albert. "An Ace is Born." *Sports Illustrated*. August 22, 2005.

Kaplan, Jim. "The Best-Pitched Game in Baseball History." *The National Pastime*, Number 27 (2007).

Paramo, Fernando. "Fernando Valenzuela." *Sport*, July 1986.

Perry, Dayn. "Pedro in the Pantheon." *The Baseball Research Journal* 30 (2001).

Price, S. L. "Sweet Sound of Santana." *Sports Illustrated*, May 23, 2005

Roberts, Jay. "Juan Marichal: An Opening Day Dandy." *The Baseball Research Journal* 30 (2001).

Sheehan, Joe. "Broken Record." *Sports Illustrated*. October 4, 2010.

Sherman, Joel. "From Nowhere to Immortality: Mariano Rivera's Unbelievable Journey." *Yankees Magazine*, April 2012.

Toot, Peter. "Breaking the Latino Barrier." *Elysian Fields* 18, no. 4 (2001).

Wulf, Steve. "No Hideaway For Fernando." *Sports Illustrated*, May 18, 1981.

Team Yearbooks

1972 Baltimore Orioles Yearbook
1973 Baltimore Orioles Yearbook
1974 Baltimore Orioles Yearbook
1981 Baltimore Orioles Yearbook
1983 Baltimore Orioles Yearbook
1999 Boston Red Sox Yearbook
1964 Minnesota Twins Yearbook
1965 Minnesota Twins Yearbook
1966 Minnesota Twins Yearbook
1992 Montreal Expos Yearbook
1970 San Francisco Giants Yearbook
1971 San Francisco Giants Yearbook
1972 San Francisco Giants Yearbook
1973 San Francisco Giants Yearbook
1959 Washington Senators Yearbook
1960 Washington Senators Yearbook

Video Reference

Countdown. Top 10 Greatest Pitching Seasons. MLB Network.
Countdown. Top 40 Players Not in the Hall of Fame. MLB Network.
"When It Was A Game III." Home Box Office, Inc. 2000.

Periodicals, Magazines and Newspapers

The Atlanta Constitution
Baseball Digest
Baseball Magazine
The Boston Daily Globe
The Chicago Tribune
The Cincinnati Enquirer
The Los Angeles Times
The Miami Herald
The National Pastime
The New York Times
The San Francisco Examiner
Sport Magazine

The Sporting News
Sports Illustrated
USA TODAY Baseball Weekly
The Washington Post

Web Articles

Baskin, Bruce. "Ramon Arano in Mexican Hall of Fame." 1800beisbol.com

Bingham, Brendon. "Fifty Best Players Not in the Hall of Fame." baseballpastandpresent.com

Díaz, George. "After Cuéllar's Death, an Outpouring of Goowill." *The Baltimore Sun*. April 12, 2012.

Finkel, Jan. *Juan Marichal,* Bioproject. Sabr.org

Johns, Greg. "After Felix' Gem, Mariners Fall in 13." mlb.com. July 27,2013.

Ramón Arano. Biographical Information. Baseball-reference.com

Rubio, Jesús Alberto. *Ramón Arano.* vozdedeporte.com. September 4, 2012

Van Hyning, Thomas. *Rubén Gómez* Bioproject. Sabr.org

_____ "Santana Unanimous Choice for AL Cy Young Award." November 18, 2006. Espn.com.

Web References

baseball-almanac.com
baseballhalloffame.org
baseballlibrary.com
baseballpastandpresent.com
baseball-reference.com
cubanball.com
dihigo.blogspot.com
espn.com
google.com
huffingtonpost.com
mlb.com
newstribune.com
ourredsox.com
paperofrecord.com
proquest.com
retrosheet.org
sabr.org
38pitches.com
vozdedeporte.com
worldatlas.com
wikipedia.org

Index